Breaking the
Appalachian Barrier

ALSO BY JOHN HRASTAR

*Liquid Natural Gas in the United States:
A History* (McFarland, 2014)

Breaking the Appalachian Barrier

Maryland as the Gateway to Ohio and the West, 1750–1850

JOHN HRASTAR

McFarland & Company, Inc., Publishers
Jefferson, North Carolina

All maps are by David Deis of Dreamline Cartography
except as noted.

ISBN (print) 978-1-4766-7044-7
ISBN (ebook) 978-1-4766-3039-7

LIBRARY OF CONGRESS CATALOGUING DATA ARE AVAILABLE

BRITISH LIBRARY CATALOGUING DATA ARE AVAILABLE

© 2018 John Hrastar. All rights reserved

*No part of this book may be reproduced or transmitted in any form
or by any means, electronic or mechanical, including photocopying
or recording, or by any information storage and retrieval system,
without permission in writing from the publisher.*

On the cover: *Workers Building the National Road,*
Carl Rakeman (Federal Highway Administration)

Printed in the United States of America

*McFarland & Company, Inc., Publishers
Box 611, Jefferson, North Carolina 28640
www.mcfarlandpub.com*

For Fran, Mary, John, Peggy, Kathy

Acknowledgments

The process of researching and writing a book on history requires the help and patience of many others who contribute in various ways. First of course, I thank my wife, Fran, for her support. She not only encouraged the project but put up with time this took away from other projects. I also thank others who contributed directly and indirectly including my colleagues at the University of Maryland libraries who assisted in finding and providing the research material used to write the book. As might be expected a Maryland university has a great deal of material germane to the early historical link between Maryland and Ohio.

However, special thanks go to three people without whose help this book would not have been possible. My brother Tim, a writer, historian, and teacher himself was one of the two major reviewers. Alzada Roberts was the other. Their reviews and suggestions helped turn my input into a readable history book. Ms. Roberts, especially, has a knack for greatly improving the presentation without changing the meaning of the ideas. Tim, Alzada, and I all realized early that maps would be necessary to make the whole story clear. I struggled at first but finally found David Deis, a cartographer who understood what I was trying to do, understood the era, and put together a wonderful array of maps to illustrate the story.

Going from the historical research to a readable book took the help of all these family, friends and colleagues.

Table of Contents

Acknowledgments vi
List of Maps viii
Preface 1
Introduction 3

ONE ◆ Setting the Stage 11
TWO ◆ Maryland to 1750 34
THREE ◆ Competition for the Ohio Country 60
FOUR ◆ The War Years 92
FIVE ◆ The Changing West 120
SIX ◆ The Waterway West 145
SEVEN ◆ Maryland as the Gateway to Ohio 170
EIGHT ◆ The Iron Link Between Maryland and Ohio 210

Chapter Notes 227
Bibliography 243
Index 249

List of Maps

1. The Appalachians and Ohio Country 12
2. Potomac and Youghiogheny Rivers 22
3. Great Valley Road 45
4. Britain, France and Spain in North America, 1750 61
5. Ohio Company Grant Request 64
6. Gist's Trace 74
7. The Virginia Second Charter, 1609 86
8. Ohio Company Second Grant Request 94
9. Braddock Road and Burd Road 102
10. Stanwix Treaty Line 117
11. Quebec Act, 1774 123
12. Northwest Territory and Louisiana Purchase 132
13. Ohio Land Subdivisions 139
14. Chesapeake and Ohio Canal National Park Service 168
15. Cumberland Road 190
16. The National Road 202
17. Baltimore and Ohio Railroad 218

Preface

I was born in Ohio but have spent most of my life in Maryland. When I first drove east with my young family from Cleveland to Maryland in 1960, we traveled on America's first superhighway, the Pennsylvania Turnpike. After we left the Turnpike we traveled east to the Washington, D.C., area on U.S. Route 40, known as the National Road, although I didn't recognize the name at the time. We made the trip to Ohio from Maryland and back many times over the years and the roads kept improving. Now with Interstates I-70 or I-68 and the Pennsylvania and Ohio turnpikes, the trip between Washington, D.C., and Cleveland can be made in just a few hours. There are some tolls, two traffic lights and no need for maps. It wasn't always this easy. For hundreds of years the Appalachian Mountains had stood as a barrier between the East Coast and the Ohio country; it had to be breached to link east and west.

> Throughout the 18th and 19th centuries, the lack of an efficient, safe transportation network kept populations—and trade—largely confined to coastal areas. At the beginning of the nineteenth century, the Allegheny Mountains were the Western Frontier [www.canals.ny.gov/history.html].

My personal connection between Ohio and Maryland is minor and of short duration, but Maryland and Ohio had a link prior to the birth of the United States. After the War for Independence ended in 1783, and prior to the birth of the new republic in 1789, the original thirteen states had to decide how the western lands ceded by Great Britain in 1783 were to be used. It was the small state of Maryland that stubbornly insisted the land should belong to all the states in confederation, not to the states originally claiming that land. Maryland was successful, with the result that the Northwest Territory was designated for new states with equal rights as the original states; Ohio was the first of these. Had Maryland been unsuccessful Ohio today might be part of Virginia, the original claimant of the Ohio country, and part of Connecticut, and its Western Reserve.

The critical link between Maryland and Ohio started about forty years earlier, in 1750, when English colonists wanted to breach the Appalachian Mountain barrier which separated the East Coast colonies, such as Maryland and Virginia, from the lush farmland of the Ohio country. The chosen path was the easiest one available, from western Maryland across the Alleghenies to the Ohio country. This path was blazed early and was used frequently in the following decades but didn't become a real, paved road until after Ohio became a state in 1803. Congress authorized and funded the road from Cumberland, Maryland, to Wheeling, Virginia, on the Ohio River, linking Maryland and Ohio. This was the Cumberland Road, which later became part of the National Road. The key purpose of the road was to finally breach the Appalachian barrier and solidly bind the western states and territories to the eastern states; in this it succeeded very well. Maryland became the gateway to Ohio.

Most of the facts about the opening of the Ohio country from the east are well covered in many history books but usually scattered through different stories such as the westward movement or the history of a state. The objective of this book is to focus on the people and events that contributed to breaking the Appalachian barrier as a single story in its own right. These efforts over a one-hundred-year interval were not accidental but were the result of a dedicated focus to open the west from the east.

The importance of binding east and west together at a critical time can't be overstated, making this story one of the building blocks of the history of the United States.

Attempting any historical research is always a challenge because cultural norms, usage, spelling, and other ideas change with time, and one cannot be sure the terms mean the same in the present as they did in the past. I have chosen some simple but I hope acceptable ground rules. I have chosen to use spelling as it is in the original source. So, for example the Youghiogheny River might be spelled Yohiogany in some places and spelled still differently elsewhere. I am confident the reader will have no trouble with the spellings in context. Similarly, I have maintained the original spelling in all quotes so as to avoid the constant use of the Latin term *sic*. There are few exceptions in which brackets are used to make the quote intelligible. Once again, the reader will have no difficulty in interpretation. For practical purposes I use the terminology of the time, present or past. For example, I use the accepted term Native American whenever possible and use colonist or settler rather than white man. However, it is not always possible to use modern terms because sometimes they would make no sense in the context of the past. For example, the settlers of the time used the appellation Indian, if not the coarser term "savage," right from the beginning. The Native Americans themselves accepted the term and used it when describing themselves as Indians. The title "French and Indian War" is well accepted in historical works but would have no meaning as the "French and Native American War." I trust the reader will understand the reasons for these ground rules.

Introduction

When Jedidiah Morse wrote his *American Geography* in 1794, he made reference to the Northwest Ordinance of 1787 and envisioned great things for the Northwest Territory, in particular what became the state of Ohio.

> In the ordinance of Congress, for the government of this territory, it is provided that after the said territory acquires a certain degree of population, it shall be divided into States. The eastern State, that is thus provided to be made, is bounded on the Great Miami on the west, and by the Pennsylvania line on the east. The center of this State will fall between the Scioto and the Hockhocking. At the mouth of one of these rivers will probably be the seat of government for this State; and, if we may indulge the sublime contemplation of beholding the whole territory of the United States settled by an enlightened people, and continued under one extended government, on the river Ohio, and not far from this spot, will be the seat of empire for the whole dominion. This is central to the whole; it will best accommodate every part; it is the most pleasant, and probably the most healthful.[1]

He described what became the state of Ohio reasonably well but perhaps overreached in the prediction it would "be the seat of empire for the whole dominion." As Joseph Wood (*The Idea of a National Road*) points out he may have been off in the particulars but not in the sentiment.[2] In 1794, and earlier, the Ohio country, defined mostly by the Ohio Valley, was regarded as almost the Promised Land. This was especially true as peace seemed to be at hand after two wars in the last half of the eighteenth century.

The challenge now was to breach the Appalachian and Allegheny mountains to enable the would-be settlers from the East Coast to reached this Promised Land, and then maintain a strong link between east and west. This challenge would occupy hundreds for the better part of a century.

The name Ohio, in one form or another, is traditionally ascribed to be of native Iroquois origin; they used the term to describe the mighty river that defined the Ohio Valley. The geography of the Ohio country had been determined millions of years ago when the collision of two continental plates caused the upwelling of land to form the Appalachian Mountains with the Ohio Valley on the western slopes. The western ridges, the Allegheny Mountains, were especially defined by accordion-like ridges and valleys. About twelve thousand years ago Asians crossing the Bering Strait began to populate North America. Eventually these people, known to us as Native Americans, spread over all of North America including Ohio and the northeastern woodlands. Sometime during that process the Iroquois named the Ohio "the great river."

Ancient cultures arose in the Ohio country, flourished, and declined. As these cultures moved farther west, parts of Ohio were left unoccupied until the more familiar historic Native American tribes including the Shawnee, Delaware, Iroquois, and Miami, moved into Ohio. These and other eastern and southeastern tribes lived on both sides of the

Appalachians, although not in them. The mountains, however, were no barrier to them as they easily moved through them for both trade and war. The Iroquois, for example, moved on foot through the north-south valleys of the mountains on well-worn paths to make war on the southern Cherokee and Catawba. Although sparsely populated by modern standards, the Native American population practiced agriculture and made good use of the flora and fauna of Ohio. Had they known the term "Promised Land" they might have used it for their Ohio country.

And then everything changed.

Late in the fifteenth century and early in the sixteenth century the Native Americans were tagged with a new sobriquet—of which they had no knowledge—Indians. Although the sixteenth century Spanish were the earliest conquerors and settlers of South America and parts of North America, the North American Atlantic coast, eastern woodlands, and Great Lakes, did not experience the European invasion until the early seventeenth century when the English and French established colonies at Jamestown and Plymouth, and in the St. Lawrence Valley respectively. At that time, the Europeans gave the Native Americans of these regions the generic name Indians. There were immediate clashes between the colonists and Indians, especially in the English colonies; the French attempted more to integrate with the native populations. Warfare between tribes had existed for centuries and was not new. If a tribe was defeated, it might have to move to a new territory or pay tribute. The Iroquois also absorbed some of their defeated enemies into the Iroquois Nation tribes. What was new was the nature of the battle with the invading colonists; it was an existential battle, one the Indians could not win.

In the east, between the mountains and the sea, the competition for the land was between the English colonists and the eastern tribes. In the west, in the St. Lawrence and Ohio Valleys, it was between the French colonists and the western tribes. Although they had a small colony on the St. Lawrence, the French claimed land all the way to the Mississippi, and, in fact, tried to work peacefully with the Native Americans of the area. The Appalachian Mountain chain separating the French and British colonies was recognized as a natural barrier and a de facto, if unofficial, border. For almost 150 years the mountains acted as an effective barrier between the two traditional enemies with only relatively small battles between them.

The mountain barrier had a larger impact on the English colonies, especially the ones east of Ohio that had boundaries reaching to the mountains including New York, Pennsylvania, Maryland, and Virginia. Virginia's second colonial charter (1609) decreed all the western lands were part of Virginia including Ohio. From 1607 to roughly 1750, the two original colonies were joined by others, and population increased. The colonies expanded west from the coastal plain, across the rivers' fall lines, back toward the mountain barrier. During this time the French had only trading posts in the Ohio country but no major population center; the English looked over the mountains and saw empty land. Although not colonized or heavily populated, the Ohio country was well known to the English; over the years there had been many expeditions and active trade with the Indians in the Ohio country. It was clear to the English colonists that Ohio had great potential for settlement. It seemed to them it would be only a matter of time before they would be able to exploit this country.

Two of the mid–Atlantic colonies in particular, Maryland and Virginia, were instrumental in opening Ohio to English colonists. The Virginia colony, chartered by King James I, had a rather expansive charter: the northern border extended on a line from the Atlantic coast to the northwest, and included most of the Ohio country. For most of the seventeenth and half of the eighteenth centuries this had little practical effect; Virginia was consolidating settlement on the eastern seaboard. However, by the 1720s and 1730s colonists were settling the Virginia Shenandoah Valley between the eastern and western ranges of the Appalachians and were looking still farther west. They took their charter seriously and considered the land of Ohio to be included in Virginia. The other mid–Atlantic colonies of New York, Pennsylvania, and Maryland had defined western boundaries, even if they were sometimes in dispute, and therefore had no "official" claims on the Ohio country. It was natural for many in the western parts of those states, especially Pennsylvania, to look across the mountains and covet the land; some moved there despite the French and Indian threat.

Maryland was a small, proprietary colony founded by Lord Baltimore in the 1630s to enhance the family estates and to provide a religiously tolerant settlement for a pluralistic society, especially for Catholics who were not welcome elsewhere in the New World. The land designated for Maryland had been carved out of the original Virginia colony. For many decades after settlement the Maryland economy depended on tobacco, and the population was clustered on the coast. That changed in the eighteenth century, when many north-south roads paralleling the mountains took German immigrant farmers from Pennsylvania through Maryland to Virginia's Shenandoah Valley to settle. Some of these farmers remained in Maryland, and western Maryland became an agricultural source for farm products, which were shipped east. The far western part of Maryland was located in the Alleghenies. This rugged country was not settled, and the mountains were a barrier to westward movement, but within the next few years it became a resource for the state because of its key geographical location. It became the gateway across the mountains to the Ohio country.

Virginia was the most populous colony in 1750, with an economy based on tobacco and trade. The original settlements were along the many eastern rivers flowing into Chesapeake Bay or the Atlantic and were dominated by the large estates of the well-to do gentry. The tobacco economy was supported by a system of slave labor that originated very early in the colony's history. Byrd, Carter, Lee, and other gentry were active in local politics and in local church affairs and they maintained an active commerce with the mother country. This gentry continued to look west and royal grants of western Virginia lands were made to those loyal to the King. Lord Fairfax, for example, received a grant in western Virginia that he sought to exploit by sale for settlement. In the first half of the eighteenth century there was a drive to sell and settle lands in the west, including those beyond the Blue Ridge Mountains in the Shenandoah Valley. This was an early indication of the leading role Virginians would take in the westward movement.

Just before mid-century the time was ripe for a group of businessmen in the Virginia gentry to join to form the Ohio Company of Virginia to try to break the mountain barrier and settle in the Ohio country on the Ohio and the Monongahela rivers. They would plan a route through northwest Maryland, starting where Wills Creek enters the upper Potomac, at present-day Cumberland, Maryland, and over the mountains to the Monongahela River. The north-flowing Monongahela River, in western Pennsylvania, joins the south-flowing Allegheny River to form the westward-flowing Ohio River at the Forks of the Ohio at present-day Pittsburgh, the entry to the Ohio country. For millennia travel by water was believed preferable to travel by land if it could get you where you wanted to go thus a water route to the Ohio country was desirable. Any map would show that the route they chose over the mountains was the shortest one between the eastern-flowing Potomac and western-flowing Monongahela. The Virginians knew that the Monongahela/Ohio route would make an impressive waterway to the west once they crossed the mountains. A route up the

Potomac River to Wills Creek, over a few mountains to the north, and to the westward flowing Monongahela River looked like a good way to enter Ohio. Although this route was their eventual goal, the first attempt to breach the mountain barrier was with a road across the Alleghenies from western Maryland to the Ohio country; the first time on an organized scale. The Ohio Company of Virginia applied for, and received, a grant of land around the Forks of the Ohio, land already occupied by Native Americans and the French.

At first, the colony of Maryland was not involved, but the Ohio Company of Virginia hired a Marylander, Christopher Gist, to blaze the first trail over the Alleghenies from Wills Creek in Maryland to the Monongahela in 1751. Others followed Gist to widen the trail, and a small number of settlers did make it across the mountains to settle near the Monongahela. The situation then became very complicated. The Ohio land was now claimed by three parties—the French, who had reasserted their claim to the country just a few years earlier, the Native Americans, who clearly predated all parties, and the English Virginians, who claimed the land based on their second charter.

The area was a tinderbox waiting for a spark. The spark came in 1754 when George Washington twice engaged the French and essentially helped initiate the French and Indian War. Prior to, and during the war, both George Washington and the English General Edward Braddock carved roads along the trail Gist had blazed over the mountains, but this time for purposes of war. The road across the mountains between Maryland and Ohio was used during the French and Indian War, but not by organized armies. It was used mainly by the Indian allies of the French who raided western Pennsylvania, Maryland, and Virginia. The road Braddock carved turned north after it crossed the mountains, away from Gist's road, which went directly to the Monongahela. Later in the war Colonel Burd cut a road off the Braddock Road to the Monongahela essentially retracing Gist's road to the river.

In 1763, following the English victory in the war, the King proclaimed a line across the ridge of the Alleghenies to be a dividing line between English settlements in the east and Indian lands in the west. This was deemed necessary because a depleted British army and treasury would be unable to defend the western frontier. The road from Maryland to Ohio was now officially closed, although many settlers kept moving into Ohio illegally; the rich land was too tempting to ignore. The troubles between the settlers and Indians continued, and in 1768 Sir William Johnson negotiated another treaty with the Indians, the Treaty of Fort Stanwix. This treaty designated Ohio as Indian land but allowed colonial settlement south of the Ohio River. This encouraged many Virginians to move west into what is now Kentucky and Tennessee. Ohio country itself, north of the Ohio River, was still considered Indian land and a colonist took risks to settle there.

The second war in fifteen years, the American War for Independence, started in 1775, less than fifteen years after the French and Indian War had concluded. One of the results of the Treaty of Paris (1783), which ended this war, was the British cession to the newly independent states of all the land west to the Mississippi River. North of the Ohio River it was the Northwest Territory, which included Ohio. Ohio was now officially a part of the territory ceded to the states, although the Native Americans in Ohio didn't see it that way. The Maryland to Ohio road was still closed for official migration although things were changing in the 1780s even before the new republic was officially born. Land ordinances in 1784, 1785, and the Confederation Congress's Northwest Ordinance of 1787 determined that the newly acquired Northwest Territory would eventually become states with the same rights as the original states. The states, through the Confederation Congress, intended to sell and settle the Ohio land.[3]

Maryland played an important part in the process of keeping the Northwest Territory, which included Ohio, open to the states in confederation rather than to individual states such as Virginia and Connecticut that had prior claims on the land. Maryland's stubborn refusal to recognize Virginia's claim to Ohio country, based on the 1609 charter, eventually caused Virginia to cede the land to the states in confederation. Ohio was now open for sale and settlement but it did not happen rapidly. The Native American population still fought hard for the land with conflict continuing well into the 1790s. The initial land offerings were also in large lots effectively blocking out the small landowner. These issues diminished, and by the turn of the century many moved to Ohio and others were planning to do so.

What hadn't changed was the mountain barrier. The mountains were no longer a border but they did provide a barrier to movement west from the east. By 1803, when Ohio had become a state, Congress knew that it would be necessary to breach that barrier with a strong link between the eastern states and the new states to be made from the Northwest Territory, Ohio being the first. Ease of migration from east to west was needed to populate the new states and to maintain commerce with them thereafter. The most important concern was that the lack of a strong east-west link would make it easier for the western settlers to look to Spain or Great Britain in the west, drift toward them, and break ties with the Union. This fear was enhanced by the ease of trade on the Ohio and Mississippi rivers. It was a fear expressed almost twenty years earlier by George Washington, who was always interested in the west. Therefore, national unity was the primary driver for breaching the mountain barrier. Doing this would require a road across the mountains that would be funded by selling lands in Ohio.

Before the road was built, an even earlier approach to crossing the mountains was considered, a canal. The mid-eighteenth century through the early nineteenth century was the age of canals. Although canals had been used for centuries they only became commercially viable in Europe in the mid-eighteenth century when they simultaneously started to receive interest in this country. Just after the French and Indian War, George Washington conceived the idea of making the Potomac usable for commerce all the way to Cumberland; he would move rocks, build sluices, and generally make it accessible for flatboats. His plans were interrupted by the War for Independence, but soon afterwards he started pursuing his dream of a navigable Potomac. Washington was seeking a way to use the Potomac to reach the mountains and find another water route onward to Ohio. He became president of the Potomac Company in 1785, a company which continued for decades after his death in hopes of completing his dream. The company was not successful, but the dream didn't die. In 1825 the Chesapeake and Ohio Canal Company began a still water canal whose objective was to provide another way across the mountains by following the Potomac, crossing the mountains and eventually reaching the Ohio country. When the canal reached Cumberland in 1850 after many difficult years of construction, the decision was made to stop there. After sixty-five years of trying it was not possible to cross a three-thousand-foot mountain barrier by canal.

Built into the statehood act for Ohio was the provision for funding the road by using five percent of the lands sold in Ohio for roads to reach the state from the east, and roads within the state. When Congress passed the act for the road in 1806 it determined that the endpoints were to be Cumberland, Maryland, and Wheeling, Virginia. The first part, from Cumberland (Wills Creek) to the Monongahela, was essentially Gist's Trace, the original path from Maryland to Ohio. Now named the Cumberland Road it was started in 1811 and complete to Wheeling in 1818, although people were using it as it was being built long before it was finished. It was built wide and with the newest broken stone technology to make sure it was sturdy for heavy travel. Although it was now the road across the mountains and the passage that breached the mountain barrier, it could not fulfill its main purpose until it was linked to the East Coast. This was accomplished not by a national road but by a series of local Maryland roads and turnpikes. Maryland started the Baltimore Pike, from Baltimore to Cumberland, simultaneously with the Cumberland Road but through a series of embarrassing delays the road wasn't complete until 1824. A solid road now existed from the East Coast at Baltimore to western Maryland and across the mountains into Ohio country at Wheeling; the east and west were now connected.

The road was heavily traveled by stagecoaches, freighters (Conestoga wagons), migrant wagons, and droves of animals, in both directions, during its heyday from the 1820s through the 1840s. Such heavy use meant frequent repairs were needed on the road but they often lagged. Many writers chronicled life on the road including activities at the many taverns, wagon houses, and, eventually toll houses. Toll houses were erected when the road was turned over to the states from the national government in the 1830s.

As successful as the Cumberland Road was it encountered competition as soon as it was completed. There now was a race to the west, especially between the states of New York, Pennsylvania, Maryland, and Virginia. The Erie Canal was started by the state of New York in 1817 and completed in 1825. It took advantage of the relatively flat east-west Mohawk River Valley, which cut a path through the mountains between Albany on the Hudson River and Lake Erie. The Hudson River then led down to New York City completing an east-west link. The canal was immediately successful and provided stiff competition for the Cumberland Road. Baltimore was now at a disadvantage with New York regarding western trade and was concerned about losing that trade.

The American Industrial Revolution was now under way and transportation technology played an important role as it had been in England for decades. Horse-drawn railways had been used for decades in England primarily to move coal or ore from a mine to a more convenient location; horse-drawn passenger railways started early in the nineteenth century. The lure of steam power for locomotion had also intrigued many and by 1825 the British had harnessed steam, starting the first passenger railway using steam locomotion. Railways in the United States lagged, with only a couple of horse-drawn mine railways in operation. Baltimoreans were now getting anxious as the Baltimore Pike and Cumberland Road, although very successful, could not compete with the tonnage that could be moved by canal. There was no access from Baltimore to the Chesapeake and Ohio (C&O) Canal near Washington, nor with any Pennsylvania canal. Even had they reached the C&O Canal it did not cross the mountains. Therefore, only months after the English steam railroad was open, Baltimore decided it had to build a high capacity freight and passenger railroad to the west.

In 1827 the Baltimore and Ohio Railroad (B&O) was formed to connect Baltimore to the Ohio River near Wheeling. It was an audacious act. It was to travel hundreds of miles through two states, through valleys, across rivers, and over the Alleghenies; nothing like it came close in the United States. It was the first general purpose railroad in the world. Although they wanted to use a route parallel to the Cumberland Road, it was not possible. They couldn't go through Pennsylvania, partly because Pennsylvania's Main Line was now in the route competition to the west. The Pennsylvania Main Line was a combination of canals, railroads, and inclined planes (to go over the mountains) to connect Philadelphia to Pittsburgh. Because Virginia was also interested in opening the west, it teamed with the B&O on the route west. The B&O went west from Baltimore, passed Frederick, crossed the Potomac at Harpers Ferry, went through the Virginia Shenandoah Valley up to Cumberland, turned west through Virginia, crossed the Alleghenies, and then continued northwest to

Wheeling; it reached Wheeling in late 1852. It was the first railroad to connect the East Coast (Baltimore) with the Ohio River without the use of inclined planes. It had happened again; Maryland had opened another gateway to Ohio, this time with an iron link.

Today little thought is given to crossing the Alleghenies as it can be done in a couple of hours using either Interstate 70 or Interstate 68, both of which duplicate parts of the Cumberland Road. U.S. 40, although not an Interstate Highway, follows the old Baltimore Pike and Cumberland Road, and therefore Gist's Trace, fairly closely, and provides scenery more like what Gist and Washington would have seen. Little thought now is given to the history of the road, the gateway, from Maryland to Ohio, the road that breached the mountain barrier, but it was the focus of the efforts of hundreds of people for the century between 1750 and 1850.

This is the story of that gateway, the one that breached the Appalachian barrier.

ONE

Setting the Stage

In the Beginning...

The Earth is over four billion years old. Although much of the early history cannot be known, it is possible to understand some of the history of the last billion years through knowledge of the geology of the area, by reading the rocks.

> The rocks at the core of the Appalachian Mountains formed more than a billion years ago. At that time all the continents were joined together in a single supercontinent surrounded by a single ocean.... About 750 million years ago the supercontinent began to thin and pull apart like warm taffy because of the expansion of the continental crust. Then about 540 million years ago the continental crust split into pieces that drifted away from each other. Seawater spread into low areas between the crustal plates and, in time, formed new oceans.[1]

The Earth's plates continued to drift so that what is now the United States was located below the equator and had vast inland seas 480 million years ago. About 470 million years ago, the crustal plates, which started to break apart 70 million years earlier, started drifting back toward one another, shrinking the intervening oceans. About 270 million years ago the predecessor continents of America and Africa collided, forming the Appalachians with the huge masses of rock pushed westward along the margin of North America. After the collision, about 240 million years ago, the continents began to pull apart again to form what is now the Atlantic Ocean.[2] The Appalachians formed at the collision remained in place along the East Coast of North America. A topographic map of the United States today shows the mountains stretching from Maine to Alabama, just a few miles from the Atlantic coast, and illustrates how they were formed by the intense pressure caused by the collision of two continental plates. Mountains form a continental divide between the flatter plateaus on either side.

The Appalachian Eastern Continental Divide had an important influence on trade and settlement when the French and English established colonies in the seventeenth century. The English colonists of the East Coast used the rivers to great effect up to the fall lines to both establish settlements and ship goods to the home country from up river. However, as the rivers did not cross the mountains, the English were limited by the mountains to their west. Similarly, the people of New France used the St. Lawrence as the major water highway for all their transportation needs and moved around easily on the Great Lakes for their trading purposes. When the French did move into the Ohio country, it quickly became obvious that trade with the outside world was possible using the Ohio and Mississippi rivers as the trade route. Because the mountains acted as transportation barriers they also became real and symbolic barriers between the French and English colonies for decades; up until 1750.

The Appalachians can best be described as a pair of roughly parallel ranges running from eastern Canada southwest down to Alabama, separated by the Great Appalachian Valley which is known by various names from north to south. It is the Cumberland Valley[3] in Pennsylvania, the Hagerstown Valley in Maryland, and the Shenandoah Valley in Virginia. The mountain ridge bounding the Valley in eastern Pennsylvania is South Mountain and is the start of the Blue Ridge Mountains, which bound the Shenandoah Valley on the east and continue into Georgia.

The western boundary of the Great Appalachian Valley in Pennsylvania and Maryland, the Ridge and Valley Appalachians, is a series of ridge-mountains, high peaks and steep valleys. This ridge and valley system provides a good visual image of how the continental collision formed the mountains "accordion" style pushing rocks up and leaving valleys between. This system starts in New Jersey and northeast Pennsylvania and arcs southwest across mid–Pennsylvania, ending in Tennessee. The westernmost part of the ridge and valley system is the Allegheny Mountain range which extends from mid–Pennsylvania down to southern West Virginia. The Allegheny Range is the biggest obstacle between Maryland and the Ohio country, creating the barrier between the Potomac River in the east and the Ohio River in the Allegheny Plateau. Nonetheless, crossing the Alleghenies provides the shortest route between the rolling hills of Maryland and the Ohio country. Once the Alleghenies were crossed the road to Ohio was open from the mid–Atlantic.

The mountains don't drop immediately to sea level but are bordered on each side by

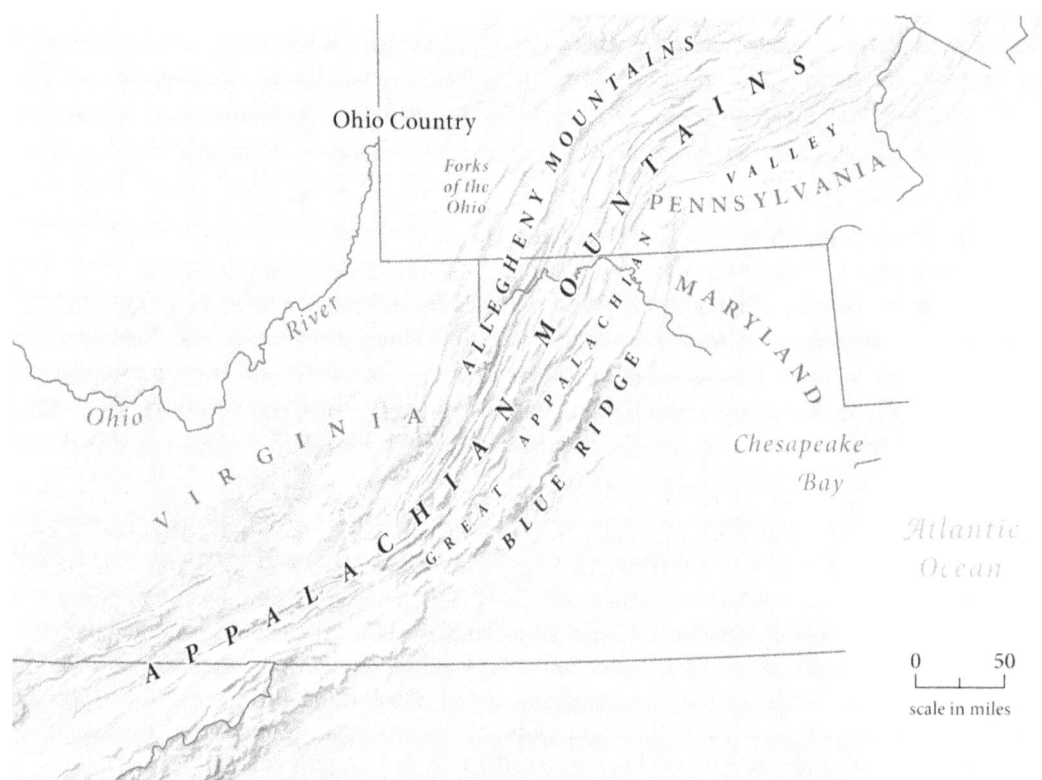

Map 1: The Appalachians and Ohio country. The Appalachian and Allegheny mountains formed a barrier between the coastal plain in the east and the flat Ohio country. The Appalachian name is derived from Native American sources.

plateaus. On the east is the Piedmont ("foot of the mountains") plateau reaching from New Jersey down through Pennsylvania, Maryland, Virginia and the Carolinas to Georgia and Alabama. East of the Piedmont is the coastal plain near sea level bordering the Atlantic coast. West of the mountains, from New York through Pennsylvania, Ohio, West Virginia, and Kentucky is the Allegheny Plateau.[4] Although not totally flat, the Piedmont and Allegheny plateaus are relatively easy to traverse, unlike the mountains. This difference is stark, and seen clearly, when one descends from the Allegheny Ridge Mountains into the plateau, as near Uniontown, Pennsylvania. The plateau looks very much like a flat plain.

Topographically Ohio is a transition state. The eastern third is part of the Allegheny Plateau, shaped by the formation of the Appalachian Mountains. The northern and western parts of the state were shaped by the relatively recent glaciers of fourteen thousand years ago. In northeast Ohio, the glaciers moved over the Allegheny Plateau as far south as the Ohio River entrance into the state. The Allegheny Plateau south of that is a more rugged and steeper area, it is the only unglaciated part of the state. In the north and west, the glaciers left flat and fertile plains. The Till Plains of central Ohio start the long series of plains that stretch out to the Midwest and to the western plains. The glaciers are also responsible for the extensive river system in the state, including the Ohio River.[5]

A few of the Ohio rivers, such as the Cuyahoga and Sandusky, flow into Lake Erie and eventually to the St. Lawrence and Atlantic. Most of the Ohio rivers ultimately flow into the Ohio River and therefore to the Mississippi and the Gulf. These include the Miami, Little Miami, Scioto, Muskingum, and Hocking. This extensive river system was another great attraction of the Ohio country. River travel was by far the easier means of transportation compared to overland travel especially before any roads existed. People could be almost anywhere in Ohio and not be far from a river they could take all the way to the Mississippi. These Ohio rivers were major trade routes.

The Monongahela River, originating in West Virginia, and the Allegheny River, of western Pennsylvania, are the two rivers that meet at the "Forks of the Ohio," where they join to form the Ohio River. This point, present-day Pittsburgh, is on the Allegheny Plateau and was considered the entry to the Ohio country, just beyond the Appalachian Mountains. In the latter part of the colonial era and early part of the republic the Ohio country was considered prime real estate for expansion although the Allegheny Mountains proved a barrier from the east to the Forks of the Ohio.

The First Americans

Early Arrivals

The first Europeans to come to North America found not only a land rich in flora and fauna but a native people. Native Americans were first encountered by Columbus, but thereafter also by every early explorer and settler from Europe. These Native Americans were at various levels of development compared to the European explorers. They varied from the relatively advanced Aztec and Inca civilizations to the Indians of the eastern woodlands who depended on hunting and agriculture, but had simpler social structures and a lifestyle integrated into the woodland. Even the Aztecs, however, had not yet invented the wheel. Yet despite the variety of cultures, all these people ultimately had come through the same route over the one-time Bering land bridge from Asia to Alaska.

Archeologists and anthropologists characterize the period from the early migrations as part of the Paleolithic period and the Indians as Paleo-Indians. It was characterized by stone tools, most notably spear points. Some of these were dated to 13,000 BCE in the Ohio Valley. The fluted Clovis point is one of the more recognizable artifacts.[6] These people were primarily nomads who survived by hunting large game and gathering from existing plants. The Paleo-Indians descended, with no clear demarcation time, into the Archaic-Indians. This period, from roughly 10,000 to about 3,000 years ago (8,000 BCE to 1,000 BCE), was still a foraging one for the Indians. Following the Archaic period the Ohio cultures evolved from the early woodland or Adena (1,000 BCE–100 CE), through the middle woodland or Hopewell (100 CE–500 CE), to the late woodland (500 CE–1,000 CE), and to the late prehistoric or Mississippian (1,000 CE–1650 CE). The dates are approximate and except for the commonly known Adena and Hopewell cultures, the nomenclature varies with authors and archeologists.[7]

As these cultures evolved over the centuries there are two characteristics that stand out. One is the lack of any permanent residential population. As the people followed these cultures (Adena, Hopewell, and Mississippian) from the northeast to the southwest they literally drained population from the Ohio Valley; they are not the ancestors of the historic Ohio Indians. It is estimated that by the beginning of the eighteenth century many old villages in the Ohio Valley were unpopulated.[8] Secondly, they left an impressive archeological record from sophisticated housing structures to earthen ceremonial and burial mounds.

It is not clear how these people, the mound builders of the Adena through the Mississippian periods, arrived and how they differed from the more traditional tribes of the north and eastern woodlands. We know that early migrations took Paleo-Indians down through Canada, the United States west coast, Mexico, Central America, and down into the South American Andes. Along the way various cultures sprang from these original travelers including the Olmec, Aztec, Maya, and Incas among many others. It is unclear when the peoples who inhabited the eastern woodlands arrived at their ultimate home. If they arrived around twelve thousand years ago they could have simply followed the lower edge of the remaining Wisconsin glacier until they reached the Atlantic coast.

Some have suggested that many of the early migrants first went south, into Mesoamerica and later returned north, perhaps to the areas of Adena, Hopewell, and Mississippian culture.[9] If both types of migration (the northern route along the glacier, and the return from Mesoamerica) took place, it would explain the difference between the mound builders and the eastern woodland people. The similarity of the Mississippian and Mesoamerican cultures would also strongly suggest this possibility. In any case, as they spread out they developed separate cultures, identities, languages, and tribes. Whether the culture and its language were part of what they carried from the old world or shaped by their new environment is unknown.[10]

Historic Indians

The Indians that most affect the narrative of the Maryland to Ohio pathways have been labeled Historic Indians and their history is roughly dated from the early seventeenth century. They are well identified tribes with specific cultural lifestyles and languages. They include tribes with well recognized names such as the Iroquois, Shawnee, Delaware, Miami, and others. A great deal is known of their customs and history in that era. These tribes started moving into the Ohio Valley in the mid-seventeenth and early eighteenth centuries. They were moving into a relatively unpopulated area from the east and the west; they were not direct descendants of previous occupants of the valley. The previous cultures, although they left some impressive monuments, had disappeared.

There is a creation myth or migration myth that comes from the Walum Olum, the sacred tribal history of the Delaware or Lenni-Lenape tribe. The story is told by George Donehoo in a 1922 paper and is attributed to Heckwelder, probably John Heckwelder, a Moravian missionary.[11] In this tradition the Lenape lived in the west and decide to migrate east. After a long journey, probably decades, they met the Mengwe (Iroquois), who were also migrating east. Historians think this was around the "the River of Fish," the Mississippi, although some believe it was the Detroit River. The Lenape had sent spies ahead who reported that the country into which they were heading was occupied by a powerful, fierce, and war-like tribe called the Alligewe. The Lenape sent messengers forward asking permission to settle in their country, which was called Alligewining [Allegheny?].

The request was refused, but they were given permission to cross Alligewe land to get to land farther east. As they crossed the river the large numbers of Lenape alarmed the Alligewe who challenged them. A fierce battle ensued in which the Alligewe drove the Lenape back across the river. The Mengwe were also traveling east and offered to help the Lenape if they could share the land gained by this conquest. The Lenape and Mengwe agreed and after many years of fighting they conquered the Alligewe. As planned, the Mengwe (Iroquois) took the northern lands around the Great Lakes and the Lenape took the lands south of the lakes. The legend suggests that the Alligewe were driven south, possibly down the Mississippi.

Later still the Lenape divided; some went over the mountains to settle on the Susquehanna and Potomac rivers, and still later some went to the Delaware River from which their English name derives (De La Warr). Some ethnologists cite the Alligewe as the ancestors of the Cherokee.[12]

This story, although a creation myth, seems to comport well with supposition that many of the eastern woodland tribes may have descended from Paleo or Archaic-Indians who took a northern route from Beringia across the continent just below the receding glaciers. Such a myth passed down orally could have covered decades, centuries, or even millennia. It puts the Iroquois, Lenape, and even the Cherokee in approximately the correct places. Recent scholarship has called the Walum Olum into question claiming the whole thing is a hoax perpetrated early in the nineteenth century. Others, however, are not convinced but believe questions might stem from the native tradition being conveyed poorly to someone not adept in the Lenape language.[13]

The area of interest for the Ohio country is the northeastern culture area, also designated eastern woodland, and can be defined as running from Nova Scotia down to the Virginia Tidewater and from the East Coast to the Mississippi, including the Great Lakes. A map of the dominant Indian language families shows this area to include two dominant languages, Algonquian and Iroquoian.[14] The Algonquian language family stretches all across northern Canada, south to around Tennessee encompassing the western Great Lakes, and down the East Coast to Tidewater Virginia.

The Iroquoian language family covers Lakes Erie and Ontario, and goes from northern Ohio, western Pennsylvania, and New York up to, and including, the St. Lawrence River valley. The Huron and Iroquois, both Iroquoian speakers, lived in that region. Interestingly, the area in Ohio, vacated by the Hopewell and left almost uninhabited for many decades, is shown as having an unknown or no-one-family-dominant designation. The Iroquois were thought, by some, to have moved up from the south, from a different migration pattern, which could explain the different language family.[15] Tribes from these two large language families were the original settlers in the Ohio Valley in historic times, from about the seventeenth century on. The name Iroquois is probably a Huron name for black snake,

Irinakhoiw, an epithet used by their enemies. The French were unable to pronounce it.[16] The Iroquois called themselves Hodenosaunee, or "people of the long house," which describes the multi-person dwellings they built.

The Ohio country was relatively uninhabited in the early eighteenth century, but the eastern woodlands surrounding that area were well populated with various Algonquian and Iroquoian tribes. North of the Great Lakes were the Algonkin, Huron, Tobacco (also called the Petun or Tionontati), and Neutral tribes. The name Huron derives from hure an old French name meaning "boar's head," presumably because of their bristly hair. The Huron called themselves Wendat or Wyandot, "peninsula people" since they resided in an area surrounded by water on three sides.[17] The Erie, sometimes called the "Cat" people, lived on the northeastern shore of Lake Erie. The nickname associated them with some animal in the area such as a raccoon, wildcat, or even panther. On the East Coast from New England to the tidewater were the Massachusetts, Wampanoag, Montauk, Delaware, Susquehannock, Nanticoke and Powhatan. To the west were the Ottawa, Potawatomi, and the Miami, and to the south the Shawnee. Most strategically located were the tribes of the Five Nations of the Iroquois: Mohawk, Oneida, Onondaga, Cayuga, and Seneca. The Five Nations were located in upper New York State near Lakes Ontario and Erie. This is a small sampling of all the tribes in the area.[18]

The Shawnee had the most influence in the area in the mid-eighteenth century. They occupied towns and villages in western Maryland, southwestern Pennsylvania, Ohio, and northern Virginia. They were a mobile people who moved across great distances. Their origin as an Algonquian tribe seems to have been around Lake Winnipeg.[19] The Lake Winnipeg location suggests they were among many migrants that may have followed the lower edge of the glaciers in moving from west to east. The Lenni-Lenape Walum Olum legend even includes the Shawnee migration to the south around 1250 CE. "When Little Fog was chief, many of them [Delaware] went away with the Nanticoke and Shawnee to the land in the south." Other Algonquian traditions of the related Sauk and Fox, describe the Shawnee moving down the St. Lawrence to the Great Lakes; also consistent with the general west to east migration below the glaciers.[20] As Clark (*The Shawnee*) notes,

> There are basically two interpretations regarding the early historic locations of the Shawnee. The first views the Shawnee as situated in the Northeast as a single tribe until the Iroquois confederacy forced them down the Ohio River and drove them to the southern branches of the Ohio by the second half of the seventeenth century. From here they split into rather autonomous divisions. The second interpretation has them drifting southward prior to European settlement along the eastern piedmont through Virginia, the Carolinas, and Georgia. From Georgia some Shawnee groups went west toward the Mississippi River. Towards the end of the seventeenth century they began moving back to the north, uniting finally in the Ohio Valley as a single group.[21]

There is no question that they spent much of the seventeenth century south of Ohio in the Cumberland River Valley of Kentucky and Tennessee; Shawnee means "southerner." They started migrating north again into southern Ohio, northern Virginia, western Maryland, and southeast Pennsylvania late in the seventeenth century.

William Mayre ("Patomeck Above Ye Inhabitants") cites the migration of the Shawnee from South Carolina from about 1677. He claims this migration took place over about thirty years. "The ancient Shawnee villages formerly on the sites of Winchester, Virginia, and Oldtown, near Cumberland, Maryland, were built and occupied probably during this migration."[22] The town now known as Oldtown was then known as King Opessa's Town or Opessa's Town. King Opessa (1664–1760) was a Shawnee chief on the lower Susquehanna until 1711 when he left his tribe to live with the Delaware, and in 1722 he moved to what became Opessa's Town.[23] The town was near the head of the Potomac River, a major Shawnee crossroads of trade with other Shawnee just across the mountains in Pennsylvania and Ohio. It was not only a principal Shawnee town but as early as 1722, had become a refuge for runaway slaves from Maryland and Virginia, much to the consternation of the two governors.[24] By 1732 the Shawnee had abandoned the town and moved to Allegheny and Conemaugh Valleys in western Pennsylvania. The town then became known as Shawnee Old Town.[25] About ten years later Thomas Cresap (1702–1790), a prominent Marylander, settled there.

As the French and English colonies grew there were clashes with the Native Americans. These happened whether the settlers befriended the Indians, as the French did, or if they treated them with disdain as the English did. These clashes and various wars have been well documented. There are many accounts of Indian tribes moving westward in Pennsylvania from the Delaware River to the Susquehanna River, and finally to the Ohio River as the colonists moved farther west. The pressure from the colonists may have caused the Shawnee to abandon Opessa's Town prior to 1732. There was also a long period in the seventeenth century that witnessed clashes between various tribes in the region, independent of the clashes with the colonists. These Indian conflicts were not spontaneous but were sparked by the intervention of Europeans into North America.

European Contact and Trade

The earliest permanent European settlements were in Virginia in 1607, Quebec in 1608, and Plymouth in 1620. These colonization attempts were all small and the colonists struggled for many years. The Dutch, well-known traders, also became interested in this new world very early, but more for trading than colonization. They started probing the St. Lawrence for furs in 1606, and by 1614 the New Netherland Company had a trading post on an island in the Hudson River.[26] The Dutch established a post at Oranje, at present day Albany, and started trading with the Mohawk. The French fur trade with the local Hurons began as New France was colonized. The Plymouth colony was late in originating trading but by the 1630s they had a thriving fur trade in Maine.[27]

New France was founded primarily to trade for furs as furs were a hot commodity in Europe, especially for hats, and the European beaver was almost wiped out. As Volwiler (*George Croghan and the Western Movement*) notes,

> The mainspring which kept the Indian Trade in North America in operation in the eighteenth century was the demand for furs and skins in western Europe. The customs and styles of dress among European nobles and courtiers, ecclesiastical and university officials, and wealthy burghers created the demand for furs; the demand for skins rested chiefly upon the needs of the more humble classes of society ...
>
> From the earliest days of the Greeks and Romans until the sixteenth century the people of central Asia and western Europe were supplied with furs and skins from the great northern plains of Eurasia.... At the time of the discovery of America, Vienna, Danzig, Lübeck and Hamburg were the great fur marts of Europe and the great navigators to Muscovy were based in part on the demand for furs. The furs and skins from the second great region of supply—northern North America—had to compete with those from Russia and Siberia in the markets of Europe. So successfully was this done that the great fur marts were shifted to London, Amsterdam and Paris, and the quest for furs took the place of the quest for gold, silver, and precious stones in luring the white man to penetrate into the vast unknown regions north of Mexico....
>
> The mutual immense profits of the trade in furs and skins ... led both savages and civilized men to desire and to maintain trading relations in spite of the heavy risks to life and property to all concerned in such trade.[28]

In 1628, William Bradford, of the Plymouth Plantation documented Dutch weapons sales to the Iroquois, so very early in the interaction between the Europeans and Indians the Indians, specifically the Iroquois, had access to modern weapons. This changed the nature of warfare for the rest of the century because stone-age weapons, such as bows and arrows were now inferior weaponry. By 1644 it was reported that the Iroquois had about four hundred guns; the English, Swedes and French also sold them guns.[29]

The weapons trade had at least three consequences. First, it provided beaver pelts to the colonists/traders who sold them in Europe and in turn provided the Indians with previously unavailable goods such as axes, kettles, tools, blankets, and firearms. The Indians quickly became dependent on these goods. Second, the trade for weapons and fur introduced diseases into the New World for which there was no Native American immunity. This would have a devastating effect on the native populations. Last, it provided competition, both between colonists seeking the furs and between the tribes attempting to supply the furs to keep the trade goods coming. The last reason was the basis for the Beaver Wars of the seventeenth century.

Beaver Wars

This cycle of violence probably started with disease. As Jennings (*The Ambiguous Iroquois Empire*) described,

> The decade of the 1630s witnessed a fearful scourge of epidemic disease among all the Iroquoian tribes that spread from the Hurons through the Five Nations to the Susquehannocks and reduced their population catastrophically by half or more. As a by-product of this horror, the tribes became increasingly dependent on trade goods from Europe, and the corollary of this dependence was heightened competition in trade.[30]
>
> No feasible way existed in the conditions of that era to prevent the competition from heightening to bloodshed.[31]

The Iroquois had another problem, the beaver supply in their neighborhood began to dry up around 1640.[32] This situation and the reduced population made them feel their existence was threatened; they had to expand their beaver territory to keep trade with the colonists going. They were fierce fighters but they had two other advantages over other tribes and confederacies. Their custom was that when they conquered a people they would not destroy them, but would instead absorb them into their nation and the conquered people would become Iroquois. This long-lasting custom served them well in increasing a diminished population.[33] The second advantage was that they were the first tribe to receive firearms, which also gave them an edge.

Beginning in the 1640s the Iroquois systematically attacked and defeated many tribes from northern New York, through the Ohio Valley, all the way to the Mississippi Valley. These tribes included the Petun, Neutral, Mohican, Huron, Erie, among others. Many of the tribes the Iroquois challenged for control of the beaver country were allied with the French, bringing the French into the fighting.[34] During these wars, which lasted decades, they cleared the Ohio country of tribes competing for the fur trade. Interaction with the Shawnee is unclear. Those who believe the Shawnee were in southern Ohio during the Beaver Wars claim they were pushed down to the Cumberland River Valley. Others say the Shawnee had never been to the Ohio Valley at that time and remained in the Cumberland River Valley, only coming to Ohio later.

During the last half of the seventeenth century the wars continued with various alliances between the Iroquois and Ottawa on one side, and the French and the western

Indians on the other. The French invaded the Iroquois homeland more than once and inflicted severe casualties. The English generally backed the Iroquois but weren't directly involved in the war. The Iroquois expanded their control over territory from Pennsylvania, through parts of Maryland and Virginia, all the way through present-day Michigan, Indiana, and Illinois to the Mississippi River.[35] Nonetheless, by the end of the century the Iroquois had been pushed back into their own land by the French and the western tribes. The French were never able to conquer the Iroquois and a stalemate developed which gave an advantage to neither party.

Peace talks began around 1700 and an agreement was reached, The Grand Settlement of 1701. This agreement was reached in Montreal in August, involving the government of New France and several hundred Indians representing dozens of tribes. The French acknowledged that after fifty years of war they could not defeat the Iroquois. The Iroquois had suffered several defeats at the hands of the French, losing population in the process, and were exhausted. The French and the Iroquois each had to compromise.

> Iroquois for practical purposes relinquished pretensions to lands west of the Maumee River and Detroit; their insistence upon hunting west of this line had been the precipitating cause of the wars after 1665. On the other hand, in these negotiations, consummating in the Montreal settlement in 1701, the French and western Indians recognized Iroquois rights to the lands east of this line.[36]

This settlement with the French changed the relationship between the Iroquois and the English. As Wallace ("Origins of Iroquois Neutrality: The Grand Settlement of 1701") explains,

> With the settlement of differences with the French and the French Indians, however, an exclusive alliance with the English would be a millstone around Iroquois necks. A better system would be the playing off of the French and British against each other, each nation protecting the Iroquois from any intrusion by the other.... Thus, in regard to the beaver country, in 1701, the French agreed to Iroquois possession of it and agreed not to invade Iroquois lands in case of a war with the English, as long as the Iroquois remained neutral; and at the same time the English contracted to protect this country from intrusion by the French.[37]

The last sentence of the Wallace quote refers to the "Deed from the Five Nations to the King of their Beaver Hunting Ground."[38] This was a "deed" from the Iroquois to the English for all, or almost all, of the land they had gained (and then lost) during the Beaver Wars. It was signed in Albany with governor Nanfan on July 19, 1701, and is also known as the Nanfan Treaty.[39] The area described is vague but seems to start in Iroquois country around Buffalo, New York and to include the area between Lakes Erie and Huron, Michigan, Detroit and south before winding around Lake Erie back to the Buffalo area. The southern boundary of the "deed" is unclear but seems to include the Ohio country down to the Ohio River. The Iroquois gave up their land claims here but expected English protection and the right to use the lands for hunting. As Jennings says though:

> This "deed" is a worthless piece of paper. It purported to set forth the rights of the Iroquois to vast hunting territories in the west by rights of conquest over the Hurons and other Indians during the beaver wars, and it conveyed these asserted rights to the English Crown. But the conveyance was made precisely because the Iroquois had been driven out of those supposedly conquered lands, which the Indians wanted the King to *re*conquer so as to provide "free hunting" for them "for ever." ... The true meaning of the Iroquois "deed" was exactly the opposite of a conveyance of property or territory. It was a challenge for the English to fight on behalf of the Iroquois for a change, instead of the Iroquois fighting for the English.[40]

Jennings points out in Chapter Two of *The Ambiguous Iroquois Empire* that the British later used this "deed," and other documents, as the basis of their claims on the Ohio country.

They claimed the Iroquois had depended on the colony of New York and therefore any Iroquois claims were British claims.[41] *This was the first major British claim to the Ohio country.*

As a result of the Beaver Wars, by the end of the seventeenth century Ohio had been cleared of Iroquois fur trading competitors. The Iroquois never occupied the territory permanently, certainly not the Mississippi River Valley, but used the Ohio country as a hunting and trapping preserve. Years later, when dealing with the much stronger French and English colonies, the Iroquois claimed the Ohio country "by virtue of conquest." This land lay relatively unpopulated for roughly fifty to seventy years, but the area around it, such as New France and the English colonies on the East Coast, was changing dramatically. It was unimaginable that this land would remain empty; it was too valuable. Various tribes started to move in early in the eighteenth century and the pace picked up later. By mid-century, three parties had intense interest in the Ohio country. It became the focal point for the competition between the three great local powers: the French of New France, the English of the eastern colonies, and the Native Americans who still saw the Ohio country as their homeland.

Ohio Tribes—Reclaiming the Ohio Country

As the native people returned to the Ohio country after the Beaver Wars they found a land of hardwoods and game. As Hurt (*The Ohio Frontier: Crucible of the Old Northwest, 1720–1830*) described it,

> The Native Americans who migrated to the Ohio country during the early eighteenth century found a land of rugged hills, dense forest, and open prairies. Above all, however, the forest dominated the landscape, and it spread with a grandeur and foreboding across Ohio like a heavy green blanket. Where the foothills of the Appalachians formed the southeastern third of Ohio, a forest of red and white oak (many six feet or more in diameter and fifty to sixty feet in height), sugar maple, hickory, black walnut, sycamore, hemlock, cedar, beech, and buckeye trees covered the rolling landscape. In this unglaciated region steep hills, narrow ravines, and sluggish streams provided an unsurpassed area for hunting and fishing to sustain Indian families. Later these lands proved less than desirable, with the exception of the rich soils in the river valleys, for white settlers who wanted to use them for farming.
>
> The glaciated plains that spread to the west also had a forest cover consisting primarily of beech, elm, cherry, and ash. Along the river bottoms natural meadows occasionally opened where deer, elk, and bison grazed on a luxuriant cover of bluegrass, white clover, and wild rye. The soils in the till plains proved the richest and most productive.... In the glaciated western and north-central portions of Ohio, the latter area known as the Lake Plains, prairies that extended several miles occasionally provided a welcome relief from the forest's canopy, and sunlight enabled the grass to grow as high as a horse's back.[42]

As Hurt observed, some of the hilly eastern foothills were not originally desirable for farmland, but ideal farming country was nearby, just a little to the north and west. One colonist who found it early was the Marylander Christopher Gist (1706–1759), who made his first trip into the Ohio country in 1750. In his journal, he noted,

> Crossed the Little Miami River … to the big Miami River … is fine, rich level Land, well timbered with large Walnut, Ash Sugar Trees, Cherry Trees &c, it is well watered with a great Number of little Streams or Rivulets, and full of beautiful natural Meadows, covered with wild Rye, blue Grass and Clover, and abounds with Turkeys, Deer, Elks and most Sorts of Game particularly Buffaloes, thirty or forty of which are frequently seem feeding in one Meadow: In short it wants Nothing but Cultivation to make it a most delightfull Country.[43]

Even before the Native Americans completed their return to the Ohio country, there were explorers who were scouting the country for exploitation by the English.

The Native American migration back to the Ohio country took place during a relatively short time from roughly 1700 through the 1750s. Some moved to Ohio after being displaced by the previous Iroquois (Beaver) Wars and others because they were displaced by colonial pressure in the east. Most common among the tribes moving into Ohio from the east or south were the Delaware, the Shawnee, and the Mingo. The Wyandot, Miami, and Ottawa moved in from the west.[44] The Mingo were an Iroquoian tribe, mostly Seneca, who migrated from the Seneca territory into northeastern Ohio and western Pennsylvania in the first half of the eighteenth century. The name is derived from the Delaware name for them, "Minqua," or "Mingwe," which means treacherous.[45] Having participated in the Beaver Wars as part of the Iroquoian war on the peoples of Ohio, and then having used the land as a hunting preserve, perhaps the Mingo decided to move back there to live because they liked the neighborhood.

The Delaware, named by the English for the Delaware River near which they originally resided, called themselves the Lenni Lenape, variously interpreted as "original people" or "men of men."[46] They were an Algonquian people apparently in that original location for hundreds of years, perhaps from the original migrations chronicled in the Walum Olum. Delaware called themselves grandfathers of tribes and were recognized by other tribes with the same title. They were among the first natives encountered by the Europeans and were gradually forced west until, by the 1740s, they settled in the Ohio Valley in southeastern Ohio.

By 1750, these tribes inhabited the Ohio country, which had been virtually uninhabited for decades. They already had experienced years, even decades, of contact with both the French and English and many tribes were in Ohio because of it. The country they now occupied was claimed not only by them, but by the French and the English. The competition for this land that … "wants Nothing but Cultivation to make it a most delightfull Country," was about to heat up. One of the key routes from the eastern seaboard to the Ohio country would be across the Alleghenies, the gateway from western Maryland to the Ohio River.

Moving Through the Mountains

The Appalachian Mountain chain, and especially the Alleghenies, proved a formidable obstacle for the early colonists. This wasn't a problem early in colonial life because there was plenty of land and few colonists. The Piedmont, up to the river fall lines, and the coastal plain provided more than enough land for the early English colonists to grow and prosper. As English colonies expanded, and as new opportunities (land) presented themselves in the west they ran into the mountain barrier. This happened quickly and, only a few decades after 1607, expeditions set out to explore beyond the mountains. The early expeditions were by individuals or very small parties who used the easiest ways to and through the mountains; they preceded any mass migration. We know they had long been preceded by the Native Americans who had occupied areas in and around the mountains for hundreds, if not thousands, of years, and therefore clearly knew how to move through them. Later, the colonists trading with the Indians would follow these same paths.

The many streams and rivers that started in the mountains flowed either east to the Atlantic or west toward the Mississippi and the Gulf. Most of them combined as tributaries to form much larger rivers, such as the Potomac, Delaware, Allegheny, Monongahela, and

Ohio before they reached their ultimate destination. While they were still in the mountains, they were small and spread out and drained large regions. In the process of running down the mountains they often cut passes into these mountains. A look at any topographical map, will show this multitude of streams and rivers covering all the states in the mountain regions. Often the waterways are close together including some that flow to different watersheds. For example, at Wills Creek, the Potomac, which flows to the Atlantic, is less than forty miles from the Youghiogheny, which flows into the Monongahela and eventually into the Ohio. It is only about eight miles from the headwaters of the North Branch of the Potomac at the southwest tip of Maryland, to the headwaters of the Youghiogheny in West Virginia. In southwest Virginia, the distance is less than ten miles from the New River, which flows ultimately into the Kanawha River and then to the Ohio, and the North Branch of the Roanoke River, which flows toward the Atlantic. Within a day's walk, a person could move from a river flowing east to the sea to one flowing west to the Ohio.

Contrary to common belief, the Indians of the Appalachian chain did not often use these rivers for transport. The dugout canoes (poplar, sycamore, walnut, elm) they used were heavy compared to the birch bark canoes used for the fur trade in New France, and could not easily be used in the rivers coming from the mountains which were often filled with rapids. The heavy canoes could not be easily portaged around the rapids or through

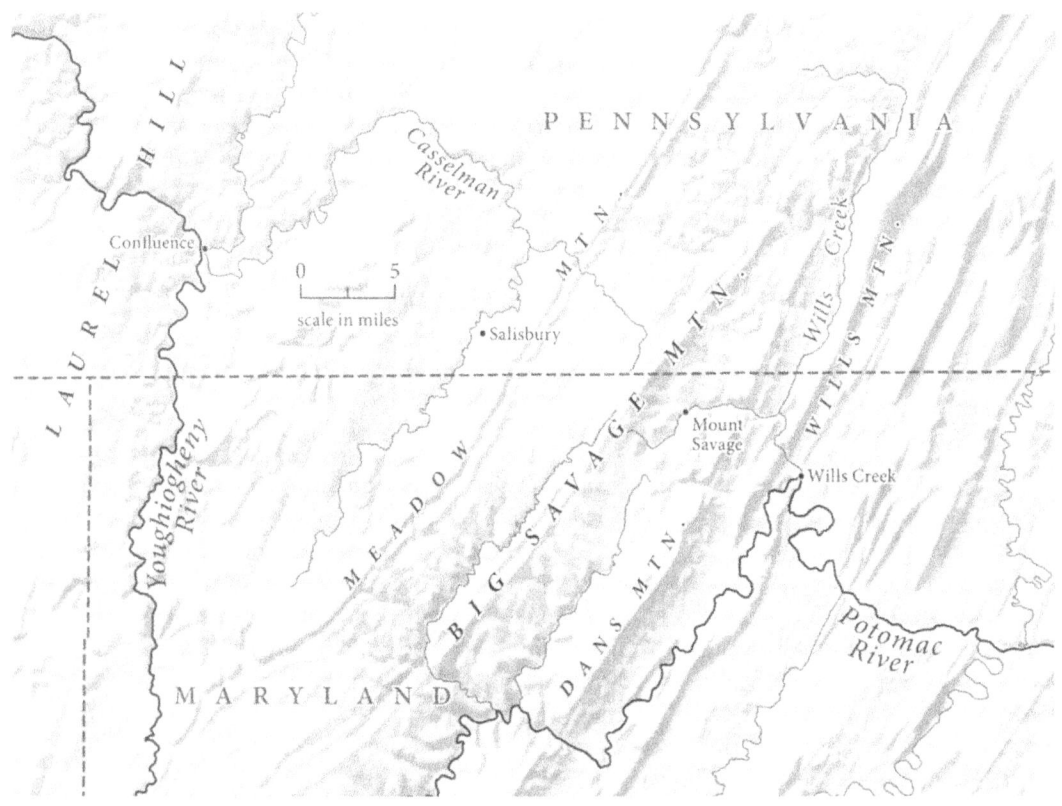

Map 2: Potomac and Youghiogheny rivers. The Potomac River, at its intersection with Wills Creek, is very close to the Youghiogheny River headwaters. Maps of these types gave the wholly inaccurate impression one could move easily over the mountains by going up the Potomac, portaging to the Youghiogheny and taking it down to the Monongahela and Ohio rivers in Ohio country.

the mountains.[47] However, these rivers and streams made easy paths through the mountains for the Native Americans as they moved for hunting, war, or trade. The rivers were often level or in valleys between the mountains. At one time there were also large animals, such bison or elk, which made trails through the woods and mountains that later were followed by the Indians. Any valley, whether cut from the mountains by water or made naturally at the birth of the mountains, was clearly an easy path to follow.

In the Appalachian chain the valleys tended to run north-south following the direction of the mountains. This was especially true of the Great Appalachian Valley which stretched between the east and west ranges of the Appalachians from New England to Alabama. In some places there were natural east-west gaps in the mountains such as the Mohawk Valley in northern New York and the Cumberland Gap in Tennessee. The Cumberland Gap was discovered by Thomas Walker in 1750 and made more famous by Daniel Boone as he led settlers to the Kentucky area in 1775. Certainly, the Indians of Tennessee and the Carolinas had used this gap centuries before the Europeans "discovered" it.

Indian Paths

The largest and most important paths acquired names first from the Indians and later from the colonists, who moved west or south on them. Any names we have are from the Historic Indians, names used after contact with the Europeans, although the paths were certainly used earlier by earlier cultures. These path names often changed later when the paths blossomed into full-grown wagon trails. The names also changed as the paths left one area for another, from north to south or from east to west. They became more anglicized as the thousands of settlers moved on them migrating south or west. Most of the well know trails moved in a north-south direction along the mountains simply because it was easier to walk in the valleys between the mountains. Obviously, many paths also had an east-west direction. Many tribes, the Shawnee for example, straddled the mountains and had moved on these trails across the mountains.

The Great Warriors Path was a north-south path starting in Mohawk country near Elmira, New York, and entering Pennsylvania near Tioga (Athens).[48] From Tioga the Great Warriors Path followed the north branch of the Susquehanna River to Shamokin (Sunbury) in east-central Pennsylvania. Once the southbound traveler reached Shamokin, he could then use any number of paths to his ultimate destination, including the Tuscarora Path. This path headed southwest following many creeks, such as the Tuscarora, and following the arc of the Allegheny Ridge, staying in the valleys between the ridges. The path continued down the Great Appalachian Valley all the way to Georgia and Alabama. Both war parties and trading parties used this corridor which explains why seashells from Florida could be found far north of Pennsylvania. The common thread for these and similar paths was that the path followed a river or streambed through any mountainous areas which minimized the steep climbs. As Hanna (*The Wilderness Trail*) noted,

> The trans-Alleghany movement of the Delawares of the Turtle and Turkey clans from the forks of the Susquehanna to the Ohio began before 1724. They went chiefly from the vicinity of Shamokin ... to a point on the Alleghany some ten miles below the mouth of the Mahoning. Here they built their first town, which they called Kithenning, or Kittanning, literally, "Great-River-Town," or "Town at the Great River." ... The route taken by the Delawares from Shamokin was in all probability the earliest important path between the Ohio and the main stream of the Susquehanna.[49]

The Monongahela River and the Potomac River, two major waterways that drain in opposite directions, are no closer anywhere than they are in western Maryland and southwest

Pennsylvania. The Shawnee, who inhabited southern Ohio, northern Kentucky, northern Virginia, and Pennsylvania, almost certainly used the paths and waterways described above to commute between these two rivers. This would facilitate trade from the Atlantic seaboard to the Ohio Valley, and if not monopolized by the Shawnee, would have been strongly leveraged by them.

English Colonization

The history of the early voyages of discovery to the east, by persons as Prince Henry the Navigator and Vasco da Gama, is well known. Similarly well-known are the voyages of discovery in the New World by Columbus and others, especially those looking for the elusive Northwest Passage. The history of the link between Maryland and Ohio begins with the colonization of eastern North America by the English in the early seventeenth century with colonies in Virginia and Massachusetts Bay. Of these two, the Virginia colony had the more significant impact on the Maryland gateway to Ohio because of its geographical location.

In 1606, King James I (1566–1625) gave a business charter to two related stock companies, the Virginia Company of London and the Virginia Company of Plymouth.[50] These were joint stock companies with the objective of making a profit by establishing colonies in America to exploit the resources therein, including gold if it was found. The leaders of the two companies were colleagues but decided to establish two separate companies. The Virginia Company of London was granted land between thirty-four and forty-one-degrees latitude; South Carolina to New York, and was called the First Colony of Virginia. The Virginia Company of Plymouth was granted the land between thirty-eight and forty-five-degrees latitude; the Chesapeake Bay to Maine, and was called the Second Colony of Virginia. The overlapping zone was available to either company as long as settlements were not established within one hundred miles of one another. These were not "sea to sea" grants but went inland one hundred miles.

Virginia

The Virginia Company of London established the well-known colony at Jamestown in 1607. The settlement had difficulty sustaining itself and had to have assistance from London, including supplies and more settlers. It established tobacco as a cash crop, which helped but did not succeed in itself making the colony self-sustaining. There were internal difficulties because some colonists expected the new world would be an easy source of riches, such as gold, as it had been for the Spanish; they were disappointed when no gold was found. Clashes with the Native Americans continued off and on for several years. At first the shortage of workers was addressed by bringing in indentured servants who were obligated by contract to work off their indenture before they could be free to set off on their own. The labor shortage was also then offset by the introduction of African slaves brought to the colony as early as 1619. Virginia survived as a colony but the Virginia Company of London did not and was a failure as a business venture. In 1624, King James I changed the status of the colony to that of royal colony to be administered by a governor appointed by the king.[51]

During this period, two other charters for Virginia attempted to help the colony survive. The second charter of Virginia, May 23, 1609, was the most consequential. It stipulated the boundaries from "sea to sea" and a northern boundary that went northwest from the coast so that all of Ohio and most of what is now Pennsylvania would be included in Virginia.[52] (See Map 7.) This second charter had a major impact over a century later when Virginians started to claim the Ohio country in their attempts to move west. It engenderd disputes not only with the French and Native Americans but also with the neighboring colony of Pennsylvania.

Massachusetts

The Virginia Company of Plymouth, led by Sir John Popham (1531–1607) and Sir Fernando Gorges (1565–1647), also tried to establish a colony in 1607, Sagadahoc, at what is now the Kennebec River in Maine. This colony did not survive for a number of reasons including weather, lack of supplies, and internal strife. The company held on for a few years because the area was still promising, but in 1619 it was finally dissolved. Following the dissolution, Sir Fernando Gorges and his colleagues received a royal patent from James I, dated November 3, 1620, for the establishment of the Council of New England.[53]

The Council made colonizing attempts but they were not successful. Interestingly, two grants they made that were successful were to two dissenting organizations, the Separatists (Pilgrims) and the Puritans. Considering Gorges's royalist tendencies these were curious grants and one wonders how they were justified. The Pilgrims sailed on September 6, 1620, and they spotted Cape Cod on November 9, 1620.[54]

In 1628, the Council of New England granted a charter to a group of Puritan businessmen for a small grant within the larger Council grant. The Charter of Massachusetts Bay, issued by Charles I (1600–1649) on March 4, 1629, first acknowledged the grant his father, James I, had issued previously to the Council of New England, and then acknowledged the grant given by the Council to the Puritans the previous year. He then granted the charter to "the Governor and Company of Mattachusetts [Massachusetts] Bay in Newe England."[55] In 1630 this group of Puritans, taking their charter with them in order to be able to control it, started the Massachusetts Bay Colony.[56]

The Massachusetts Bay Colony was founded primarily by religious dissenters who established the colony in order to practice their religion without interference. It was not established for commercial purposes so any expansion westward was to accommodate the expanding population. There was no desire to find gold or to find the westward passage to India.

The colony in Virginia was a different story. Established for profit it almost failed and began to thrive only when tobacco became a valuable commodity. The Virginia colonial mindset was to constantly look for more opportunities especially to the west, including more trade, with the Indians and the still lurking idea of the passage to the South Seas, to India.

Virginia Looks West

The Virginia Tidewater area was quickly settled up to the fall line of the numerous rivers. Ocean going ships were able to sail up the Virginia rivers and directly service the tobacco plantations located on the rivers. This easy access to the plantations is one of the reasons large cities, such as Philadelphia or New York, did not develop as they did elsewhere; there was no need. Exploration beyond the fall line began early in the colony's history, but moving beyond the falls took longer, perhaps because of the frequent colonial-Indian wars.

Not until the 1640s was a series of forts established at the falls of the rivers, including the James and Appomattox rivers, situated to protect against the Indian uprisings, the latest of which was in 1644.

Fort Henry was established in 1646 at the falls of the Appomattox River, near present day Petersburg, Virginia, and was headed by Captain Abraham Wood (c. 1610–1680). Although he initially was an indentured servant, common in Virginia at the time, Wood became independent and a trader, and acquired a great deal of land near the river. He entered politics in the House of Burgesses, as many landowners did. He was appointed to head Fort Henry through a unique, almost semi-feudal arrangement. Fortifying lands on the frontier was an expensive proposition, so a public-private arrangement was made, Wood would have to maintain and man the fort at his own expense for at least three years, in consideration for release from certain taxes. He did this and stayed for the next thirty years. During that time, Wood was instrumental in sending out numerous trading parties and at least four expeditions. The trading parties were sent west for commerce with the Indians.[57]

Another purpose of the expeditions was to discover what was beyond the mountains, and especially to seek the South Sea. Alvord (*The First Explorations of the Trans-Alleghany Region by the Virginians 1650–1674*) cites the governor in a 1626 letter to the Privy Council, "discoveries by land … are of great hope both for the riches of the mountains [gold] and probabilities of finding a passage to the South Sea."[58] That hope was still alive in the 1640s. The South Sea was thought to be only a few days' journey beyond the head of the James River. Wood continued to send out trading parties and some small expeditions into the 1650s but little was known and still less written about them.

The most significant expedition initiated by Wood started in September 1671. It was led by Captain Thomas Batts (c. 1630–c. 1690) and included Thomas Wood and Robert Fallam (1623–1702), who kept the record of the expedition. The South Sea lure was still alive. According to Alvord, "The three gentlemen bore a commission from Major-general Wood 'for finding out the ebbing and flowing of the Waters on the other side of the Mountains in order to the discovery of the South Sea.'"[59] This Batts and Fallam mission was the first English mission to cross the mountains in western Virginia and find a river that flowed west into the Ohio. The entire trip lasted from September 1 to October 1. They were clearly not the first ones to travel the area because they found some trees that had been marked (with the letters MANI[60]), but they were the first to record their travels. They reached the New River on September 13, near the present border between Virginia and West Virginia.[61]

The New River arises in North Carolina, cuts northeast into southern Virginia, and then heads northwest to present-day West Virginia, which was then still part of Virginia. It flows into the Kanawha which then flows into the Ohio. The New River is unusual as it is just west of the eastern continental divide, and therefore flows toward the west, toward the Mississippi, rather than toward the east and to the Atlantic. The nearby Roanoke River flows to the Atlantic as most eastern rivers do. The New River is actually very old sharing its headwaters with the old Teays River, which dates back millions of years. The Teays flowed from the same source as the New River, but it flowed west across Ohio to the Mississippi. It was overrun and diverted by the many glaciers that covered Ohio over millions of years. These glaciers, and part of the Teays River, are what eventually gave rise to the Ohio River.[62]

Alvord's description of the Batts and Fallam expedition is based on the journal kept by Fallam, which is included in section five of Alvord's book. However, others have also reconstructed the expedition using the same journal and have come to different conclusions on where the expedition ended. Some thought it might have gone farther up the New River to the Kanawha River. Another account has the expedition ending far west of the New

River at present-day Matewan, West Virginia, on the West Virginia-Kentucky border. This account also claims the names of Batts and Fallam had been erroneously changed from Batte and Hallam.[63] Despite these discrepancies on the final leg of the expedition, all agree that they had discovered the New River and, therefore, the Ohio River Valley.

In 1716, years after the Batts and Fallam expedition, another westward expedition was mounted by Virginia Lieutenant Governor Alexander Spotswood (c. 1676–1740). The objective this time was not the discovery of the South Sea, the goal of Batts and Fallam, but to popularize the westward expansion of the Virginia colony. The South Sea now was not presumed to be quite as close as originally thought. Spotswood departed Williamsburg and traveled northwest before the expedition into the west really began in Germanna, Virginia, near the Rapidan River. He was joined by several prominent Virginians and was prepared for a rather comfortable trip.

> The whole number of the party, including gentlemen, rangers, pioneers, Indians, and servants, was probably about fifty. They had with them a large number of riding and packhorses, an abundant supply of provisions, and an extraordinary variety of liquors.[64]

This was the first organized expedition into the Shenandoah Valley, but it did not cross the eastern continental divide and did not reach the Ohio Valley. The Shenandoah River flows north, ultimately to the Potomac, which flows into the Atlantic. To encourage expansion to the Shenandoah Valley, Spotswood had a rather expensive trinket struck, a golden horseshoe with precious stones that could be attached to a watch chain, and presented one to each member of the party. Large-scale expansion did not happen for years although some claimed there were some settlers in the Shenandoah Valley within a year after the Spotswood expedition. Whereas the Batts and Fallam expedition could be, and was, used years later to claim the Ohio Valley for Great Britain, Spotswood's expedition to expand Virginia colonization could not be used for such a claim, because it never reached the Ohio Valley.

New France

Before they became successful in the early seventeenth century, the French, like the English, made some early unsuccessful attempts at colonization in the sixteenth century. The first of these efforts was by the explorer and would-be colonizer Jacques Cartier (1491–1557). Cartier made three voyages, starting in 1534. On his first voyage he discovered and explored the Gulf of St. Lawrence and planted a cross on the Gaspe' Peninsula claiming the territory for France. He was unsuccessful in discovering the coveted Northwest Passage, but he started to trade European goods for fish and other food. On his second voyage (1535–1536), Cartier followed the St. Lawrence down to Stadacona (Quebec) and then to Hochelaga (Montreal), areas which would become the heart of New France. On his third voyage (1541–1542) Cartier started an unsuccessful settlement. His voyages were the first hint this new land could supply beaver pelts for France; fur was to become the new gold for New France. Although he, like his predecessors, was not successful in finding the Northwest Passage his voyages did set the stage for the colonization of New France about seventy years later.[65]

Champlain and New France

After Cartier's unsuccessful attempt at settlement there was little movement until the turn of the century. On December 18, 1603, the French king, Henry IV (1553–1610), granted an exclusive charter to Pierre du Gast, Sieur de Monts (1564–1628), to inhabit the lands of Acadia for the purpose of trading with the natives especially in furs.[66] The grant covered the area from the fortieth parallel to the forty-sixth parallel, roughly from the latitude of New Jersey and central Ohio to New Brunswick, Canada. Ironically, the northern boundary did not include the present-day city of Quebec. Others would be prohibited from that area for ten years.[67] New France was to be colonized to support the fur trade.

De Monts took Samuel de Champlain (1574–1635) with him and in 1604 started a settlement on Sainte-Croix Island, an island between what is now Maine and New Brunswick, Canada. The Sainte Croix settlement was a failure because of harsh weather, lack of fresh water, and disease. In 1605 Champlain moved the settlement to Port Royal on the north coast of what is now Nova Scotia, to a land that was fertile with moderate weather. Here the French established their policy of friendship with the Indians. This intention to coexist peacefully with the Native Americans continued in later colonies in New France. The Port Royal settlement was more successful than the one at Sainte-Croix, but still not permanent as the company failed and the settlers of Port Royal returned to France in 1607.[68]

Champlain was still interested in colonizing New France and once again appealed to the king for support. Part of his argument was that English had founded colonies in Virginia and Maine and were in danger of encroaching on the territories claimed for New France. Part of Maine was included in the French claim of Acadia. The king concurred with the proposal and on January 7, 1608, Henry IV issued a new decree, this time with a monopoly of only one year.

> On the basis of "information that has been given to us by those who come from New France, regarding the good quality and fertility of lands in that country, and that the inhabitants thereof are disposed to receive the knowledge of God, we have resolved to continue the settlement which has already begun there."[69]

Champlain sailed again to the St. Lawrence and in July 1608, and established the first permanent French settlement in New France at Quebec. He spent most of the rest of his life in New France trying to make a go of the fur trade and to increase the population, but he made little headway. In 1629, Champlain was forced out by the English and returned to France, but he returned to Quebec in 1633 and served as governor, holding this post from 1633 until his death in 1635. The fur trade thrived but the settlements did not. By the time of his death there were fewer than two hundred permanent settlers in the colony.[70] Well after Champlain's death the French crown made a more determined attempt to increase the presence of colonists in New France.

Growth of the Colony

Despite the almost coincidental years of settlement, 1607 and 1608, the colonies of England and of New France were very different from one another and developed along different lines. These differences would have an impact on the future of New France. One difference was the interaction with the aboriginal people, the Native Americans. The New England and Virginia colonists saw these people as savage foes, a group to be avoided and kept at a distance. Although this eventually changed, it was a source of much early bloodshed.

On the other hand, Champlain sought to cultivate relations between his colonists and the Native Americans. He wanted to expand the fur trade, which meant doing business with these tribes and he set up numerous trading posts throughout the country to facilitate this interchange. The colonists of New France quickly established friendly relations with the Huron nation, which occupied the land of the upper Great Lakes. To foster this trade Champlain encouraged young men to interact with the tribes very closely. They became known as the *coureurs de bois* or "runners of the woods." These Frenchmen traveled far and wide for months at a time to gather beaver pelts. They often integrated into the tribes, including intermarriage; they became as much Indian as they were French.[71] Many turned outlaw in order to sell furs they obtained through unofficial channels.

Like the Spanish, the French saw the opportunity to convert the heathen aborigines and invited the Jesuits to undertake this task and set up missions in the territory.

The most telling difference between the French and the English involved the growth of the colonies and the dramatic differences in the growth rate. Fischer (*Champlain's Dream*) notes this problem.

> Its population was very small and in most years grew scarcely at all. In the winter of 1627–28, Champlain wrote that "55 people, men, women, and children depended on the habitation for subsistence, not including the native inhabitants." Other European settlements, by comparison, were expanding rapidly. By 1628, the Dutch had 270 colonists in New Netherland. The English Pilgrims at Plymouth were 300 strong in 1629. A census of Virginia counted 1,275 English settlers and 22 Africans in 1624. Massachusetts had 506 English Puritans in 1630.[72]

The census of Canada estimates that the population of Quebec in 1629, just a few years before the death of Champlain, was 117.[73] There were not enough settlers from France to grow the population, and there was simply no reason for most to emigrate from France to a wilderness area. The religious turmoil at the time in France involved the dissenting Huguenots. To escape persecution, they began emigrating from France in the late sixteenth century and continued to emigrate in the seventeenth century. However, as dissenters they were explicitly denied entrance to New France, a Catholic country. Charles Prestwood Lucas (*A Historical Geography of the British Colonies, Vol. V, Canada-Part I (New France)*) claimed this was the fatal flaw explaining the failure to achieve a robust colonization of New France.

> The most fatal mistake made by the French in regard to North America was the exclusion of the Huguenots. The men who wished to leave England went to the present United States. The men who wished to leave France were not allowed to go to Canada, and went in considerable numbers to England and her colonies. The effect, therefore, of Roman Catholic exclusiveness was that, though France had a far greater population than England, the greatest French colony failed for wont of colonists. Nor was it only a matter of quantity, but a matter of quality also. The Huguenots were the type of men who would make homes, create business, and build up communities beyond the seas. They were of the same strong fibre as the New England Puritans. In the competition of the coming time, New France was doomed in consequence of being closed to French Protestants.[74]

This is the exact opposite of the situation in New England where the population increased dramatically after the Puritans established the Massachusetts Bay Colony. According to estimates of the U.S. Census Bureau there were about 4,700 colonists in America in 1630. By 1640 that had grown to almost 27,000, with 9,000 of this increase in Massachusetts alone.[75]

The issue of colonization was not a temporary one but lasted for the entire existence of New France; it was a major factor in the eventual replacement of the empire of New France in America by the British Empire. The original purpose of the foothold in North America was trade, especially in beaver pelts and the interests that promoted this trade held sway for years. Ultimately, the French did come to a realization that to take de facto possession of the land it was necessary to increase the population. This took many forms over the years. The first attempt at reinvigorating the colony came in 1627 when Cardinal

Richelieu (1585–1642), first minister to Louis XIII (1601–1643), started the Company of New France, better known as the Company of One Hundred Associates for the number of investors it had. One goal was to increase the population, but the objective of stabilizing the fur trade was still present.[76]

At the same time, the seigneurial system was established by Richelieu as a means of increasing settlement. This was a semi-feudal system in which seigneurs were granted land and expected to obtain inhabitants to work the land. Most of the land was along the St. Lawrence between Montreal and Quebec. The Company of One Hundred Associates managed this system. Although not basically oppressive, it was still a top-down semi-feudal system without the incentives the English colonists were seeing for new opportunities and self-government. The Company of One Hundred Associates lasted until 1663 when Louis XIV (1638–1715) made New France into a royal province, again to boost colonization. By then the population of New France was about 2,500 and the population of the English colonies was about 100,000. The colony started to grow slightly under this direct royal control.[77] One step the king took was to establish the *Filles du Roi*, or Daughters of the King. He paid for hundreds of young unmarried women to go to New France to marry male settlers already there, and therefore increase the population internally; this action helped.[78] However, by 1754, at the start of the French and Indian War, this royally governed, semifeudal system, which still depended more on furs than on agriculture, had a population of only about 55,000 compared to the English colonies' population of almost 1,500,000.[79]

Expanding New France

Shortly after taking royal control of New France, Louis XIV appointed Jean Talon (1626–1694) to be the Intendant of justice, police, and finances. The Intendant was the administrator of the internal affairs, just under the governor. In his two terms, 1665–1668 and 1670–1672, Talon vigorously attempted to expand settlement, commerce, industry, and territory in the colony. One of his goals was to increase settlement and in that regard he was the administrator of the *Filles du Roi* project. He was successful and the population doubled from 1663 to 1673, from 2,500 to 6,800; this was still very small compared to that of the English colonies.[80]

Talon was aware of the potential of North America. When he arrived in 1670, he wrote to the French minister, Colbert,

> This country is laid out in such a way that by means of the St. Lawrence one can go everywhere inland, thanks to the lakes which lead to its source in the West and to the rivers into it along its shores, opening the way to the North and the South.[81]

He was also concerned about the strong presence of the English on the coast and even suggested conquering New Holland in order to give France another entrance into the country. The charter for the Hudson's Bay Company was issued just before Jean Talon returned to New France and may have been the reason for the widespread exploration and territorial expansion he initiated during his second term as Intendant starting in 1670. He sent out many expeditions to accomplish the expansion, first looking westward. On September 3, 1670, he sent Daumont de Saint-Lusson (d. c1677) to take possession for the King of France the, "whole central region of America." Talon was not one to shun lofty goals. By June 1671 Saint-Lusson and his party reached Sault Ste. Marie at the edge of Lake Superior. Saint-Lusson did not shirk his duty either; he raised his sword and a handful of earth and proclaimed:

> In the name of the Most High, Mighty, and Redoubted Monarch, Louis, Fourteenth of that name, Most Christian King of France and of Navarre, I take possession of this place, Sainte Marie du Saut, as also of Lakes Huron and Superior, the Island Manitoulin, and all countries, rivers, lakes, and streams contiguous and adjacent thereunto,—both those which have been discovered and those which may be discovered hereafter, in all their length and breadth, bounded on the one side by the seas of the North and of the West, and on the other by the South sea.... *Vive le Roi*."[82]

Thus the claim was made for New France to extend from the St. Lawrence to the west coast.

Talon was also interested in exploring and claiming lands in the south, still expecting to reach the South Sea by moving in that direction. However, in exploring southward he was anticipated by Robert Cavelier de La Salle (1643–1687), traditionally the discoverer of the Ohio River (*la Belle Rivière*).

La Salle was born in Rouen in 1643 and was a Jesuit for several years. He left the order to pursue more adventurous activities, ultimately traveling to New France in 1666, where he was assigned a seigneury near Montreal. While there, he heard about a river in the south that might be the imagined route to China. Excited by the idea, he approached Governor Courcelle for permission to make the exploration.[83] Although he got the patent to do it he received no backing from Courcelle regarding funding; he was on his own. A Sulpician priest, Dollier de Casson (1636–1701), had a similar idea and broached it with the governor. De Casson was encouraged to combine his exploration with La Salle. There was mutual agreement, so on July 6, 1669, they set off to look for the Ohio.[84] This was a year before Talon arrived for his second term.

Several weeks into the expedition, in October, the priests were persuaded of a mission opportunity farther west in the Great Lakes region and they split with La Salle leaving him alone or with a small party. The story then became a little more confusing. La Salle kept journals which were known to have existed years after the expedition, but these have been lost. Some recent accounts claim he had not carried out his mission to look for the Ohio River and the Gulf of California.[85] However, Francis Parkman (*La Salle and the Discovery of the Great West: France and England in North America, Part Third*) makes a good case that, in fact, he did reach the Ohio. According to Parkman, we have the accounts of the Ohio exploration from a second party who heard the story from La Salle years later in Paris, and also from La Salle's claim in 1677 to Count Frontenac, governor at the time, that he did reach the Ohio and followed it all the way to the falls near present-day Louisville. Parkman had maps which had been made by a La Salle contemporary, Louis Joliet who also attributed the exploration of the Ohio to La Salle. This would have been in the latter half of 1669 or the winter of 1669–1670.[86] It is not clear when La Salle returned but it might have been late summer of 1670.[87] From Parkman's accounts it appears that La Salle did reach and explore the Ohio, the first European to do so.

Others, including Charles Hanna (*The Wilderness Trail Or The Ventures and Adventures of the Pennsylvania Traders on the Allegheny Path*), vigorously dispute the La Salle claim that he reached the Ohio and claim that the first European to do so was a Dutch trader, Arnold Viele, who did it in 1692.[88] Hanna puts forth four arguments including the claim that the Joliet map was later amended with an addition. Arnold Viele was an interpreter and trader operating out of Albany, at that time a Dutch settlement. He had been captured earlier (1687) by the French but apparently was released.

> In 1692 Governor Fletcher of New York sent him and some other Christians to accompany a small band of Shawanese to their homes in the West. Viele remained among these Indians for fifteen months.... While on this tour of duty, Viele is presumed to have explored the country between the Susquehanna and the Ohio, and part of the Ohio Valley.[89]

Other evidence cited is a letter by Pierre Le Moyne d'Iberville (1661–1706), founder of the French colony of Louisiana, written in Rochelle, France, August 30, 1699, to the French minister acknowledging the Viele expedition of 1692.[90] This evidence is as credible as that of Parkman. Although it is not clear who the first European was to see the Ohio, it happened within a twenty-three-year span near the end of the seventeenth century. It is clear that France considered it within the vast territory she claimed throughout the center of North America. The claim was reinforced by a later mission down the Ohio in 1749, which will be covered in a later chapter.

In the autumn of 1670, shortly after he returned to New France, Talon sent La Salle on another mission south to search for the China Sea. This was probably the trip during which La Salle traveled the Great Lakes eventually ending up on lower Lake Michigan. From there he portaged to the Illinois River and followed it downstream. Again, some claim he followed the Illinois River to the Mississippi, but there is no hard evidence that he did. Although La Salle was back in Montreal in August 1671, apparently he did not meet with Talon before Talon again left for France in 1672 after his second tour as Intendant. This prompted a claim that La Salle did not complete his mission.[91] La Salle apparently had a reputation for unreliability.

Talon was not finished pushing the boundaries of New France, and was desirous of challenging the Spanish near the mouth of the Mississippi. Shortly after Saint-Lusson's mission and while still waiting for La Salle, he commissioned Louis Joliet to find the river they knew was there which they were sure flowed into the China Sea. Planned in 1672, it was 1673 before the expedition started. Accompanied by the Jesuit Jacques Marquette, Joliet started in Lake Michigan and through various river routes finally found and followed the Mississippi. This was the first documented discovery of the Mississippi by France. Their intention was to follow the river all the way to the Gulf, for Joliet was now certain that the Gulf of Mexico was the destination, not the China Sea. When they reached the Arkansas River they met some Indians who convinced them that either hostile Indians and/or hostile Spanish would put them in danger. Joliet and Marquette turned around and made their way back. The mission was partially accomplished.[92]

Completing the Link from the St. Lawrence to the Gulf

The New France expansion in North America was basically complete in April 1682, when La Salle canoed down to the mouth of the Mississippi and claimed the whole Mississippi River basin for France, naming it Louisiana in honor of Louis XIV. France now claimed about a third of the present-day North America. The land stretched from the northeast, including Newfoundland and Acadia, down to the Gulf of Mexico. It was bounded on the east by the Appalachians, on the other side of which were the English colonies, and on the west by the Mississippi River basin. This basin included the Missouri and Arkansas rivers and parts of the present states of Montana, Wyoming, Colorado, New Mexico and Texas. It went as far northwest as the present-day Manitoba and Saskatchewan Provinces. New France was considered made up of Canada, Acadia, the upper country (*pays d'en haut*), and Louisiana. Canada, which included Newfoundland, had as its heart, the St. Lawrence River Valley. The name Canada is from the Huron-Iroquois word "Kanata" meaning village or settlement. Jacques Cartier started using it in 1535.[93] The upper country included the land above the Great Lakes all the way to present Provinces of Manitoba and Saskatchewan. The upper Louisiana territory was considered to be Illinois country.

This was the maximum extent of New France in North America. The French could move easily between the St. Lawrence and the Gulf of Mexico via the many lakes and rivers. This expansion did not take overwhelming force because the terrain was easy and they had no natural opposition. As they moved, they set up a series of forts but not settlements; the area was sparsely settled which would become a disadvantage later. The population around 1690 was about 12,000, compared to the population of the English colonies which was twenty times that at around 250,000.[94] New France was rigidly controlled by the mother country and its inhabitants did not experience the economic and political independence afforded the English colonies. Both these factors would be pivotal when the competition heated up in the mid-eighteenth century.

Two

Maryland to 1750

Maryland is a small state, ranking forty-second out of fifty states in area, but it was right in the middle of the thirteen original colonies in size, with six larger and six smaller colonies. It was considered the third of the major English colonies after Virginia and Massachusetts.[1] Although there was a religious aspect to the founding of Maryland, it was not a primary factor as it was in in the Plymouth Colony and the Massachusetts Bay Colony. Founded by Catholic gentry in an age when Catholicism in England was not viewed favorably, this religious aspect was unusual.

Maryland was founded in 1634, less than thirty years after the founding of the Jamestown colony and New France. Geographically the colony was favorably located in the mid–Atlantic region, just above Virginia; in fact, it was carved out of the Virginia colony. Its location, and more importantly its shape, determined that it would be a major factor in the opening of the Ohio country from Maryland, although the Ohio country was unknown and unnamed at the time. Its shape can be viewed, figuratively, as a closed fist with its open forefinger pointed directly at the Ohio country. Maryland stretches from the Atlantic coast, westward across mountain ranges and fertile valleys, all the way to the tip of its panhandle in the Allegheny Mountains.

The founding and initial settlement of the colony went smoothly, but growth did not follow the original plans of the Proprietor, Lord Baltimore, who envisioned a feudal province with large manorial holdings. A feudal province was difficult to establish in the New World and initial growth was slow. Almost forty years after bring founded, Maryland had only about thirteen thousand inhabitants. The settlement in southern Maryland quickly evolved into an insular tobacco producing economy that did grow and prosper.

Western Maryland, beyond the coastal plain, lay undeveloped for decades. It began to prosper in the third and fourth decades of the eighteenth century when the potential of that region was recognized by many immigrant farmers. By 1748, the province had more than ten times the 1675 population and was doing well. Maryland had reached its geographical limits and was boxed in by Virginia and Pennsylvania, neighbors with ambitions for the Ohio country. It was soon realized that Maryland's location was the key to the entrance to the Ohio country, because of the proximity of the upper Potomac (Maryland) and Monongahela (Ohio country) rivers. By the middle of the eighteenth-century Maryland was playing a key role in opening Ohio.[2]

Founders

George Calvert (c. 1580–1632) was a member of the English nobility. After receiving both a Bachelor of Arts and a Master of Arts degree from Oxford, he toured Europe before entering the King's service; he was a friend of King James I (1566–1625). This was an unlikely friendship since James was a survivor of the Gunpowder Plot, hatched by Catholic dissenters, and sponsor of the King James protestant version of the Bible, and Calvert was a Catholic. Their friendship predated Calvert's conversion to Catholicism. However, their friendship started because James trusted Calvert even as a young man. He sent Calvert on a special, but unspecified, mission to Louis XIII (1601–1643) at his accession in 1610, and engaged Calvert in his religious battle with Conrad Vorstius, a professor of divinity at Leiden, the Netherlands, whose theological and political theories were obnoxious to James.[3]

Calvert's service to the King included being in charge of correspondence with the governments of Spain and Italy. He was knighted in 1617 and made Secretary of State in 1619.[4] He remained an advisor to James and may have given an early hint of his view on religious toleration. According to Andrews (*History of Maryland: Province and State*), the Separatists (Pilgrims) had not made any progress on their emigration plans until Calvert became Secretary of State: "The inference is at least natural that as Secretary of State Calvert must have aided the Separatists either directly or indirectly, in obtaining their patent." The King's confidence in Calvert was again displayed in 1624 when Calvert was appointed by the King to transform the Virginia Company colony into a royal colony.[5]

Either through his contacts as Secretary of State, or through other friends, Calvert grew interested in, and invested in, stock companies including the Virginia Company. He also became interested in starting his own colony and did so in 1623 when he obtained a charter for a colony on Newfoundland, which he named Avalon. Later, after a visit there, he was convinced it was not a hospitable place for a colony and he pulled out apparently losing his £25,000 investment. Calvert then petitioned the King for lands in a more hospitable place, such as in Virginia. He had visited that area and was convinced it was his future. Prior to the petition, however, he had converted and became a Roman Catholic in 1625. Although he resigned his post as Secretary of State, because of that conversion, he remained James's friend. Just prior to James's death in 1625, James raised him to an Irish peerage, Baron of Baltimore.[6] In doing so James also dispensed with the oath of ecclesiastical supremacy and kept Calvert on the Privy Council.[7]

It was on August 19, 1629, that he requested the Virginia land. Charles I (1625–1649) was now the King, and he was also friendly with Baltimore. Without waiting for a reply, Calvert, the new Lord Baltimore, made a visit to Virginia. He was not well received, not only because he was looking for his own land there, but also for his "romanish religion." He originally looked at land in the middle of the colony near the James River, but finally selected and plotted a piece near the northern end of the colony and the Potomac River. King Charles I supplied the name Terra Maria, Maryland, after the queen.[8]

The charter passed the privy seal just a few days before George Calvert's death on April 15, 1632. The charter was issued to his son Cecilius (Cecil) Calvert (c. 1605–1675), the second Lord Baltimore, on June 20, 1632, and provided palatine, almost monarchical, powers to Cecil Calvert. In short, this was not to be a self-governing colony like Massachusetts Bay or a stock company colonization like Virginia, but a private domain where the Proprietor had rights similar to a feudal lord. These rights were spelled out in the charter.[9]

The area chosen and described in the charter was fairly straightforward.[10] It was to include all of the land, "between the Ocean on the East ... and between that Boundary on the South [Watkins Point], unto that Part of the Bay of Delaware on the North, which lieth under the Fortieth Degree of North Latitude."[11] In other words it was bounded on the east by the Atlantic Ocean and the Bay of Delaware up to the fortieth parallel. From the Bay of Delaware, it was to go west, "in a right line, by the Degree aforesaid, unto the true meridian of the first Fountain of the River of Pattowmack." The southern boundary was then to follow the far shore of the Potomac River to where it discharges into the Chesapeake Bay and then to Watkins point, a point on the eastern shore of Chesapeake Bay, and from there eastward to the ocean, to complete the province. It included the entire Chesapeake Bay. A contemporary map of Maryland will show that it does not follow these original charter boundaries. At one time or another all of Maryland's boundaries were challenged and many changed. As a result, Maryland is much smaller now than it was as specified in this charter.

Religious Toleration

The early seventeenth century was a time of severe religious strife. There was a strong and expected relationship between the monarchy and the established church, thought to be a necessary bond ever since the Reformation. It was not imaginable that a kingdom could exist with more than one established church; wars were fought to assure one church would dominate under one monarch. The toleration of multiple religions was never considered by either church or state. The king existed to enforce the will of God and the people of the realm were expected to practice his religion if they expected to practice any religion openly; if they did not, they were expected to leave. These practices carried over to the New World.

All the Spanish colonies were set up to be Catholic and missionaries were sent to convert the heathen. New France was Catholic and the dissenting Huguenots were not allowed in. Certainly, the Pilgrims and Puritans of Massachusetts were not tolerant of other religions and were especially hostile to Catholics. They left England precisely to practice their own religion, but would not tolerate others; they were fortunate to be granted land patents that allowed them to settle in the New World. Virginia was slightly different since it was set up as a commercial colony, not a religious one. Although not established for religious purposes, the default position was to follow the Church of England and later that link was made official. From the beginning, there was antipathy to Catholics in Jamestown.

Cecil Calvert remained a friend of King Charles, just as his father had been a friend of King James. Although both Catholics and Puritans were dissenters from the Church of England, James and Charles seemed to have had more trouble with the Puritans, and there was a slightly more lenient attitude toward Catholics than Puritans, at least by the King. The friendship of the King of England and a Catholic Baron was still unusual, and must have raised eyebrows on both sides of the religious divide. Despite the friendship, it is unlikely that Calvert ever thought of establishing a "Catholic colony" as some have claimed; it would not have been possible. Maryland's immediate neighbor, Virginia, was a royal colony with the established religion of the Church of England and was hostile to Catholics. The New England colonies were not royal colonies, they were established through a private company, but they were hostile to Catholics. Despite Charles's friendship with Calvert and his leniency toward Catholics a proprietary Catholic royal colony under King Charles, the Head of the Church of England, would not have been possible.[12]

Nevertheless, Calvert did want to provide some refuge for his co-religionists in the colony he was establishing in America. He was in the minority, and despite his friendship with the King, was hindered in his religious practice. He did not desire a colony that would establish his faith but one that would be tolerant of all faiths, at least Christian faiths. That would be the best he could expect to achieve. The charter, which Calvert wrote and the

King approved, had an explicit goal of "extending the Christian Religion" but did not impose a state church. Had the charter been intended to establish a state religion it would have been very explicit on this point. There was no secret here either. As William Thomas Russell (*Maryland: Land of Sanctuary, A History of Religious Toleration in Maryland from the First Settlement until the American Revolution*) notes, "Charles was in no uncertainty as to Calvert's religious convictions and intentions any more than he had been regarding those of the father of Cecilius." In other words, Charles was aware of the establishment of a colony that would tolerate all Christian religions.[13]

Despite the approval, if not the blessing of the King, Cecil Calvert had to be careful in the implementation. Although he would have liked to be a member of the first group to settle in Maryland, he decided he must stay home and look after his interests. He sent his brother Leonard to be among the first colonists and instructed Leonard to minimize the religious aspects. "He assuredly did not wish religious dissension to jeopardize the expedition and bade his brother Leonard, designated as governor, to 'cause all Acts of Romane Catholique Religion to be done as privately as may be and ... [to] instruct all the Roman Catholiques to be silent upon all occasions of discourse concerning Religion.'"[14] Calvert was careful to achieve a balance of Catholics and Protestants on the first voyage to avoid provoking hostility from either the homeland or the existing colonies which remained hostile to Catholics.

The Province of Maryland had a reputation for religious tolerance in an era when neither the state nor church would accept toleration. As seen by the early efforts of the Calverts this reputation was well-deserved even though it had a somewhat shaky start. As with other provinces, things changed in Maryland and religious tolerance was not always observed. For example, at the time of the English Glorious Revolution in 1688, a group known as the Protestant Associators ousted the Calvert Proprietor, and turned the province into a royal colony, which lasted for about twenty-five years. The Church of England was established as the official church and Catholics were forbidden to hold public office. Nevertheless, despite this interval, Catholics did survive and the early precedent for religious tolerance in Maryland was still recognized. Although it took more than 150 years, that precedent led to the First Amendment.[15]

Maryland Charter

The Maryland Charter is a remarkable document for more than just its silence on an established church. The Proprietor, Sir George Calvert, Lord Baltimore, was given vast, almost monarchical powers. Some speculate that this was not only because he was a good friend of James I, but because things did not go as planned with the Virginia Company, originally set up as a stock company. After a few years Virginia had been converted to a royal colony. More control was recognized to be a necessary component for a new colony, so James I granted Lord Baltimore more control over his province than the Virginia Company had over its province.[16]

The charter was an aristocratic document conferring great powers on the Proprietor. The extent of the grant was broad and the Lord Proprietor controlled all the lands and waters of the province, and was granted the right to initiate legislation, and enact laws,

> with the Advice, Assent, and Approbation of the Free-Men of the same Province, or the greater Part of them, or of their Delegates of Deputies, whom We will shall be called together for the framing of Laws, when, and as often as Need shall require.

Of course, popular assemblies of the early seventeenth century, if they existed at all, were expected to be directed by the crown's representative, unlike today's assemblies of freemen.

The Proprietor was entitled to establish courts of justice, appoint judges and magistrates, and pardon offenses. He had the power to set up towns and harbors and impose import taxes, and to confer titles. He could sell or rent land. He could set up militias, wage war, and, if need be, declare martial law. Furthermore, the crown pledged,

> that We ... at no time hereafter, will impose ... any impositions, Customs, or other taxations, Quotas, or Contributions whatsoever, in or upon the Residents or Inhabitants of the Province aforesaid for their Goods, Lands, or Tenements within the same Province.

In other words, the crown would not tax the land of the settlers. For all this Calvert was to pay two arrowheads per year and one-fifth of any gold or silver that might be found.

Sprinkled among the vast proprietary powers the charter conferred were forward looking aspects, such as a representative assembly, that seemed to work against some of the prerogatives of the Proprietor. Since George Calvert wrote the charter, approved by James I, Calvert was recognizing the right of an assembly to frame laws. Some sort of self-government was essentially inevitable in these colonies on the Anglo-American frontier, because they were so far from the mother country and day-to-day business could not be overseen by England. Nevertheless, it is still remarkable to have it included in the original charter. Cecil Calvert did exercise many of these rights, but not all; for example, he did not confer any titles.

Russell suggests that Calvert's "intention in so wording the charter as to give himself and his successors such sweeping sovereignty, was not to make use of that power for self-aggrandizement, but to defend his colony from royal interference, and preserve intact for his colonists that principle of religious toleration which he had desired should always be theirs."[17]

Or, as Andrews suggests, his idea was more to protect from Parliamentary interference than from royal interference.[18]

Maryland continued the string of remarkably innovative reasons for establishing the Anglo-American frontier: from a business community (Virginia), to religious communities (Massachusetts), to a fishing settlement (New Hampshire), to a Proprietary province that tolerated multiple (Christian) religions, and accepted a popular assembly to frame laws (Maryland). Given the evolution of these and other future colonies generally without interference from England it is not surprising they eventually came together in a country that embodied all of these characteristics.

Border Disputes

Every one of Maryland's original borders has been changed, except one, since the grant was given to George Calvert in 1632. Each major or minor change has made Maryland smaller; thousands of acres of the original grant were eventually lost. Most of these changes took place in the seventeenth century, so it is difficult to determine what the impact might have been if the territory had not been lost. Maryland is a small state and its geography, with the western panhandle pointing toward the Ohio country, is what allowed it to become the gateway to the Ohio country. However, except for a couple of prominent Marylanders, most of the people taking advantage of that gateway were from other colonies. With a larger territory and correspondingly larger population, the colony, and then the state, might have had more resources to settle the western lands earlier.

The border disputes began early on Maryland's eastern border at the Delaware Bay. The English had claimed all the land on the Atlantic coast by virtue of discovery by John Cabot in his voyages in 1496–97. The King had made grants to the Virginia Companies along the East Coast early in the century with claims on the Atlantic coast all the way from Virginia to New England. The Maryland grant followed a couple of decades later. As Maryland would find out, receiving grants and claiming the land were two different things. The Maryland charter granted the land "between the Ocean on the East and the Bay of Chesapeake on the West" but Maryland would not long hold this total peninsula.

Others claimed land in Maryland territory on the west bank of the Delaware River. First the Swedes who were expelled by the Dutch who in turn were expelled by James, Duke of York (1633–1701), brother of Charles II. James crossed from the land given to him on the eastern shore of the Delaware River to the western shore, Maryland Territory, to claim land. Lord Baltimore recognized the danger and tried to bolster his claim to that area by getting Marylanders to settle on the peninsula between the Atlantic Ocean and Chesapeake Bay. He was unsuccessful and the Duke of York, soon to be James II of England, was in de facto control of the west bank of the Delaware River, part of Maryland.[19] It got worse for Maryland when William Penn (1644–1718) received his grant.

In 1681, William Penn was granted a charter for land north of Maryland. Although the Maryland charter was very clear that the fortieth degree of latitude constituted its northern border, the Pennsylvania charter relied on poor maps and its lower border was vague. Penn's first settlers laid out Philadelphia at the confluence of the Schuylkill and Delaware rivers in Maryland territory, a few miles *below* the fortieth degree of latitude. Although that gave Penn access to Delaware Bay, he soon realized that his colony might not have an outlet on the Chesapeake Bay, which he also thought necessary. Unlike Lord Baltimore, Penn was friendly with the Duke of York and tried to persuade James to cede to him the peninsula between the ocean, and Chesapeake Bay, clearly Maryland territory in 1682.[20]

Lord Baltimore objected and the dispute was referred to the Board of Trade which rendered a decision in 1685. In short, the ruling went badly for Baltimore. He lost the entire northeast section of the peninsula to Penn, today's southern Delaware. Clearly Penn's friendship with King James II was an advantage in this dispute. The details of this boundary were not settled for decades until the other border dispute between Maryland and Pennsylvania was settled.[21]

As important as this transfer of peninsular territory from Baltimore to Penn was, it was not the primary border dispute. The Pennsylvania charter stipulated that the southern boundary of Pennsylvania was to be determined by "a Circle drawne at twelve miles distance New Castle Northward and Westward unto the beginning of the fortieth degree of Northern Latitude." The problem was that this circle does not intersect that latitude but is below it, the result of the poorly drawn maps available.[22] More importantly, the forty-degree latitude line ran *above* Philadelphia, the primary city of Penn's colony, which put Philadelphia in Maryland. As a result, there was a disputed area of very valuable land between Pennsylvania and Maryland just south of the fortieth degree of latitude. Penn also claimed land below even the present-day border with Maryland. If his claim had been upheld, it would have put his colony very close to the upper reaches of the Chesapeake Bay giving Pennsylvania another water access besides Delaware Bay.[23] Penn offered to buy the land that would give him access to the Chesapeake Bay; Lord Baltimore refused.[24]

Baltimore and Penn both died before the dispute was settled but their descendants carried it on well into the eighteenth century. During this time both the Penn and Calvert families encouraged settlement in the disputed area and claimed sovereignty over these settlers. The primary area of conflict was in the Conejohela Valley, along the west shore of the Susquehanna River for the last thirty miles before it enters the Chesapeake Bay. That dispute gave to the conflict the name of Conojocular (Conojacular) War or Cresap's War, and Thomas Cresap entered Maryland history for the first time.[25]

Border Agreements

The Pennsylvania-Maryland border was eventually settled—to the distinct advantage of the Penn family. After Lord Baltimore petitioned the King in 1732 for a resolution a boundary adjustment was reached in 1732 that gave the Penn's all their claims. The boundary was to be fifteen miles south of the southernmost point of Philadelphia.[26] It was in the same agreement that split the peninsula previously. There were agreements in 1738 and 1750 which further refined the boundaries. The boundary between Maryland and Pennsylvania wasn't finally settled until the famous Mason-Dixon survey of 1763–1767.

In addition to losing land on the north and east Maryland also lost land on the west and south. In the west, the Baltimore grant was to the farthest head of the Potomac River, initially believed to be the head of the North Branch of the river. It was later discovered that the South Branch extended farther west. The head of the South Branch would have given Maryland more land in the west but its later discovery, by Daniel Dulany, was too late for the boundary to be changed. On the southern border with Virginia, the border was to be due east from Watkins Point across the peninsula. The surveyor, however, ran the line not due east but five degrees and fifteen minutes north of east, costing Lord Baltimore another fifteen thousand acres.[27]

These boundary changes to the original Calvert grant for Maryland cost the Proprietor over eight thousand square miles of territory, or over forty percent of the initial grant. This land, especially the twenty-mile strip across southern Pennsylvania, would have provided Maryland substantially more resources, especially in the west, and probably would have made the more populous Maryland much more involved in blazing the gateway to Ohio. Marylanders, including Cresap, were the leading figures in blazing that trail, but the main push to go through that gateway came from other provinces, most notably Virginia. Partly because of the very narrow longitudinal strip of Maryland in the west, the province had a very poor record of defending the western part of the colony in the various wars with the French in that area, especially during the French and Indian War.[28] Another reason for Maryland's lack of interest in a westward movement was its fixed western border. Virginia had a charter that extended "sea to sea" which meant that Virginians believed the land on the other side of the mountains belonged to them. Marylanders knew they had a fixed border in the west.

The Land

After Calvert abandoned his Avalon colony in Newfoundland because of the harsh climate he settled on the present site of Maryland, in the northern part of the Virginia grant. Although he didn't know the land first-hand, he had chosen well.

Maryland originates on the Atlantic with the Atlantic Coastal Plain, dominated by the

Chesapeake Bay estuary, which drains most of the Maryland rivers. The Bay literally divides the Eastern Shore from the Western Shore uplands. The Eastern Shore is low and generally flat, sandy soil at sea level which drains well. It is very good for a variety of crops. It is so flat that "An elevation scarcely thirty feet above sea level became a landmark to be dignified by the name Windy Hill."[29] The colony temperature was moderate, varying from freezing in winter to quite warm in the summer. The rainfall supports a good growing season. There are fresh water springs but the rivers on the Eastern Shore, the Nanticoke, Choptank, and Chester are tidal rivers, which provided ship access far upstream, allowing access to much of the land.

The first settlement in Maryland was on the western shore of the Chesapeake Bay at the very tip of the province where the Potomac River meets the Bay. After exploring the Potomac, they settled on what they called St. Mary's River and named the settlement St. Mary's City. Calvert had learned a lot from the mistakes of the other colonies. First, on the trip they had about twice as many colonists as did the Jamestown colony, and all were expected to work, unlike in the Jamestown colony. Next, they came early in the year, March 1634, and planted their first crop right away, which put them in good stead for the coming winter. They immediately erected a palisaded fort at St. Mary's. They knew of the trouble some of their neighboring colonies had with Indians and intended to avoid that sort of trouble. They made contact with the Indians to establish good relations and to "purchase" the land for their settlement, or at least exchanged trade goods for it.[30]

The western shore of the Chesapeake Bay is part of the Atlantic Coastal Plain up to the fall line of the rivers. This fall line goes through present-day District of Colombia and Baltimore up to the head of the Bay. The two main rivers, the Potomac and Patuxent, are tidal rivers below the fall line and allowed ocean going ships to go up the rivers to that line. The Susquehanna River, mostly in Pennsylvania, drains into the Bay in northeast Maryland, is the primary river that flows into the head of the Chesapeake Bay estuary. The land on the Western Shore is more upland than the Eastern Shore, at a slightly higher elevation. The whole Atlantic Coastal Plain is green, flat, and well-suited for agriculture.

Moving west past the fall line, the land rises in elevation and is hillier. This is the Piedmont region, the "foot of the mountains." This section, like the rest of the province, would have been densely wooded when the first settlers arrived, but was eventually made into good agricultural land. The Piedmont, as well as the land farther west, was not settled early. For many decades, the Atlantic Coastal Plain, on the eastern and western shore of Chesapeake Bay was the center of population and agriculture.

West beyond the Piedmont is the easternmost range of the Appalachians, the Blue Ridge Mountains. The Blue Ridge starts in Pennsylvania and extends down through Virginia bordering the Shenandoah Valley on the East. South Mountain, starting in Pennsylvania, goes down through Maryland as part of the Blue Ridge. The Great Appalachian Valley dividing the Appalachian range from Vermont to Georgia extends through Maryland between the Blue Ridge on the east and the Ridge and Valley Allegheny mountains on the west. In Pennsylvania and Maryland it is called the Cumberland Valley, and also the Hagerstown Valley in Maryland. See Map 1. If the Piedmont was not settled early, western Maryland was settled even later.

The mountains of western Maryland provided a formidable barrier to travelers and remained open only to Native Americans, trappers, and traders for about a century after the first settlers reached Maryland. In the mid eighteenth century, the section of the Great Appalachian Valley in Maryland was settled when Hagerstown was founded. Until about 1750 there was little thought given to moving past the Alleghenies, not only because of the mountain barrier, but because the land was claimed by others. People then started to realize there was life beyond the Alleghenies and if that barrier was breached one would be at the entrance of the Ohio country. The Ohio country not only promised rich farmland but also a route to the Mississippi and, eventually world trade.

Growth of the Colony

Calvert had hoped to do two things to get the colony functioning as soon as possible. First, to establish a landholding aristocracy similar to the one in England, one that would support his own palatine in Ireland. Second, he wanted to bring as many settlers as possible to the colony so it could start to pay off financially; the more settlers, the more quitrents paid to the Proprietor.[31] He promised two thousand acres to anyone who transported five adult males as settlers and proportionally smaller acreage for fewer people. He was trying to establish manors, but he also made it very easy for other land-hungry settlers to obtain a land patent. This system essentially worked against the establishment of large manors and frustrated his intention of a landed aristocracy. Instead of manorial lords the single-family freehold of 250 acres or less, prevailed.[32] Nonexistent in the previous or succeeding colonies, the feudal or semi-feudal system failed in the one chance it had in the English colonies, with a generous royal grant to a sole Proprietor. The wildness of this country and the people attracted to it precluded a feudal establishment.

The Proprietors Calvert ran into another problem they didn't anticipate ... democracy. The charter mentions laws made by an assembly of free men. However, the Calverts believed the practices of all such assemblies of the time would be followed, that is, the assembly would take directions from the governor, appointed by the Proprietor:

> both George and Cecil Calvert sincerely held it was much better for the Proprietary, with his superior wisdom and experience, to initiate legislation, than to have such matters proposed and handled in more or less irresponsible fashion by popular "factions." They felt that the masses of the people were much less likely to know what was good for them than the Lord Proprietor and his deputies.... Furthermore, up to that time, experience had seemed to prove conclusively that the people could not be trusted to maintain a strong or stable government.[33]

Andrews continues, "From the beginning, however, the Maryland colonists thought one thing was fundamental and essential, and that was the directing of legislation by their chosen representatives, and the establishment of local self-government." The religious tolerance experience may have given the settlers the confidence to demonstrate their rights in other ways, such as with the Assembly. This clash started in the very first Assembly in St. Mary's City in February 1635. The Assembly framed a series of laws as they believed was their prerogative from the charter. Lord Baltimore saw it differently and used the same article of the charter to support his position. He claimed the right to make laws and asserted the Assembly could only approve or suggest changes. He refused to ratify their laws, proposed his own, and called for the Assembly to meet again in 1638. When the Assembly met in 1638, it was a gathering of freemen from across the province; they sat as a representative body in a unicameral manner in a single chamber. They debated the Proprietor's proposals and promptly voted two to one against them.[34] Representative government had come to Anglo-America. The Proprietor and the Assembly eventually compromised, but the tone had been set.

This tension between the Proprietor and the Assembly was to continue as long as there was a Lord Baltimore. The primary conflict was about money with the Calverts insisting their proprietary rights took precedence over matters of state so they should be paid first. Because the Assembly had to pay the Calverts first it was unable to raise enough revenue even to wage some of the wars against the French in America in the late seventeenth century, and especially for the French and Indian War in the eighteenth century. The consequence was that the province was unable to defend western Maryland at times. The lack of defense in the west was one reason Marylanders did not migrate westward. A couple of individual Marylanders, Thomas Cresap and Christopher Gist, were exceptions. Many settlers of western Maryland and/or of the Ohio country came from other colonies.[35]

One other lesson Maryland learned from Virginia was that tobacco was a good cash crop and easily grown in the tidewater area on the Chesapeake Bay. There had been a lull in the tobacco market but it picked up in the 1630s, just in time for these colonists to take advantage of it. By 1637 tobacco had become the medium of exchange and by 1639 it was the main cash crop.[36] The province exported one hundred thousand pounds of tobacco that year. These tobacco "planters" were the small freeholds of just a few acres that the planters worked alone after clearing the land. They were poor by later standards, with personal estates worth £100 or less. These were not the planters of the large Virginia estates with many servants and slaves. Some rose to affluence over time but most stayed poor.[37]

Indentured servants were brought to the colony to supplement the labor force. As they worked off their indentures they became freemen and went on to establish their own households. Eventually some slaves were brought in, especially to work the tobacco fields, but slavery was never as an important part of the economy as it was in Virginia. Indentured servants were mostly young adult males who outnumbered women four to one.

Because of the imbalance between men and women, the colony did not grow quickly and remained centered around St. Mary's City for many years. The small agricultural colony had no need to expand from the original area. Population estimates vary widely for most of the seventeenth century. There were perhaps 250 in 1634, the year of settlement. One estimate sets the population at 2,500 in 1660; another estimate has the population at 8,000, over three times higher.[38] Even in 1660, almost thirty years after initial settlement, Charles County, just north of the original St. Mary's County, and Baltimore County were frontier wildernesses. After that, population estimates started to converge. In 1675 the population was estimated at 15,000, then 25,000 in 1688 and about 32,000 in 1700.[39] Most of the increase was due to immigration. Population was still concentrated on the Atlantic Coastal Plain, not even extending as far as the Piedmont; Marylanders were not moving west. After 1700 population picked up because of internal migration from other provinces.

Maryland Paths and Roads

Indian Paths

The Indian paths discussed in Chapter One, including the Great Warrior's Path, spread over the entire eastern half of the country. However, there were some paths, usually starting in Pennsylvania, which had a more direct impact on Maryland.

The Maryland roads all started as Indian paths, then became paths for the colonists, first as walking paths, then as paths for packhorses, and finally as wagon roads. Paul Wallace (*Indian Paths of Pennsylvania*) identifies almost two hundred Indian paths in Pennsylvania many of which drop into Maryland. These paths were often used by the Indians for trade or statecraft negotiations. Prior to European arrival the Indians used the most convenient paths, generally at moderate elevations according to Wallace. "Indian paths were dry, for the most part because they followed ... well drained ridges. It must be understood, however, that these ridges were not usually mountain spines like Kittatinny or Blue Mountain.... On the contrary, they were more often modest elevations in the midst of wide valleys overlooked by the mountains."[40]

One of these paths, later to be known as the Monocacy Path, followed multiple routes southwest from Wright's Ferry (Wrightsville), Pennsylvania, on the Susquehanna River down through Maryland to Virginia. There were at least two Monocacy paths from Wright's Ferry through Maryland; one had two branches. The first of these paths arced southwest from Wright's Ferry through present day York, Gettysburg, and Fairfield, Pennsylvania. It crossed South Mountain near Blue Ridge Summit, Pennsylvania, into the Hagerstown Valley to Hagerstown and then to Williams Ferry (Williamsport), Maryland. There it met other paths and crossed the Potomac into the Shenandoah Valley of Virginia. The second path left Wright's Ferry just southeast of the first one. It passed through York and Hanover, Pennsylvania, into the Monocacy Valley, Maryland toward Frederick, Maryland, where this path split again into two branches, one ending at Harper's Ferry and the other at Williams Ferry.

All these paths are not parallel by coincidence. A terrain map of Pennsylvania (Map 1) shows the eastern range of the Appalachian Mountains arcs in this manner in central Pennsylvania and these paths follow along in the valleys between the mountains, with two of them crossing the Catoctin and South mountains at key points. All four of these paths ended in the Shenandoah Valley which itself presents an easy walking path deeper into Virginia and points south. It is likely that all four were at one time or another "Warrior's Paths" originating in eastern Pennsylvania.

Wallace identifies at least three other Indian paths entitled Warrior's Paths that come down from *central* Pennsylvania to the Potomac, and beyond. They were all parallel and very close. One went through Everett, Pennsylvania, down to Oldtown, Maryland, on the Potomac. The second went from Frankstown (Hollidaysburg), Pennsylvania, down to the Potomac at Cresaptown.[41] Between these was the path through Raystown (Bedford) Pennsylvania to Wills Creek on the Potomac, the site of the future Cumberland, Maryland. These were all in the narrow valleys between the steep mountains of the Allegheny range.[42]

The path from Raystown to Wills Creek follows the Cumberland Valley, a narrow valley between Wills Mountain and Evitts Mountain. (This is a different Cumberland Valley than the one in east-central Pennsylvania that is part of the Great Appalachian Valley.) These paths, unlike the paths in the Hagerstown and Monocacy Valleys, remained busy Indian paths and traders' paths; they were too rugged to become emigration trails. They also provided valuable information about the area around Oldtown and Wills Creek, information that would lead to the Wills Creek and Potomac junction as the jumping off point toward the Ohio country.[43]

Evolution from Path to Road

At the turn of the eighteenth century all these trails crossing western Maryland in the north-south direction started in Indian settlements on the Susquehanna River and led to Virginia. The emigrant settlers moved from the Delaware River to the Susquehanna River then down these paths to Virginia. They then quickly transformed these paths into roads back east, from Paxtang (Harrisburg) and Wright's Ferry back through Lancaster, to Philadelphia. By the late 1720s and through the 1730s the rush for land in the west was on;

it peaked in the 1740s. These Indian trails became first walking paths, then packhorse paths carrying settlers and trade goods, and then roads between Pennsylvania and Maryland. The Monocacy Road, in all its branches, was one of them.

> In 1739 the Monocasy Road, or certainly the Pennsylvania part of it, was laid out as a wagon-road, connecting at Lancaster with the road from Philadelphia. From Lancaster it ran westward, crossing the Susquehanna at Wright's Ferry, now Wrightsville, thence through the settlement upon the Big Codorus, afterwards laid out as York, thence through Hanover, crossing the Maryland near Kreutzmiller's Mill on Conewago creek, and so on to the Potomac....[44]

The best known of these routes became known as the "Great Valley Road," the "Great Wagon Road," or the "Philadelphia Wagon Road."

The Great Valley Road, in the 1720s and 1730s, followed various routes through Pennsylvania, the most common from Philadelphia to Lancaster to York to Gettysburg.[45] From Gettysburg it crossed a gap in South Mountain to Chambersburg, Pennsylvania, in the Cumberland Valley. From there it moved south through Hagerstown to Williams Ferry, across the Potomac to the Shenandoah Valley. In the following decades, the road lengthened farther south eventually reaching Georgia. Over its peak years, from 1740 on, the Great Valley Road carried thousands of immigrants, not only Germans to the Shenandoah Valley, but also Scots-Irish who entered the country in Philadelphia and followed the road into the Carolinas. During its growth. other roads branched from it, some heading west. One

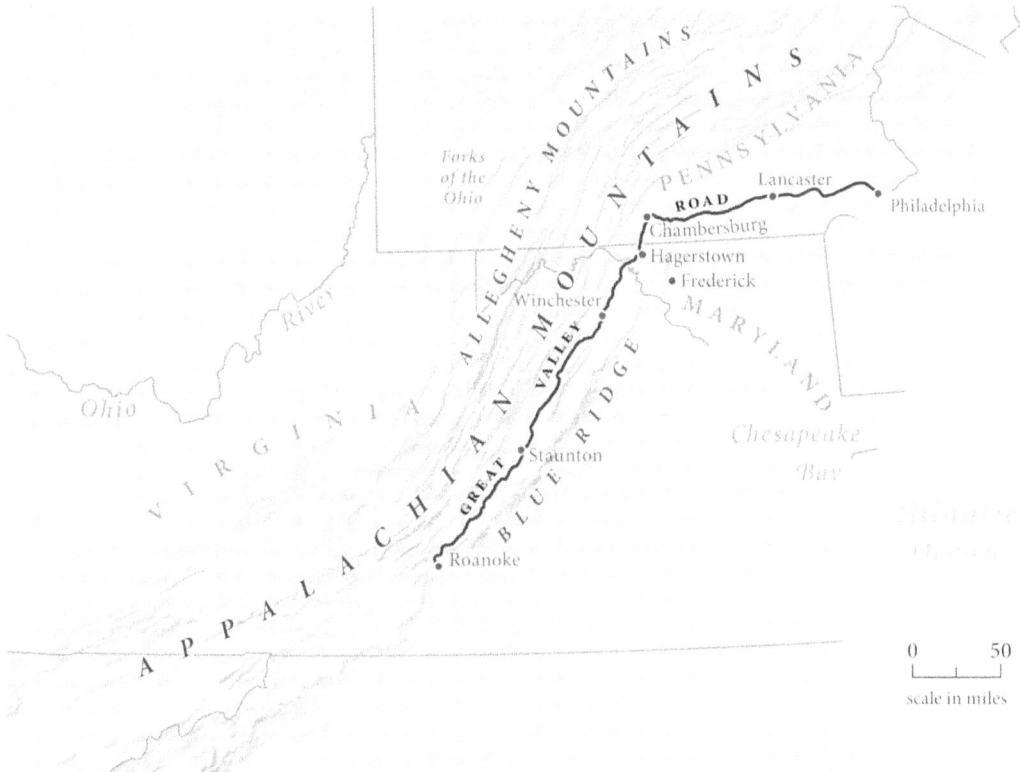

Map 3: Great Valley Road. The Great Valley Road or Great Wagon Road went from Philadelphia to Roanoke. Using the Great Appalachian Valley made it relatively easy for settlers and traders to move north and south between the mountains.

of these was the Wilderness Road which branched west near Roanoke, Virginia. On this road, through the Cumberland Gap, Daniel Boone led various settlers west into Kentucky. However, that wasn't until 1775, well after others had started the move into the Ohio country through western Maryland and Pennsylvania starting around 1750.[46]

From around 1730 to 1750 Maryland provided many north-south roads for settlers who were passing through and some who were settling in western Maryland. Once towns such as Frederick sprang up, it became necessary to carve out some east-west roads for the western farmers to use to get their crops such as corn and wheat, to eastern markets, and to receive supplies. The tidewater area had for years used water transportation, especially for tobacco the main product of Maryland. Roads developed along the waterways to serve the tobacco trade, but did not reach toward the west.

In *Money and Transportation in Maryland 1720–1765*, Clarence P. Gould has pointed out there were two streams of settlement into western Maryland. One was through Pennsylvania; for years, the Great Valley Road and Monocacy Road were the only connections to the outside for the western settlements. However, there was another stream of settlers pushing up the eastern side of the Potomac. The base of that settlement was on the Potomac in the tidewater area. As they pushed farther up the river the road they built extended communication with the interior for the first time. "By 1728 a road had been pushed as far back as the Monocacy, and shortly thereafter an elaborate system was developed connecting western settlements with the county seat and with the tide-water on the two branches of the Potomac."[47] However,

> Neither the Philadelphia wagon road nor the Potomac River were suitable to the needs of the western communities. A road directly across from the Monocacy to the Chesapeake would be much shorter, consequently in 1739 there were sent to the assembly "a Petition of the Inhabitants about Monocacy, and above the Mountains on Potowack River, A Petition of the Inhabitants on the west side of Potomack River.... By which Petitions the several Petitioners pray that a Road may be cleared through the Country from the City of Annapolis, for the more easy Carriage of their Grain, Provisions, and other Commodities."[48]

This petition went nowhere in the Assembly, consistent with the policy in Maryland of basically ignoring roads, probably because the rivers in the tidewater took care of most needs. The counties were in charge of the roads and depended on volunteer labor to construct and maintain them. In the west construction was difficult as they had to deal with rocky ground and forests. Most roads were built with private funds, because they were needed before the province could finance them. That is probably how the road between Annapolis and Frederick was built, within ten years of the founding of Frederick in 1745. There was a flurry of road building in the east around this time but the roads going west remained in poor shape and traveling west was a real chore. It improved later when the Baltimore Pike started in Baltimore, went to Cumberland, Maryland, and went through to the Ohio country as the Cumberland Road. The improvements really didn't start until the French and Indian War in the 1750s because of the need to ship supplies from the east to the west.[49]

By 1750, western Maryland was populated with farming communities and had commercial centers at Frederick, and later Hagerstown. There were some east-west roads, although poor, that allowed trade in western agricultural products with the eastern ports of Annapolis and the relatively young town of Baltimore. Philadelphia was still a major trading hub because the Great Valley Road and the Monocacy Road connected western Maryland with this city more easily than western Maryland connected with eastern Maryland. The trails west of Hagerstown into the Ridge and Valley Alleghenies were still primitive.

Although there were traders in Pennsylvania, Maryland, and Virginia that crossed the mountains into the Ohio Valley, there was no large-scale movement of people across the Alleghenies claiming land in the Ohio country.

Barriers to Moving West

The Atlantic Coastal Plain of Maryland is much like that of Virginia; it is a tidewater area. As in Virginia this meant that even the growth of towns was stifled; ships could move right up to the tobacco plantations where tobacco could be loaded and other goods offloaded. There was no need to build towns for the tobacco commerce. Though Lord Baltimore encouraged the settlers to plant a variety of crops, the temptation to grow a high profit crop like tobacco was too great. Although the population grew, mostly through immigration, for most of the seventeenth century, this tobacco economy guaranteed an insular colony bounded by the local river fall lines.

One of the factors that made it difficult to open western Maryland was the realization that none of the streams had access to larger rivers leading to the sea. St. George Leakin Sioussat (*Highway Legislation in Maryland and Its Influence on the Economic Development of the State*) quotes the philosopher Blaise Pascal, "Rivers are roads that move, and carry us whither we wish to go," and a rejoinder by another, "Yes, provided we wish to go whither they carry us."[50] Clearly the rivers west of the coastal plain did not flow in the correct direction for tobacco growers. Not only were roads nonexistent in the east-west direction tobacco was very difficult to move over roads because of its bulk and weight. As a result, the roads that developed along the tidewater rivers became "rolling roads," where tobacco casks were "rolled" along the roads to the ships, rather than carried.

Factors other than lack of suitability for tobacco precluded a western movement. One was the border dispute with Pennsylvania which had been going on for decades and peaked in the 1730s. Pennsylvania settlers moving west from the Delaware River area to the Susquehanna River area, were just not sure to which province they would be moving. The area just southwest of the Susquehanna River, Conejohela Valley, was one of the disputed areas and the dispute wasn't settled, for all practical purposes, until 1738. The violence of the dispute clearly disturbed many families and precluded them from moving into western Maryland at the time.

There was some concern about danger from Indians in the far western part of the province; there was little problem in the east, such as the Piedmont. There were no sedentary tribes, no residents, in Maryland in the 1730s. In the west, the Shawnee lived in Maryland for a while at Opessa's town on the Potomac but moved out around 1730. The Iroquois frequently moved south from New York to the Carolinas to fight the Catawbas. They used the Warrior's Paths, which went through the area near Opessa's Town, the future Old Town (Oldtown), Maryland. They were always considered dangerous and during the many wars between the English and the French, up to and including the French and Indian War, far western Maryland was often under threat. The French were constantly stirring up trouble between the Indians and the English colonists on the western frontier. However, this was in the far west and there were other problems closer to the more populous part of the province that slowed development of the west.[51]

Baltimore County, established in 1659, was still the frontier at the turn of the century. North and west of the county, from roughly the Susquehanna River to the Monocacy and Potomac rivers, there was an area called the Maryland Barrens. Most of the New World was heavily forested when the settlers arrived. The Barrens, however, were not. Unlike either the heavily forested areas, or the prairie grasses of the Shenandoah Valley, the Barrens were mostly scrub brush and small saplings. At first this was a deterrent because many believed that scrub indicated infertile soil. There was also a need for timber to build houses and barns; the Barrens did not have the timber for these buildings. The soil was later found to be very good for farming, but the perception of the infertile Barrens helped delay movement toward western Maryland well into the eighteenth century.[52]

Roads were very primitive in the colony for many years. The first road-law of Maryland was in 1666, over thirty years after the founding of the colony. It remained in effect almost unchanged until 1696. Many of the "roads" were nothing but footpaths, unsuitable for wagons. Although the capital, St. Mary's City, was on a river, it was extremely difficult to reach. It could take many days, including a lot of walking, to get to the Assembly meetings. The capital was moved to Annapolis in 1694 for political reasons, but one also suspects because it was easier for travel. Some St. Mary's County inhabitants sent a petition after the move of the capital to Annapolis in which one article said, "the petitioners suspected the chief dislike of the location of the capital at St. Mary's to be on account of the inconvenience of its situation, because the gentlemen, the members of the house, have been forced to their great trouble oftentimes to travel on foot from Patuxent to St. Mary's and so back again."[53] In 1683 the legislature ordered the erection of over one hundred towns, but within a quarter of a century most had disappeared and many had never existed. Roads were not built to "nowhere" and neither could towns be ordered into existence. When people found a need to move to a place only then would a town or road be built to serve that need.[54]

One of the other barriers to development of the west was the speculation in land warrants, mostly held by the eastern gentry. Speculators could take out warrants on vast amounts of western land and hold them anticipating an increase in value before selling them.[55]

> The quitrent frustrated, or made prohibitive, speculation in land but not in warrants. By taking out a warrant an individual held the exclusive right to have the specified area surveyed. He could hold on to this privilege or have the tract surveyed but not patented. In each instance the speculator maintained possession of the land without paying quitrent.[56]

Daniel Dulany, a member of the Assembly, observed the practice and found it an obstacle.

> "Great Quantities of Lord Baltimore's back Waste Lands (now of no Use or Advantage to Him) from being taken up and paid for." Many of the inhabitants who would willingly have settled in such locations had been deterred from doing so "for fear of Engaging in Disputes with the Proprietors of the Said Warrants." Instead, they had chosen to reside in Virginia and elsewhere rather than involve themselves in "Disputes of which they could not Hope Easily to see an End."[57]

He saw these settlers passing through Maryland and settling in Virginia instead; the land was being wasted.

In 1732, Charles Calvert, the Fifth Lord Baltimore and Proprietor, feeling pressure from both Virginia and Pennsylvania, issued a proclamation to try to open up the back country of western Maryland. Hopefully, the settlers moving to Virginia would see western Maryland as a settlement option.

> Lord Baltimore, the proclamation announced. "being desirous to Increase the Number of Honest People within…Maryland and willing to give Suitable Encouragement," offered 200 acres of land in fee, subject to a quitrent of four shillings sterling per year, payable at the end of three years, for every 100 acres, to any person having a family who would within three years actually settle on the land between the Potomac and Susquehanna rivers. To each single person he offered 100 acres.[58]

The proclamation, by itself, was not successful, and only lasted for three years which was not enough time to have an impact. Prior to the proclamation, the cost of settling in Maryland was higher than the cost of settling in Pennsylvania or Virginia. The land quitrents were much higher and there was a clergy tax in Maryland to support the established Anglican Church that was not imposed in Pennsylvania.[59] Finally there was a rather stiff land fee with each land grant. Although the proclamation was a more liberal inducement to settle there were still high quitrents, fees, and taxes that imposed a heavy burden on any settler. The difficulty was compounded by the fact that the payments were required to be paid in sterling and there was a scarcity of money in Maryland.[60]

Until 1747 the Assembly would only accept tobacco as a substitute for sterling for taxes and fees. This aided the planters in the coastal plain who had been using tobacco as currency for years but did nothing for those trying to settle in western Maryland from other provinces. The immigrant German farmers who did try to stay quickly fell behind in these payments. The apparently more liberal land grant system was basically a chimera for poor immigrant farmers. Although some stopped in Maryland on their way south most continued to Virginia where the terms for land were more favorable. Western Maryland settlement was stalled.[61]

All these factors were in play in the first decades of the eighteenth century and had the effect of stifling settlement in the west. The proclamation of Lord Baltimore in 1732, although not a panacea in itself, started to change things. He and some prominent Marylanders, such as Daniel Dulany and Philemon Lloyd, Secretary of State, became concerned about the land distribution activity going on in Virginia, just across the Potomac. The activity of the Virginia governor caused distress, not only with some of his own constituents, but also with Marylanders. The aggressive moves westward by Virginia in the 1720s and 1730s spurred Maryland to encourage settlement in order to keep that land.

Virginia Pressure in the West

In 1716, Virginia Governor Spotswood led an expedition to the Shenandoah Valley to promote settlement there and beyond. Within a decade of the expedition, there was a serious move into the Shenandoah Valley, just over the Blue Ridge Mountains. One of the factors that propelled settlement across the Blue Ridge was a dispute that had its roots in the past but played out in the early 1730s.[62]

In 1649, as a political payoff for support, King Charles II granted all the land in Virginia between the Rappahannock and Potomac rivers, known as the Northern Neck, to Lord Culpepper. The grant was later renewed by James II in 1669, and eventually passed on to Lord Fairfax through marriage. This Fairfax Grant was essentially the land across the Potomac from Maryland and included at least part of the Shenandoah Valley. There was always a conflict between the colonial government and the grantee, Fairfax. "Under terms of the grant, the colonial government and General Assembly retained political and legal authority over the Northern Neck, but the grant owners ... had the authority to sell and collect quitrents." However, colonial officials did not want to lose authority to grant colonial land in that area also and to collect fees from processing such grants. The colonial officials started to grant land. The uncertainty of the borders, again caused by rudimentary maps, allowed this dispute to go on for many years; it wasn't clear who owned what part of the land, Fairfax or the colonial government. This did not deter William Gooch, the Lieutenant Governor of Virginia from 1727 until 1749, from embracing the position that was most favorable to the colonial government and acting on it. Gooch's strategy was to grant much of the land and require settlement to assure government control. Under Lieutenant Governor Gooch the colonial government became very active with land grants in the Northern Neck.[63]

The first white settlement of the Shenandoah Valley was around 1725. The first recorded colonial government grant under Gooch was to John Van Meter, originally from Holland but more recently from New York, in June 1730 for ten thousand acres, "on the West side of the great Mountains [Shenandoah Valley]." This was on the condition that he and his family would settle on it within two years. If he could get twenty other families to come, they were to get an additional plot of twenty thousand acres. He was said to have sold his original grant to Jost Hite (Joist Hite, Joost Heyd).[64]

Jost Hite, originally from Germany, was an activist in Pennsylvania and did not like how the German settlers were being treated there. The Quaker authorities were indifferent to the safety of the German settlers in the backcountry who suffered from Indian raids. The settlers petitioned the government but received no help. Hite set out to look for more favorable conditions in Virginia.

> Jost Hite made an agreement with the Van Meters and became a partner in the plan to found a German colony in Virginia, and in 1732, with his family, his son-in-law, George Bowman ... with their families, and several others—sixteen families in all—left York, crossed the Potomac, and settled near where Winchester now stands.[65]

This was the beginning of the German migration to the Shenandoah Valley from Pennsylvania through Maryland that would continue for many years and have a major impact on the settlement of western Maryland.

In the 1720s and 1730s, German immigration to the colonies was heavy. Pennsylvania was their primary point of entry, but they faced some barriers there from both the people and the land. Southeast Pennsylvania was becoming crowded and some residents felt they were being overwhelmed with immigrants, especially those that spoke a foreign language, so the immigrants were encouraged to move on. As the Germans moved farther west from the Delaware River to the Susquehanna River, they faced an Indian threat. They were farmers, not Indian fighters, so they requested help with this threat. Although the Quakers were happy to have the German immigrants as a buffer between them and the Indians, the pacifist government was not interested in fighting Indians for them, and in fact felt that since they would be encroaching on Indian land they deserved what they got. Lord Baltimore invited some Germans into the contested lands near the Susquehanna to help bolster his position in the Maryland-Pennsylvania border dispute. Once it became evident that settling there was no longer a desirous destination because of the dispute, the Germans looked for other places to settle. These were the people, led by men such as Van Meter and Hite, which Gooch was trying to attract.[66]

The Virginia grants were also dangerous for Maryland because they encroached on Maryland territory. In November 1730, the Virginia Council granted land

> Upon peticon of William Beverly, Joseph Smith & Joseph Clapham, Gent.: leave is granted them to take up twenty thousand acres of Land upon Cohongaratoon [Potomac river], beginning at the mouth of Conecachigh [Conococheague] River, and up both sides thereof along the Bank of Conhongaratoon to include that quantity.... On the Peticon of Aug. More [Moore] & John Robinson. Gent, leave is granted them to take up thirty thousand acres of Land upon the River Cohongaratoon, beginning at the mouth of Andirton [Antietam] River, & extending to within three miles of the mouth of Conecakigh River.[67]

Cohongoranta was the Iroquoian name for the Potomac west of the Blue Ridge. Finally, in May 1732 the Council granted land, "To John Robinson, Esqr. 20,000 acres on Monocassie, on the North Side Cohongaratoon River, if Sd. Lands appear to be within the Bounds of this Colony."[68] All these grants were a problem because they were on the Maryland side of the Potomac, and had been since the Maryland charter was issued. At least in the last grant Gooch and the Council acknowledged that it might not be in Virginia. Gooch was being aggressive in pushing Virginia west, even into Maryland.

This was not the only attempt by Virginia to acquire Maryland land, and even Pennsylvania land. At one point Gooch claimed there was uncertainty about the source of the Potomac and contended before it passed the Shenandoah River it came from the northeast, from the Susquehanna River. This is not true; it came from the northwest and all the maps of the day showed that. Had Gooch prevailed he would have provided Virginia with most of western Maryland, ultimately crossing the fortieth parallel and claiming some of Pennsylvania. Baltimore and Penn could not remain passive to this challenge. Baltimore made his own claim that, in fact the true fountain of the Potomac was actually the Shenandoah River and, therefore, the land north of that river was actually granted to Maryland in its charter. Frank W. Porter III (*From Back Country to County: The Role of Economics and Politics in the Settlement of Western Maryland*) covers this dispute well in his discussion of the settlement of western Maryland.[69] These claims and counter-claims were not upheld and the Maryland-Virginia border remained as it was. However, these aggressive moves did alert the Maryland Proprietor not only of the danger of losing his western lands, but also of the value of the lands.

Thomas Cresap—Maryland Frontiersman

There is disagreement on when Thomas Cresap was born, anywhere from about 1694 to 1702, but there is agreement that he came from Skipton in Yorkshire, England when he was about fifteen years old. He lived to be over ninety, and possibly as old as one hundred. During his lifetime, he had a major impact on Maryland history. There is also agreement that from the time he landed, he was a full-fledged Marylander vigorously supporting the Maryland land claims. He married in his mid-thirties and lived at the time in what is now Havre de Grace Maryland, on the Susquehanna River, at the head of the Chesapeake Bay.[70]

Cresap fell into some debt and fled to Virginia to escape creditors. He met some people there who played an important role in his later adventures, men such as Thomas Lee, Lawrence and Augustine Washington, and others. He wanted to stay in Virginia but his wife, who had remained in Maryland, was adamant about staying in Maryland so he returned.[71] As Lawrence Wroth ("The Story of Thomas Cresap, A Maryland Pioneer") notes,

> ...and he who in later years was to become the "Maryland monster" to his neighbors in Pennsylvania, and who was to be known far and wide as an Indian fighter and regarded justly as a stumbling-block in the onward path of French Empire was in this domestic interlude forced to surrender to a woman's wish.[72]

He had a well-deserved reputation as being mean, nasty, and very tough; his later adventures show she was as tough as he was.

In 1730, Cresap moved farther up the Susquehanna to land on the west bank near Wright's Ferry, Pennsylvania, between present-day Lancaster and York, a ferry operated by a Pennsylvanian. This was at the farthest northern reaches of the land claimed by Baltimore, and was probably just over the fortieth parallel. The tract was named Pleasant Gardens. Cresap either bought this land, although he had recently been in debt so it begs the question on how he had the money, or, as others claim, Maryland granted him five hundred acres. Lord Baltimore was trying to challenge the Penns, and Cresap would have been seen as an ideal person to settle there in order to help support the challenge. He was tough, feisty, and always willing to push the envelope. He was definitely a Baltimore supporter in this dispute, so a grant from Lord Baltimore is not unreasonable. This rich land just west of the Susquehanna, the Conejohela Valley was the main area of conflict. Soon after he moved there Cresap received a patent from Annapolis to act as justice of the peace and captain of the militia. The combination of the land grant and appointments by Maryland started a reasonable speculation that he was an agent of Maryland in this dispute.[73]

In 1730, the border dispute, which had been dormant for almost fifty years, erupted again in earnest with Cresap's move. As soon as he arrived, he started a ferry business across the Susquehanna in competition with Wright's Ferry just upstream. The competition for the ferry business heated up. One morning in October 1730, he was attacked midstream by two Pennsylvania men who admittedly tried to kill him. He barely survived that attack, and was attacked numerous times over the next several years. He also was an aggressor, at one time killing a neighbor's livestock that had been allowed to run loose in his cornfield. In another incident, he tried to take land from a neighbor by building a cabin on it only yards from the neighbor's house. In one raid in 1733, Cresap's house was attacked and he shot and killed one of the intruders. Kenneth P. Bailey's *Thomas Cresap, Maryland Frontiersman* chronicles many of the battles he and his wife had with both the government of Pennsylvania and some of its citizens.[74] These back and forth attacks were acknowledged by both sides to have been territorial disputes over the uncertain border.

In one such attack in November 1736 the Lancaster Sheriff and a large number of men came to Cresap's house to arrest him. He fought back but in the attack one of his servants was killed and his house was burned down. He was arrested and taken to Philadelphia where he was shackled and put into prison. By then Cresap was infamous and the whole town turned out to jeer the "Maryland monster." "As much to irritate the spectators as anything else, Cresap turned to one of the Pennsylvania guards, George Aston, and made the remark: 'Damn it, Aston, this is one of the Prettyest Towns in Maryland.'"[75] The war went on as Maryland retaliated for the attack, partly by raiding a Pennsylvania jail and releasing some Maryland prisoners. Cresap made himself so obnoxious in the Pennsylvania prison that they offered to release him. He refused unless the King would order that it should be done. The British government stepped in on August 18, 1737, and Cresap was released.[76] Carrying on "Cresap's War" was the first service this frontiersman performed for Maryland; it was not to be the last. He would, from 1737 on, figure prominently in the westward expansion of the province.

Re-enter Thomas Cresap

After Thomas Cresap was released from jail in 1737, he and his family packed up their belongings and moved west, past the Blue Ridge into the Cumberland Valley, later Hagerstown Valley, in Maryland. It is rich farmland, and across the Potomac becomes the equally rich Shenandoah Valley in Virginia. He settled on Antietam Creek, only a few miles from present-day Hagerstown.

Cresap had a five-hundred-acre tract he named "Long Meadows." It is not clear exactly when he got the land, sometime between 1737 and 1739, or how he paid for it. After his troubles in the east he was probably short of money. However, the war in the east made him famous in Maryland and this might have helped. Sources differ on how he paid for it with one source maintaining it was given to him by Lord Baltimore for his services against Pennsylvania in that border dispute, and another source claiming he received it from Daniel Dulany with whom he soon entered into a business arrangement.[77] From about 1739 to at least 1744, Cresap acted as an agent for Daniel Dulany, the holder of land warrants in the Antietam Valley. "Between 1732 and 1739 a tremendous increase in the purchase of land warrants occurred."[78] Dulany probably acted as a traditional land speculator and purchased these warrants in the Antietam Valley, later patenting the land and selling it. Cresap sold farmsteads on the spot for Dulany thereby saving the new owner from an eighty-mile trip through rugged land back to Annapolis to negotiate the sale. The land in the Valley was very rich loam three-feet deep and was most often sold to German farmers coming down the Monocacy Road from Pennsylvania.

Cresap built a house on Antietam Creek, which like all houses he subsequently built, were more like small forts for protection. His forts as homes always seemed to mark the English frontier. This strategy served him well later. This home as a fortress might have been based on his experience back east during the Conojocular War. Here he started trading with the Indians and became well known by both the Indians and white settlers for fair trading. He was very ambitious and sought other business deals, some successful and others almost driving him into bankruptcy; he was always a risk taker. Once when he tried fur trading, his pelts, ready to be shipped to England, fell into French hands and he again lost a fortune. However, he recovered and became a successful trader, which allowed him to buy more land.[79]

After he settled Long Meadows, he purchased more land, still farther west. Called "Skei Thorn" it was located on the Potomac on land that later became Fort Frederick. This three-hundred-acre tract was west of the present-day Hagerstown. Cresap was buying and selling more land well into the 1740s, always looking west for his own home. His attachment to his land was reflected in some of the names he gave these tracts, such as, "The Barrons," "Johnson's Desire," "Anderson's Delight," "Crabtree Folly," and, "Hart's Delight." In addition to his trading skills and his frontiersman's acumen, he was clearly a savvy businessman. By 1753 Cresap owned at least two thousand acres in Maryland in addition to land he owned in Virginia.[80]

For his final home, he continued his proclivity for moving west. On May 20, 1740, Cresap purchased a two-hundred-acre tract for £100 from Captain John Charlton of Pennsylvania, who had purchased it just the year before. It was called "Indian Seat" but was also known by other names and was on the Potomac River about fifteen miles southeast of the present-day Cumberland, Maryland. This was clearly the westernmost settlement in Maryland at the time. He built his usual "fortress" home there. It was also known as "Shawanese Old Town," or "Opessa's Town," which had been abandoned by the Shawnee just a few years earlier. It became known as "Old Town" and later, Oldtown.[81] It was no accident Cresap settled there. It was on the Warriors Path, a trail frequently used by the Five Nations in their north-south movements, mostly to make war on the southern Catawba. At this location, the Potomac was easily fordable. Cresap was a successful Indian trader and this was an ideal trading location.

There were many paths or trails that crossed western Maryland in the 1730s, but most of them were in the north-south direction. The Indian trails for trade and war later became colonial paths for walking or packhorses, then wagon roads. Cresap's movements were different. He literally blazed the first east-west trails across Maryland through his own westward land purchases and sales. He certainly knew he was in the farthest reaches of the western Maryland panhandle. At first, he probably didn't realize he was within a few miles of the key jumping off point from Maryland to the Ohio country, what would become Cumberland, Maryland, although that fort and town had not yet been established. Thomas Cresap one of the key players in the opening of Ohio. As Wroth has noted, "When in later years Virginian settlers began to press into the Ohio region, following the lines of easiest travel, they found it more desirable to cross the Potomac somewhere near Cresap's house and so on to the Monongahela by the road he had blazed in that direction than to struggle over mountain ranges beset with every difficulty known to man and beast."[82] Cresap had a key role in in opening the Maryland west, but he wasn't alone; he worked with Daniel Dulany.

Daniel Dulany and Western Settlement

Enter the land development entrepreneur, Daniel Dulany with his new colleague—Thomas Cresap. Dulany was both a land speculator and a land developer. Land speculators often have an unsavory image because they make no improvement to the lands they hold, simply keeping the land until the price goes up and it can be sold for a profit. A land developer, on the other hand will make improvements in the form of town development or by lending credit to small borrowers who want to develop the land. The static situation Lord Baltimore faced with his western lands needed some imaginative approach to encourage settlement. Dulany was the person to supply it.

Daniel Dulany (1685–1753) was an immigrant from Ireland who had read law and worked himself into very prominent positions. He became a member of the Maryland Assembly and later was chief judge of the court of vice admiralty; in 1742 he was elevated to the Lord Proprietor's Council of State. He was also a businessman who was a partner of Charles Carroll of Carrollton, and others, in an iron producing company, the Baltimore Company. This was a major industrial concern in an agrarian province and by 1750, along with other iron works in Maryland, was producing approximately one-seventh the output that England was producing. He had acquired about twenty thousand acres of plantations in the tidewater area but was also interested in western land. Prior to 1721, he partnered with Major John Bradford to acquire two thousand acres along the Potomac. Bradford would scout it out and Dulany would take care of the warrants and patents.[83]

These lands were on the lower Potomac. As William B. Mayre points out ("'Patowmeck Above Ye Inhabitants,' A Commentary on the Subject of an Old Map") in 1721 western Maryland all the way to the eastern edge of the Monocacy River Valley was wilderness with no colonial settlement. The Monocacy is a tributary of the Potomac with headwaters in Pennsylvania. There were Indian tribes in the area, including three Shawnee villages and one Tuscarora village. The villages seemed to be of recent origin, that is, not of prehistoric lineage. The area was controlled by the Five Nations and the Susquehannocks, although neither lived in the area.[84] Aside from the settlements on the Potomac, which used the river for transportation, the interior was not settled.

This began to change in Maryland around 1727 when Benjamin Tasker patented seven thousand acres, which he called "Tasker's Chance," on the west side of the Monocacy. Around that time, Charles Carroll of Carrollton began to suggest to Lord Baltimore the need to occupy the western lands; this suggestion led to Baltimore's 1732 proclamation.

Dulany also bought some land on the other side of the Monocacy but did nothing with it for a few years.[85]

Things were changing for the Maryland west in the early 1730s. Virginia's push to occupy the Northern Neck, the stream of German settlers crossing Maryland to get to those lands, the growing scarcity of desirable land in the tidewater, and the interest of Marylanders who saw the value of these lands came together to boost interest in western settlement. Sometime in the mid–1730s Daniel Dulany met Thomas Cresap and another partnership was born. Cresap and Dulany may have met in 1736 while Cresap was in jail. Dulany was one of the commissioners the governor sent to Philadelphia in an unsuccessful attempt to free Cresap.[86]

Dulany had always been interested in expanding or preserving Maryland's boundaries, and he had been one of those encouraging Lord Baltimore to settle the western lands in order to protect them from the expanding Virginia settlements of the Northern Neck. In July 1744, he travelled west to inform himself of the "first Fountain" of the Potomac, the western limit of the province. He discovered it quickly and reported to Lord Baltimore, "Potomack River above the Mountains divides into two Large Branches, one called the South and the other the North branch. The first is the longest, and (as I am inform'd) the Main Branch of the River, and consequently your Lordship's boundary."[87] Once again it was observed that the Maryland border should have been farther west, but nothing came of it. The border remained at the meridian of the source of the shorter North branch.

Dulany went back in the fall but it was too late in the year to explore the source of the Potomac. However, he did explore some of the lands in the area, probably the land that he and Cresap had been selling. He was enthusiastic about what he saw.

> I have not been long return'd from a journey into the back woods, as far as to the Temporary line between this Province and Pennsylvania, where I had the pleasure of seeing a most delightfull Country, a Country My Lord, that equals (if it does not exceed) any in America for natural Advantage, such as a rich & fertile Soil, well furnished with timber of all sorts abounding with lime stone, and stone fit for building, good slate and some Marble, and to crown all, very healthy.[88]

He also saw many Germans migrating through to Virginia's Shenandoah Valley. This combination must have convinced him the area was ripe for more development. He went on a land buying spree much to the surprise of his neighbors who thought perhaps he had lost his mind. He began by acquiring Tasker's Chance. He purchased seven thousand acres from Tasker for £2,000 currency, including land north-south along the Monocacy and stretching west toward the Catoctin Mountains. This was the largest single tract of his subsequent purchases. He divided the land and sold it in one to three-hundred-acre units. He sold most of it, five-sevenths, at a loss, but profited on the remaining two-sevenths. Some of those sales were to squatters who were already farming the land.[89]

The operation was as simple as it was profitable. Dulany patented the land for £5 sterling per hundred acres plus fees; he turned the land over to buyers in small tracts at £30 sterling per hundred acres. No money changed hands in most transactions: the purchaser simply obligated himself to parts of the principal at stated intervals with interest at six percent. In a single one-hundred-acre deal, the landlord "created" added value of £25, or five times the original cost, secured against an unimpeachable asset, the land itself.[90]

Dulany had seen and appreciated the value of the western lands and continued to increase his holdings and to resell them to small farmers. He was a speculator for he did make good profits from the land he sold. He was also a land developer because he was getting small farmers to settle on, and increase the value of, the land. An additional advantage was to preclude encroachment on Maryland territory by the aggressive settlement in the

Northern Neck in Virginia. He had been warned by Tasker that, under the authority of the Fairfax grant, Virginians were moving into land near the upper Potomac. He, in turn, warned Lord Baltimore, "Several People in Virginia under that Right [Fairfax grant] is getting into that part near the Fountain head of Potowack ... and in time will do as our Northern Neighbors has done unless timely care is taken to prevent them."[91] He, of course, was referring to the Pennsylvania-Maryland border dispute. The best way to preclude encroachment was for Marylanders to settle the land. Dulany was implementing what he had encouraged Lord Baltimore to do for some time.

Cresap continued to scout lands for Dulany in both the Monocacy and Antietam Valleys. Around 1740, Cresap moved farther west to Old Town and mortgaged his Antietam tracts, including Long Meadows, to Dulany. Cresap found and surveyed "Buck Forest" (1,600 acres and later 3,000 acres) on a Monocacy tributary; "Locust Level" (3,180 acres); "Spring Garden" and "Addition to Spring Garden" near the Monocacy.[92] Just the names suggest Cresap may have had a hand in all of these acquisitions. Cresap had a fondness for poetic names for the tracts he acquired. In that buying spree Dulany had acquired over nineteen thousand acres of land in the Monocacy and Antietam Valleys with the objective of populating these lands with Germans.

In the seventeenth century, small numbers of Germans had immigrated into the colonies, particularly Maryland; there was not a major German influx until the early and middle years of the eighteenth century. The seeds of this migration were in the European Thirty Years War (1618–1648) which ravaged the Rhine River region known as the Palatinate. It began as a religious war in the Palatinate but, over the years, involved many of the countries of Europe. The violence was renewed late in the century after the revocation of the Edict of Nantes[93] in 1685 by Louis XIV, when many Huguenots fled France to the Palatinate. French forces followed them with the intention of destroying the Huguenots and the Palatinate. More violence followed in the War of the Spanish Secession (1701–1714). The net result of this continued violence was a vastly reduced, poverty-stricken population in the Palatinate and a strong desire to move out ... anywhere.[94]

This was also the moment the agents of William Penn, were looking for settlers for his province, and one place they looked was Europe. They had an overwhelming response. The Palatines quickly jumped at the chance to move on, because immigration offered asylum from the Palatine violence. The first stage of their journey, in 1709, was to London, England and from June through October, between thirteen thousand and fourteen thousand Germans arrived there. They were destitute, with no job prospects so the English government tried to move them on as quickly as possible. Some were sent to Ireland, some were sent back to the Palatine, and some were sent to New York. Many of the latter found their way to Pennsylvania. This was the beginning of a constant stream of Germans to Pennsylvania. By 1717, the Pennsylvania authorities became alarmed at the large number arriving. In 1729 the Penn's wrote to Pennsylvania Secretary Logan, "As to the Palatines, you have often notice to us, wee apprehend have Lately arrived in greater quantities than may be consistent with the welfare of the Country."[95]

There was a nativist backlash against the Palatine Germans. Even Benjamin Franklin was worried as late as 1751,

> Why should the Palatine boors be suffered to swarm into our settlements, and, by herding together, establish their language and manners, to the exclusion of ours? Why should Pennsylvania, founded by the English, become a colony of aliens, who will shortly be so numerous as to Germanize us, instead of our Anglicifying them, and will never adopt our language or customs any more than they can acquire our complexion?[96]

This attitude has repeated itself many times during our history, even to this day. Later Franklin recanted, but many of these Germans had moved on by that time. With the Pennsylvania-Maryland border dispute still going on many were encouraged to move south to Maryland to occupy the disputed lands. Others, such as Jost Hite, were sought by Virginia to occupy the Shenandoah Valley,

In 1732 Lord Baltimore made his land offer. As the German migrants moved through Maryland to Virginia, some decided to stay especially in the Monocacy Valley, because of the rich lands there. It is not clear how many came and stayed because they received land from Lord Baltimore or if they simply became squatters. Dulany met these people on his later western trip and was one of many who were impressed with their farming, farm structures, and their industry.

> In a region known for wasteful and slovenly farming, contemporaries praised the Germans' industry and good management. "It is pretty to behold our back settlement," wrote Lewis Evans in 1753, "where the barns are as large as palaces, while the owners live in log huts; a sign though of thriving farmers." "The farms on the river are owned chiefly by the Germans, & bear all marks of their industry," added Dr. Benjamin Rush, and are "equal in point of cultivation to any perhaps in the world."[97]

Even Benjamin Franklin changed his mind, "Their occupation is mostly husbandry, and they are reckoned excellent farmers, have made great improvements in the countries where they reside, and some few of them, by their diligence and skill in agriculture, have gained very considerable estates."[98]

Dulany was convinced, so when he started his expansion in the west in 1745, he wrote to both Lord Baltimore and Governor Ogle,

> With a "little Encouragement," he began, "the most remote parts of your Lordship's province will be filled with quiet, honest, and Industrious Inhabitants." But in order to accomplish this, Lord Baltimore would have to imitate a practice which the proprietor of Pennsylvania had found to be very successful. Lord Baltimore was to permit "newcomers" who were unable to buy their own land to settle on the "most distant country" where they would be able either to pay, at a future date, for the land, or by their "Improvements" increase the value of the land. Either way, Dulany added, "I need not tell your Lordship how advantageous such an Enterprise will be to yourself and your family." What Dulany was, in fact, telling the proprietor and the governor, was that they would be "Surprised" to see how "the back parts of the Province are Settled and Improved beyond what could be expected."[99]

Dulany was telling the proprietor that the original feudal concept of holding the land tight, looking for large landowners, and charging high fees and rents would not work for the backcountry. He knew that the land in the west was not good for tobacco and had no waterways for moving tobacco to the ships, unlike the tidewater. Dulany knew that farming in grains and other crops would work very well in the backcountry, and the only way to do this was to attract poor, but industrious farmers to settle and improve the land. Dulany, was willing to follow that plan, and in the process not only improved western Maryland but made a fortune in his own right.

Dulany knew that a commercial center would have to be established to help the farmers and consumers to meet. He had the surveyors set up lots for a town on the eastern side of Tasker's Chance, near the Monocacy River. He surveyed 350 to 400 feet by 60 feet lots. He offered them to artisans and tradesmen for a fee of £4 or £5 currency with a ground rent of one shilling per year, payable to him, which was allowed by Lord Baltimore. Most of the lots went to German immigrants. Dulany donated lots to both the Lutheran and Reformed churches for their church buildings. Local political and administrative posts were filled with his appointees. The town was called Frederick Town and later Frederick, probably after the son of Lord Baltimore.[100] Frederick wasn't the first German settlement in the Monocacy Valley, but it quickly became the most important.

Frederick, the Monocacy Valley, and the Cumberland (Hagerstown) Valley farther west grew rapidly, mostly populated by German immigrants. By 1750 Frederick was estimated to have about one thousand residents, exceeding the population of Annapolis at eight hundred; it was the largest town in Maryland. "Lord Baltimore heartily extended his gratitude 'for the Laudable and Acceptable Service' Dulany had rendered him with the establishment of Frederick." A member of the Braddock expedition in 1755 noted that although Frederick had been settled only seven years there were about two hundred houses and two churches because of the "industrious but imposing people." Later, in 1773, Governor Eden noted "that Frederick had, at one time, been the extreme boundary of 'cultivated establishments,' but after the efforts of an 'industrious laborious people' was a 'Wilderness' turned into 'well-stocked plantations.'" Western Maryland continued to grow not only with German immigrants from provinces like Pennsylvania, but with immigrants coming directly from the Palatinate through the port of Baltimore.[101]

Frederick and the Monocacy Valley are just east of the Catoctin and Blue Ridge mountains. Just west of these mountains is the Great Valley of the Appalachians or, as it is known in that area, the Cumberland or Hagerstown Valley. Some of the German settlers went over the Blue Ridge to this valley, even farther west of Frederick. They settled at Conococheague near a creek by that name, near the present-day Clear Spring, Maryland. For a short time, they were likely even farther west than Thomas Cresap who had moved to his permanent home in Old town in 1740. The Conococheague Creek flows into the Potomac at Williamsport, Maryland, where Williams Ferry was located. Conococheague was the farthest settlement in western Maryland until the French and Indian war.

The other prominent town in western Maryland was established by Jonathon Hager, in the Cumberland Valley. Hager arrived in Philadelphia from Germany, probably the Palatinate, in 1736. He spent three years in Pennsylvania moving down to Maryland in 1739 to patent two hundred acres in the Cumberland Valley near Conococheague. He gathered more land over the years until he had almost 2,500 acres. He laid out a town in 1762, intending to name it Elizabeth-Town after his wife. The town prospered but the name did not; it became known as Hagerstown. The Cumberland Valley in this part of Maryland became known as the Hagerstown Valley.[102]

Both Frederick and Hagerstown prospered, not because of east-west intra-province traffic, but because both were on major north-south roads which saw a lot of traffic between New York and Pennsylvania, to Virginia and the Carolinas. The Hagerstown Valley is the major farmland area farthest west in Maryland; west of that valley is the Allegheny Ridge and Valley mountains. Of necessity, after Frederick was founded east-west roads between Frederick and Annapolis and Baltimore were constructed.

New Adventures

By the mid-eighteenth century the colony of Maryland was much more diverse in its population and economy than it had been just a few decades earlier. Tobacco, though still very important, was not the only crop. Wheat and other grains were grown in the western part of the state and shipped east. There was an iron industry near Baltimore, and Baltimore was growing fast, on its way to becoming a major eastern port. The population had increased with many migrants coming from Pennsylvania and settling in the west; many of these now were landowners. The political system had become more sophisticated over the years. The Governor and the Assembly had become experienced in dealing with the Proprietor. These skills would prove to be valuable in later years when all the colonies became independent. Although Maryland grew and prospered, it was still bounded in area in an era that was about to become expansionist.

All the English colonies had expanded to the limits set by the Appalachians. In any situation where there are limits that people can see beyond, there are many who want to go beyond those limits. This was true in the middle-Atlantic colonies of Pennsylvania, Maryland, and Virginia. Many traders had crossed the mountains, especially in Pennsylvania and Virginia, and conducted an extensive business with the Indians and the few white settlers in the Ohio Valley. For many settlers, the status quo seemed unreasonable because they knew of the rich lands in the Ohio country just beyond the mountains. The situation facing the inhabitants of these mid–Atlantic colonies, especially the entrepreneurs, was different in all three colonies.

The Virginia charter was from sea to sea, so right from the beginning many in Virginia assumed there would be a western movement, mountains or not. The expeditions to the west illustrate this, first to look for the South Sea, and then to push for settlement in the Shenandoah Valley as a prelude to further expansion. Furthermore, the northern boundary of the second Virginia charter went northwest from the sea so that it included the major part of the Ohio country. It is doubtful the King had even a vague idea of the implications of that charter when it was issued in 1609. Clearly many Virginians saw the Ohio country as a natural part of their colony.

Pennsylvania had a different problem. The Pennsylvania charter had defined a western boundary but it had not been defined clearly. It was not clear if it was a true meridian line or a jagged line following the shape of the Delaware River. This was important because Pennsylvania claimed the Forks of the Ohio, present-day Pittsburgh, was in their colony. The Forks were clearly in the Ohio country so Pennsylvania also laid claim to the Ohio country.

Maryland, on the other hand, was not so lucky. It had a fixed western border with no claim to the Ohio country. Nevertheless, its location was key. Western Maryland was the location of the key route from the mid–Atlantic colonies to the Ohio country.

Three

Competition for the Ohio Country

In 1798 some boys playing in southeastern Ohio, where the Muskingum River meets the Ohio, found a square lead plate three or four feet below the surface, which had been exposed by the rushing water. They dug it up, noticed it had some writing they did not understand, and took it home to use part of it to make bullets. Similar plates were eventually found, including one by a boy named R. P. Hereford discovered in 1846, where the Kanawha River enters the Ohio. This plate was approximately eleven inches by six inches and varied in thickness from about one-eighth to one-quarter of an inch. Buried August 18, 1749, the plate had been there almost one hundred years. Inscribed in French the plate contained this information:

> In the year 1749, of the reign of Louis XV, of France, We, Celeron, commandant of a detachment sent by the Marquis de la Galissonier, Captain-General of New France, in order to re-establish tranquility among some villages of savages of these parts, have buried this plate at the mouth of the river Chi-no-da-hich-e-tha [Kanawha], the 18th August, near the river Ohio, otherwise beautiful river, as a monument of renewal of possession, which we have taken of the said river Ohio, and of all those which empty themselves into it, and of all the lands of both sides, even to the sources of said rivers; as have enjoyed, or ought to have enjoyed the preceding kings of France, and that they have maintained themselves there, by force of arms and by treaties, especially by those of Riswick, of Utrecht, and of Aix-la-Chapelle.[1]

This was the proverbial stake in the ground or plate in the sand, by which the French were claiming the entire Ohio Valley, whether La Salle had discovered it or not. Article two of the Treaty of Aix-la-Chapelle (1748) ending King George's War stipulated that everything after the war was to revert to the status quo ante. To France that meant the Ohio Valley was theirs. The French expedition by Celoron de Bienville was the French reaction to the plans of the Ohio Company of Virginia, to do more than just trade in the Ohio country, but to promote settlement there as well. It was time for France to show a presence in Ohio.

By 1749 the importance of the Ohio River to the future of both New France and the English colonies was recognized by all. The English claimed the Ohio Valley through the discoveries of the Batts and Fallam expedition almost one hundred years previously and by the more recent Treaty of Lancaster in which they claimed the Iroquois had ceded the land to them. The only clear way to establish ownership was to occupy the land. The French expedition by Celoron de Bienville (or Blainville) was a rather weak attempt to show possession, but it hardly qualified as occupation. It would take more than some lead plates to do that.

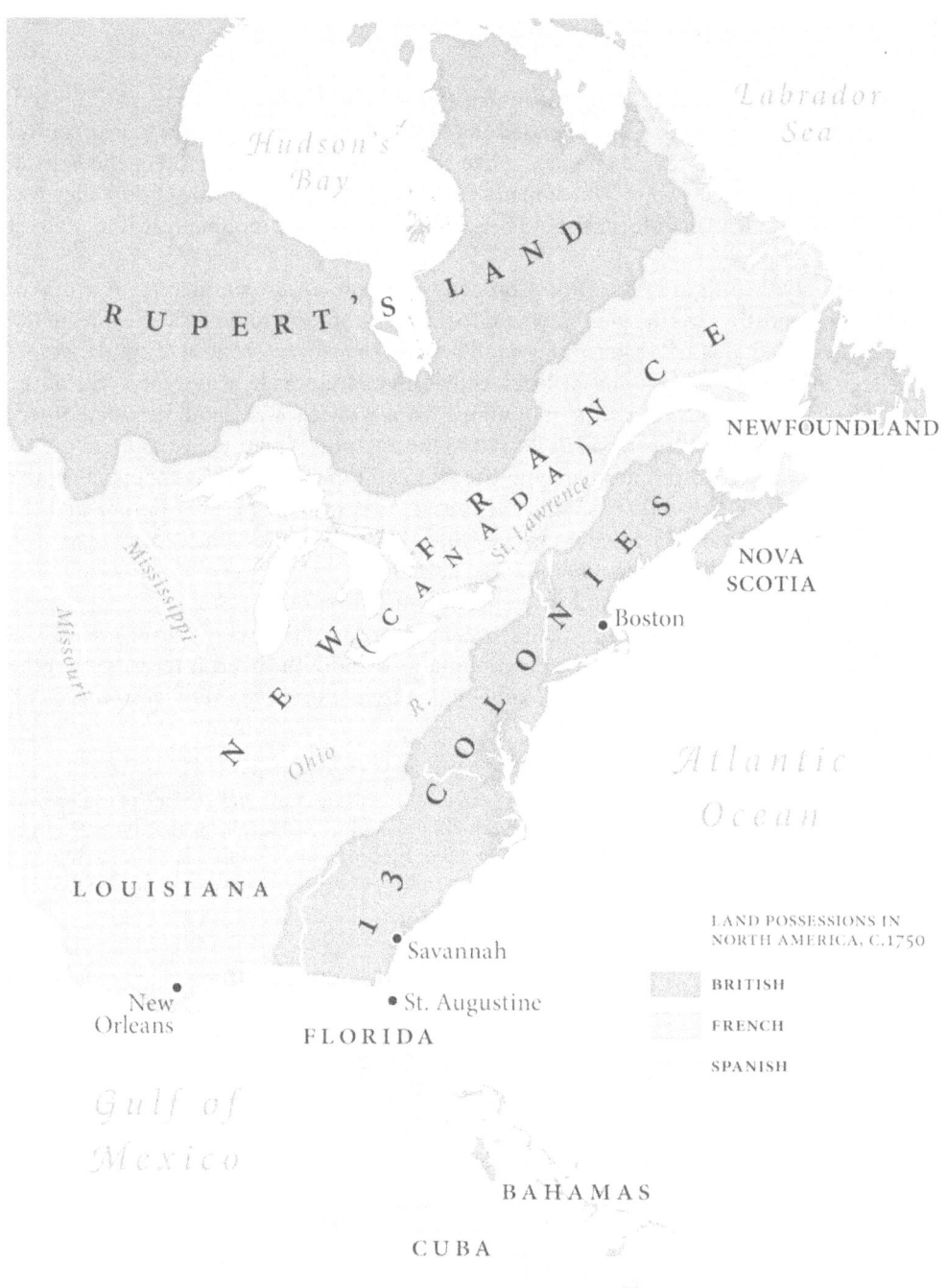

Map 4: Britain, France, and Spain in North America, 1750. This depicts the relative land claims by the British, French, and Spanish around 1750. It does not indicate settlement density as large parts of Louisiana and Canada were sparsely settled whereas the British East Coast was densely settled.

The Ohio Company of Virginia

The eighteenth century was one of almost continual war between France and England. Although King George's War had just ended and both countries were anxious to take control of the Ohio Valley, each feared an overt move could reignite the conflict. For the British, the establishment of a commercial company that would claim land in the Ohio Valley was an ideal approach. British influence could be extended west of the mountains without direct government action.

Ostensibly the origin of the Ohio Company of Virginia was commercial. A group of businessmen, mostly Virginia gentry, would form a corporation to move settlers from the relatively crowded area of western Maryland and the Northern Neck of Virginia, across the Alleghenies to the Ohio country, specifically to the Monongahela and the Forks of the Ohio. The shortest route across the mountains from western Maryland, originated near the head of the Potomac River, which flowed to the Atlantic. The route would end on the Monongahela, which flowed ultimately to the Ohio and then to the Mississippi. The first objective would be increased trade with the Native Americans, especially in furs, and the second objective would be settlement in the Ohio Valley. To achieve the second objective, they would build settlements, roads, and forts, developing the country and increasing their wealth through the sale of land and the collection of quitrents.

This was land speculation but it did serve the interests of the British government. The English colonies would extend across the mountains without the overt intervention of the king. As noted by Bailey (*The Ohio Company of Virginia and the Westward Movement, 1748-1792*),

> But a study of the Ohio company is far more than a study of a scheme in land speculation. It is a study of explorations, of Indian problems and policy, of colonial jealousy and conflict, of traders and traders' problems, of the closing struggle between France and England for the possession of North America, of British colonial and imperial policy, and of Virginia and Pennsylvania boundary disputes. Therefore the history of the Ohio company is a factor of major importance in the story of frontier advance into the Ohio country.[2]

Founding the Ohio Company of Virginia

Thomas Cresap was not an easy man to get along with, and he made enemies easily, as had happened with the Pennsylvanians. Originally, he lived near the present-day Havre de Grace, Maryland, but he had moved to Virginia in 1730 to avoid creditors on a rather small sum he owed. While in Virginia he met some of the Virginia gentry, including Thomas Lee and Lawrence and Augustine Washington. Even during his brief stay in Virginia, he was not well received. He was confronted by a number of other people, who suggested he remove himself from Virginia. Apparently his personality was as abrasive as ever; once again he got into a fight. He returned at his wife's request and lived in Maryland thereafter.[3]

Cresap built his fortune in land in Maryland as he continued to move to the western frontier, first to Antietam, and then to Old Town in far western Maryland. During that time, he also purchased some land in Virginia, probably near the Potomac, where he also had land on the Maryland side. In the late 1740s Cresap once more was in contact with the Washingtons and Lees. It is not clear if this had been a continuous relationship over the intervening years, or if it arose because of the common interest they all had in western land. In any case, in their meetings the idea of a land corporation was broached. Once again Cresap's charming personality showed through. It was claimed by a Richard Peters, "that vile fellow Cresap who had suggested a scheme to Col. Lee and other great men in Virginia to make trading houses at Alleghenny."[4] Whether or not Cresap was the one who made the initial suggestion to establish a corporation to move across the mountains, it was completely in his character to promote moving farther west; he had been doing it all his life. The scheme that Peters was referring to was the founding of the Ohio Company of Virginia.

Although Cresap was indeed a founding member of the company he was an outlier compared to the others in the group. The exact number of members at the birth of the corporation is not clear.[5] It could have been thirteen or fourteen or twenty, as there are sources for all these numbers. The distinguishing feature of the group, however, was that they were almost all members of the Virginia land-owning class. At one time or another in the early years the company included Thomas Lee, Robert Carter, George Fairfax, Richard Lee, Robert Dinwiddie, George Mercer, George Mason, and Lawrence and Augustine Washington, among others. These names are writ large in Virginia history, a group with substantial financial backing as well as political influence.

Cresap, and his son Daniel, did not have the wealth of the Virginians but they did hold great deal of land in Maryland and Virginia by this time, something the Virginians would have respected. He was welcomed into the corporation, despite his boorish reputation, which he must have held in check, probably because of his expertise in pushing the western frontier, and in frontier land acquisition.

If Cresap was not the one with the original idea for the corporation then it was certainly Thomas Lee, probably in 1747. Lee was the first head of the corporation and came with a broad base of experience in the westward movement. As a member of the Lees of Virginia, he had opportunities others did not have. At twenty-three he became resident manager of the five-thousand acre Culpeper-Fairfax holdings in the Northern Neck. His support of the western movement included encouraging the movement of German immigrants into the Shenandoah Valley. In 1732 he was elected to the Virginia Council, a position that made him one of Virginia's commissioners negotiating the Treaty of Lancaster in 1744. He frequently expressed his opinion about the French as "enemy" in the Ohio country. As senior councilor in 1749 he became acting Governor of Virginia when Lieutenant Governor Gooch returned to England. His eye toward expansion in the west, and his positions of influence, made him a natural leader for the company.[6]

The company lost little time and quickly made their first petition for land, as a list of patents and grants shows: "Oct, 20th 1747. Thomas Lee, Esq., and Eleven others, for 200,000 acres to be laid out from ye Branch called Kiskomanett's and Buffalo creek on the south side of the River Alligany, and between the two creeks and the yellow creek on the north side and on the main River of Alligany als. Ohio. [The Boundry of Pensylve.]"[7] Governor Gooch was a little leery of making the grant as New France also claimed the land and the grant might lead to conflict. He backed it though; and thought it would be beneficial for the crown so in November he sent it to the Board of Trade to ask permission from the King. To help their petition the company sent a request to John Hanbury, a London merchant, to join the company and make the case for them in London. On January 11, 1749, Hanbury made their case to the King and Council. They requested,

> A tract ... of five hundred thousand acres of land betwixt Romanettos and Buffloes creek on the south side of the river Aligany otherwise the Ohio, and betwixt the two creeks and the yellow creek on the north side of said river or in such other parts to the west of the said mountains as shall be judged most proper by your petitioners for that purpose. And that two hundred thousand acres be granted immediately ... as soon as these two hundred thousand acres are settled and the fort erected

that three hundred thousand acres more residue of the said five hundred thousand acres may be granted to your petitioners adjoining the said two hundred thousand acres of land.[8]

The King received the proposal well. Over the next several months the petition went back and forth between the Board of Trade and the Privy Council, specifically addressing the question of whether or not it would be good for Virginia and British interests. They agreed it was a positive move. Further stipulations were made during this process, including the requirement for the Company to set up a fort on the new land using their own funds. Finally, on March 16, 1749, the Council ordered the instructions to Gooch be drawn up for the King's signature. On July 12, 1749, Gooch made the grant to the Company as instructed.[9] Although probably not thought important at the time, the phrase, "or in such other parts to the west of said mountains as shall be judged most proper by your petitioners for that purpose," would become important later when the company had trouble fulfilling its obligations for the first two hundred thousand acres.

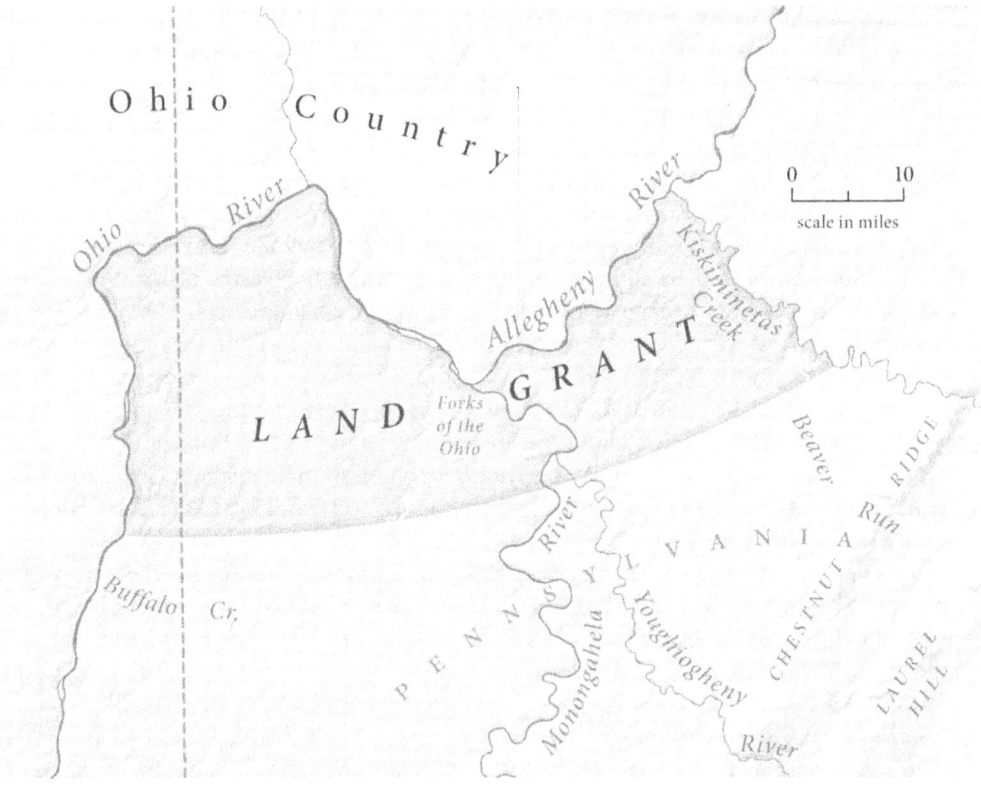

Map 5: Ohio Company Grant Request. The grant the Ohio Company requested spans the area east of the Ohio and Allegheny rivers from Kiskiminetas Creek, a tributary of the Allegheny River, westward to the Ohio River. It is centered on the Monongahela River and the Forks of the Ohio, present-day Pittsburgh, considered the heart of the Ohio country. The Allegheny River comes from the north, and the Monongahela River from the south, to meet at the Forks of the Ohio to form the Ohio River. Some land is mentioned north of the river with the reference to Yellow Creek, which enters the Ohio from the west just a few miles upstream of Buffalo Creek, near present-day East Liverpool, Ohio. No northern border is mentioned for the land north of the river, so it is likely it was meant that some land on the other side of the river from the main grant was desired. The main grant of five hundred thousand acres is south and east of the river.

The Hanbury petition emphasizes some interesting points. First, in part it reads like a realtor's brochure when it describes the land in question, as it takes some liberties. He claims,

> that the lands to the west of the said mountains are extremely fertile [true] the climate very fine and healthy [true] and the waters of the Mississippi and those of the Potomac are only separated by one small ridge of mountains easily passable by land carriage [not true] so that by the convenience of the Navigation of the Potomac and a short land carriage from thence to the west of the mountains and to the branch of the Ohio and lake Erie British goods may be carried at little expense [not true][10] [Comments in brackets are the author's].

Although overly simplified, this document shows what the members of the company were thinking. The land they proposed to occupy and sell was just west of the mountains, on the Allegheny and Ohio rivers, and spanned the Forks of the Ohio. They were proposing, not only a settlement, but a trade route up the east flowing Potomac and, over the mountains to the west flowing Monongahela. Jared Sparks (*The Writings of George Washington*) made the same observation, "The Company conceived, that they might derive an important advantage over their competitors in this trade, from the water communication of the Potomac and the eastern branches of the Ohio, whose headwaters approximated each other."[11] Their competitors included the French.

The petition was careful to point out the trade and territorial advantages to the empire,

> it will not only be made the best and strongest Frontier in America but will be the means of gaining vast addition and increase to your Majestys subjects of that branch of the peltry and furr trade which your petitioners propose by means of the settlement ... and will at the same time greatly promote the consumption of our British manufactures enlarge our commerce encrease our shipping and Navigation and extend your Majestys Empire in America.[12]

This was more hyperbole, similar to the real estate description, but this is what probably sold the crown on the project.

The first point Hanbury made clear in his petition before the crown was the justification for being able to cross the mountains and claim land on the western slope. The British had never been beyond the mountains in any numbers before, but claimed land in the Ohio Valley by reason of the Batts and Fallam expedition about eight decades earlier. That was a weak link in their claim to the Ohio Valley as it was only an expedition and left no permanent presence. Others who had wanted to go farther previously did not, partly out of fear of French retaliation. One of Governor Spotswood's objectives in his 1716 expedition was to push farther west. That expedition only reached the Shenandoah Valley, not part of the Ohio Valley, but Virginians were moving in the right direction.

There were many British traders but no large British settlements in the Ohio Valley. In theory, Hanbury could have claimed the land by virtue of the second charter of Virginia issued in 1609. That charter would have included most of the Ohio Valley as it was "sea to sea." However, the charter was about 140 years old, would have been considered useless by the French, and would have been challenged by Pennsylvania's claim to the same land.

Hanbury made the strongest justification possible in the petitions because the Ohio Company knew they would be breaking new ground. He claimed in the July 1744 Treaty of Lancaster, the Six Nations of the Iroquois, "did yeild ... and forever quit claim to your Majesty ... all the lands west of Virginia with all the rights thereto, so far as your Majesty should at any time thereafter be pleased to extend the said colony."[13] The Iroquois had claimed the Ohio country by right of conquest. The treaties with the Native Americans, especially the Iroquois, were complicated, and not all were interpreted the same way by both parties. The movement by the Ohio Company into the Ohio Valley was soon challenged by the Six Nations, leading to another treaty, the Treaty of Logstown (Loggstown) in 1752. Logstown is a few miles downstream on the Ohio from the Forks. That treaty was required after the Ohio Company sent out explorations for land in the Ohio Valley.

Blazing the Trail

Expanded trade with those already in the Ohio country was one of the main objectives of the company. In competition with other land companies such as the Loyal Company, and especially with the Pennsylvania traders conducting the existing trade, they knew they had to move quickly. Lee realized the Ohio Company had the advantage of coming from Virginia and crossing the mountains at the closest point to the Monongahela.

They knew they wanted to start their road across the mountains at Wills Creek, a point on the upper Potomac, a few miles upstream from the Cresap place. Wills Creek, named after a local Indian, enters the Potomac from Maryland after cutting its way from the north through Wills Mountain. Near its source the Potomac is shallow and easy to ford so it would be easy to cross the river from Virginia to Maryland at that point. Cresap knew of Wills Creek because he had made an early survey on the Maryland side for Governor Bladen. Cresap called the area—the location of present-day Cumberland, Maryland—Wills Town. As Bailey says of the route they were considering, "Wills' Creek had dug a deep ravine through Savage Mountain, and thus served with this principal range as the divide between the headwaters of the Youghiogheny, a branch of the Monongahela, and the Potomac. As a result it had become one of the favorite Indian paths from the Potomac to the Ohio river and its head tributaries."[14] The company chose this accessible and strategic position for their headquarters and in 1749 built a storehouse on the Virginia side of the Potomac just opposite Wills Creek. They had invested four thousand pounds sterling in goods which they intended to ship across the mountains to the traders in Ohio. When the goods arrived, the storehouse was not yet built, and the goods were not yet ready to be shipped across the mountains. The company was successful in selling these goods from the storehouse location to the traders and Indians who inhabited this trade route.[15]

In addition to increased trade, the other objective of the company was to settle the land. The grant required they settle one hundred families on the land and build a fort on it within seven years. Upon accomplishing that, they would be granted an additional three hundred thousand acres on the Ohio.[16] This meant they needed to explore and survey the land.

In 1749, the company sent out a party including Thomas Cresap and others, to look for suitable land and settlement sites. These men were mostly traders who were unfamiliar with surveying and were unsuccessful in finding appropriate land. The Ohio Company then turned to two surveyors more familiar with seeking and laying out sites for settlers. One of these was a Virginian, George Washington, and the other a Marylander, Christopher Gist. Washington had apparently previously surveyed some company land on both sides of the Potomac.[17]

Gist eventually made two critical journeys into the Ohio country for the company, the first was in 1750. On the second journey, starting in 1751, he blazed the trail from Wills Creek through Maryland and Pennsylvania to the Ohio Valley, the trail that eventually linked Maryland and Ohio. The importance of the trail that Gist blazed across the mountains cannot be over emphasized. Its importance was not manifest immediately, because packhorses were perfectly adequate for the trade going on at the time. Gist's intention to blaze a path for settlers was a clear indication of the need for a real road across these mountains, not just a path. Once settlement started, it would be necessary for a good road, not only to move settlers west, but also to move goods east.

George Washington and Christopher Gist

Washington was not a trailblazer like Gist but he was interested in western lands and eventually he acquired large land holdings in the west including the Ohio country. Washington had great interest in acting for the benefit of his country, but often, especially concerning land acquisition, those actions also coincided with his interests. There is no evidence he ever put his interests above his duty to country, but at times he protected his land interests while he was on duty. When Washington's will was executed in 1800 it listed 52,194 acres to be sold or distributed in Virginia, Pennsylvania, Maryland, New York, Kentucky, and the Ohio Valley; he was land rich.[18] According to Forrest McDonald (*The Presidency of George Washington*) regarding speculators,

> One worked or connived to obtain a stake, then worked or connived to obtain legal title to a tract of wilderness, then sold the wilderness by the acre to the hordes of immigrants, and thereby lived and died a wealthy man. Appropriately, the most successful practitioner of this craft was George Washington, who had acquired several hundred thousand acres and was reckoned by many as the wealthiest man in America.[19]

This was the result of his desire for land acquisition, a taste he had developed early.

Washington was born in February 1732 into a moderately well-to-do family, but not one that matched the wealth of the Virginia gentry such as the Lees, the Fairfax's, and the Carters. His was an extended family; where George was one of six born to his father's second wife; he had three stepbrothers and one stepsister from his father's first marriage. He was close to two of his stepbrothers, Augustine and Lawrence. The family moved around a lot and George did not receive the classical education that his brother Lawrence had received in England. He was not broadly read in the classics but did well in mathematics. Washington envied the urbane manners of his brother and others of the gentry, and embarked on a series of self-improvement efforts in reading, manners, and bearing, generally trying to make a good impression.[20]

His father died in 1743 when George was only eleven. Although he lived with his mother at Ferry Farm, he frequently sought the company of his brother Lawrence who lived at an estate Lawrence would name Mount Vernon. George was ambitious and was not really interested in staying at Ferry Farm although it would have afforded him a comfortable life as a mid-level planter. He was also lucky. He became acquainted with the Fairfax family and got his first break.

During his self-education efforts, George became interested in surveying, apparently helped by his interest in mathematics. He got an opportunity to put his knowledge to use when in 1747, Thomas, Lord Fairfax, arrived from England to look over his holdings in the Northern Neck. Fairfax put together a surveying party in 1748 and sixteen-year-old George was invited to participate. Up to this point Washington had only done some practice surveys, but now he would actually get paid for some of his surveys. George enjoyed surveying and the outdoors, and he made the most of this opportunity. By July 1749, he was commissioned a county surveyor of Culpepper County. He had a reputation for honesty and fairness as a surveyor and was financially successful. By the time he was eighteen he made his first land purchase, 450 acres in the Shenandoah Valley. This was followed closely by the purchase of one thousand acres on a tributary of the Shenandoah River.[21] These were only the first of many land purchases he would make, mostly in the west.

George was only fifteen in 1747 when his brothers Lawrence and Augustine became founding members of the Ohio Company. There must have been many interesting discussions between George and his brothers about the western lands. These discussions, plus George's interest in surveying, may have led to his life-long fascination with opening the western lands. He was never a shareholder in the Ohio Company, but over the next several years, as a young officer in the Virginia regiment, he interacted with the company and its members. All the while he kept his eyes open for promising land in which to invest.

Although surveying gave him some autonomy he was still ambitious to prove himself in some well-recognized profession, such as the military. This opportunity came indirectly in the late 1740s when his brother Lawrence became ill with tuberculosis and George spent a great deal of time helping him by looking for cures, or at least relief. They tried various diets and warm locations such as Barbados; nothing worked. After Lawrence died, and after the later deaths of his wife and daughter, George eventually inherited Mount Vernon. While he was taking care of Lawrence George became interested in a position Lawrence held, that of an Adjutant General of Virginia. He started lobbying Governor Dinwiddie for the position even prior to Lawrence's death. Eventually he gained the position, receiving the Northern Neck adjutancy in February 1753 just before his twenty-first birthday; his title was Major. Just a few months later, Dinwiddie was looking for an officer to head an expedition to warn the French to stay out of Ohio. Washington heard of this plan, raced to Williamsburg to ask for the commission, and received the job. Thus by 1754 Washington was on the world stage although not in a very auspicious manner. He was blamed by many for starting the French and Indian War.[22]

Christopher Gist and George Washington started working together in the early 1750s after they met through the Ohio Company. Gist was over twenty years older than Washington but they worked well together for several years and became friends. Gist became familiar with Washington's military assignments and he was a perfect match for the guide duties Washington would need.

Gist was, like Thomas Cresap, a Marylander through and through, but unlike Cresap Gist was a third-generation Marylander. A member of a prominent English family named Christopher Guest had immigrated to Lord Baltimore's Maryland sometime between 1660 and 1682. He moved to the Patapsco River, south of present-day Baltimore, acquired a lot of land in the area, became a force in politics, and married Edith Cromwell, of the famous English Cromwell family. Their son Richard became a justice and commissioner of Baltimore as his father had been. Richard changed the spelling of his surname to Gist. Christopher, born in 1705 or 1706 was one of the four sons of Richard Gist and Zepporah Murray; Christopher also had three sisters.[23]

By all accounts the young Gist was successful as a fur trader with the Indians, an explorer and a ranger. He married at age twenty-three, and he and his wife had six children. Two of the boys, Nathaniel and Thomas, became well-known frontiersmen in their own right. His family life was interrupted at times with ranging on the frontier where he gained valuable experience for his very important role in opening the path from Maryland to Ohio. Over the years, the family was friendly with George Washington. Gist was tall for the age, and physically strong making him well suited to take care of himself in the wilderness. Washington, himself an outdoor person of some skill, attested to Gist's abilities. Gist got along well with both colonists and Native Americans projecting an aura of integrity, and was well-trusted by Washington. Well educated, primarily in surveying but also mathematics, Gist also wrote well as evident in in the journals he kept on his travels. Not as abrasive as Cresap in personality, he worked well with Cresap, Washington, and the members of the Ohio Company. Gist and Cresap together played critical roles on the Maryland frontier and deserve to be remembered for their accomplishments as Marylanders.[24]

Lord Baltimore had learned from the mistakes of previous English colonies and was determined to avoid conflict with the Native Americans, establishing friendly contacts which paid off in the long run as Maryland was not troubled by bloody conflicts with the native people. Nevertheless, there were some problems. The Six Nations' Senecas frequently raided the frontiers and Baltimore County found it necessary to organize a militia of rangers. These men would "range" the frontier to repulse or preclude raids. Gist made his reputation in this role and developed his skills in dealing with the Native Americans. Through his fur trading he covered a lot of territory in western Maryland, western Pennsylvania, and even the Ohio country. Rangers, were also responsible for maintaining the county roads. At one time Gist was put on trial for failing to take care of a road, but he was acquitted. This may have shown he was distracted by some of his other businesses, which included his surveying business, a trading boat, and serving at one time as Baltimore County coroner.[25]

Gist's father owned a fur trading business where Christopher learned the trade. When he was thirteen, his father was put out of the fur trading business when his fur warehouse burned down. Christopher, nevertheless entered his own fur trading business and, ironically, lost his own warehouse full of furs in a 1732 fire. He continued with his other business ventures but some of these enterprises also failed and his most successful work continued to be on the frontier. Like Thomas Cresap, he longed to be on the frontier and was planning to move farther west.[26]

It was probably in the early 1740s that he sold his failing businesses to relatives and moved his family to the Yadkin River on the North Carolina frontier near present-day Wilkesboro. The family became acquainted with the Boone family and Christopher knew Squire Boone, father of Daniel. Daniel was closer in age to Cristopher's son Nathaniel and they used to hunt together. A few decades later Daniel would lead settlers through the Cumberland Gap to Kentucky, making his own opening to the west from Virginia.[27]

The Ohio Company found Gist in North Carolina around 1750 and made him their chief frontier scout, undoubtedly because of his reputation and the recommendation of Thomas Cresap.[28]

Gist's Journeys

FIRST JOURNEY, 1750–1751

Although they received the approval for the grant in July 1749, the Ohio Company lost time taking advantage of it, a problem since the grant was to expire in seven years. After Cresap was unsuccessful in finding suitable land in 1749 he recommended the company hire Christopher Gist, a qualified surveyor, to explore the Ohio country for lands to settle. They accepted Cresap's recommendation and on September 11, 1750, the Ohio Company gave Gist his expedition instructions. They were of a general nature because they weren't sure what to expect. This cost them more time as this was to be only his first journey.[29]

He was to explore west to at least as far as the Falls of the Ohio, near present-day Louisville, a significant distance. He was to "observe the Ways & Passes thro all the Mountains you cross, & take an exact Account of the Soil, Quality, & Product of the Land, and the Wideness and Deepness of the Rivers." He was to observe the Indians and their strengths and numbers. Most of all when he found good land he was "to measure the Breadth of it, in three or four different Places, & take the course of the Rivers and Mountains on which it binds in Order to judge the Quantity.... You are to draw as good a Plan as you can of the Country You pass thro."[30] The broad scope of the instructions is curious considering the original two-hundred-thousand-acre grant stretched from the Kiskiminetas Creek and the Allegheny River, just above the Forks, down to Buffalo Creek, just below present-day Steubenville, Ohio, on the Ohio River. This grant was all east of the Ohio and Allegheny rivers yet the instructions took in all of Ohio. Although they had presented to the King that the land they were seeking was just over the mountains from the Potomac, Gist was not instructed to follow that route.

These instructions came late in the season and Gist got a late start. He went first to Cresap's place at Oldtown, then he left from there on October 31, starting north and slightly east along an old Indian path, up to the Juniata River in Pennsylvania. The Juniata River is a tributary of the Susquehanna arising in central Pennsylvania. This was the origin of a large northwest arc that took him through a large part of Ohio until he ended the journey at his home on the Yadkin River in North Carolina. From the Juniata he headed west along Loyalhanna Creek, a tributary of Kiskiminetas Creek and then farther west to Shannopin's Town, a Delaware Indian village on the Forks of the Ohio.[31]

It took Gist twenty days to travel to Shannopin's town. Many days he didn't travel due to illness, and he rested at the town before starting out again. Now in 1750, the competition for the Ohio country between the French, English, and the Native Americans was coming to a head. He noted in his journal how careful he had to be in using his compass as he could not let the Indians see him using it. He knew that the compass would indicate he was looking for land to settle and that would put him in danger from the Indians who were now becoming wary of white settlers. He presented himself to the Indians as a Virginia agent looking for closer alliances with the Indians.[32]

On November 24, 1750, he left Shannopin's town and traveled a little farther down the Ohio to Logstown, a mixed Indian village (Shawnee, Seneca, Delaware, Wyandot and Mohawk), home of the Seneca "Half-King" Tanacharison. Tanacharison played an important part in the region a few years later when he accompanied George Washington on a trip considered by some to be the start of the French and Indian War.

Gist then left the Ohio River and went straight into central Ohio where he met the well-known Pennsylvania trader George Croghan and interpreter Andrew Montour. As he moved generally west and south Gist found better land. Near the Muskingum River, in Ohio, he found fairly good land for farming although in some places it was hilly and rocky. This is not surprising as the eastern section of Ohio is part of the Allegheny Plateau, the transition from the mountains to the plains. As he moved farther west he noted on Sunday March 3, "I left the path, and went to the South Westward down the Little Miami River or Creek, where I had fine traveling thro rich Land and beautiful Meadows, in which I could sometimes see forty or fifty Buffaloes feeding at once—The Little Miami River or Creek continued to run thro the Middle of a fine Meadow, about a Mile wide very clear like an old Field, and not a Bush in it."[33] In the valleys of the Great Miami and Little Miami rivers, in southwestern Ohio, he entered the very fertile Till Plain of Ohio, a flat plain which was the beginning of the plains that stretched to the far west. This was the type of farmland everyone was looking for and Gist recommended it for settlement upon his return.

From his location in south-central Ohio Gist made a side trip up to the Miami town of Pickawillany or Twightwee Town (English) or Demoiselle (French). The Miami people were also known as the Twightwee people. Pickawillany was located on the upper Great Miami River, near the present-day Piqua in western Ohio. It was a trading town established by the Miami in 1733 and included French traders who took great pains to keep out the English. Nevertheless, by 1747 the Miami Chief Nicholas was friendly with the English and started the move toward welcoming the English, possibly because French trade goods were more expensive than those of the English. They openly traded with the English and encouraged Pennsylvania traders, especially George Croghan, to come to trade.[34] Pickawillany was a large trading town, one of the Miamis' largest and included more tribes than just the Miami. The location of the town in far western Ohio shows just how far west both French and English, specifically Pennsylvania, traders had traveled into the Ohio country. As per his instructions Gist made a point of visiting Pickawillany to strengthen relations with the powerful Miami.

Gist started his return on March 12 when he crossed the Ohio River into Kentucky. He didn't reach the Falls of the Ohio although he was within fifteen miles of that area when he saw troubling signs of Indian activity including some traps. Gist thought he could sneak closer but was afraid to leave his only traveling companion, a servant boy. He missed one of the objectives of his instructions and this caused him some concern as he was conscientious.[35] He made his way back through northern Kentucky, passing near the Red River where Daniel Boone would make his first trip into Kentucky some eighteen years later. As Yadkin River neighbors, it is probable Gist informed Boone about Kentucky. Through April he travelled across Kentucky, southern Virginia, over the mountains and to his home in the Yadkin River Valley arriving on May 18. Because of Indian trouble his family had fled to Roanoke where he found them the next day.[36]

On May 14, while still on his journey, Gist wrote to Thomas Lee that he would meet the company on June 15. From May 21 to May 24, prior to the Gist report, the company held a meeting at which they made some important decisions. Apparently, they had second thoughts about sending Gist as far out as central Ohio and decided to petition for specific grants closer in, including on Kiskamonito and Lowelhanning Creeks and on the three forks of the Youghogane River in western Pennsylvania. They thought this would "greatly contribute to the security of their Settlements and increase of their Trade."[37] This was an indication they were again focused on settling on the original grant between the mountains and the Ohio River. Another resolution at the same meeting reinforced this change of strategy, "Resolved that it is necessary to have a Road cleared from the mouth of Wills Creek to the three forks of Youghogane and that Colo. Cresap be empowered to agree with any person of persons willing to undertake the same so that the expence thereof does not exceed twenty five pounds Virginia currency."[38] This was the first step in making a road across the mountains from Maryland to the Ohio country; which eventually became the Cumberland then National Road.

SECOND JOURNEY, 1751–1752

Gist met the committee on July 15 (a month late) to turn in his journal report. The committee clearly had anticipated the results and had been making plans. They were not satisfied with his recommendations on settling lands around the Miami Rivers, as good as the land might be. Worried about Indians, the French, and long supply lines they apparently didn't want to extend that far west at first. They needed to settle their first two hundred thousand acres closer in and they were running out of time. The grant was made two years earlier and they only had five more years to meet its obligations. They immediately gave Gist two more charges for his second journey. First, as he was on the journey he was to invite the Indians to a meeting at Logstown in May of 1752.[39] The Logstown conference was to clarify the terms of the Lancaster Treaty of 1744 because some Indians were complaining about how the treaty was being interpreted by the English.

Second, the instructions were now much more specific concerning area to be explored. He was to get company horses from Cresap for himself and whomever he took with him and "you are to look out and observe the nearest and most convenient road you can find from the company store at Wills creek to a landing on Monongahela, from thence you are to proceed down the Ohio on the south side thereof as low as the Big Conhaway and up the same as far as you judge proper, and find good land." As before he was to keep a good journal and look for good land.[40] The Big Conhaway is the Kanawha River which enters the Ohio River from West Virginia in southeast Ohio. They were expecting a very detailed look at the two hundred thousand acre grant they had originally received but the Kanawha was well south of the original grant.

Although he received his orders on July 16, once again Gist got a late start that year. He had to go to Cresap's home in Oldtown, on the Potomac a few miles southeast of Wills Creek, to pick up horses and supplies and probably to wait for his son who accompanied him on his second journey; they left on November 4. This time he traveled directly to the path all were expecting would become the road over the mountains to Ohio. Crossing the Potomac from the Company storehouse in Virginia, just across from Wills Creek, at present-day Cumberland, Maryland, they traveled west through a gap in Wills Mountain and then through a gap between Piney Mountain and Dans Mountain. Reasonably early they had to have gone over Big and Little Savage mountains, Meadow Mountain, through Little Meadows, and over Negro Mountain, although they had not yet been given those names. One travels this route, across these mountains, on the present U.S. Route 40, the National Road.[41]

This was the heart of the Allegheny Ridge and Valley system that formed the western borders of the Appalachian range. Although they were moving generally west and north, it is not known exactly where they crossed these areas as they were also moving laterally always looking for land. We do know they arrived at the middle branch of the Youghiogheny River, the Casselman River, by November 22. Laurel Run and the Casselman join the Youghiogheny about six miles north of the Maryland line. Each day he made some comment on the quality of the land, which was still "stony" because they were still in the mountains.[42]

They continued west going through Great Meadows and finally crossing Chestnut Ridge, the last mountain, to reach the Allegheny Plateau. It is not clear where they crossed Chestnut Ridge, but it might have been near Laurel Run. They camped at a Laurel Creek on November 25. Laurel Run, on the west side of Chestnut Ridge, flows into the Youghiogheny, between present-day Uniontown and Connellsville. This is near where Gist later made his home. The journal from November 30 to December 6 describes the land they explored after they crossed the Ridge.

> We searched the Land several Miles round and found it about 15 M from the Foot of the Mountains to the River Mohongaly the first 5 M of which E & W is good level farming land, with fine Meadows, the Timber white Oak and Hickory—the same Body of Land holds 10 M, S, to the upper Forks of the Mohongaly, and about 10 M, N, towards the Mouth of Yaughyaughgaine—The Land nearer the River for about 8 or 9 M wide, and the same Length is much richer & better timbered, with Walnut, Locust, Poplars and Sugar-Trees, but in some Places very hilly, the Bottoms upon the river 1 M, and in some Places near 2 M wide.[43]

They explored the land between the mountains and the river during those seven days. From Redstone Creek and the Monongahela down to the Forks of the Monongahela, where the Cheat River joins the Monongahela, is about twenty miles. From Redstone Creek up to the mouth of the Youghiogheny, where it meets the Monongahela, is also about twenty miles. From the river to the mountains is about fifteen miles. Today the land is as he describes, except less timbered. Gist describes the start of some good farmland in the Ohio Valley, which obviously pleased him; a few years later he received some of this land and, with a few other families settled on it. The Gist Plantation was just north of present-day Uniontown, Pennsylvania.

On December 7 Gist went to and stayed at an Indian camp on a creek at that time known as Nemacolin's Creek, later called Dunlap's Creek, which empties into the Monongahela at present-day Brownsville, Pennsylvania. It is not clear where on the creek the camp was located, that is, whether or not it was near the mouth at the Monongahela. Although his purpose was to invite the Indians to the Logstown meeting the coming year, he received an earful from the leader of the camp who complained that white people had taken over land without compensation that they, the Indians, had been given. He wanted Gist to tell the king about this. "I was obliged to insert it in my Journal to please the Indian."[44] Clearly, the planned meeting at Logstown, to clarify the terms of the Treaty of Lancaster, was needed. This Indian chief was called Nemicotton by Gist but is more commonly known as Nemacolin, a Delaware Chief who later worked with Thomas Cresap to enlarge the trail Gist opened into a path known as Nemacolin's Path.

Sources indicate they got to the river on Monday, December 9, after their stay at the Indian camp. "Gist reached the Monongahela several miles up the river from the mouth of Redstone Creek. The direction and distance given indicate that his place of crossing was in the vicinity of Jacob's Ferry, Fayette County, Pennsylvania."[45] Darlington (*Christopher Gist's Journals*) indicates a similar location where they reached the river because of a cave near there similar to the one Gist describes. "'The Cavity in a Rock' was probably on the river bank, on the east side, six miles from Brownsville, up the river, on the farm now owned by Captain Jacobs."[46] Dunlap Creek enters the Monongahela River at Brownsville and Redstone Creek enters the Monongahela one mile downstream (north) of Dunlap Creek. Gist's party crossed the Monongahela on December 15. Although he may have crossed the river at Jacob's Ferry, a short distance north of Redstone Creek, the traditional location of Gist's arrival at the Monongahela is Redstone Creek.

Gist had just cut the path destined to be the first road across the Alleghenies from Maryland to Ohio country.

In his journal for November 22 Gist seems to indicate he camped at the Forks of the Youghiogheny which is slightly north of the trace shown in Map 6.[47]

He continued southwest after crossing the Monongahela, toward the eastern bank of the Ohio into present-day West Virginia. They were slowed by bad weather and his son's frostbitten feet. By mid–February they made it to the Ohio and Kanawha rivers and started back, all the while noting the qualities of the land for settlement. On Thursday March 12, they crossed back over the Monongahela heading back for the Potomac.[48] Once again Gist met some Indians who questioned him on the ownership of the land.

> While I was at Mohongaly in my Return Home an Indian, who spoke good English, came to me & said—That their great men the Beaver and Captain Oppamylucah ... desired to know where the Indian's Land lay, for that the French claimed all the Land on one side of the River Ohio & the English on the other Side; and that Oppamylucah asked me the same Question when I was at his Camp in my way down, to which I had made him no Answer ... that I was at a loss to answer Him.[49]

Gist attempted an answer, but in fact all the Indians he encountered all had the same unanswerable question. Where was the land for the Indian?

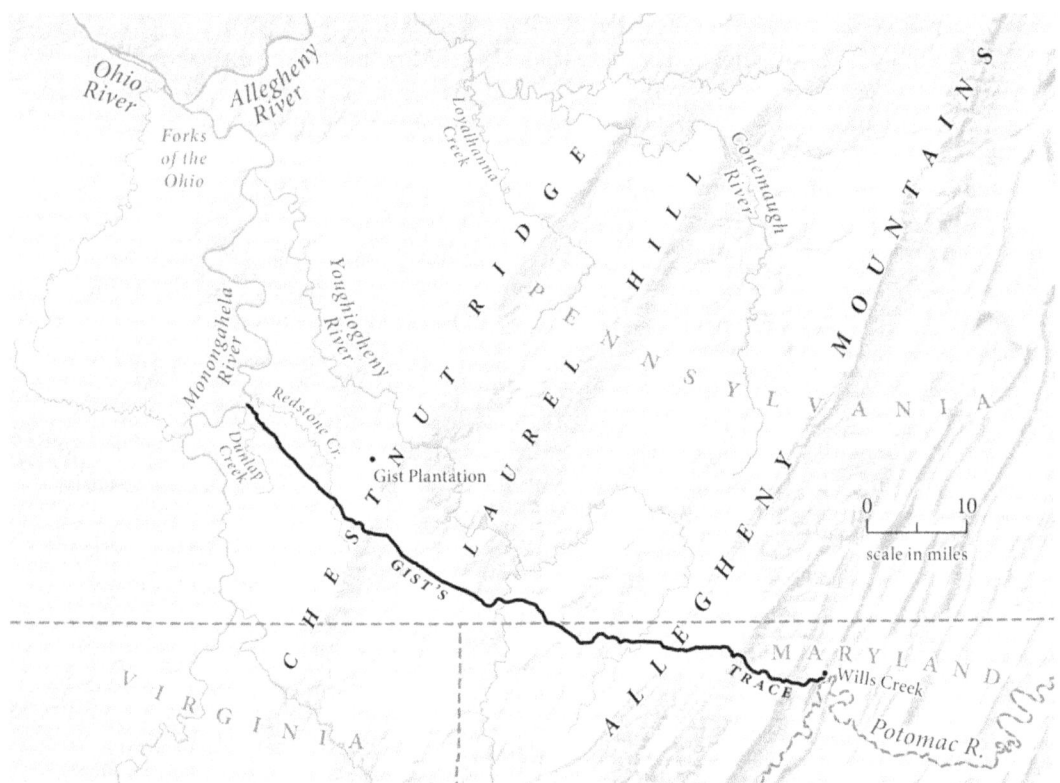

Map 6: Gist's Trace. Gist's Trace ran from Wills Creek and the Potomac (modern Cumberland, Maryland) to Redstone Creek on the Monongahela River near present-day Brownsville, Pennsylvania. This trace of Gist's path across the mountains, and any trace, should be considered an approximation of the actual route because, as was noted, he traveled laterally as he moved forward. He did this because he was looking for good land. For example, in his journal for November 22 Gist seems to indicate he camped at the Forks of the Youghiogheny, which is slightly north of the trace shown (trace courtesy of Frederick Siler, Historical American Trails, Roads and Migration Routes, http://tinyurl.com/ozya453).

He knowingly kept a less detailed record of his return trip to Wills Creek because he thought that had been covered in his journal on the way out. He did observe that he did not go home by the same route, apparently traveling east from the Forks of the Monongahela back to Wills Creek, a distance he rightly estimated at seventy miles.

> I did not keep exactly my old Tract but went more to the Eastward & found a much nearer Way home: and am of Opinion the Company may have a tolerable good Road from Wills Creek to the upper Fork of Monhongaly, from whence the River is navigable all the Way to the Ohio of large flat bottomed Boats—The Road will be a little to the Southward of West, and the Distance to the Fork of Mohongaly about 70 M.[50]

The company apparently liked the road to the Monongahela, at Redstone Creek better and did not take his recommendation for this alternate route. The return trip was slow due to bad weather and the load of skins they were carrying to trade, from March 12 until their arrival at Wills Creek on March 29, 1752.[51]

It had taken almost three years from the grant in 1749 for Christopher Gist to discover the path across the Alleghenies and explore the land. The Ohio Company of Virginia had lost a lot of critical time, and within two years a war intervened that would change forever how the Ohio land would be exploited. Nevertheless, they proceeded to the next steps that needed to be taken to transform the path into a road.

Cresap's Road—Nemacolin's Path

The Hanbury petition had been put before the King in January 1749 with the land grant following in July. During those months the Ohio Company had not been idle, holding a meeting on June 21 during which they charged Hugh Parker and Thomas Cresap to employ persons to build a road "between those places as should be most for the Company's advantage."[52] They didn't specify a location of that road and they couldn't act until the grant was made, but in various other meetings they authorized the purchase of land around Wills Creek and the building of a storehouse for trade goods near there.

Two years later the May 1751 resolution concerning the road was more specific ... to the three forks of the Youghiogheny. Bailey claims that in 1751 the company did open a narrow trail from Wills Creek to the "three forks of the Youghiogheny, a spot known as Turkey Foot."[53] Just north of this trail two tributaries join the Youghiogheny to form what looks like a "turkey foot." Why to the three forks? Gist had just returned from his *first* journey but had not gone anywhere near the three forks and he could not have recommended that location at that time. It is possible that Cresap had taken the trail from Wills Creek to the three forks during his unsuccessful exploration looking for suitable land for settlement. Cresap was also very familiar with that country since he lived nearby and it is likely he opened that foot trail. In the summer of 1751, between the two Gist journeys, the company reiterated the need for a road in the direction they now favored. Their instructions to Gist for the second journey explicitly stated he was to go to a landing on the Monongahela. Aware of the company's May instructions to Cresap about the road to the three forks Gist undoubtedly made sure his path would include that route.

If Cresap opened a trail to the three forks in 1751 as Bailey claims, possibly in response to the company's May resolution, Gist did not acknowledge it in his journal. On November 4, 1751, Gist left from the company storehouse opposite the mouth of Wills Creek on his second journey, but he does not mention a road or path in his journal. It is possible Cresap had opened the trail late in 1751, after Gist departed, or Bailey was mistaken about the date. Gist returned from his second journey on March 29, 1752. Apparently at that time the company had received no feedback of progress on the road, if any, so they issued instructions for Gist to take the road farther, to the Monongahela based on the results of his second, and more successful, journey. On April 28, 1752, the company instructed Gist, "If Colo. Cresap has not agreed with any person to clear a road for the Company, You are with the advice and assistance of the said Colo. Cresap to agree with the proper Indians who are best acquainted with the ways Immediately to cut a Road from Wills Creek to the Fork of Mohongaly at the cheapest rate you can."[54] This time the Fork of the Monongahela was referring to the Monongahela, not the intersection of the Monongahela and Cheat to which Gist referred.

Both James (*The Ohio Company, Its Inner History*) and Bailey say the road was at least laid out and partially cleared in 1752, probably in the summer.[55]

Tradition, and many historians, ascribe the building of the road from Wills Creek to the Monongahela to the trio of Gist, Cresap, and Nemacolin, the Delaware Indian. Mulkearn (*George Mercer Papers*) acknowledges these accounts but disputes the assertion that Nemacolin helped the Ohio Company lay out the road. She correctly claims, that Nemacolin is mentioned nowhere in the history of the Ohio Company as presented in the *George Mercer Papers*, except in passing in one entry of Gist's second journal. These accounts, however, are not necessarily in conflict. It is quite probable that Nemacolin was never employed by the Ohio Company. He was a friend of Thomas Cresap and, according to Bailey, "Cresap engaged Nemacolin" to help with the road.[56]

We know little about Nemacolin except that he was a life-long friend of Thomas Cresap and his family. Nemacolin's father, Checochinican, was born into the Lenape (Delaware) Nation, Turtle Tribe and Fish Clan and moved to the Susquehanna River after his marriage in 1714. Nemacolin, born in 1715, was planning on becoming a Fish Clan Chief as his father was. They were apparently still on the Susquehanna when Thomas Cresap and his family moved to the area in 1730. The families lived near each other and became good friends, each family moving west again at a later time. Cresap settled in far western Maryland and Nemacolin and his tribe lived for a while near present-day Uniontown, Pennsylvania. It is probable that Nemacolin moved west because of colonial settlement pressure in eastern Pennsylvania.[57]

His father had written to the Governor of Pennsylvania as early as June 1729 protesting the taking of Indian lands.[58] Similarly, Nemacolin had protested to Christopher Gist about the same issue when they met on Gist's second journey. By this time Nemacolin had moved even farther west to the site on Dunlap's Creek where Gist visited him. Moving west from the Susquehanna over the Alleghenies, Nemacolin certainly became familiar with these mountains, a valuable asset to Cresap and Gist when, along with Nemacolin, they laid out the road from Wills Creek to the Monongahela.

The 1752 road from Wills Creek to the Monongahela followed the path Gist took on his way west on his second journey crossing Chestnut Ridge into what is now Uniontown, Pennsylvania, and directly to the Monongahela River near Redstone Creek. Bailey and others provide similar descriptions of the route although the names of some mountain ridges and streams have changed over the years. This path was very rough, probably suitable only for horses because Bailey suggests that the following year (1753) William Trent widened the path so packhorses could pass. He also suggests that in 1752 the company built a second storehouse at Redstone Creek and the Monongahela after the one built at Wills Creek.[59] Since they had just completed the road in 1752 and it wasn't widened for packhorses until 1753, it seems more likely the date was 1753. The Red Stone Old Fort, a blockhouse combining a storehouse and a fort was built in the same location.

Seventeen fifty-two was a busy year, including the meeting at Logstown in June that Gist attended. Probably after the treaty meeting Gist moved his home from the Yadkin River on the North Carolina frontier, to land clearly within the Ohio Company grant and very close to the path he recently opened on his second journey. His home, and the area surrounding it, was called Gist's Place or Gist's Plantation and shows up on maps of the time. It was located just west of the Alleghenies and north of what is now Uniontown, Pennsylvania, between the Monongahela and Youghiogheny rivers. Gist's home was only ten or fifteen miles from the blockhouse at Redstone Creek. He convinced at least eleven families to work the area with him. These were the first white settlers resulting from efforts of the Ohio Company of Virginia to open the Ohio Valley to English settlers.[60]

There was not a flood of settlers at first, but after two wars they eventually came. As Wroth ("The Story of Thomas Cresap, A Maryland Pioneer") points out,

> The threatened French War discouraged a steady settlement of the lands, but the fact that a visitor to Cresap's house at Old Town in 1754 found him away from home visiting the company's settlers on the Ohio, is evidence that the activities of this organization were the point of the wedge that entered

the wilderness and laid it open to the inrush of emigrants which occurred in the years following the Revolution.[61]

Indian Cessions and Treaties

The British and French were not the only ones vying for the Ohio country. The Native Americans, there long before either European power, claimed the land. Whenever the Europeans pushed out from the coast there was conflict with the Native Americans reluctant to give up their lands. The concept of ownership was different for the Indians and the Europeans. The Indians did not recognize land ownership; the land was free to anyone who could claim it and use it. By virtue of conquest they claimed the right to control territory for hunting, trapping, and farming. The land itself, however, could not be bought or sold. The Europeans came from a society where land was limited, owned, and controlled by a few people. Europeans recognized the ability to buy and sell land by paying for it with goods or gold, making the land exclusively theirs. The two concepts were incompatible.

As the colonies expanded, the conflicts between Europeans and Native Americans increased. Both groups ultimately realized that continual warfare was not only inimical to the health of the factions but impossible to sustain. Gradually they came to agreements on territorial limits accepted by both parties. Although reluctant to lose land, the Native Americans avidly desired European trade goods including iron pots, axes, knives, blankets, cloth, firearms, and especially liquor. Once exposed to these goods they were very reluctant to go back to stone axes, spears and arrows so they became more willing to trade beaver and other pelts for the goods.

Unfortunately, the availability of European trade goods was not the only result of the contact between these peoples. The Native Americans had no immunity to European diseases, which did immense damage to some of their populations. In some regions, the reduction in tribal population made it easier for the European to move in. The lucrative trade for European goods also led to bitter competition between some tribes. Tribes began to align with one colony or another and become the chief trading partner for that colony. Native Americans had been battling each other for centuries but now the colonists became part of the competition.

Shortly after the colonization started, early in the seventeenth century, lands were ceded and treaties signed. Often the different concepts of ownership or the description of the land in question would lead to confusion and eventually to new treaties. Although these negotiations included many tribes and colonies, gradually one Native American nation became more dominant.

The dominant Native American group was the Five Nations of the Iroquois: Seneca, Onondaga, Oneida, Cayuga, and Mohawk. In 1722, it became the Six Nations, when the Iroquois speaking Tuscarora came up from North Carolina. They called themselves Haudenosaunee, house builders or people of the long house, and were skilled in both war and diplomacy. They had fought for years with varied success against the Catawba in the south moving along the Warrior's Paths through the mountains. They were one of the earliest tribes to acquire firearms, when the Mohawk traded with the Dutch as early as the 1620s. When the Iroquois defeated an enemy they sometimes absorbed them into their confederacy instead of destroying them. This allowed them not only to maintain population in the face of losses from disease, but to extend their control over an area greater than they could occupy. By virtue of this conquest they claimed the Ohio country even though they did not occupy it afterwards.

The Covenant Chain to the Treaty of Logstown

The Covenant Chain is a metaphor that described the relations between the Iroquois Six Nations Confederacy and the colonies of New York, Massachusetts Bay, Connecticut, Maryland and Virginia. It lasted from the late seventeenth century to the mid eighteenth century. This relationship was an outgrowth of how the Confederacy worked together among themselves and how they related to other tribes, describing them in terms of brother, uncle, father or nephew. The term was first used around 1677 in treaties between the Confederacy and the colonies, but its use began years earlier in their dealings with the Dutch. The Mohawk talked about an "iron chain" that bound them to the Dutch in a 1643 treaty. That terminology had evolved from the description as a "rope" and later as a "chain of silver." When the English ejected the Dutch in 1664 the Iroquois quickly bound themselves to the English with the same metaphor. The contacts within the chain were mostly between the Mohawk, the diplomats of the Confederacy, and New York; most of the meetings were in Albany and occurred on a regular, almost yearly basis.[62]

As Virginians moved west in the first half of the eighteenth century there was inevitably more contact between them and the Indians, and therefore more conflict. This necessitated more meetings and treaties under the umbrella of the Covenant Chain. In 1722 Virginia Governor Spotswood sponsored a conference with the Iroquois in Albany to discuss conflicts in the Shenandoah Valley. They came to an agreement and a treaty resulted. However, many of the terms used to describe boundaries were ambiguous, whether purposeful or unintended, and clarification was not attempted. A later conflict, precipitated by the Albany misunderstandings, resulted in another meeting in 1744, this time in Lancaster, Pennsylvania. The meeting was hosted by the Pennsylvania Lieutenant Governor and included Thomas Lee as one of the commissioners representing the Governor of Virginia.[63]

The treaty meetings continued for several days in late June and early July with some minor agreements achieved. The Six Nations agreed to cede to Maryland some land in northwest Maryland. The Virginia commissioners agreed to allow passage on the Great Valley Road in the Shenandoah Valley. Once this business was concluded the commissioners stated their case again and then opened their chest of gifts the Six Nations would receive provided they agreed to the new deed. The gifts included about two hundred pounds of goods and two hundred pounds of gold. The Six Nations agreed, accepted the gifts, and signed the deed on July 2, 1744.[64] The treaty included the following cession,

> the said Sachims or Chiefs on behalf of the said Six Nations Do hereby renounce and disclaim not only all the Right of the said Six Nations but also *recognize* and acknowledge the Right and Title of our Sovereign the King of Great Britain to all the Land within the said Colony as it is now or hereafter may be peopled and bounded by his said Majesty our Sovereign Lord the King and his Heirs and Successors.[65]

This was the treaty that Hanbury cited in the request for the Ohio Company of Virginia land grant. The Six Nations thought the "said colony" was the Shenandoah Valley up to the Alleghenies. It is not clear why the Six Nations gave up any claim to Virginia for just goods and gold. They may have seen they were losing the battle for control of the Shenandoah Valley and got what they could for it. The Virginians were satisfied that this gave them the access to the Ohio country that they sought because the "said colony" to them meant "sea to sea." Within a year grants were being made of lands that were in the Ohio Valley. It was probably also no coincidence that within three years, one of the Virginia commissioners, Thomas Lee, would be the head of the Ohio Company of Virginia. Lee was the other person, besides Cresap, who is credited with the idea of the Ohio Company of Virginia.

When the Ohio Company of Virginia started moving into that country it quickly became evident that still another meeting would be necessary to clarify what Virginia thought was concluded at Lancaster. The 1752 meeting at Logstown (Loggstown) resulted in the Treaty of Logstown which was instigated by and for the benefit of the Ohio Company. The company's objectives and interests were backed by Virginia, so the Virginia commissioners represented the company's interest as well as the colonial government at those meetings. The mixing of private and government business was common at the time.

Logstown was an Indian village located on the Ohio River just a few miles downstream of the Forks of the Ohio and included members of several different tribes. For almost a year during his travels Gist had been inviting all the Indians he met to a meeting at Logstown in the spring of 1752. The Ohio Company was anxious to start settlement in the Ohio Valley but had been hearing complaints from the Indians about the English violating the Treaty of Lancaster. Prior to moving settlers to the area, the company felt it was necessary to reiterate the terms of the treaty, as they saw it, and to once again get agreement from the Indians. It was clear the Indians did not have the same interpretation of the treaty terms and this would be a chance to clarify these terms.

The Virginia Commissioners, Joshua Fry, Lunsford Lomax, and James Patton, were there representing Virginia as this was an official government meeting; Christopher Gist was also there representing the Ohio Company. Tanacharison, a Seneca Chief, who was to play an important role in the expeditions of George Washington a few years later, was also there. After the formal opening ceremonies in June 1752, the Commissioners focused on the purpose of the meeting.

> Brethren, at the Treaty of Lancaster, in the year 1744, between the Government of Virginia, Maryland, & Pennsylvania, you made a deed recognizing the King's Right to all the Lands in Virginia, as far as it was then peopled, or hereafter should be peopled, or bounded by the King, our Father, for which you received the Consideration agreed on.[66]

The Virginia Commissioners clearly thought the Indians had conceded the Ohio country in the Lancaster Treaty and they immediately got to the point. "Brethren, it is the Design of the King, our Father, at present, to make a Settlement of British Subjects on the South East Side of Ohio, that we may be united as one people, by the strongest Ties of Neighborhood." This was now an explicit statement of their plan to settle in Ohio. They set out the advantages for the Indians of this Ohio Company settlement, including greater availability of trade goods, protection from the French, and others.

The Indian response, by Tanacharison, was direct.

> We are well acquainted that our chief Council at the Treaty of Lancaster, confirmed a Deed to you for a Quantity of Land in Virginia which you have a Right to ... we assure you we are willing to confirm any Thing our Council has done in Regard to the Land, but we never understood, before you told us yesterday, that the Lands then sold were to extend further to the Sun setting than the Hill on the other Side of the Allegany Hill.[67]

In other words, they didn't believe the land they sold in 1744 went past the Alleghenies into the Ohio Valley. This seems to be a rather calm response to losing that land. The Indians may have felt they had lost effective control because things had changed so rapidly over the previous eight years. Virginia could have pressed its claim more strongly and possibly could have avoided paying anything for it, but the Virginians knew they were vying with New France for control of this area and they wanted to substantiate their claim by right of purchase.

The treaty was signed at the end of the meeting with the "Consent and Confirmation of said Deed" with the Indians understanding that the Ohio Valley was now open to Virginia. The Indians agreed to allow British settlement on the south-east side of the Ohio and promised that they would not molest these settlements. The Indians made the request, that the British should build a fort at the Forks of the Ohio, probably in anticipation of trouble with the French they saw coming.

In all the treaties covered here, and in many others, it is difficult to say if deliberate deception was involved or just carelessness. There was clearly ambiguity, which may have been purposeful or may have come from a lack of precision due to language differences. For whatever reason, it took many treaties and many years to resolve these issues. It is not coincidental that as the colonists moved farther west, and gained strength, their land claims became more expansive.

Claims on the Ohio Country

New France

By 1750 the French had established a trade route from Quebec and Montreal in New France down through the east and Midwest to the Mississippi River and to Louisiana. It was a vast territory but easily traveled via the many rivers flowing north-south including the Ohio and Mississippi. There were no mountains for the French to cross to get to the Ohio Valley as there were for the English. As there was no incentive for people to leave France and move to a wilderness area, they did not have the resources to colonize the land, unlike the English. The French were content to exploit the land for its furs and other resources, and to trade with the Native Americans.

By mid-century trade with the Indians was becoming problematic because French trade goods were much more expensive than comparable English goods. The long trip these goods made from France through the St. Lawrence to Quebec and Montreal was costly because the river was frozen and closed for much of the year. Due to the abundance of goods available from both England and the British colonies, there was more competition and therefore British goods were cheaper.

The French became more concerned when the Ohio Company of Virginia was formed in 1749. Although they still had little intention of colonizing Ohio they knew it was vital to their link between New France and Louisiana and a show of force would be necessary to warn off the English. This effort began with an expedition in 1749, followed by construction of a string of forts a few years later.

CELORON EXPEDITION

In 1749 the Governor-General of New France, Marquis de la Galissoniere, sent one of his officers, Celoron de Bienville, on an expedition to seal France's claim to the Ohio Valley. Celoron was to use the traditional method of claiming the land by burying lead plates at the mouths of key rivers emptying into the Ohio. He started on the upper Allegheny, because at that time the Allegheny River, with headwaters in northern Pennsylvania, was also called the Ohio. In La Salle's time the French knew the Ohio River as la Belle Riviere, the beautiful river. In his journal, however, Celoron called it by the Iroquois name, Oyo.[68]

Celoron left the Montreal area on June 15, 1749, with a company of two hundred officers, soldiers, and Indians. Over the next month, they made their way south, by canoe or by portaging their supplies around Niagara, onto Lake Erie, and to Lake Chataquin (Chautauqua). Their purpose was not only to mark the land for New France but to win or regain the confidence of the Indians.

> I communicated the intentions of M. the Marquis de la Galissoniere to the officers, who saw that it was of great importance for the execution of the orders with which I was charged, to reassure the nations of these countries; and the unanimous sentiment was, to send them word to remain quiet in their cabins and to assure them that I came only to treat with them of good things and to explain to them the sentiments of their Father Onontio.[69]

For the entire journey, Celoron would be sorely tested in trying to gain the confidence of the Indians, but even at the earliest villages he visited, the Indians, anticipating their arrival, would leave all their goods behind and disappear into the forest, unsure why this large French military force was coming. The Indians knew that a large part of their trade was with the English and they feared the worst. Celoron was frustrated from the beginning and discussed with officers and chiefs, "the most suitable measures to dissipate the terror which our march has spread."[70]

They buried their first lead plate at what is now the confluence of Conawango Creek and the Allegheny River in northern Pennsylvania. The inscription was similar to the one quoted previously but with the river name Kanaaiagon (Conawango) instead of Kanawha.

As Celoron moved down the Ohio he met many English traders and some English soldiers whom he warned off the land. In the face of this force the English meekly submitted, at least for the present. He came across an Indian village flying three French flags and one English. As in every instance when he met the Indians, he warned them against the English and ordered them to destroy the English flag. "They hide from you their idea of establishing themselves therein in such a way as to render themselves of that territory, and drive you away, if I should let them do so."[71] He was correct on that. The English were interested in taking possession of the land and excluding the Indians. The French, more interested in trade and the exploitation of the resources, would be content to share the land with the Native Americans. As noble as this might seem in hindsight, the lack of French settlement from New France down to Louisiana would be the French Achilles heel in the battle for North America. Population was important.

Celoron was frustrated that the Indians didn't see the long-term issue, coming to the conclusion that "their personal interests make them look with favorable eyes on the English, who give them their merchandise at one-fourth the price; hence there is reason to think the King of England or the country makes up the loss which the merchants sustain in their sales to draw the nations to them."[72] In other words, the King of England was subsidizing the trade goods to capture market share.

In July and August Celoron continued his journey, burying plates at various rivers along the Ohio including the Muskingum and Kanawha. They moved past the Indian village at the Scioto River, and left the Ohio River at the Great Miami River where they planted the last of their six plates. They moved up the river to Pickawillany known to the French, for unknown reasons, as the village of the Demoiselle and the chief as La Demoiselle (the Young Lady). From there, Celoron went back through Detroit and on to Montreal, completing the trip in September.

It was obvious to Celoron as he completed the circuit that the Indians he had hoped to reassure along the way felt almost universal fear and contempt for the French. He knew he had failed.

> The journey is twelve hundred leagues. I was still more happy in my own esteem and in that of my officers of the detachment. All I can say is, that the nations of these localities are very badly disposed towards the French, and are entirely devoted to the English. I do not know in what way they could be brought back.... A solid establishment would be useful in the colony, but there are many inconveniences in being able to sustain it.... I am in doubt as to the feasibility of the undertaking without incurring enormous expenses. I feel myself obliged on account of the knowledge I have acquired of all these places, to put these reflections at the end of my journal, so that one may make use of them as he shall judge proper.
>
> Signed,
> Celoron[73]

He had put his finger on the vulnerability of the French in the Ohio country. He recognized the English trade advantage and felt that a larger French population through an established French colony would help, but he knew it would be expensive. Some of the six leaden plates he buried have been recovered. They served absolutely no purpose in marking the territory as they were ignored. At least one plate did serve a purpose in that part of it was melted down and made into bullets.

Defense of the Ohio Country

In 1749 events were starting to move rapidly in the Ohio Valley. Celoron started his expedition in June, in July the Ohio Company received its grant from the King, and the Ohio Company built its first storehouse just across the Potomac from Wills Creek. Cresap and others were sent out by the English in 1749 to look for suitable land for settlement. Although they were unsuccessful that year, in the following summer Gist got his orders to find that land, starting his first trip late in 1750. Although that trip did not identify specific settlement areas it did show him the vast riches of the Ohio country. He also made it as far northwest in Ohio as the Miami town of Pickawillany. His second journey, over the winter of 1751–1752, was more successful in identifying promising land near the Monongahela and up to the Forks of the Ohio. He was a British citizen from Maryland who had been all over Ohio.

All these British incursions into what they considered their Ohio country did not go unnoticed by the French. After the largely unsuccessful Celoron expedition, in 1752 the French initiated a series of actions that further exacerbated tensions especially in the Ohio country. This started in a trading town in northwest Ohio on the Great Miami River near what is now Piqua, Ohio.

As the Shawnee and Delaware moved back into Ohio to avoid crowding in the east, some of their earliest settlements were along the Ohio River. They gradually spread northward along other rivers and settled other areas. The English traders followed them west. Other tribes such as the Miami moved in from the west. The Miami settled Pickawillany on the Great Miami River close to Loramie Creek, near present-day Piqua. By 1751 the town had about four hundred families. Originally, like many other Ohio tribes the Miami traded with the French, but they became disenchanted with the cost of French trading goods and started to befriend English traders. As a result, they were not inclined to welcome the overtures of Celoron when he visited in 1749.[74]

Pickawillany was near several trade and portage routes, making it a good location for a trading post. In 1747 George Croghan, a Pennsylvania trader ("king of the Pennsylvania traders") set up shop there, building a fortified trading post. Trading also grew because of the chief, known as La Demoiselle by the French, Old Briton by the English, and by various Indian names including Memeskia, Pianguisha, and others. He was very cooperative in sending word to tribes, ranging from Detroit to Kentucky, about the trade available at Pickawillany. The French had long held the monopoly on trade with the Ohio tribes and the recent widespread poaching by English traders was seen as a provocation by New France. The incursion by Croghan may have been the proximate reason for Galissoniere to send out the Celoron expedition. Celoron had asked the Miami to return west to the Maumee where they had come from; they refused.[75]

The English showed no signs of backing off. The Cresap expedition of 1749 to look for land was followed by the two Gist journeys, the second one ending in the spring of 1752. The conference at Logstown followed immediately in June 1752. Apparently this was too much for the French and an order was issued for an attack on British interests in Ohio. The Celoron expedition might have been a restrained response to first incursions but the response to the Logstown Treaty was not.

The conference at Logstown, which resulted in the Logstown Treaty, ended on June 13, 1752. Probably not coincidentally, Charles Langlade led a force of about 250 French Indian allies including, Ottawa, Ojibwa, and Potowatomi, in an attack on Picawillany on June 21, 1752. The mixed-blood Langlade was from Michelimackinac in New France. On that day, the Miami women were working the fields and most of the men were on a hunting trip. The Langlade forces breached the lightly defended stockade and damaged houses in the village. The raiders held the women briefly but were primarily after the chief, La Demoiselle, and the English traders. They killed a few Miami, and took five English traders prisoner. Mostly, however, they wanted to make a statement. The French Indian allies killed one of the traders and ate his heart, as well killing, dismembering, boiling, and eating the chief La Demoiselle. This was the French response to the English trading post, and the Miami refusal of Celoron's request that they return west. The Miami got the message and moved back west. Most of western Ohio was now back under French control and subject to their trading practices. Many English traders moved back to Pennsylvania.[76]

The next steps to consolidate French control of the Ohio country came in 1752 under the new Governor-General, Ange Duquesne de Menneville, Marquis de Duquesne. As Anderson (*The Crucible of* War) notes Duquesne was "A man utterly unaffected by self-doubt" when he arrived in Quebec in July. He was under orders to "to make every possible effort to drive the English from our lands." He was to "make our Indians understand … that we have nothing against them, [and] that they will be at liberty to go and trade with the English in the latter's country, but that we will not allow them to receive [the English] on our lands." Duquesne started efforts to fortify the Ohio country by requiring the Canadian militia of eleven thousand men to begin drilling every week.[77]

Duquesne's intention was to provide a military force in the Ohio country to enforce this directive. He ordered the building of four forts in the Ohio Valley for this purpose. Two of these were under construction by the spring of 1753, Presque Isle on Lake Erie near present-day Erie, Pennsylvania, and Fort Le Boeuf, near present-day Waterford, Pennsylvania, a portage away on the upstream part of French Creek, which is a tributary of the Allegheny River. The third fort, Fort Machault at present-day Franklin, Pennsylvania, was started in the autumn and was near the village of Venango at the confluence of French Creek and the Allegheny. The fourth fort was to be named Fort Duquesne, and was to be built in 1754 at the Forks of the Ohio. Fort Duquesne was not as easily built because things had heated up and there was military competition for that critical junction.[78]

Virginia and Pennsylvania

The Ohio Valley lies west of the Appalachian Mountains with rivers flowing into the Ohio River from the east, where they originate in the western slopes of the Appalachians, and from the west. (Map 1) The French claim on the Ohio country seems clear as they had claimed and settled New France and Louisiana moving easily between them through this country. Although they did not settle the country in great numbers, the expeditions of La Salle and others proved French claims reasonable to Europeans if not to Native Americans. They would have faced resistance from the Ohio tribes if they had moved in large numbers of settlers as the Indians were feeling more and more constrained by European settlements. Moreover, the French in North America were spreading from New France to Louisiana guided by a coherent, if not aggressive, colonization policy.

In contrast the English claim on the territory was more tenuous. It was based on the Batts and Fallam expedition of the previous century but it was weak because settlement never followed. They also claimed the country because the Iroquois had conquered the tribes in Ohio and the English claimed the Iroquois as English clients. Once again there was no consequent English settlement and the Iroquois had withdrawn from most of Ohio. By mid-century the English settlements east of the Appalachian Mountains were pushing west but were blocked by the mountains and provincial western boundaries. Each province was independent and there was no unified British policy on expansion west past the mountains into Ohio country. The colonists, as well as many in London, were well aware of the potential of land in Ohio. London, however, was reluctant to force the issue militarily for fear of starting another war; the treaty (Aix La Chappelle) from the previous war was only a year old in 1749. When the Ohio Company of Virginia applied for a grant in the Ohio country both the home government and Virginia's colonial government saw an opportunity to break through to Ohio in a commercial, less threatening manner, and they welcomed the approach.

Why Virginia? Why did the Ohio Company of Virginia lead the way for the English in the competition for the Ohio country? The reasons are linked to the original nature of the colony and the Second Charter of Virginia in 1609.

The colony was originally set up as a land company to profit London investors. This capitalist venture proposed to increase wealth by discovering gold or improving and selling land. Although the colony was taken over by the crown in 1624 when the land company failed, the colonial mindset didn't change. This was demonstrated, for example, in 1716 when Governor Spotswood led the expedition to the Shenandoah Valley in order to promote settlement there. In the 1730s Lieutenant Governor Gooch similarly hoped to promote settlement in the Northern Neck, near Maryland by issuing land grants. Virginians always saw the west as an opportunity.

The first charter of Virginia in 1606 employed degrees of latitude to define the northern and southern boundaries of the land grant. The grant was from thirty-four degrees to forty-one degrees north latitude, roughly from Cape Fear, South Carolina to New York City. The company was to choose a location within that swath and have rights to land fifty miles north and south. The inland distance granted was one hundred miles so the total area was to be one hundred miles square.

However, when the charter was reissued in 1609 it was much more generous. The charter granted land,

> being in that Part of America, called Virginia, from the Point of Land, called Cape or Point comfort, all along the Sea Coast to the Northward, two hundred miles, and from the said Point of Cape Com-

fort, all along the Sea Coast to the Southward, two hundred Miles, and all that Space and Circuit of Land, lying from the Sea Coast of the Precinct aforesaid, up into the Land throughout from Sea to Sea, West and Northwest.[79]

The key provision of this grant was the northern boundary. Present-day Atlantic City, New Jersey, marks a point about two hundred miles north of Cape Comfort, which is near present-day Hampton, Virginia. If one draws a line *northwest* from that point the Virginia grant, which extended from sea to sea, would include most of today's Pennsylvania, and *all* of the Ohio country. Map 7 shows this area and helps explain why the Virginians felt they were entitled to the entire west.

Within the next several decades the Virginia grant was diminished by grants to other colonies, especially Maryland and Pennsylvania. Some minor differences over the western boundary were resolved and the Potomac River boundary between Maryland and Virginia was never an issue. Maryland's major boundary disputes were with Pennsylvania and Delaware.

That wasn't the case between Virginia and Pennsylvania. When William Penn was granted land for the Pennsylvania province, border definitions were confusing, at least partly due to the poor maps of the time. The northern and southern borders of Pennsylvania engendered disputes with New York and Maryland, which would require time, sometimes decades, to settle. The eastern border, the Delaware River, was fairly clear, but the western border, was problematic.

The Charter for the Province of Pennsylvania says, "the same is bounded on the East by Delaware River.... The said Lands to extend westwards five degrees in longitude, to bee computed from the Eastern Bounds."[80] In other words, it seems the western border was always five degrees longitude from the meandering Delaware River and this quickly became confusing. Using a river as the border between provinces was fairly common, as with the Potomac between Virginia and Maryland. There was no confusion about the Delaware River as the eastern border but having a border over two hundred miles west follow the meanderings of the Delaware River was unusual if, in fact, that was the meaning in the charter. How would that line be marked out accurately in the wilds of western Pennsylvania? A much more reasonable interpretation would be to use a longitudinal line as the western border, which was how the western border of Maryland was defined. If this was to be the case, then where would the point be on the Delaware from which the five degrees of longitude would be measured?

Initially the meandering western border seemed to be the default position, but early on it didn't really didn't matter. This line was west of the mountains and there were no settlers there, only traders. The border became important in mid-century when Pennsylvania traders were much more active in the Ohio Valley, Pennsylvania, settlers were moving closer to the mountains, and the Ohio Company of Virginia was granted land along the Ohio. Competition for the Ohio country now existed not only between the Indians, French, and English colonies, but also between the two English colonies of Pennsylvania and Virginia.

After the Logstown conference in June 1752 Christopher Gist was appointed the official surveyor of the Ohio Company and he settled his family in the grant area where he was ordered to lay out a town and a fort at Chartiers (Shurtees) Creek on the Ohio, a few miles downstream from the Forks. It was the one the company was to establish on their land grant. The Pennsylvania Proprietor, Thomas Penn, soon heard about the fort and believed this was too close to what he considered Pennsylvania territory, although the border was still undetermined. According to Craig (*Lecture upon the Controversy between Pennsylvania*

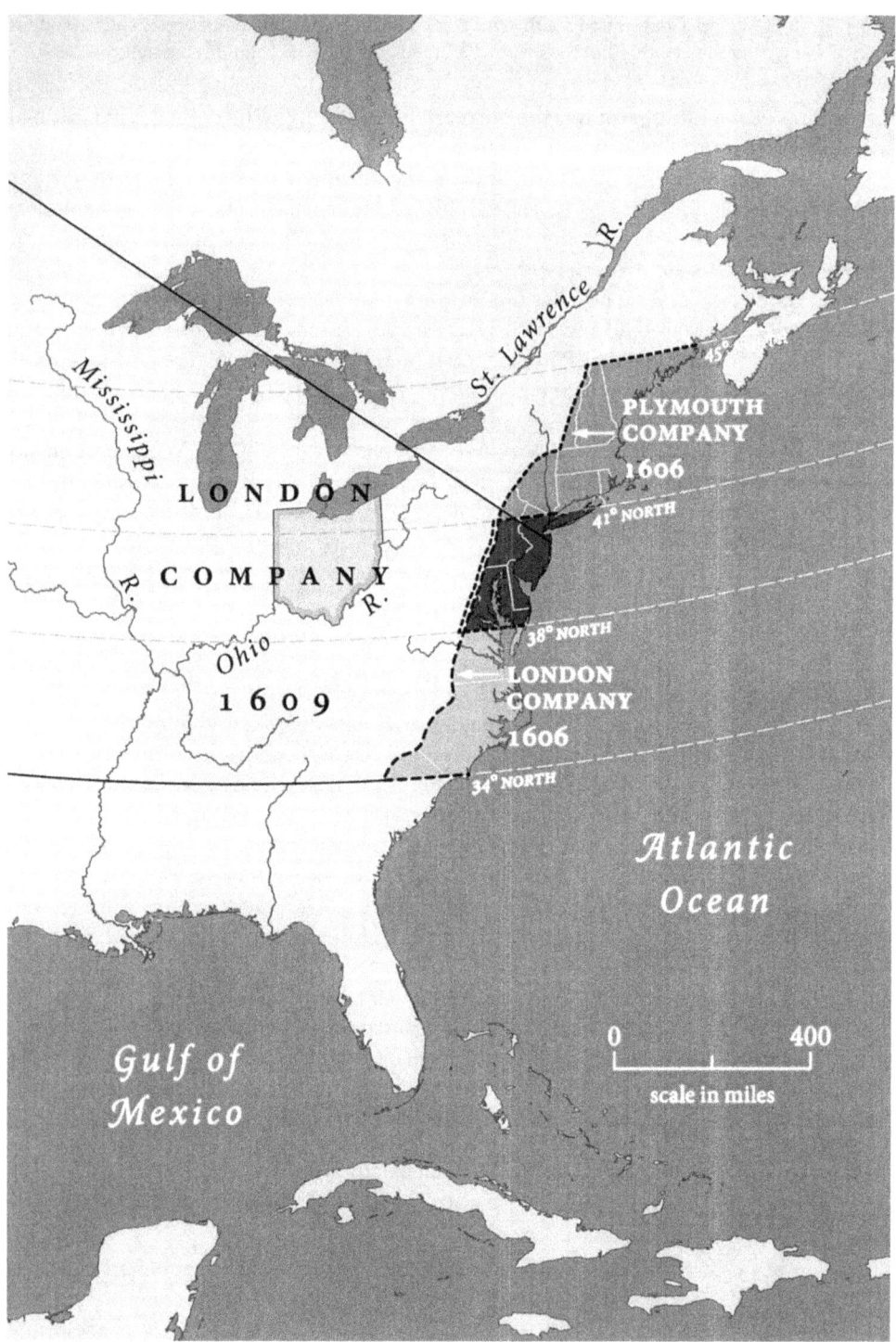

Map 7: The Virginia Second Charter, 1609, set the southern boundary at the latitude of Cape Comfort, Virginia, and the Eastern boundary up the seacoast for 200 miles, near present-day Atlantic City. From there the boundary went northwest. There was no western boundary; the grant was "from sea-to-sea." Virginians rightly saw these boundaries as including Ohio country.

and Virginia about the Boundary Line) Penn was of the opinion that the fort was being put there to repel the incursions of the French, which he approved, and he instructed his Governor, Hamilton, "to render any assistance in his power, taking, however, an acknowledgement from Virginia, that any settlement made should not be construed to the prejudice of the rights of the Penns. Of these instructions, Gov. Hamilton immediately gave Dinwiddie notice."[81]

The Governor of Pennsylvania made clear to the Governor of Virginia that although he could cooperate in repelling the French, he wanted to make sure Virginia would not infringe on Pennsylvania territory. The contest for western Pennsylvania, and specifically whether the Forks of the Ohio were in Pennsylvania or Virginia, would go on for decades, just as the Maryland-Pennsylvania border dispute would continue. These issues would not be settled finally until after the War for Independence.

PENNSYLVANIANS IN OHIO

France claimed the Ohio country by virtue of discovery and exploration. Virginians laid claim to the Ohio country based on the 1609 charter granted by the King to Virginia and the claims of their Iroquois clients, and Maryland, with a fixed western boundary, had no claims to the Ohio country although two of its frontiersmen, Gist and Cresap, were instrumental in opening the country. Pennsylvania's claims to the Ohio country were somewhere between those of its neighbors. Officially, the western boundary of Pennsylvania, five degrees of longitude from the Delaware River, included at least part of the Ohio country. According to Pennsylvania, this included the Forks of the Ohio, but not much beyond them. Pennsylvania did not have a provincial claim to the country beyond the Forks, but similar to Virginia, individual citizens of Pennsylvania did provide much de facto control of the country.

Three Pennsylvanians in particular were influential in providing a major English presence in the Ohio country through their dealings with the Indians of Pennsylvania and Ohio. George Croghan was a trader, Andrew Montour was an interpreter, and Conrad Weiser was an Indian agent for Pennsylvania. All three won the respect of the Indians with their diplomacy in treating the Indians as equals deserving their regard. Although Pennsylvania and Virginia, and their respective traders, were competitors for Ohio country, these three men worked well with the Virginians and Marylanders.

Trade for beaver furs and deerskins slowed just before the troubles broke out in the 1750s, but it was still big business. The Pennsylvania traders dominated the market, especially in Ohio. New Yorkers didn't travel far into the interior and the Virginia traders were less numerous, prompting Virginia's creation of the Ohio Company of Virginia to increase trade in Ohio. Pennsylvanians competed with the French in the central and upper Ohio Valley south of Lake Erie. Many traders were stationed near the Susquehanna and moved far west for the trade. As Volwiler ("George Croghan and the Westward Movement") observed,

> the Pennsylvania traders had assumed the aggressive and, in spite of the Appalachian barrier, had pushed the trader's frontier 500 miles westward in less than half a century; in 1750 this line was near the Wabash and Maumee rivers, nearly 500 miles in advance of the settler's frontier in Pennsylvania.... Nor had the expansive force of this movement been exhausted when it reached the Wabash and Maumee: it began to cross this line—a weak barrier at best—and move on toward the Mississippi, bringing anxiety into the hearts of the best French officials.[82]

George Croghan, one of these traders, had migrated to Pennsylvania from Dublin in 1741, and although from Ireland, was not Catholic but Church of England. His religious affiliation and some education gave him access to provincial officials other less refined traders might not have had. He patented some land in Lancaster County after moving from Philadelphia, and speculated in land very early. He settled on a tract close to the Susquehanna River near Harris's Ferry (Harrisburg) and quickly became a trader as this was near a trading path used to cross the mountains. That path used the Juniata River which led to the Kiskiminetas Creek then entered the Allegheny just above the Forks. Using such paths as these the traders moved their packhorse trains into Ohio.[83]

Croghan set up a trading post on the Allegheny at Pine Creek to use as his second base of operations. He built a storehouse at Logstown and spread out into Ohio country setting up other trading posts including one on the Muskingum and one at Pickawillany. Only five years after immigrating, he was trading on Lake Erie and had multiple employees and packhorse trains. He ventured so far west that the Governor of New France, Jonquiere, complained to the Governor Clinton of New York, that the traders were even in sight of Detroit. Croghan and his rivals, who were usually friendly, saturated the Ohio country with English goods because of their friendly relations with the Indians, and of underpricing the French with English quality trade. They traded with the Miami, Shawnee, Delaware, Wyandot and Mingo all across Ohio. This provoked a response from the French, first with Celoron's 1749 expedition, the attack on Pickawillany, and then with the building of the forts. These activities can be cited as a proximate cause for the French and Indian War, which started a few years later.[84]

Croghan's good relationship with the Indians did not go unnoticed by the Pennsylvania provincial authorities. Soon he was providing unofficial service as an Indian agent, and later in an official capacity, sitting in on numerous conferences for the province in the late 1740s. The Indians had a great deal of confidence in him and at times would not meet unless either Croghan or his good friend Andrew Montour was present. His name was recognized and invoked when the officials wanted to make an impression with the Indians. On one of Gist's journeys he met some Indians who made him feel uneasy and threatened. He told them he was going to meet George Croghan and apparently that was a good enough recommendation for the Indians to treat him well. Although they were technically competitors Gist and Croghan were friends.[85]

The Ohio trade was almost cornered by the Pennsylvanians to the extent that Croghan did not feel threatened by the Virginians. He traveled with Gist on his first journey through Ohio when they met and traveled from Muskingum to Pickawillany, a major Croghan trading post; they often met on the frontier. Croghan was at the Logstown conference in 1752 representing Pennsylvania as was Gist, who represented Ohio Company interests. Although primarily called for the benefit of the Ohio Company, the conference was beneficial for trade overall so the competing traders, Gist and Croghan, worked together on the treaty.

Another person intimately linked with the English incursion into the Ohio country was Andrew Montour, a mixed blood French and Indian. His mother, ultimately known as Madam Montour, was the child of a Frenchman and Huron woman in Canada. Madam Montour was abducted early in life and was raised as an Indian. One of her sons, Andrew, was her child with an Oneida chief. Andrew was uneducated but both he and his mother became well-known interpreters and therefore important at various conferences. Her last major conference was at Lancaster in 1744, which her son also attended. The interpretation function was as important as the trading function in maintaining peaceful relations with the Indians. Montour was well recognized for this skill and became a good friend of George Croghan. His kinship with the Indians also helped his credibility.[86]

Montour, like Croghan, was employed by Pennsylvania but did occasional work for

New York and Virginia. His expertise was so widely recognized that the Ohio Company instructions to Gist for the Logstown conference explicitly required him to engage Montour as an interpreter. He took a leave of absence from Pennsylvania to work for the Ohio Company at the conference and it has been suggested that he was instrumental in persuading the chiefs at Logstown to accept the pact. Just prior to the conclusion of the conference Montour had a private meeting with the Indians, including Tanacharison, after which they came out and the Indians agreed to sign the treaty.[87] This intervention could explain why they signed the treaty when on the face of it there seemed very little incentive for them to do so. The company was so grateful that at a meeting near the end of the year they "Resolved that Mr Montour be allowed thirty pistoles for his trouble at the Loggs town … and that if he will remove to Virginia and Settle on the Companys Land and Use his Interest with the Indians to encourage and forward our Settlements that the Company will make him a present of one thousand Acres of Land to live on, and make him a legal title to the same."[88] Montour often traveled with Croghan and, like Croghan, accompanied Gist on the trip from Muskingum to Pickawillany. Both men would also aid George Washington in the early campaigns of the upcoming French and Indian War.

The third prominent Pennsylvanian to be involved with the Indians and the Ohio country at this time was Conrad Weiser. He was one of the Palatines that immigrated to Pennsylvania following the violence in the Palatinate, arriving on the ship *Lyon* at age thirteen in 1710. He was introduced to the Mohawk as an adolescent, and later became Pennsylvania's chief diplomat dealing with the Six Nations. Weiser also dealt with the numerous other tribes in disputes with the European settlers who were constantly moving farther west in the province.[89] In 1745 he failed in one of his missions, gaining peace between the Six Nations and the Catawba, but as Wallace (*Conrad Weiser, Friend of Colonist and Mohawk*) notes,

> but it was so important in its consequences to Conrad himself that it may be called the turning point in his public career. It brought him for the first time into contact with the main forces that were henceforth to be opposed to him, French intrigue and New York politics; and it set him off on a long trail of international adventures that shaped his career to a climax during the last round of struggle between the French and English in America.[90]

Weiser, like Croghan and Montour, had a good reputation with the Indians and as chief Indian agent attended many conferences. At times, he worked with them on the frontier, although he probably did not spend quite as much time on the frontier as they did. As with Montour, Weiser was also respected by the Virginians. He was once asked by Thomas Lee, head of the Ohio Company, to attend an Indian conference as an interpreter.

At the conference, at Logstown in June 1752, Weiser was notable by his absence. Governor Dinwiddie of Virginia and Thomas Cresap of the Ohio Company requested he attend as an interpreter. Weiser requested permission from Pennsylvania Governor Hamilton to be able to attend and Hamilton gave the permission although he had mixed feelings. In a letter to the Penns, Hamilton wrote Weiser's presence would keep him better informed:

> and by the means of Conrad, I shall be better inform'd, than I could otherwise be, what the designs of the Virginians tend to. I do, intend to instruct Conrad that if he finds the Virginians desirous to Obtain leave from the Indians to build a Fort in any convenient place, to assist them with all the Intrest of this Government, as being a thing that would be greatly serviceable to the English in General, and particularly to our Province.[91]

This sums up the political situation rather succinctly. Hamilton would like Weiser to be there so he could keep an eye on the competing Virginians. On the other hand, he supports building a fort because it would be "serviceable to the English," helping both Pennsylvania and Virginia in their competition with the French.

Weiser did not go to Logstown. The Indians at that conference were Ohio Indians who were sometimes at odds with the Six Nations and Weiser probably saw it as a conflict of interest because his main concern was keeping peace with the Six Nations.

These three Pennsylvanians—trader, interpreter, Indian agent—officially or unofficially represented Pennsylvania interests on the Ohio frontier. They worked very well with the Indians and often with the Virginians as unofficial actors encouraged by the provinces to open the Ohio country. In one sense, they served the same function for Pennsylvania that the Ohio Company did for Virginia and all were successful. The crown remained in the background but supported the moves. By 1752 the English presence in Ohio was strong and supported by the Ohio Indians over the French. The only thing the English did not yet have was a settlement, or permanent presence in Ohio.

The End of Peace

For almost 150 years, until about 1750, two European powers, France and England, had occupied the eastern half of North America. There were brief conflicts in some areas but the borders between them were mostly stable. They had come as colonists and traders and assumed control of the land as if they owned it. In doing so they often conquered and displaced the Native Americans who had been there for millennia. At other times, they worked with these Native Americans and negotiated with them for land. Nevertheless, they were competitors with them for the same land.

By an accident of nature, the French and English were separated and weren't competitors at first. The natural dividing line or natural border, was the Appalachian Mountain range that separated the English colonies east of them from the French inland empire west of the mountains. By 1750, the mountains were not enough of a barrier. Almost by osmosis the English had seeped across the mountains to saturate the Ohio country with traders. The next logical step for the English was for someone to recognize the opportunity the land in the rich Ohio country offered, and therefore try to settle it.

That took place in 1749 when the Ohio Company of Virginia was formed and started plans to move across the mountains in numbers to settle the land. The plans of the Ohio Company to settle hundreds of thousands of acres in Ohio country would require a radical increase in the numbers of people crossing the mountains. That could not be achieved with individual packhorse trains crossing on mountain trails but would require a road to accommodate the hundreds, then thousands that were expected to move to Ohio. In 1752 the Ohio Company cut a road from the headwaters of the Potomac River across the Alleghenies to the Monongahela River. That path had been a Native American path across the mountains to Ohio, probably for millennia, at the time it was considered to be the easiest route.

It might be an exaggeration to say that the formation of the Ohio Company, and the road it cut, were the immediate cause of the French and Indian War that followed a few years later, but one could make that case. The French had been concerned for years about the English trading activity in land they had considered theirs since the time of La Salle. At the time the Ohio Company was formed, the French started taking steps to reassert their authority in Ohio. The first step was the Celoron expedition in 1749 to mark out their claim along the Ohio. After the Logstown Treaty in 1752 in which the Ohio Indians agreed to allow the Ohio Company settlers to settle on the east side of the river, a French raiding party carried out a massacre at the English trading town of Pickawillany in Ohio. This was followed, in the same year, by the French initiative in building a series of forts from Lake Erie down toward the Forks of the Ohio.

The competition for the Ohio country led to bloodshed in 1754 and shortly thereafter to the French and Indian War in America, part of a worldwide conflict known as the Seven Years' War (1756–1763), which decided the fate of the French Empire in North America. A major arena of conflict was on the American frontier between the British and their Indian allies and the French and their Indian allies. The frontier included the Allegheny Mountains and would impact the English attempt to colonize Ohio.

The road to Ohio was closed for the duration except for wartime activities.

Four

The War Years

Events started to move rapidly in 1752, the year Gist, Cresap, and Nemacolin laid out the path from Wills Creek to the Monongahela. In July, the Marquis de Duquesne arrived in Quebec with orders to preserve the link between the Canadian and Illinois settlements, and by extension those in Louisiana. To do this he would have to secure the Ohio country. Events picked up speed in 1753 when William Trent was tasked by the Ohio Company of Virginia to widen the road just cut to the Ohio country. Duquesne's series of four forts were started early in 1753.[1]

Although there was now a road to Ohio, better described as a widened path, there was not to be time for a peaceful use of it. Starting with confrontations and ultimatums in 1753, leading to actual fighting in 1754 and 1755, the road would be a war road for many years. The Ohio Company plans to settle Ohio changed dramatically in those years.

Washington's Road

Lawrence Washington took over the Ohio Company after the original head, Thomas Lee, died in 1750. He wanted to induce German immigrants (Pennsylvania Dutch) to settle the land. They would agree to take fifty thousand acres of the land and settle two hundred families on it if they could be relieved of the tax on them that would be required to support the English clergy. Although Washington was in favor of this, Lieutenant Governor Dinwiddie was opposed fearing it would set a bad precedent.[2] This was just one of their organizational problems. By late 1752, realizing they were running out of time they took another step to jump-start the program, they sent a petition to the Governor and Council of Virginia asking permission to settle their first two hundred thousand acres in Ohio. They claimed they had cleared a road from Wills Creek to one of the branches of the Ohio (Youghiogheny). This was Cresap's Road, Nemacolin's Path, and was a major step forward in their mind. This new request also included more of the Ohio country; it went farther down the Ohio River. The request went now from Kiskominettos Creek down to the great Connaway (Kanawha) alias New or Woods River. They promised they would settle there by December 1753. This petition was either disregarded or rejected by the governor and Council.[3]

As things were heating up on the frontier, the Virginia Council was now bypassed when the Ohio Company sent a second petition to the King, who referred it to the Committee of Council for Plantation Affairs on March 28, 1754. This was a substantial rewrite of the 1752 petition. It was broad, listing a lot of the past history of the company and included complaints about others intruding as well as complaints on the lack of action on the 1752 petition. The petition mentioned Gist's travels and, importantly, the construction of a road, "and laid out and opened a wagon road thirty feet wide from their Store house at Wills Creek, to the three branches on the Ganyangaine (Youghiogheny) River, computed to be near eighty miles." The thirty-foot width was an exaggeration as Washington discovered when he needed to cut a road for his wagons on the trip he was starting.[4]

In this petition to the King the Ohio Company offered to settle three hundred families instead of the one hundred originally required, and also to erect two forts instead of one. One would be at Chartiers Creek (which they said was being built) and the other at the Kanawha. They laid out a more precise boundary, unlike in previous petitions, because there were challengers for land in Ohio country from others, English and French interests:

> from Romanettos or Kiskomenetto Creek on the South East side of the Ohio, to the fork at the entrance of the great Conhaway River to the entrance of Green Briar River, and from thence in a straight Line or Lines along the mountains to the South East Spring of Mohangaly River; and from thence Northward along the Mountains to the North East springs of Romanetto or Kiskominetto Creek or till a west Line from the Mountains intersect this said Spring and along it to its entrance into the Ohio.[5]

This definition would include the original five hundred thousand acres requested and much more, it would be the largest area requested by the Ohio Company. If it seems like a desperate land grab by a company in trouble it was. By the time the petition reached the Board of Trade on April 2, 1754, it was moot, overtaken by events.

The second grant requested by the Ohio Company is shown in Map 8. The northern boundary is similar to that of the first request but the southern boundary goes many miles down the Ohio River, and the eastern boundary is much closer to the mountains. The original grant request is a small section near the top of this area. This area is estimated to be approximately seven million acres, over ten times the original grant request.

As this second petition was making its way through the system in London, events in America were occurring that would lead to different results than those being requested in the petition. Ironically, on April 2, the same day the petition reached the Board of Trade, George Washington started out with a force of 160 men heading to the Forks of the Ohio to oust the French. In the next few weeks he encountered two different French forces, experienced his first battles, and was unsuccessful in both. The petition to the King was officially rejected on June 25, 1754.[6]

Virginia Lieutenant Governor Dinwiddie was a stockholder in the Ohio Company. Whether for this reason or because he was anxious to take action against what he saw as a threat from the French in Ohio, late in 1753 Dinwiddie decided to act against the extension of French forts into that country.

He and other governors had received a letter from London written by the Southern Secretary, the earl of Holdernesse, which acknowledged the string of French forts being erected and authorizing force.

> You are warranted by the king's instructions to repell any hostile attempt by force of arms; and you will easily understand, that it is in his majesty's determination, that you should defend to the utmost of your power, all his possessions within your government, against any invader. But at the same time, as it is the king's resolution, not to be the aggressor, I am, in his majesty's name most strictly to enjoin you, not to make use of the force under your command, excepting within the undoubted limits of his majesty's province.[7]

This was a warrant for the use of force, not with his majesty's troops but with Virginia troops only, and with caution. And, by the way, make sure you are in his majesty's province.

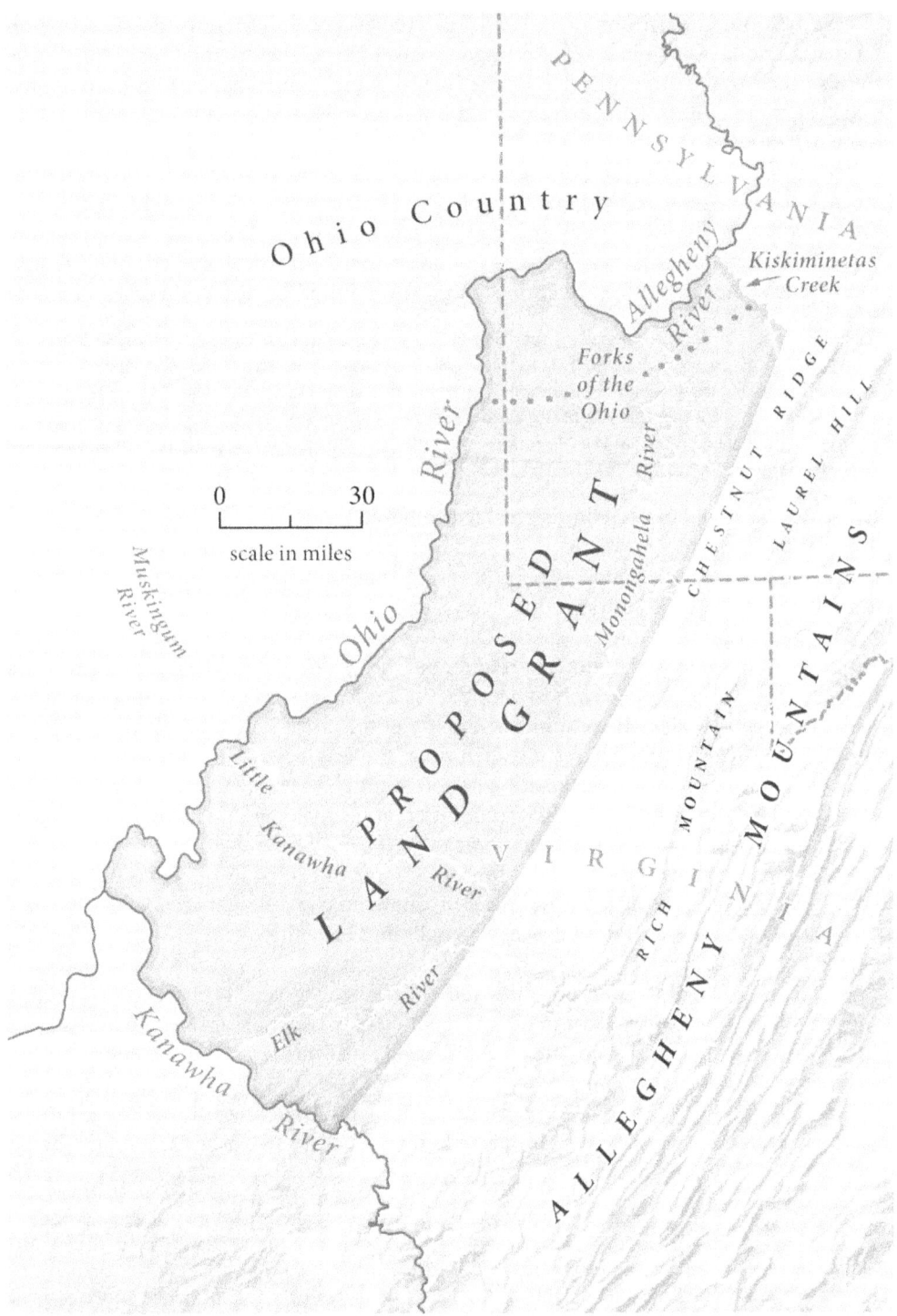

Map 8: Ohio Company Second Grant Request. The northern boundary is similar to that of the first request but the southern boundary goes many miles down the Ohio River, and the eastern boundary is much closer to the mountains. The original grant request is a small section near the top of the shaded area (above the dotted line).

Dinwiddie also had to be careful for other reasons. He was a shareholder in the Ohio Company and there were those in his own legislature who suspected any action he was considering was for company reasons rather than colony reasons. Dinwiddie had come from England in 1751 to become Lieutenant Governor of Virginia. He had been a member of the Ohio Company, and after the death of Lawrence Washington in 1752 had become one of the leaders of the company.[8] He tried to steer a middle course by deciding to send an emissary with a small, non-threatening party to the French to warn them out of Ohio country. The new adjutant, Major George Washington, heard about the mission and hurried to Williamsburg to request and receive this diplomatic mission from Dinwiddie on October 31, 1753. Remarkably, Virginia entrusted this rather delicate diplomatic mission to a twenty-one-year old who had absolutely no military or diplomatic experience.[9]

The mission was to travel to one of the new French forts, Fort Le Boeuf, to hand-deliver a message from Governor Dinwiddie to the French demanding they leave the Ohio country because it was English territory. Fort Le Boeuf is in northwest Pennsylvania on French Creek which flows into the Allegheny River. Washington gathered a party of about six or seven, including a French interpreter. They started immediately and in two weeks were at the Ohio Company storehouse at Wills Creek where he obtained the services of Christopher Gist as a guide. They left by horseback almost immediately as it was late November and they would face some harsh weather conditions.[10]

The Washington party used the trail Gist had blazed, which was carved into a path by Gist, Cresap, and Nemacolin, and recently widened by William Trent. It started by crossing Wills Mountain, next to Wills Creek, and successively went between Dans and Piney mountains, then over Savage, Meadow, and Negro mountains. These are all part of the Alleghenies in western Maryland. It passed over Winding Ridge, still in Maryland, and then into Pennsylvania over the Youghiogheny River, through Great Meadows, over Chestnut Ridge and into the Ohio country near the Monongahela River.[11] All these mountains and ridges are part of the Allegheny chain. Before the use of this route to facilitate a diplomatic meeting, the intention had been to use the road for Ohio Company settlers. Gist and his fellow settlers most likely had used this route when they moved and settled on the Gist Plantation the year before. Following this mission and another later in 1754 it also became known as Washington's Road.[12] See Map 6.

Washington's party did not go toward the Monongahela after they crossed the mountains as Gist had done, but instead went north toward the Forks of the Ohio. Washington was tasked with additional duties on the trip, one of which was to look for a good fort location at or near the Forks. Whether this task was from Dinwiddie as Lieutenant Governor of Virginia or Dinwiddie as head of the Ohio Company is not clear. Gist had been asked by the Ohio Company to lay out a town and fort at Chartiers (Shurtees) Creek, three miles downstream from the Forks, just the year before, as required by the grant. Washington was also asked to gather intelligence information from the Indians. His party traveled to Logstown, then downstream on the Ohio to meet with the Delaware chief Shingas and the Seneca chief Tanacharison (Tanaghrisson). The Indians were not very happy to meet yet another white party in the Ohio Valley as they could see the trouble brewing between these new people and the French who were reasserting their own presence in this country. They could see nothing good coming of it.

Washington persuaded Tanacharison to accompany him to Fort Le Boeuf to help show Indian-English solidarity. Tanacharison, originally a Catawba, had been captured in an Iroquois raid in the south and was adopted by the Seneca. After the Iroquois pulled out of Ohio following the Beaver Wars some Seneca and Cayuga moved back in. The Six Nations sent representatives to live with these Ohio tribes to convey direction from the Six Nations in New York. Tanacharison was one of these Six Nations' representatives. When he represented the Ohio Indians at conferences, such as the recent Logstown conference, he had to clear any agreements with the leaders of the Onondaga back in New York. He was known to the English as the Half King, probably because he had one foot in the camp of the Six Nations and one foot in the camp of the Ohio Indians. The Ohio Indians did not always see eye to eye with the Six Nations so this could be a tense relationship. The Ohio Indians felt the Six Nations were too amenable to ceding Ohio land, land that they, the Six Nations, did not inhabit. This was an issue that would come up again and again.[13]

The party moved on and stopped at Venango a trading post at the confluence of the Allegheny River and French Creek. From there they traveled to Fort Le Boeuf, near Lake Erie, reaching it after dark on December 11, 1753. Although they were received cordially by the commander Captain Jacques Legardeur de St. Pierre, the message Washington brought from Dinwiddie was anything but cordial.[14] "The lands upon the Ohio River are so notoriously known to be the property of the Crown of Great Britain that it is a matter of equal concern and surprise to me to hear that a body of French forces are erecting fortresses and making settlements upon that river, within his Majesty's dominions ... it becomes my duty to require your peaceable departure."[15] Legardeur wrote an equally uncompromising French response, "rights of the King, my master ... to the lands situated along the Ohio [were] incontestable." However, he said he would forward the message to the Marquis Duquesne.[16] Washington received the sealed reply and started his return.

After a rather perilous return journey in which he and Gist endured a fall in icy river waters, and were attacked by an Indian, Washington reached Williamsburg in mid–January 1754 and gave the sealed French reply to Dinwiddie. Washington's return on Nemacolin's Path would be the last peaceful use of that path. Washington also completed a rather thorough intelligence report, which included his observations; the report was well done and well received. The report and letter were enough to cause Dinwiddie to convey concern to London. By the end of the month Dinwiddie was again prepared to act on his own to preclude further French incursion into Ohio and he alerted London.[17]

In the meantime, the Ohio Company was speeding up work on a fort because of the rapidly changing political situation. The Company had met on November 2, 1753, and soon had equipment and supplies moving toward the Ohio. On January 6, 1754, when Washington was traveling back to Wills Creek, from his diplomatic trip, he met a party from the Ohio Company who said they were going to build a fort on the Forks. The original plan was to build the fort not at the Forks, but at Chartiers Creek, a short distance downstream. While on his trip, Washington had seen the Forks and had observed that it was a better location for a fort than Chartiers Creek, but he did not have the time to communicate that to the Ohio Company. If Washington was correct on what the party said, the Company must have changed their mind in the November 2 meeting and decided to build on the Forks instead of Chartiers Creek. The information to motivate the change could have come from any of a number of sources including Croghan, Trent, or Cresap.[18]

William Trent, who was working for the Ohio Company, was building the company's storehouse at Red Stone[19] Creek in February 1754. The company was concerned about the aggressive response by Legardeur, probably hearing about it from Dinwiddie, sent word to Trent to go with Gist and Cresap and work on construction of the fort at the Forks immediately, apparently to supplement the party already working there. This was the fort required by the Ohio Company grant that was originally planned for Chartiers Creek. It had the backing of the government of Virginia, and was a rush job because of the French move toward the Forks. Trent was informed that he would soon be joined by a company of men headed by George Washington.[20]

Dinwiddie acted quickly after receiving Washington's report in January. He ordered the mobilization of two hundred men, promoted Washington to Lieutenant Colonel, and ordered him to prepare to march to the Forks to support Trent and his crew in building the fort. Although Washington was to be second in command to Colonel Joshua Fry on the expedition, Fry was not readily available and Washington started training the troops.[21]

By mid–March the French were closing in on the Forks and Trent and his company were running out of supplies. Dinwiddie ordered Washington to leave immediately, without Fry, and gave orders that "you are to restrain all such offenders and in case of resistance to make prisoners of or kill and destroy them."[22] Washington left on April 2, 1754, with 160 green recruits, and was three weeks out when news came that the French had taken the Forks. The normal route at the time was to travel from Williamsburg to Winchester, Virginia, to, and across, the Potomac to Wills Creek. From Wills Creek they would then take Nemacolin's Path to the Ohio country. Since Washington's force included supply wagons he had to cut a road to and past Winchester. It is doubtful he was even up to Wills Creek when the news came.[23]

On April 17, the English construction crew at the Forks capitulated to an overwhelming French force of over one thousand troops armed with cannons. There was no battle as it would have been useless. The English were allowed to march off with honor, even being allowed to take their tools. The French then proceeded to build Fort Duquesne at the Forks of the Ohio, one of the largest and strongest in their western empire.[24]

Washington now faced some decisions. He could retreat, wait for reinforcements which were supposedly on the way, or inform the governor and wait for instructions. He did not know the size of the French contingent at the Forks so he didn't know what he would encounter. Here is where his inexperience showed. He was young, only twenty-two, in command of a stronger force than he could have hoped to command, and still looking to make his mark as an officer. He decided to continue with the mission according to Dinwiddie's orders.

They moved along Nemacolin's Path—the Ohio Company path—making only about two or three miles a day because they had to cut a road to allow their wagons to pass. Sixty of his force cleared the road and widened it to six feet.[25] He was improving the path into a road as they marched. Washington's army reached Great Crossings at the Youghiogheny River on May 18, 1754, where he wrote a letter to Dinwiddie commenting on the road he was pushing through to Ohio country: "The road to this place is made as good as it can be, having spent much time and great labor upon it. I believe wagons may now travel with 15 or 1800 w't in them by doubling at one or two pinches only."[26] Washington planned to go to the Ohio Company's fortified storehouse at Red Stone Creek for supplies, which was only about forty miles from the Forks. The path they were following, laid out by Gist, Cresap, and Nemacolin, passed through a meadow, now known as Great Meadows, between Laurel Hill and Chestnut Ridge.[27] Chestnut Ridge is the last mountain on the road before it reaches the Allegheny Plateau and Ohio country, only a few miles from Gist's Plantation. The meadow was good foraging for the horses and Washington planned a fortified post there. They had reached Great Meadows by May 24.[28]

Captain Contrecoeur, commandant of the French contingent at the Forks, had been scouting their progress. He did not want them to reach the Forks where the fort was still under construction and not ready, so on May 23 he sent out a small detachment, headed by Ensign Joseph Coulon de Villiers de Jumonville, to warn them off. Washington was building a palisade for his own troops in Great Meadows when Gist rode in on May 27, to inform him of the proximity of the de Jumonville party. Assuming they were hostile Washington decided to engage this party; he did not know they were only coming to confer.[29]

The events of the following day resulted in bloodshed and many believe initiated, or at least was the first battle in the French and Indian War. These events have been well researched and described by others such as Anderson.[30] In short, Washington did surprise and attack the de Jumonville party, but having captured many of the French soldiers he lost control of the situation. In a surprise attack Tanacharison, the Seneca chief who had accompanied Washington to Fort Le Boeuf, and had his own personal animosity towards the French, killed the prisoner de Jumonville by a hatchet to the head. Other Indians in Washington's party then attacked and killed more prisoners while Washington stood by, taken by surprise. This was his first military action and his inexperience was evident as he did not stop the attack. This massacre took place in a glen, now known as de Jumonville's Glen, just off the road the Virginians were traveling. Washington sent a letter to Dinwiddie trying to put the best spin on the situation, but decided to continue forward after completing his small palisade in Great Meadows, which he aptly named Fort Necessity, on June 2.

Despite losing many Indian allies, horses, and supplies he pushed on and continued the road building, toward Gist's Plantation and the Red Stone Creek storehouse on his way to Fort Duquesne. He still had Dinwiddie's orders. He intended to improve the road from Gist's to Red Stone Creek along the way. Before he could do that, while near Gist's place on June 28, he received word of a large French force coming to push him back over the mountains. He considered making a stand at Gist's but thought better of it and retreated to Fort Necessity where he would make a stand.[31]

Done in haste, Fort Necessity was flimsy and not large enough to hold all his men. Tanacharison tried to convince Washington that the fort was a "death trap" but Washington ignored him. Tanacharison and up to one hundred Mingos joined Washington on June 1 but left prior to the battle.[32] The men who could not fit in the fort lined trenches they dug outside the fort to prepare for the fight. Washington's inexperience showed again in the poor location he had chosen for the fort. It was in an open field surrounded by woods in which the French took cover and fired on the flimsy structure. After a short battle on July 3, 1754, Washington capitulated to a much superior French force. The French commandant, Coulon de Villiers, did not take Washington as a prisoner but allowed the Virginians to retreat after Washington signed the capitulation paper, which required them to leave the Ohio country and not return within a year. Why only a year is not clear. It was July 9 before Washington's defeated force returned to Wills Creek.[33] On the return to Fort Duquesne the French force burned Fort Necessity, and destroyed the only two vestiges of the Ohio Company in the Ohio country at the time, Gist's Plantation and the Red Stone storehouse. Gist was unhurt.

On U.S. Route 40, just off the road in Great Meadows, is a United States National Park, the Fort Necessity National Battlefield, which has a reconstructed replica of the original Fort Necessity.

Braddock's Road

The news of Washington's defeat reached London in early September. Thomas Pelham-Holles, Duke of Newcastle, and secretary of state for the Northern Department, reacted immediately and sought support from William Augustus, Duke of Cumberland, captain-general of the army and son of King George II. Deciding they had to act, they quickly received support from the King and ordered two regiments under Major General Edward Braddock go to Virginia. This force was to take Fort Duquesne from the French, and to eliminate other forts in Ohio they deemed aggressive. They hoped that by taking quick, decisive action in North America they could forestall a wider war with France.[34] As Anderson continues,

> In fact, events had reached a stage at the beginning of 1755 that made a war between Britain and France all but inevitable…. [Many factors] would take such comparatively minor episodes such as Jumonville's death and the Battle of Fort Necessity and make something much larger, much more dangerous, than even Newcastle at his most pessimistic could have foreseen. How the clash of tiny numbers of men in a frontier conflict would grow into a world war, how that war would redraw the map of Europe's empires, and how it would transform the relationship between England and her American colonies—such a chain of events would have defied the most exuberant imagining.[35]

Braddock acted quickly and by February he was in Williamsburg, Virginia; his two regiments arrived in America in March, and sailed up Chesapeake Bay and the Potomac to Alexandria, Virginia. In the weeks before he left for Wills Creek, Braddock had several meetings with colonial officials discussing strategy and asking for support. His troops left Alexandria in early April and started toward Wills Creek, using two different routes, one through northern Virginia, via Winchester through the Shenandoah Valley, and one through Maryland, which included a route through Frederick. Frederick is where Braddock joined the troops after his meetings.[36]

Colonel Dunbar's regiment, which traveled through Maryland, used a new road that Governor Sharpe had recently built from Rock Creek and the Potomac, adjacent to Georgetown, up to Fort Cumberland. Just prior to reaching Wills Creek, on May 8, this regiment stopped at Cresap's place at Oldtown to pick up supplies. An unknown seaman traveling with Dunbar kept a log of the journey. Either by reputation or personal discussions with Cresap, the author of the log was impressed. He aptly described Cresap and his home:

> we found a Maryland Company encamp'd in a fine Situation on the banks of the *Potomack;* with cleared ground around it; there lives Colonel Crefsop, a Rattle Snake, Colonel, and a D—d Rascal; calls himself a Frontiersman, being nearest the *Ohio;* he had a Summons some time since the French to retire from his settlement, which they claimed as their property, but he refused it like a man of Spirit; This place is the Track of Indian Warriours, when going to War, either to the Noward. Or Soward. He hath built a little Fort around his House. And is resolved to keep his Ground.[37]

They made their way to Wills Creek on the Potomac by late May. A fort had been built on the west side of Wills Creek in 1754–55 by Colonel James Innes, which he named Fort Mount Pleasant. When Braddock arrived, representing the king, he renamed it Fort Cumberland in honor of the king's son the Duke of Cumberland.[38] Cumberland, Maryland, retains the name today.

Braddock had the services and advice of many people with experience in this area of the country. Christopher Gist was hired as the expedition guide and Thomas Cresap was hired to supply provisions. George Washington was offered the job of head of the Virginia Regiment under Braddock but he rejected this offer as he knew of the disdain in which the royal military held the colonial regiments. Washington was a proud man with a lifelong desire to have a commission in the regular royal army; he wanted more than to be part of the subsidiary Virginia Regiment. He did, however, join Braddock as a volunteer military advisor, hoping more would come out of it later.[39]

Braddock, by his actions, would lose the support of one group that would have made a difference later, the Indians. The Indians, led by the Oneida Scarouady who had succeeded Tanacharison, and the Delaware chief Shingas, offered their help although their support for the British was tepid. Nevertheless, they wanted the French out of the valley. Braddock was headstrong and arrogant. He saw no good in the Indians, and did not think they could help; he had no confidence in their fighting ability. Later that British attitude would change dramatically when both sides courted the Indians for the fighting that was to come. The separation between Braddock and the Indians was sealed when the land question came up. The Indians were still trying to consolidate their claim to the land, the Ohio country, after challenges by the British and French. Braddock was asked by a Delaware chief "what he would do with the land if he could drive the French and their Indians away." Braddock was brusque and declared that no Indian should inherit the land as it was only for the English to settle. This clearly angered the Indians and many went directly over to the French.[40]

Braddock's force consisted of two regiments of royal troops numbering seven hundred men each, and provincial companies from New York, the Carolinas, Virginia, and Maryland. The addition of sixty artillery pieces and thirty seamen brought the total to approximately two thousand, with over one hundred wagons.[41]

This large body of troops started leaving Fort Cumberland on May 29. They intended to follow Washington's Road and started that way from Wills Creek over Wills Mountain. Gist, Nemacolin and Cresap had all gone this way, straight west from Wills Creek. Washington had also used this route and supposedly had cut it to accommodate wagons. However, there was clearly a difference in the wagons that Washington used, because Braddock's large army wagons could not make it through without falling apart while going over the rough and rocky road over Wills Mountain. As they were also wider, Braddock had to widen the road to twelve feet.[42] "Captain Orme wrote of the debacle: 'The ascent and descent were almost a perpendicular rock; three wagons were entirely destroyed, which were replaced from the camp; and many more were extremely shattered.'"[43]

This was unacceptable. The wagons had only gone a couple of miles the first day and would fall far behind the advance party he had sent out if they all didn't fall apart first. He sent out a small party to look for a better route. On June 2 Lieutenant Charles Spendelow, attached to Braddock's force from the Royal Navy, found a way *around* Wills Mountain, along Wills Creek. As Wills Creek came down from the north to the Potomac it had cut a narrow gap in Wills Mountain just before the creek entered the Potomac. That gap, now known as the Cumberland Narrows, seems to be an obvious route around the mountain for any army with wagons because it was level with Wills Creek. Although explorers such as Gist, Nemacolin, and Cresap didn't need it because they just used packhorses, one would think that Washington would have found it for use by his wagons, but he did not. After Braddock's search party found it, one hundred men took only four days to complete the road along Wills Creek around the mountain; it was only a couple of miles longer than going over the mountain, but it was much easier for the wagons.[44]

This set the tone for the rest of the expedition. It was long and tedious process headed by the engineer Sir John St. Clair, but it was necessary. The inexperienced George Washington was impatient at times not realizing the difference between building a road for a large army and one for the small expedition he headed the year before. He was part of the advance party but became frustrated at how slowly things were moving.

> We set out ... with less than thirty carriages, including those that transported the ammunition for the Howitzers, and six-pounders, and all of them strongly horsed; which was a prospect that conveyed infinite delight to my mind.... But this prospect was soon clouded, and my hopes brought very low indeed, when I found, that, instead of pushing on with vigor, without regarding a little

rough road, they were halting to level every mole-hill, and to erect bridges over every brook, by which means we were four days in getting twelve miles.[45]

"Leveling every mole-hill" and "erecting bridges over every brook" was necessary for the heavy wagons that were following.

Braddock was taking the same route that others had taken before him, including Gist, Nemacolin, Cresap, and Washington. Now he was turning it into a real road, one that could take heavy military wagons. His army was over ten times the size of the force that Washington had moved over this route just one year earlier.

They had gone around Wills Mountain but still had to cross the other mountains of the Allegheny range. Next they went through Sandy Gap between Piney Mountain and Dans Mountain. The road continued over Big and Little Savage mountains, then Meadows Mountain and, the later named Negro Mountain. They crossed Winding Ridge and on June 24, forded the Youghiogheny River at Great Crossings where the water was about three feet deep and the current swift. They passed through Great Meadows, the site of Fort Necessity, with little or no mention of the fort. One wonders what Washington thought as he passed near the ruins of the Fort, from which he had been ousted less than a year ago. On June 26, they reached Chestnut Ridge, the last of the mountains before the Allegheny Plateau. They didn't continue westward on the path Gist had laid out toward the Monongahela, but instead headed north, directly toward Gist's Plantation which they reached on June 27.[46]

Depending on how one counts the mountains and ridges there were at least five or six that could not be avoided, but had to be climbed; some as high as 2,900 feet. The route did not follow the Gist route exactly but deviated from it at places just as the National Road, the present U.S. Route 40, later deviated slightly from the Braddock Road. The distance from Fort Cumberland to Chestnut Ridge is approximately sixty miles. It had taken them a month to cut and travel the road to this point. The total distance from Fort Cumberland to the Forks of the Ohio is about 120 miles.[47]

The road was now a real road, and at that time the only one from western Maryland to the Ohio country. What started out as Gist's Trace then became Cresap's Road, Nemacolin's Path, and Washington's Road, could now be legitimately called Braddock's Road. Many in the intervening years, including books and articles by Hulbert, Laycock, and Baker, have traced the road. The Braddock Road was almost identical to the Gist-Cresap-Nemacolin Road from Cumberland to Chestnut Ridge. At Chestnut Ridge, however, it veered north toward the Forks instead of forging west or northwest to the Monongahela.

Braddock's objective was to take Fort Duquesne at the Forks of the Ohio. In the next few days he crossed and re-crossed the Monongahela. On July 9, the Battle of the Monongahela took place a few miles from Fort Duquesne and was a catastrophic loss for the British. The French Indian allies attacked the British regulars in a forest, an arena in which the latter were unprepared to fight. The dismissal of the British Indian allies by Braddock now loomed as an important blunder.

Braddock was mortally wounded in the battle and only lived for a few days. He died on July 13 and Washington supervised the burial on July 14. Because they wanted to assure the opposing Indians would not desecrate the body, Braddock was buried without ceremony in the middle of the road and wagons were driven over the gravesite to cover all traces of it. Most of the British forces wound their way back to Fort Cumberland and arrived to muster there on July 25. There were still over one thousand British troops at Fort Cumberland but there was no leader and no will to return to Fort Duquesne. The troops disbanded, dispersed or deserted; Dunbar and his regiment fled to Philadelphia. Fort

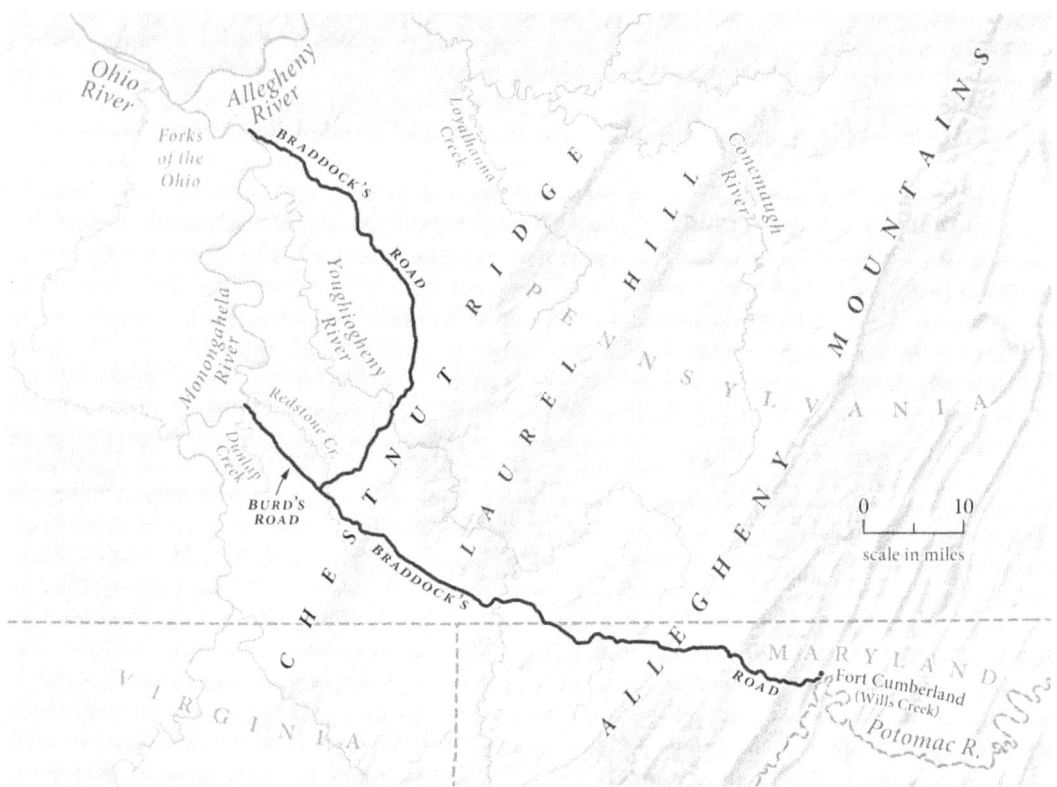

Map 9: Braddock Road and Burd Road. The Braddock Road follows Gist's Trace over the mountains, near Gist's Plantation, but then swings north to the battle site on the Monongahela. This map is based on several different sources. For a more detailed description of the route see *Braddock's Road: Mapping the British Expedition from Alexandria to the Monongahela,* by Norman L. Baker. See also Map 6.

Cumberland was in the hands of a few of the Maryland militia. For now, the Braddock Road had been abandoned.[48]

War in the West

The Seven Years War between France and England was a worldwide conflict lasting from 1756 to 1763. The French and Indian War, as this conflict was commonly called in North America, is synonymous with the Seven Years War, but it began earlier. There is disagreement whether the war started with Charles Langlade's attack on Pickawillany in 1753, Washington's attack on Jumonville in 1754, or Braddock's defeat in 1755. There is no question that by July 1755 the war for North America was on in full force in the Appalachian region and in the Ohio country.

The early successes in the war on the frontier were by the French, not by any French military action but by the depredations of their Indian allies on the undefended English settlers in western Pennsylvania, and Maryland. The Pickawillany raid had separated the Miami from the English, and Braddock's attitude that the Indians had no right to Ohio country had separated the Ohio Indians from the English. The Shawnee, Delaware, and

Mingo in Ohio allied with France but considered themselves fighting for their homeland, the Ohio country, not for the French.

Over the next three years there was no peace on the road from Maryland to Ohio. There were numerous deadly Indian raids with no pushback from Virginian or royal troops or from the militias of Pennsylvania or Maryland. The Quaker government in Pennsylvania was not interested in arming anyone for war. Consequently, the western raids pushed settlers east, all the way to Carlisle and Harris's Ferry on the Susquehanna River. The Pennsylvania frontier became a no-man's land. Pennsylvania Governor Robert Morris spoke of "'a vast Tract of Territory' laid waste by French and Indian raiders. Years later John Heckwalder … entered a 'howling wilderness' where, in every direction, the 'blackened ruins of houses and barns, and remnants of chimneys' confronted him."[49] The devastation was so complete that Canadian Governor-General, Marquis de Vaudreuil later complained that "raiders entering the Susquehanna Valley near Shamokin in mid–1757 found nothing to attack: the region contained only abandoned farms."[50]

Maryland and Virginia fared no better. Small stockades were built in which people crowded for safety. "To the south Winchester, at the northern end of the Shenandoah Valley and Fort Cumberland on the upper Potomac stood alone, the small settlements beyond the Blue Ridge having been overrun or abandoned in the early raids." Later some four hundred captives repatriated to Maryland, Virginia, and Pennsylvania gave an indication of the total losses.[51]

The struggle in Maryland between the Proprietor and the Assembly continued. The Assembly did not want to appropriate any funds for the war until the Proprietor contributed as well. Except for one or two small bills there was no Assembly support for the war in the west. The province did build one fort, Fort Frederick, on the Potomac, but it was far east of Fort Cumberland, almost to Conococheague Creek and saw no real action in the defense of western Maryland.

Fort Cumberland was of no use in the defense of western Maryland either. The Indians, the primary threat, easily moved around it, harassed it, and raided many nearby settlements. During the war it was the headquarters of various Maryland and Virginia detachments. Shortly after the Braddock defeat Washington was made commander-in-chief of the Virginia forces. He made his headquarters at Fort Cumberland for a while but was not impressed with it; it was too vulnerable in his opinion. The Indian raids were reaching as far back in Virginia as Winchester. Washington wanted to abandon Fort Cumberland and fortify Winchester instead as part of Virginia's fort-building project along the Alleghenies. He claimed, "Fort Cumberland is of little use; there is not an inhabitant living between it and Winchester, except a few settlements around the Fort…. At Fort Cumberland I would have one company to garrison the place to secure it, to procure the intelligence, and to cover the detachments sent to the Ohio River, which is all the use it can ever be put to."[52] Governor Dinwiddie of Virginia, still a member of the Ohio Company, wanted Fort Cumberland to remain open and he formed a council, with Washington as a member, to assess its status. The council concluded, with Washington's agreement, that even though the Fort was defenseless and poorly constructed, it should remain open and maintained, "since the only road to the West for wheel carriages passed in this direction."[53] This would be the road back to Ohio after the war. Washington had concurred with keeping the fort open, but he wanted to build a fort further along the road, perhaps at Great Meadows, the Fort Necessity site. Washington still wanted to retake Fort Duquesne.

The presence of an undefended wagon road between Fort Duquesne and Fort Cumberland remained a concern. Washington had his headquarters at Fort Cumberland in early

1757, but in April he and his regiment were called back to Virginia. Captain Dagworthy and Maryland militia troops replaced the Virginia Regiment at the fort. A few days after Washington's departure Dagworthy received reports that a large body of French troops had left Fort Duquesne with large guns, wagons, and horses and were headed to attack Fort Cumberland. Dagworthy took the threat seriously and called in reinforcements to strengthen the fort. This report turned out to be a rumor, but it was believable because an attack by a French force down the existing road was credible.[54] The Indians undoubtedly used the road even though they did not need a wagon road as it had been a path between the Potomac and Monongahela for centuries.

The Indian raids in western Maryland caused many settlers to head back east. Even Thomas Cresap left Oldtown with his family and neighbors to live with his son on the Conococheague Creek farther east. Cresap raised a party of volunteer rangers, and went back to Fort Cumberland to start his own raiding. He followed the Braddock Road back to Savage Mountain in one raid, and engaged in a fight with an Indian party during which his son Thomas was killed. In a later raid in the same area, farther up the road, Cresap was accompanied by two other sons and with a man described as a "negro of gigantic stature." On this raid, they moved past Savage Mountain and engaged in another Indian battle. The unnamed black man was immortalized in the name of the mountain, which is now known as Negro Mountain, one of the highest ridges on the Braddock Road. According to his son this was Cresap's last battle during this war and he settled back at Oldtown.[55]

Forbes Road

William Pitt returned to the British government in 1757 as Secretary of State for the Southern Department and immediately took active control of the prosecution of the war in all of its theaters including Europe and America. One of his initiatives was a push for better use of the colonial troops in North America. He also sent more royal troops to North America for operations in three different theaters, one of which was in Pennsylvania. Pitt's intention was to defeat France in North America so he appointed Brigadier General John Forbes to command a force to take Fort Duquesne. Forbes was astute enough to recognize that the first thing to be done was to make peace with the Indians that Braddock had alienated, and make agreements with them. The departure of those Indians not only diminished Braddock's force but caused them to ally with the French. Forbes had to deal with some old history, including fraud, in order to restore relations with the Native Americans.[56]

In 1737 Penn family members had agreed to purchase land west of the Delaware River from the Delaware tribe, based on the distance a man could walk in a day and one-half. It was called the Walking Purchase. This formula seemed reasonable to the Delaware as they knew how limited that should be. The fraud was in how the plan was implemented. Using multiple, speedy runners along a straight line to a distant point and then projecting a line northeast, perpendicular to the original line of walk, back to the Delaware River, the Penn's claimed 1,200 square miles of prime Delaware River land. One doesn't have to know the shape of the area claimed to understand that one man walking a day and one-half could not enclose 1,200 square miles. Although the Delaware were client Indians of the Six Nations, the Six Nations did not back the Delaware against this fraud because it was not Iroquois land that was lost. This was another example of the Six Nations giving away land that did not belong to them; it happened repeatedly. This trick was not easily forgotten by the Delaware who now started to look at land farther west in the Wyoming Valley of Pennsylvania.[57]

The claim on Pennsylvania Indian lands did not end with this fraudulent purchase. A conference was held in Albany, New York, in June and July 1754, referred to as the Albany Congress. Coincidently, it took place at the same time George Washington was being pushed back by the French force at Fort Necessity. The prime purpose of the Congress was to discuss a stronger union between the colonies; the Congress failed in this primary goal; there was no colonial agreement. (Had the participants known of Washington's defeat it might have encouraged an agreement.) The interesting results of the conference were in the "side" meetings that were going on.

A Connecticut land speculation company was trying to get title to five million acres in the Wyoming Valley of Pennsylvania. They plied the Indians with liquor and offered two thousand pounds of New York currency for the land. Not to be outdone the Pennsylvania proprietors sent their own diplomat, Conrad Weiser, to acquire the cession of *all* the land claimed by the Iroquois in Pennsylvania. "Weiser also succeeded in obtaining a deed to hitherto unceded Iroquois lands—in this case everything west of the Susquehanna between 41° 31' north latitude and the Maryland boundary—in return for a nominal sum (four hundred pounds New York currency) and the promise of further payments to follow."[58] Everything west of the Susquehanna" would have included all of the Ohio country. This was an egregious grab that would have displaced all of the Ohio Indians.

Weiser was successful, at least temporarily, by dealing directly with the Six Nations, who once again were giving away land that wasn't theirs. This poisoned relationships for years between Connecticut, Pennsylvania, the Six Nations, and the Delaware.

A conference to address these fraudulent deals took place in Easton, Pennsylvania, in 1757 between the Delaware chief Teedyuscung and Pennsylvania officials. For the Delaware, Teedyuscung sought the revocation of the Walking Purchase and 2.5 million acres in the Wyoming Valley. No significant resolutions were made although there was some progress and it set the stage for a meeting the following year.[59]

Forbes's purpose at the Easton Treaty conference of October 1758 was to win back the Indians through negotiations. He invited delegates from the Ohio Indians, Shawnee, Delaware, and Mingo to the conference. The Indians were justifiably skeptical but the English delegates tried to convince them

> that the English had undertaken military operations in the west only after the French had established forts there, and by reading to them the provisions of the 1757 Easton agreements that offered aid and presumably guaranteed land, to Teedyuscung's people in the Wyoming Valley. These facts he argued, could be taken as proof that the English did not intend to colonize beyond the Alleghenies, but only to expel the French and revive the trade that the Ohio tribes desperately needed.[60]

This was disingenuous, as early as 1750 the Ohio Company had planned to move into the Ohio country to settle English colonists. In fact, the opposite was true and the English were always the ones to seek more land for the colonies, not the French. Braddock baldly acknowledged this reality when he dismissed the Indians prior to starting his expedition to the Forks. The Indians of Ohio knew this and remained skeptical. Once again, they reminded the English that it was the Indian land they wanted: "It is plain," they insisted, "that you white people are the cause of this war; why do not you and the French fight in the old country and on the sea? Why do you come to fight on our land? This makes everybody believe, you want to take the land from us by force, and settle it."[61] Despite the hypocrisy the Ohio Indians heard, they knew the French were weak and that Forbes was already advancing on the road he was building to Fort Duquesne, so they agreed to meet in Easton in October. Forbes didn't attend as he was ill, but Pennsylvania was represented by Lieutenant Governor William Denny and Conrad Weiser, the Pennsylvania Indian agent. The Governor of New Jersey, Sir Francis Bernard, also attended. George Croghan was there as a representative of Indian Agent William Johnson, and Andrew Montour as an interpreter. The Indians were well represented by an estimated five hundred chiefs, including Iroquois and Ohio Indians, led by Teedyuscung.[62]

Teedyuscung sought the same land he had sought the previous year but he was unsuccessful and was marginalized at the meeting. Once again, he submitted to Iroquois authority. Agreement was reached when Conrad Weiser then proposed to *return* to the Iroquois all of the land from the Albany purchase *west* of the Allegheny Mountains. At Albany in 1754 Weiser had obtained for Pennsylvania *all the land west of the Susquehanna*, including Ohio country, from the Iroquois. Now he proposed returning the part of this land that was Ohio country west of the Alleghenies, satisfying Ohio Indians who now thought they would be safe from English settlements in Ohio. This proposal satisfied all who were present. The Pennsylvanians would keep the land ceded to them in Albany, except the Ohio country. The Iroquois in New York were disinterested in the Pennsylvania land, which they had ceded in Albany. The Ohio Indians thought they now had title to all lands in Ohio west of the Alleghenies, and General Forbes now had a peace settlement with the Indians prior to his assault on Fort Duquesne.[63]

When Forbes was ordered to take Fort Duquesne he was given the same objective as Braddock had been given just three years previously, although a lot had changed during that time. Braddock's was the first British attack against the French and he hadn't realized the importance of Indian allies; he paid for this misjudgment with his life. Forbes had learned the lesson and ensured peace with the Ohio Indians prior to his attack on Fort Duquesne. He also faced the same challenge as Braddock of crossing the Alleghenies to get to the fort but he chose to go directly across Pennsylvania rather than using the Braddock Road. This route, over well-established roads from Philadelphia to Carlisle, was slightly shorter than the Braddock Road, but he still had to cut a new road over the mountains.

Forbes had learned from Braddock's experience and planned more carefully. He also had more men, seven thousand, compared to Braddock's two thousand. He started his diplomatic effort to convene an Easton conference about the same time he started on the road, in late spring, 1758. He knew he wanted to complete the Easton conference before his assault on Fort Duquesne but he did not hesitate to start road construction. Forbes's planning included careful logistic support and the establishment of Fort Bedford at Raystown and Fort Ligonier along the route. Washington was garrisoned at Fort Cumberland with his Virginia Regiment at this time and he received information on Forbes's plan to move directly overland to Fort Duquesne on July 24. He immediately wrote a letter to Colonel Henry Bouquet, Forbes's second in command, suggesting a new road could not be made, at least in time.[64]

On August 2 Washington sent a much longer letter to Bouquet outlining in detail why the Braddock Road was a preferable route to Fort Duquesne. He claimed that the Indians long-time use of this trail had shown the value of the route from Wills Creek to the Monongahela demonstrating its superiority. The road was opened by the Ohio Company and was improved by himself, and the following year by Braddock. "A road, that has so long been opened, and so well and so often repaired, must be much firmer and better than a new one." He acknowledged that the shorter distance between Raystown and Loyal Hanna (near the Forks) was an argument for the direct road but, he said, "I must beg leave to ask, whether it requires more time, or is more difficult and expensive, to go one hundred and forty-five miles in a good road already made to our hands, than to cut one hundred miles anew, and a great part of the way over impassable mountains."[65] Washington then laid out a meticulous table comparing the distances from Carlisle to Fort Duquesne by way of Raystown with the distances from Carlisle to Fort Duquesne via Forts Frederick and Cumberland. He showed the latter, the Braddock Road, to be only nineteen miles longer and much preferable because of the existing road. His letter went on for many pages and listed many reasons for using the Braddock Road.[66]

Forbes dismissed Washington's argument because he saw it as promoting the provincial interests of the Ohio Company over British royal interests. He reprimanded Washington and his colleague (Colonel Byrd) for having "showed their weakness in their attachment they belong to" above "the good of the service." However, he was having some doubts that Washington might be right in worrying about completing the mission before the end of the year. Forbe's men still had to cross Laurel Ridge a formidable peak. Laurel Ridge ranged down across central Pennsylvania to the Braddock Road path where it was much diminished, so much so that some accounts of the Braddock Road don't even mention it. Forbes Road would have to contend with the high part of Laurel Ridge whereas the Braddock Road did not. Washington lost his argument but eventually joined Forbes at Raystown, only about thirty-five miles from Fort Cumberland, and was instrumental in the final push to Fort Duquesne.[67]

The battle for Fort Duquesne was one of the turning points of the war. For 150 years, since the start of both the English and French colonies, the population of New France was minuscule compared to that of the English colonies. When Pitt reorganized the war effort he put fifty thousand troops on the ground, the equivalent to two-thirds of the total population of Canada, in North America with the intent to completely conquer New France. Against this force New France could put only 6,800 regular troops in the field. The numerical inferiority of population finally caught up with New France.[68] By November 1758 Fort Duquesne held a garrison of three hundred although only a third of them were fit for duty and their Indian allies had abandoned them. On November 23, anticipating Forbes's army, the French evacuated the fort and destroyed it with explosives, an explosion the Anglo-American force heard ten miles away. It is likely that Washington was one of the first to enter the remains of the fort the next day.[69]

Following the destruction of Fort Duquesne, the British built their own fort at the Forks and called it Fort Pitt. Colonel Bouquet was now in charge of Fort Pitt and the surrounding area known as Pittsburgh. General Forbes, who was in poor health for the entire campaign, and had to be carried about, made it back to Philadelphia but died shortly thereafter. George Washington resigned his commission in the Virginia Regiment and did not put on a uniform for several years. He never achieved his dream of a commission as an officer in the regular British army. The Forks of the Ohio were now removed from the wrangling between the provinces of Pennsylvania and Virginia and in the hands of the regulars of His Majesty George II. This would have ramifications for the settlement of the Ohio country.

A Road from the Ridge to the River and One Back East

The path between Chestnut Ridge and the Monongahela, the last part of Gist's Trace, was an Indian path during the war and had been for years before, but it was unimproved as a road. That was to change because of the exigencies of war.

Fort Pitt was being constructed in early 1759, but it and other forward British garrisons were difficult to supply. The Indians were still very active and the Forbes Road was vulnerable to attacks on supply trains. It was decided to reopen the Braddock Road in the summer, in order to bring supplies to Fort Pitt from Virginia as well as along the Forbes Road. Bouquet was skeptical if the advantages of this route would outweigh the need to garrison Fort Cumberland which the Virginia troops had previously evacuated leaving a small number of Maryland militia to garrison it. Competition still existed between Pennsylvania and Virginia over the ownership of this land in Ohio country, so Bouquet was hesitant to give Virginia any advantage by reopening the Braddock Road. When it was finally decided to open the road, the Virginians also insisted, on the construction of a new road from the Braddock Road to the Monongahela.[70] Their reasoning was that there would then be three ways to get supplies to Fort Pitt—by the Forbes Road, by the Braddock Road to the Forks, and by floating bateaux down the river from a new fort at Redstone Creek.[71]

The Virginians reopened the Braddock Road on August 20, 1759. This was probably just an announcement that the road was now open with no corresponding attempt to improve it. The road had not been used for wagons in over four years. Two days later Colonel Bouquet wrote to General John Stanwix, who had succeeded General Forbes after the latter's recent death that he had ordered Colonel James Burd to open the road between the Braddock Road and Redstone Creek and to build a fort there. This road was to veer off from the Braddock Road after it crossed the mountains, and head straight to the Monongahela instead of north to the Forks.[72]

Map 9 shows the Burd Road extension from the Braddock Road to the Monongahela, essentially duplicating the latter half of Gist's Trace.

On September 1, Burd and his two hundred men were at Fort Cumberland, ready to start up the Braddock Road. As he traveled the road he complained bitterly of its poor condition. It was "not more than 10 feet wide and carries up every Hill almost without a turn and Hills almost perpendicular." This is not surprising. It had been four years since Braddock cut a road that would take heavy military wagons into a virgin forest, ample time for the road to almost revert to its primitive state. Nevertheless, Burd's troops made good time, passing Fort Necessity on September 10 and arriving at Gist's place the same day.[73]

Burd started the new road to the Monongehela immediately and by September 23 he had built a road over sixteen and a quarter miles long to Dunlap's Creek, one mile upstream from Redstone Creek. Dunlap Creek enters the Monongahela at present-day Brownsville, Pennsylvania. Veech (*The Monongahela of Old*) credits the route of Burd's road to a trader named Dunlap who used a trading road from Wills Creek to the Monongahela. Dunlap was the eponymous trader whose name supplanted Nemacolin's on the Creek.[74] Dunlap's Road was identical to the Braddock Road up to Chestnut Ridge but went from the top of Chestnut Ridge northwestward to the river in almost a straight line instead of going toward the Forks. Burd was told to go to Redstone Creek but chose the Dunlap Creek location for defensive purposes and constructed a fort there. They tried to name it Burd's Fort but the more traditional name of Redstone Old Fort stuck. It is not clear if the original Redstone Old Fort, built by the Ohio Company, and destroyed by the French, was at Dunlap Creek or at Redstone Creek, which were close to one another.

Burd's Road, from the mountains to the Monongahela followed the same path to the Monongahela that Gist had laid out a few years before for the Ohio Company. It would have taken Ohio Company settlers right to the heart of the first grant of Ohio land on the Monongahela River. As the French and Indian war was winding down in 1759 and 1760 settlers started to move into the Ohio Valley in numbers. This improved road and its extension to the river provided an ideal route for this expansion. At the intersection of the road and the river the settlers, mostly squatters, could either settle near the east side of the

Monongahela or board flat boats to float up to the Forks and from there downriver on the Ohio to western Ohio or Kentucky. For those who did not want to float down the river the road was later extended through western Pennsylvania across the Monongahela to Wheeling, Virginia, and eventually across the Ohio River, first as the Cumberland Road and later as the National Road. Of course it was also still possible to follow the Braddock Road all the way to the Forks instead of going to the Monongahela via the Burd Road.

There was now a road over the Alleghenies, the Braddock Road to the Forks of the Ohio, and a spur directly to the Monongahela, the Burd Road. However, one still had to get to Fort Cumberland to be able to use it, and the fort was isolated. There were also some Allegheny ridges between the Hagerstown Valley and Fort Cumberland including Sideling Hill, Polish Mountain, Warrior Mountain and others, although they were not as high as ones west of Fort Cumberland. The fort was fairly easy to get to on horseback or to supply using packhorses, but to move heavier military equipment was another matter. As yet there were no wagon roads through these Maryland mountains. Originally the Potomac was seen as a possible route to Wills Creek but the upper Potomac was not navigable and therefore could not be used for heavy equipment. When Braddock's regiment traveled through Maryland they had a fairly easy time going from Georgetown up through Frederick. However, because there were no wagon roads going directly over the mountains to Fort Cumberland, they had to detour, moving northwest to the Potomac at present Williamsport, and crossing the river. They then traveled about seventy miles along the Potomac in Virginia and re-crossed it at the Little Cacapon River, near present-day Paw Paw, West Virginia. From there they followed the river through Oldtown to Fort Cumberland.[75]

Maryland built Fort Frederick on the Potomac in 1755, in response to the Indian uprisings following Braddock's defeat. A road was built from the fort to Frederick town, which was already connected to Baltimore by road. The road from Frederick to Fort Frederick was also relatively easy to build. The two Forts, Frederick and Cumberland, which were critical for defense, were still isolated from each other in Maryland; to travel between them one would have to cross the Potomac, travel in Virginia and re-cross the river again as Braddock had done. In 1758 the Maryland Assembly finally got around to authorizing a Maryland road across the mountains between Forts Frederick and Cumberland. This road passed through present-day Hancock, Maryland, and followed the river past Oldtown to Fort Cumberland; it was entirely in Maryland.[76]

This road, sixty-two miles long, was not much but at least it could take wagons. There were now primitive roads from Baltimore to Frederick, from Frederick to Fort Cumberland, and from Fort Cumberland to the Monongahela. Although not exactly on the same roads, this was to eventually be the route of the Baltimore Pike and Cumberland Road from Baltimore to the Monongahela. There was also a road from Georgetown on the Potomac to Frederick. The Maryland Assembly recognized the importance of the road, not only for the war, but for after the war, when they appropriated money for the road: "will contribute much to lessen the Expence of carrying Provisions and Warlike Stores from Fort Frederick to Fort Cumberland; and will induce many People to travel and carry on a Trade in and through this Province, to and from the Back Country."[77]

Pontiac's Rebellion and the Proclamation of 1763

Forbes's victory at Fort Duquesne in late 1758 was the first major crack in French control of the Ohio country. The building of Fort Pitt, much larger than Fort Duquesne, was an indication that the English planned to stay despite their assurances to the Ohio Indians at Easton that they only wanted to drive out the French and they would then pull back over the Alleghenies. The country, however, was not yet secure. There was an expectation that there would be a counterattack by the French to try to retake the Forks. The British also did not yet completely control the countryside. Bouquet's forces controlled the fort but not all of Ohio country. The Ohio Valley was further secured in 1759 when the British forces took Fort Ticonderoga, Fort Niagara, and won the Battle of Quebec in September. Although the Seven Years' War would continue a few years longer, the French and Indian War in North America was coming to an end.

All the early attempts at colonization of Ohio country had been completely stopped by the war. The Braddock Road was undoubtedly used by war parties but no peaceful traffic utilized the road. Not only was Ohio country unavailable, but all the western settlements of Pennsylvania, Maryland, and Virginia had been pushed east by the war, and the western parts of these provinces were a wasteland. Nevertheless, the desire to move west and the pressure to do so did not diminish during the war but actually built up during the war years.

The Ohio Company lands were devastated and its buildings destroyed during the war. It is on record as issuing only one company order from 1753 to 1759. After six years of forced inactivity they did not give up, "the Ohio Company renewed its interests and vigorously explored all avenues which might lead to a legal title or patent to a huge tract of land on the Ohio." There was now a large British fort at the Forks, "yet the Company to all intents and purposes had lost its great land grant 'west of the Alleghenies.'" The Ohio Company tried to recoup. If nothing else the war had run out the clock on the original grant's seven years to settle the granted land. In their July 6, 1759, meeting, they ordered their secretary, John Mercer, to draw up the case on why they were unable to meet their obligation to settle. Presumably this would be persuasive and they would get their original grant back.[78] It did not happen.

The war, as they say, changed everything. The pressure for new settlement had built up and people were starting to move. They were moving to a new environment, one set up by the British Home government to prosecute the war, rather than one set by provincial governments. The British government and regular troops had set up forts including, Fort Cumberland, Fort Bedford, Fort Ligonier, and most conspicuously, Fort Pitt. It had constructed roads, such as the Braddock Road and the Forbes' Road, to move troops into battle. Although there was still a conflict between Virginia and Pennsylvania on the ownership of the Forks of the Ohio that was now was overshadowed by the presence of His Majesty's regulars in Fort Pitt. The Indians surely noticed that. They had had assurances, as recently as Easton, that once the French were driven out, the Indians would have the land west of the Alleghenies. Now they began to wonder.

This military presence and the diminishment of Indian attacks by French allies had consequences. People now started taking advantage of the roads and forts, especially traveling these two main roads, Braddock's and Forbes's, and settling around the forts. This was advantageous for both parties, the military and the settlers. The farmers felt safer because of the presence of the forts. They were able to grow large crops and found willing buyers in the occupants of the forts, who, for their part, didn't have to go far for provisions. The army encouraged this arrangement for cost reasons. As early as 1759, the German migration from Pennsylvania, down through Maryland and into the Shenandoah Valley, resumed. Farmers and hunters traveled even farther, into the Carolinas. They avoided areas in the south where there was still violence, such as where the war with the Cherokee was still going in the Carolinas.[79]

The British had won the competition for the country by defeating the French. The Indians still assumed the land was theirs but their competition now was only with the British. It was an unequal contest in which the stronger party sets the terms. This was obvious when the traders were the first ones back into Ohio. They came in great numbers and the prices for their trade goods was higher. "George Croghan reported that the Indians 'complained of the price of strouds [a coarse woolen cloth] saying it was dearer than what they formerly gave the traders for it.'"[80] There were also other constraints on trade. Now that the British had taken over many smaller French forts, the Indians lost their bargaining positions because they were required to travel to these forts to complete their trades.

By the end of the war in 1763, "the movement of traders throughout the Ohio country and beyond had gotten completely out of control; a list of traders killed that year showed they had been in virtually every town west of Fort Pitt. In the meantime, Johnson was forced to admit that he was 'at a loss what steps are to be taken' to regain control over the trade and, th[r]ough it, the Indians."[81] In addition to the traders, the Ohio Valley was now invaded by large numbers of hunters looking for hides and meat, competing with Indian hunters on Indian hunting grounds. Most of these hunters were Virginians, which meant they had crossed the mountains using the Braddock Road. This movement started in 1759 after the British erected Fort Pitt and was impossible to ignore by 1761: "From Redstone Creek Sergeant Angus McDonald reported 'Crowds of hunters' moving through the Monongahela Valley in October of that year. To the north, at Fort Pitt, Bouquet tried to cope with 'repeated Complaints from the Indians about hunters who were Making the natives' fall hunt more difficult—and more dangerous.'"[82] The numbers of settlers around the forts were becoming overwhelming. Anderson distinguishes between "licensed," and "unlicensed but tolerated," and "illegal" settlers. Presumably the licensed ones were licensed by the fort to remain and the illegal ones were squatters. Some of the squatters were on land that George Croghan owned on the Allegheny. The irony is that many of these "illegals" were providing substantial food and fodder for the forts. They were demonstrating the fertility of the Ohio Valley itself, the reason everyone wanted to go there. "Only fourteen families were reported to be living in the vicinity of Red Stone Old Fort in 1761, forty or so miles from Pittsburgh; but they floated a thousand bushels of corn down the Monongahela to the Forks."[83]

The invasion became so overwhelming that early in 1760 Colonel Bouquet complained to the governor of Virginia that the Monongahela was being "over run by ...Vagabonds, who under pretense of hunting, were making settlements." He was still trying to abide by the Treaty of Easton, which allocated all the land west of the Alleghenies to the Indians. Attempting to stop the settlement Bouquet issued a proclamation in October 1761, No. 4— PROCLAMATION AGAINST SETTLING,

> Whereas by a Treaty held at East town in the year 1758, and since ratified by His Majesty's Ministers, the Country to the West of the Allegany Mountains is allowed to the Indians for their Hunting Ground, and it is of the Highest Importance to his majesty's service, the preservation of the peace and a good understanding with the Indians, to avoid giving them any just cause of Complaint, this is therefore to forbid any of His Majesty's subjects to Settle or Hunt to the West of the Allegany Mountains on any Pretence Whatsover.[84]

It didn't work. People were on the move not only the Ohio Valley but all along the frontier, from Nova Scotia to the Carolinas. As Anderson points out,

> The fundamental force at work in them all, was the dynamism of a farming population seeking opportunity.... American farmers moved to take up new lands regardless of virtually every factor but the safety of their families.... With the defeat of the French accomplished and the Indians

unlikely to mount effective military resistance, therefore, both governments and private enterprises tried to position themselves to take advantage of population movements that no one could control.[85]

The Ohio Company was one of the private enterprises trying to get Bouquet to budge. Colonel Bouquet was aware of Thomas Cresap's efforts to get settlers from Virginia and Maryland to move to Ohio. In the process Cresap offered Bouquet twenty-five thousand acres for himself, which Bouquet refused. Whether Cresap made this offer on his own or on behalf of the company is unknown. Twice the Ohio Company made the offer of a share in the company, once through Cresap and once through George Mercer an officer in the company. Bouquet refused both.[86]

As the war wound down on the frontier, between 1760 and 1763, many more people simply moved to Ohio either as squatters or as settlers who thought they were on land they had rightful title to. There was no count so the number of migrants is unknown. The tribes of the Ohio country were increasingly resentful of these intrusions they believed should be precluded by the Treaty of Easton. Part of the responsibility for this problem was the lack of policy from the British government. Prior to the war there had been no British policy regarding land in Ohio, London allowed the colonies to determine their own policy. This set colony against colony as, for example, Pennsylvania and Virginia who competed for both trade and land in Ohio. There had been a tacit acknowledgment by the British government that it was a good idea for the Ohio Company to claim the Ohio land in order to preclude the French from actually taking possession of the land, which they also claimed. At the close of the war the situation was now very different. One of the three competitors for the land was no longer a factor; it was now only the British and the Indians. This was a problem for the Indians, because unlike the French, the English intended to settle the land and the Indians knew it.

The fighting on the frontier had ended, the formal end to the Seven Years' War (the French and Indian War) was concluded in the Treaty of Paris on February 10, 1763. France ceded, and Britain claimed, all the land in North America east of the Mississippi (except New Orleans), and thus *all* of Ohio country. This provision shocked the Ohio Indians. As Hurt (*The Ohio Frontier: Crucible of the Old Northwest, 1720–1830*) relates, "Newcomer, head of the Delawares, reportedly was 'struck dumb for a considerable time.' Croghan reported that the Ohio Indians insisted that the 'French had no Right to give away our Country; as, they Say, they were never Conquered by any Nation.'"[87] This was the final insult. Since the British had won control of the Ohio country there had been restrictions on Indian movement, including trading restrictions, increases in the cost of trade goods, colonial hide hunters, and settlements on the Ohio. With no French counterweight the Indians lost all leverage. The Indians anticipated this; as in other times of stress, a religious prophet emerged in 1761, preaching a religious revival. The Delaware prophet Neolin advocated a return to nativist culture and a rejection of European culture and goods. His people should return to their original clothing and farming, the boys should learn to use the original weapons the bow and arrow. He urged the separation of whites and Indians and rejected trade between them. Neolin had followers far across the Ohio country, but the signing of the treaty was the event that convinced the Indians that the only way to keep, or regain, their Ohio land was to separate the Indians and whites.[88]

Neolin's idea of separation inspired others to take back their land by force. The fighting started in the far northwest where the Ottawa chief Pontiac led a band of western Indians, Ottawas, Potawatomies, and Wyandots, against the garrison at Fort Detroit and put it under siege. In a series of local uprisings rather than a coordinated assault, they quickly overran all the other forts west of Detroit. The Ohio Indians, Delaware, Shawnee, and Mingo started raiding the eastern forts in late May 1763, all the way from Fort Niagara down to Fort Pitt, which was also besieged. Forts Venango, Le Boeuf, and Presque Isle fell in June. The Indian raiders hit settlements on the Forbes Road and attacked as far east in Pennsylvania as Carlisle. They roamed and raided the Virginia back country from the Potomac to Carolina. This activity resembled the early days of the war just concluded, the days of the frontier Indian raids of 1755–1757. Although Pontiac was not directly leading the total war it took his name as the nominal leader, it was becoming Pontiac's War or Pontiac's Rebellion.[89]

This was a bloody, furious reprisal by the tribes who had lost land over the years through a series of treaties, but now lost it all without even being party to the negotiations for this treaty. The British leadership was clearly taken by surprise and those on the frontier, the traders, settlers, and hunters while less surprised, were no less devastated by the attacks. After the war the British forces had been reduced at all the forts, replaced by less experienced regulars or militia. The British knew they had one major advantage—time. In the previous conflicts the Indians had French allies and French suppliers, but now they did not. If the British could hold onto the major forts they knew the Indians would soon run short of ammunition and food. The three largest forts, Fort Detroit, Fort Niagara, and Fort Pitt, did not fall, but all had to be resupplied and reinforced. Colonel Bouquet had this responsibility regarding Fort Pitt.

The Indian sieges of the forts continued and the conflict was prolonged due to the lack of overwhelming force by the British. It took Bouquet months to fight his way to relieve Fort Pitt. The war continued deep into 1764 as the British missed opportunities to settle and the Indians, suffering from a lack of supplies, disagreed among themselves over prolonging the war or making a truce. Finally, in the summer of 1764 the British sent out two expeditions, one from Fort Niagara led by Colonel John Bradstreet, and one from Fort Pitt led by Colonel Bouquet. Bradstreet was to go to Detroit via Lake Erie and Bouquet was to subdue the Ohio Indians through the Muskingum Valley. Over the next several months, truces were made and fighting decreased, largely due to the exhaustion of the two parties. The Indians knew they could inflict damage and win some battles but recognized they could not prevail in the long run. A peace was reached in 1765.[90]

The uprising stung the British government. Although the war with France was over, a new one had taken its place caused by their own Native American policy. This policy was one of domination demanding sovereignty over the Indians and confiscation of their land, which the Native Americans naturally resisted. The French, never trying to "own" Indian land had a much better rapport with the Indians explaining why the natives were surprised that their father in New France, Onontio, had abandoned them.

These wars had two effects. The first was the British realization that they could not draw down the army after the war with France as they had hoped. The British force had grown very large and was expensive to maintain, but the Indian wars convinced them they would need to keep troops in the colonies to protect the frontiers. The second effect was that the British finally acknowledged they had some responsibility toward the Native Americans and began to reexamine their Indian policy between 1761 and 1763.

George III, a keen supporter of the army, conceived how to do both. In the new British policy, very few troops would remain in Britain but twenty of the new battalions would be stationed in America. Parliament would pay for their troops in America in 1763, but thereafter taxes on the colonies would support them. Not long after the Peace of Paris, and while Pontiac's War was still going on, these acts to increase revenue were implemented. A very willing Parliament passed the American duties Act of 1764, the Sugar Act. There was almost no dissent and as Israel Maudit the representative of Massachusetts in London, noted,

> There did not seem to be a single man in Parliament, who thought that the conquered provinces ought to be left without troops, or that England after having run so deeply in Debt for the conquering those provinces ... should now tax itself for the maintenance of them. The only Difference of opinion ... was that Mr. Grenville said he did not expect that America should bear more than a good part of this expense; whereas other leading Members not of the Ministry said it ought to bear the whole.[91]

To Parliament, the Sugar Act seemed to be a rather easy and inconsequential law, but the reaction in the eastern parts of the colonies was anything but inconsequential. This was the first of many acts of Parliament over the next twelve years that would eventually lead to a war even more consequential than the one just ended.

The second change after the war having to do with British Indian policy led to more near term effects. As adept as they had been in dealing with the Iroquois through the Covenant Chain for seventy years, especially through the Indian agent William Johnson, and as successful as they had been in smoothing over previous land acquisition treaties, the British still had hypocritical and conflicting policies with the Indians. During the recent war, they realized they had mismanaged relations with the Indians by allowing the colonies to come up with inconsistent policies and allowing them to compete for Indian land without any central direction from London.

The response to this perceived mismanagement was the Proclamation of 1763. The Proclamation, issued by George III, was hastily put together and was issued on October 7. The news of Pontiac's Rebellion reached London in early August and on August 5 the Board of Trade decided they had to issue a proclamation to assure the protection of the Indians' hunting ground. They sent a letter to the King suggesting exactly that.[92] The Proclamation included the instructions for the new colonies of Quebec, East and West Florida, and Grenada, but it was focused primarily on Indian lands by laying out those boundaries. That was done in two paragraphs,

> no Governor or Commander in Chief in any of our other Colonies or Plantations in America do presume for the present, and until our further Pleasure be known, to grant Warrants of Survey, or pass Patents for any Lands beyond the Heads or Sources of any of the Rivers which fall into the Atlantic Ocean from the West and North West, or upon any Lands whatever, which, not having been ceded to or purchased by Us as aforesaid, are reserved to the said Indians, or any of them.
>
> And We do further declare it to be Our Royal will and Pleasure, for the present aforesaid, to reserve under our Sovereignty, Protection, and Dominion, for the use of the said Indians, all the Lands and Territories not included within the limits of Our said Three new Governments ... as also all the Lands and Territories lying to the Westward of the Sources of the Rivers which fall into the Sea from the West and North West as aforesaid.[93]

These paragraphs define the crest of the Appalachians, specifically the Alleghenies, the crest of which constitutes the Eastern Continental Divide, as the boundary between the colonial lands in the east and the Indian hunting grounds in the west. The colonists were not permitted to settle west of this boundary.

This action was taken in haste and many have claimed it was only meant to be an interim step to stop the surge of migration into Ohio. This is evident even in the above paragraphs which include phrases such as "do presume for the present, and until our further Pleasure be known," and "for the present aforesaid." It also violated the legitimate proprietary grant to Pennsylvania, which, although still in dispute with Virginia, was known to go beyond the Appalachians. It apparently was never contested but presumably a royal proclamation would take precedence over a colonial grant. The Board of Trade members were aware of these issues and there were discussions beforehand that specifically addressed some purchases and grants that were objectionable to the Indians. These included some New York purchases, the grant of land on the Ohio the British government made to the Ohio Company, and the various patents in Ohio given by the Virginia governor.[94] The Proclamation was issued despite these concerns.

There was also the issue of the many white settlers already in the prohibited area. What was to become of them? By the Proclamation they were "forthwith to remove themselves from such Settlements." This was not only impractical in general but especially so for these settlers who came from Northern Ireland and the borderlands between England and Scotland (Scots-Irish or Scotch-Irish) during the last four decades. For centuries, these people had known war and the hardscrabble existence on the border and in the highlands. They were used to that hard life and sought border frontiers. When they immigrated to America, they were the first to take the Great Valley Road to the borderlands of Virginia and the Carolinas, and the first to settle on the distant western Pennsylvania borders. They sought to destroy Indians, and to settle on any land they could take, without regard to title. They fit well into the mountains of Appalachia. They would not voluntarily leave the Ohio land they had settled, and there was no practical way for the government to remove them.[95]

Simultaneously London had to address the policy that was implicit from the time of the grant to the first colony, Virginia, when it was granted "sea to sea" rights. Pennsylvania and Maryland had limited western borders but Virginia and other colonies had charters that went to the Pacific. Many decisions, such as the Ohio Company grant, also presumed a westward movement; there was a built-in bias toward expanding westward. Already there were those in the British government who thought the colonists in the existing eastern colonies needed room for expansion.

For all these reasons the Board of Trade knew the Proclamation of 1763 was a temporary expedient, as signaled by the words, "for the present." They were already considering moving the boundary line to include the upper Ohio River because of all the settlers already there. As this could not be done in a timely manner, it was kept off the table and the easily defined mountain ridge was set as the boundary. Others had the same "temporary expedient" attitude, whether because of the incompleteness of the document or what they saw as its unenforceability. George Washington was angry when he first heard of the Proclamation as he had always considered the need for the country to move westward, and he owned land in the Ohio country he was afraid of losing. In a letter to his friend William Crawford Washington says, "I can never look upon that proclamation in any other light ... than as a temporary expedient to quiet the minds of the Indians. It must fall, of course, in a few years especially when those Indians consent to our Occupying the Lands."[96] Washington was prescient as that is exactly what happened.

Treaty of Fort Stanwix 1768 and Lord Dunmore's War

Colonial settlers and traders ignored the Proclamation of 1763, moving into the Ohio Valley in large numbers, thousands. As Hurt notes,

> These "Frontier People" sought not accommodation with the Ohio Indians but rather their removal. Compromise did not enter their thoughts, and magnanimity never governed their actions. British officials in the west considered them to be the "very dregs of the people" and "lawless banditti." General Gage contended that these frontier men and women were "a Sett of People ... near as wild as the

country they go in, or the People they deal with, & by far more vicious & wicked." Respecting personal freedom more than law and advocating their right to take unused land rather than to await negotiated settlements with the trans-Appalachian Indians, these frontier people moved relentlessly into the Ohio Valley and soon cast covetous eyes to the rich lands west of the river.[97]

The situation on the frontier had changed dramatically in only thirteen years. Prior to 1750 the mountains had been both a real and symbolic dividing line between the French western empire and the British colonies on the East Coast. In the mid–Atlantic the French never made a claim to land east of the mountains. The British, on the other hand, always had eyes on the west especially the Virginians who took their "sea to sea" grant seriously.

Once the Indian threat subsided along these roads, even before the Treaty of 1763 formally ended the war, there was no natural brake on migration to the Ohio country. Neither Bouquet's proclamation in 1761, nor the king's proclamation in 1763 put a stop to that migration. It was if the gash only widened and the flood of people increased. As Hurt notes, "By 1774 approximately fifty thousand whites lived on the trans-Appalachian frontier and the British army could not control them, being in the words of Gage 'too Numerous. Too Lawless and Licentious ever to be restrained.'"[98] The Proclamation of 1763 was at least an acknowledgment by the British government of some responsibility to the Indians; that was new. Knowing that the Proclamation was only an expedient stopgap, and ignored by settlers another attempt to settle the boundary with the Indians was needed. So far most of the squatting in the Ohio country had been east of the Ohio River. There was hope that this trend could be maintained.

British Indian policy was examined once more after the Proclamation of 1763 in an attempt to better define the ambiguous line set forth in the Proclamation. The next attempt at clarification was in 1768 at a conference at Fort Stanwix, present-day Rome, New York. This conference would also address trouble with the Cherokee in the south. The Board of Trade gave specific instructions to William Johnson, Superintendent of Indian Affairs for the Northern department, and Colonel John Stuart, Superintendent for the Southern Department on how they were to draw the lines. Colonel Stuart completed his work and the Treaty of Hard Labor was signed by October 1768, creating line separating Indians and settlers that went from the mouth of the Great Kanawha River (on the Ohio) south through the Carolinas, Georgia and Florida. Johnson was directed to run the line from Owegy, Pennsylvania, on the Susquehanna River, down the Susquehanna to Shamokin, up the west branch to the Kittanning Creek on the Allegheny, down the Allegheny and Ohio to the mouth of the Great Kanawha River where it would meet the line drawn by Stuart. This would have provided colonial access to all the land east of the Ohio River, a sizable portion of the Ohio country, but would leave all of the present state of Ohio and all of the future Tennessee and Kentucky in Indian hands.[99]

William Johnson, well-respected Indian agent and acknowledged friend of the Iroquois, did not follow his orders. Instead he drew a line that started farther north in Pennsylvania, near Fort Stanwix, snaked its way through Pennsylvania and reached the Allegheny River at Kittanning Creek, the point that was included in the instructions. Then his line went down the Ohio, not stopping at the Great Kanawha, but continuing all the way to the confluence of the Ohio and Tennessee rivers, near present-day Paducah, Kentucky. This forced Stuart to reopen negotiations to include the Tennessee River boundary. There were many secret negotiations and much speculation on why Johnson unilaterally changed the boundary he was instructed to negotiate. Billington ("The Fort Stanwix Treaty of 1768") covers the topic well, basically concluding that there were favors given to some land companies in the area.[100]

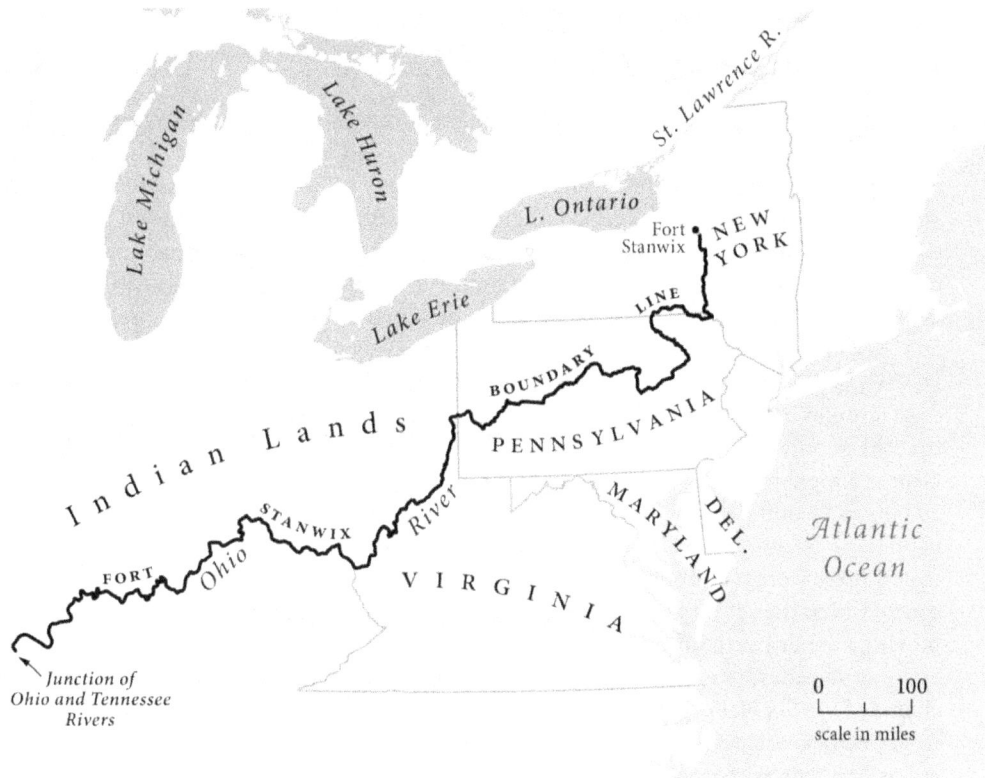

Map 10: Stanwix Treaty Line. This map, with the Stanwix line following the Ohio River, shows the clear demarcation between the territory reserved for the Indians in Ohio, and the territory reserved for colonial expansion in Kentucky and western Virginia. This separation was the reason Kentucky was settled several years earlier than Ohio.

The Loyal Land Company and the Greenbrier Company were formed in the late 1740s, about the same time as the Ohio Company of Virginia and for the same reason, to enjoy profits from land sales on the other side of the Alleghenies. Competitors of the Ohio Company, their grants were in western Virginia, past the Alleghenies but well south of the Ohio country. The Greenbrier grant was on the Greenbrier River. Their lands and settlers suffered the same wartime depredations by the Indians as were experienced in Pennsylvania, Maryland and Virginia. The traders who had been doing business in the Ohio country, including George Croghan, also suffered loss of their trade goods estimated to be in the tens of thousands of pounds sterling. A number of these traders, again including Croghan, banded together after the war to try to get recompense from the Indians. This group, known as the "suffering traders," later known as the Indiana Company petitioned for land from Pittsburgh down the Ohio to the Little Kanawha, then back to the Monongahela and to Pittsburgh. This territory was clearly in Ohio country.[101]

The common denominator of these claims was that they were all on the west side of the Proclamation line of 1763. Had the Proclamation line been maintained or Johnson's orders from the Board of Trade been followed, these claims would all be invalid because these lands would have remained Indian lands. Johnson was urged to change his line to comport with his orders, but he did not. The Stanwix treaty opened *all* the land below the Ohio River to white settlement all the way to the Tennessee River. This includes the present states of Kentucky and Tennessee. Stuart negotiated the Treaty of Lochaber with the Cherokee in 1770 to adjust the boundary of the Treaty of Hard Labor line and make it compatible with the Fort Stanwix line.

The Allegheny Mountain barrier, which had held for decades between the colonists in the east and the Ohio Indians in Ohio country, had been breached. The settlers came pouring across the mountains in large numbers, many undoubtedly using Braddock's Road and Forbes' Road. There was no company in operation to mark off and sell the land. The Ohio Company tried to renew their grant after the war but it was unable to do so. The other land companies were just starting or never began. It probably made little difference as the settlers assumed they could just settle on any land they wanted to; most were squatters. Because of the lack of any organization there was no way to tell how many migrated. In 1767, even before the Treaty of Fort Stanwix, merchants estimated there were four hundred families living in the Monongahela Valley. "By 1771 those traveling in the west claimed that the 'Country beyond the Laurel Hill as far as Redstone' was already 'full of People.' George Croghan, attempting to be more specific, reported that some 5,000 families, perhaps 20,000 to 25,000 people, lived west of the mountains."[102] The rush of migration was also happening farther south, in Kentucky. In 1774 Lord Dunmore, Governor of Virginia, estimated there were ten thousand people south of the Ohio River, which was now the barrier across which the settlers and the Ohio Indians faced each other. The demarcation line was moving farther north and west.[103]

For decades, the Ohio Indians, Shawnee, Delaware, and Mingo, had been treated as clients of the Six Nation Iroquois. They had grown farther apart in recent years, especially when the Iroquois willingly traded client lands for their own benefit. This is what happened at Fort Stanwix where the Iroquois ceded all the lands south and east of the Ohio River to the British because were not lands the Iroquois used. They were lands of the Ohio Indians and these tribes did not concur with the terms of the Treaty of Fort Stanwix thus breaking with the Six Nations. A familiar pattern was developing as another boundary settlement with the Indians, farther west, was settled in a treaty with terms which, understandably, did not sit well with the Ohio Indians. The prospect for more violence was inevitable.

> What neither the Indians nor the Crown proved able to effectively confront was the one frontier problem they shared: the rising tide of border settlements that, after 1765, threatened to engulf Kentucky and other parts of the Ohio Country. For the next decade the Ohio country became the scene of an increasing cycle of violence as settlers from Virginia staked their claims in the west. Their moves were encouraged by a declining imperial authority as the few troops in the west were sent to confront the incipient rebellion in the east. Moreover, the Virginians carried into the west not only an insatiable appetite for land but virulent Indian hating and a territorial dispute with Pennsylvania that made another war all but inevitable by 1774.[104]

Violence erupted in May 1774, based on a provocative act when some Mingo were lured across the Ohio River at Yellow Creek, near present-day Steubenville, Ohio, by Virginians who murdered them. The Shawnee and Mingo retaliated and once again the frontier was a bloody battlefield. In Virginia, Governor Dunmore started to raise a force to pursue Ohio Indians, but this time he was motivated by an added twist.[105]

In 1772 the government had abandoned Fort Pitt, knowing there was no danger from France in the west which allowed them to put their time and resources toward dealing with the controversy engendered by the crises in the east. Jurisdiction for the fort passed to Pennsylvania, reawakening the colonial issue of the Pennsylvania-Virginia border dispute about who owned the Forks of the Ohio. In January 1774, Virginia Governor Dunmore asked Dr. John Connolly to raise a militia, go to the fort, and claim it for Virginia. After a short legal battle with Pennsylvania, Connolly and the militia remained at the fort when Dunmore rechristened it Fort Dunmore on April 25, 1774. Dunmore was anxious to get militia into the area to solidify the Virginia claim to land west of the mountains including Pennsylvania land. Dunmore was interested in having Virginians settle in the west and may have been a land speculator himself. All these interests came together when he decided to act against the Ohio Indians.[106]

Dunmore quickly raised two armies of about one thousand men each to be deployed to Ohio. He sent one army under Colonel Andrew Lewis down the Kanawha toward the Ohio, and he commanded the second army himself. He led his northern army from Fort Cumberland, across the Braddock Road to the Redstone Creek, on to Fort Dunmore (Pitt), and down the Ohio. They were to meet Lewis's army at the mouth of the Hocking River in Ohio and attack the Indians from there. These plans were disrupted when the Shawnee, under chief Cornstalk, attacked Lewis at the Kanawha and Ohio in the Battle of Point Pleasant on October 10, the only real battle of what became known as Lord Dunmore's War. Dunmore pursued Cornstalk up the Hocking River and a few days later an armistice was signed. The terms required the Shawnee to yield their hunting rights in Kentucky, which meant they had now de facto agreed to the terms of the Stanwix treaty. This was the first direct land cession by the Ohio Indians. Previously the Six Nations had ceded many of the Ohio Indian lands, but the Ohio Indians never did so until this time. The Virginians agreed not to hunt north of the river in Ohio.[107] The Ohio River was now the new border.

Although it was always difficult to raise militia in the colonies, Dunmore was able to raise a force of two thousand. Part of his success was probably due to the threat posed by the Indians on the western frontier and part was probably the desirability of the land that would be available once the Indians were removed. Another factor which was making people more sensitive to the need of a militia was the increasingly volatile situation in the east. The Tea Act of 1773 and the resulting Boston Tea Party had taken place in May and December of 1773. As a result of the Tea Party, the government closed down Boston with the Boston Port Act in March 1774. The first Continental Congress met in September 1774 and was in session during the Battle of Point Pleasant. Dunmore must have had mixed feelings about helping the Virginia colony protect its western frontier. He was a Loyalist and within the next six months he would be at war with the very colony he was presently leading.

Dunmore's march on the Braddock Road is the last known military use of this road. Of course, settlers into the Ohio country were still using it, but the war, which started in April 1775, would slow that movement for the duration. Another war had once again closed the door to Ohio.

Five

The Changing West

There was no peaceful movement of settlers to the Ohio country during the French and Indian War because the war zone extended on both sides of the mountains, as far as Carlisle, Pennsylvania, in the east. Before the end of the war and the neutralization of the French threat, impetuous hunters and settlers started to move in large numbers into the Ohio country even though it was unorganized, illegal, and unsafe. Their routes were dangerous, and may have been by the Forbes Road through Fort Pitt, the Braddock-Burd Road to the Monongahela, or through Kentucky, probably all three. Pontiac's Rebellion in 1763 and Lord Dunmore's War in 1774 created a constant state of conflict until the American colonies rebelled in 1775.

The fighting after Lord Dunmore's War never stopped, continuing after the colonies declared their independence and became states. Throughout the War for Independence fighting went on not only in the east, but in Ohio. During this war, the Ohio Indians felt most threatened by the Americans and tended to support the British operating from Fort Detroit. The Americans operated out of Fort Pitt. There was a great deal of bloodshed and brutality on both sides with guilty and innocent suffering alike. An American raid on a Moravian village in Ohio resulted in about one hundred innocents, Indians and whites, being trapped and slaughtered, one of many similar incidents. The war ended in 1783 but the violent clashes in Ohio did not stop.[1]

The last quarter of the eighteenth century was a turbulent one for the original thirteen colonies, later states, as well as for the land west of the Alleghenies. That land was in an almost continual state of war for over forty years after 1755; the conflict with the Indians continued into the 1790s. But by the end of the century the main fighting had ceased and there was an organized way for people to move into Ohio and beyond, land they had been coveting for over fifty years.

Westward movement started in earnest during this period.

Western Virginia

The treaty that William Johnson negotiated at Fort Stanwix in 1768 was different from previous treaties. It did not use the mountains as a boundary between the colonists and the Indians, but by following the Ohio River westward, the boundary was essentially perpendicular to the mountains in the west. As usual there was land reserved for the Indians, in this case the Ohio country north and west of the Ohio River. The land south of the Ohio River was considered part of western Virginia and therefore open to Virginia settlement. It would not be easy to settle there but there was now a clear distinction that one could settle legally in western Virginia but not in Ohio. Although eventually many more settlers moved to Ohio than Kentucky, this explains why Kentucky, originally part of western Virginia, became a state over a decade earlier than Ohio.

The French and Indian War interrupted, but did not stop, the plans of Virginians to move west, but they had to accept the new reality that British lands were limited to the area east of the Mississippi and they could no longer claim the colony went from "sea to sea." Since by this time the extent of the land beyond the Mississippi was known it is doubtful there were any who thought that "sea to sea" was possible anyway. This still left a vast part of the Virginia claim to the west (Kentucky) and the northwest (Ohio), all the way to the Mississippi and the Great Lakes. The Fort Stanwix Treaty did not change the boundary of Virginia, but as far west as the Tennessee River it did separate the Indians and the colonists, the northern territories from the southern. The area above the Ohio River was Indian land, but the area below was now open to development by Virginia.

Into the 1770s, Virginia was still claiming and naming counties in the west and northwest. From 1738 to 1770 the west and northwest from the Blue Ridge through Ohio to the Mississippi was shown on Virginia maps as one county, Augusta.[2] As early as 1767 the Virginia House of Burgesses considered a new county to be carved out of Augusta County. They created Botetourt County in December1769 with a northern border from the Blue Ridge northwest and west to the Mississippi. The remainder of Augusta County still covered Ohio.[3] These were indications Virginia intended to continue its move west, including into Ohio, after the war with the French.

The people were moving faster than the General Assembly could keep pace and the Assembly acknowledged that many settlers had already moved west.[4] Three years later, in April 1772, once again a county would have to be subdivided and Botetourt County was divided into Fincastle and the new Botetourt County. The people who had moved cited the fact they were very far from the eastern counties and needed their own representation in their own county.[5] Virginia was recognizing that governing the western lands from Williamsburg would be difficult, the land would require division into smaller counties.

Quebec Act 1774

The effects of the French and Indian War lingered on in many forms years after it was officially ended in 1763. One effect was the lack of resolution concerning the ownership of Indian lands; Pontiac's Rebellion of 1763–1764 had picked up where the war left off. One of the motives for the Proclamation of 1763 was to appease Indian concerns about the obvious British land grab that was taking place. The Indians knew settling these lands had been a British policy from the beginning. They considered the land to be theirs and believed the French defeat in the war should not impact them because they didn't lose the war. Another effect of the war was the British government's need to raise revenue to cover the war expenses, leading to a series of acts beginning with the Sugar Act of 1764 and then the Stamp Act of 1765 designed to raise revenue from the colonies to pay for the recent war. Initially these acts were seen by London as benign. When the colonists resisted, the acts became more coercive. This created a cycle of violence that eventually led to the colonies rebelling and declaring themselves independent states.

These and other royal acts not only coalesced the colonial anger against the taxes being imposed but also had the colonists rethinking their relationship with the mother country. Although the proximate cause of this cycle of rebellion, war, and independence was the revenue and coercive acts, a longer view suggests this break was inevitable. The English colonies had 170 years of experience on the American mainland, an ocean apart from the mother country. They had learned how to cope by themselves, how to govern themselves, and they had developed a culture unique to their circumstances and geography. If not in 1776, the split would have happened eventually anyway. Metaphorically, it was not unlike an adolescent growing, learning, maturing and eventually leaving home to start his or her own future.

These acts weren't the reason some settlers started crossing the mountains as the war subsided, but they did cause the colonists to rethink their colonial rights, including their initial charter rights. Faced with the Proclamation of 1763 they now became more protective of their western rights.

The earlier treaties with the Indians did not involve changing any colonial boundaries but simply set lines of demarcation between the colonists and the Indians. Most of these agreements were negotiated by the colonies themselves. This changed with the Proclamation of 1763 when the British Home government unilaterally drew a line through some colonies and prohibited those colonies from expanding their settlements west of the line into an area reserved for the Indians. In the view of the colonists their colonial charter was being violated because they would be prohibited from using their own lands. Although a colonial government might respect such a boundary many settlers and squatters, did not; they crossed into Ohio country and settled along the Monongahela and the east side of the Ohio River. The Proclamation of 1763 had no practical effect.

The history of the next few years from the Stamp Act of 1765 through to the colonial rebellion, which started in 1775 is well known. The Boston Tea Party in December 1773, was followed by a series of acts, called the Intolerable Acts by the colonists, by which the royal government intended to bring the colonies in line. The first law was the Boston Port Act of March 1774, which closed Boston with the demand that Bostonians pay for all the tea destroyed in the Tea Party. The last of the Intolerable Acts was the Quebec Act of June 1774. This act had a major impact on the west.

As part of the Proclamation of 1763 after the defeat of France, four new provinces were established by the British government: Quebec, East Florida, West Florida, and Grenada. The original boundaries of Quebec were approximately those of New France with the southern boundary just below Montreal; it did not intersect the existing East Coast colonies. A civil government was set up with an assembly and English law was the law of Quebec; they expected a large influx of English immigrants. When that English population did not materialize the governor, Guy Carleton, thought it would be easier to rule without an assembly because the majority French population had no experience with a democratic assembly. He also feared another French uprising in Quebec and wanted to ensure the loyalty of the populace. His suggested solution was to go back to the semi-feudal autocracy, state church (Catholic), and French civil law.[6]

The British government also saw an opportunity to apply more pressure to the increasingly recalcitrant colonies and to provide more stability for the Indian lands of Ohio, which were being invaded by more and more settlers. They enacted the Quebec Act of 1774, which enlarged the boundaries of the Quebec province down to the Ohio River and west to the Mississippi. It included all the Indian lands north and west of the Ohio River. The eastern colonists were infuriated. Not only were they angry that the new province would have no assembly and revert to the religion and laws of the country they had just defeated, it would also literally move the western parts of some provinces, especially Virginia, into the province of Quebec. The colonists saw this as a violation of the original charter and was one the leading causes of the upcoming break between Great Britain and her American colonies.

Five. The Changing West

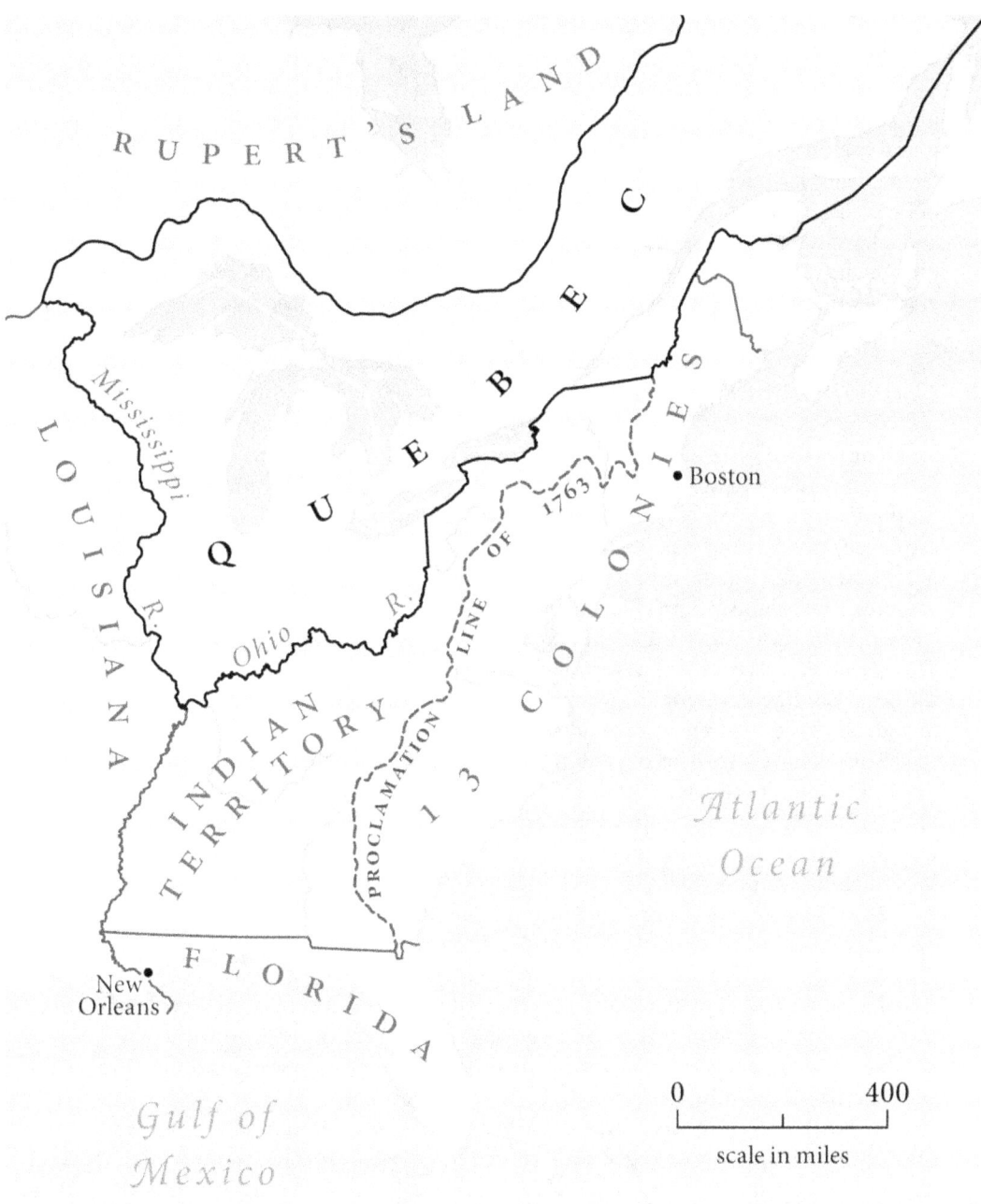

Map 11: Quebec Act, 1774. The vastly expanded province of Quebec then included all of the Ohio country.

It is not a coincidence that the War for Independence started in April 1775, only ten months after the Quebec Act. It is also not a coincidence that the two leaders in this rebellion were Boston, concerned about loss of personal liberty, and Virginia, concerned about the loss of property. The grievances about the suspension of English law and the loss of property found their way into the Declaration of Independence, penned by Virginian Thomas Jefferson, who was referring to Quebec when he complained, "For abolishing the free System of English Laws in a neighbouring Province, establishing therein an Arbitrary government, and enlarging its Boundaries so as to render it at once an example and fit instrument for introducing the same absolute rule into these Colonies." The Quebec Act was in effect for only two tumultuous years during the struggle for independence.

Confederation Congress

The Quebec Act of June 1774 was the tipping point to colonial rebellion, it precipitated the meeting of the First Continental Congress in September 1774, only three months later. As these acts were imposed over the previous decade, the colonies felt more and more estranged; the Atlantic was getting wider. They acknowledged King and Parliament, but felt they were more than keeping their part of the bargain between the mother country and colonies. The colonists didn't like the feeling of being "pushed around." Moreover, they had learned to be mostly self-sufficient and were outgrowing what they saw as a partnership. They resented certain royal governors and royal interference in internal colonial affairs. The First Continental Congress was an attempt to decide how the colonies could cooperate to address the issues they were facing.

This Congress met for only about a month before adjourning. The colonies kept in touch throughout the crises but did not reconvene with the Second Continental Congress until May 1775, just weeks after the bloodshed at Lexington and Concord in April. This Congress began the preparations for war. They established the army and appointed George Washington as commander.

After Tom Paine's "Common Sense" pamphlet in January 1776 the intense desire for declaring independence picked up and was seen to be most likely, although not yet inevitable. By June 1776, *prior* to the vote on independence, the Continental Congress established a committee to prepare for a confederation of the states that would enable them to work together to defend themselves. However, they were in no mood to come under a national government similar to that of the British Monarchy. In the meantime, independence was declared on July 4.

By July 12, 1776, the first draft of the Articles of Confederation was presented to Congress. This document was the definition of how these new states would work together during and after the War for Independence. Inevitably there was much discussion among the thirteen independent states and the Articles weren't adopted by the Continental Congress until November 15, 1777. Unanimity was required for ratification, and the document wasn't ratified until March 1, 1781, almost four years later, mostly due to the stubbornness of Maryland. The Continental Congress became the Congress of Confederation or Confederation Congress and they named themselves, "The United States of America."[7]

The Confederation was a loose one. Each colony was extremely jealous of its own history, heritage, and government, and each valued its independence. They would act together when necessary to prosecute the war but remain independent states after the war while continuing the Confederation. The foreign policy of the Confederation was exclusively the province of the Congress, states were explicitly prohibited from their own foreign policy. One of the main reasons for the Confederation was, to present a united front to foreign countries, projecting the image of a nation-state entitled to make treaties and request loans. It had the power to raise an army and issue money. The Achilles heel of the Confederation, however, was the inability to lay taxes on the states or individuals; imposing taxes was anathema to all. The tax policy of George III was the reason they were in this conflict and they were not going to put themselves back in the same situation. Instead, there would be a common treasury to which the states would contribute money when requested. In practice this did not work, time after time the states failed to provide the funds requested by the Congress. The army was destitute at times, because of the lack of funds, almost costing them the war.

Although the Confederation had a weak national government, there were a number of important agreements with significant consequences, especially for the Ohio country, which were made in that era. One significant achievement was the peace with Great Britain negotiated prior to, and concluded by, the Treaty of Paris in 1783. The American team of John Adams, Benjamin Franklin, and John Jay, negotiated a treaty in which Great Britain ceded the territory from Massachusetts and the Great Lakes down to Florida, and from the East Coast to the Mississippi River; the latter being one of the chief objectives of the American negotiators. This area was approximately four times the size of the original thirteen colonies and clearly included all of the Ohio country and much more.

The Confederation survived the war, signing the Paris Peace Treaty in 1783. In the years that followed it became more and more difficult for the states to operate under the Articles of Confederation. One reason being the inability to raise money by voluntary contributions. By 1786 leaders including George Washington, James Madison, Alexander Hamilton, and John Jay recognizing the inadequacy of the Articles, and recognizing the need for a stronger central government, led the effort that resulted in the Constitutional Convention of 1787, and eventually to the new republic in 1789.

The years from 1776 to 1789 were consequential, not only because of the success of the Revolution and the creation of a new Constitution, but also for the future of the Ohio country. Despite the dysfunction of the Confederation Congress, often suffering from lack of interest and the inability to muster a quorum, it did manage to produce some significant decisions that had a major impact on the land west of the original colonies, beyond the mountains.

One of the challenges the newly independent states faced was how they would deal with this new bounty in land that included the Ohio country—the Northwest Territory. By the time the new republic started in 1789, they knew how they would apportion the land and how they would admit new states. These decisions were made under the Confederation Congress. Although no new states were admitted under the Articles of Confederation, after 1789 the new republic lost little time in admitting new states. Ohio, among other others, was formed through this process.

Land Cessions—Maryland Assures There Will Be an Ohio

Clearly the early work of the Continental Congress after the Declaration of Independence concerned the prosecution of the war in progress; but the discussions in Congress prior to adoption of the Articles of Confederation also considered broader issues in anticipation of the situation after the war. The new states, especially Maryland, considered the western lands.

On October 15, 1777, it was moved by Maryland in Congress, "That the United States, in Congress assembled, shall have the sole and exclusive right and power to ascertain and fix the western boundary of such states as claim to the Mississippi or South Sea, and lay out the land beyond the boundary, so ascertained, into separate and independent states, from time to time, as the numbers and circumstances of the people thereof may require."[8] The motion received only one vote, that of Maryland. By this action, Maryland became the first to propose these western lands become states. This issue of western lands was not something new that Maryland had just recognized, but was an issue that had been stuck in their craw for over twenty years. In late 1753, and early 1754, when Maryland Governor Horatio Sharpe wanted to support Virginia Governor Dinwiddie's attempt to raise a force to attack the French at the Forks of the Ohio, Sharpe's Assembly rebuffed the funding request. He blamed two factors for the denial; one was an imminent election.

> The other was the fact that "our people could not as yet see things in their proper light & seemed to think the Occasion of the present Dispute was who should possess Lands ... of which they would reap no Benefit seeing the lands were already granted by his Majesty to the Ohio Company." With a definite western boundary and no opportunity to acquire territory as a result of war, Maryland refused to tax herself for the benefit of Virginia and the Ohio Company.[9]

That was over twenty years earlier, but in October 1777 Maryland was still in the same situation with a fixed western boundary, and was still worried about the other states moving to claim Ohio country after the war. The move to reserve the western lands was a rather audacious move. General Gates had just won the Battle of Saratoga, one of the few decisive victories the Americans would win, but the survival of the newly independent states was still in question, let alone that of any land beyond their borders. Nevertheless, Maryland was asserting the royal charters were now void and the Confederation Congress should take charge, fix the western boundaries of the states, and furthermore should make independent states of all the land west of those borders extending to the Mississippi. The Treaty of Paris which ended the Seven Years War in 1763 had acknowledged the Spanish claim to lands west of the Mississippi put an end to the Virginia claim of a "sea to sea" colony although Virginia still claimed Ohio country by virtue of the 1609 charter. Article II of the Articles of Confederation states, "Each state retains its sovereignty, freedom, and independence, and every other power, jurisdiction, and right." Thus the Congress had no power to tell the states what their borders were. No wonder Maryland cast the only vote for the move.

Maryland was looking ahead, as were all the states that had claims on the Ohio country and had plans for settlement there. De facto settlement had already happened in many places beyond the mountains. Maryland was making a statement and making it early. It was a small state with a definite western boundary; Marylanders knew they could not expand. They were concerned that the western land would be gobbled up after the war by the larger states, Connecticut, New York, and Virginia. Maryland would then become much smaller relative to these states with their new western territory. Other small states such as New Jersey and Delaware had similar concerns, but Maryland was much more willing to stand up and be counted.

The reaction to Maryland's effort to have the western lands laid out into states by the Congress was demonstrated by the lack of support it received and the change made to the still pending Articles of Confederation. On October 27, only twelve days after the Maryland motion, a provision was added to Article IX that said, "no state shall be deprived of territory for the benefit of the United States." That should have been the end of it, after the war

Virginia should have been allowed to claim and sell all the land they had prior to the war but that is not what happened.[10]

Maryland had the theoretical support of small states such as Delaware, New Jersey, and Rhode Island, but not for what they were proposing. "What these states desired was either a share in the revenues arising from the western country, or, that funds accruing from the sale of western lands should be applied towards defraying the expenses of the war."[11] Although this is part of what Maryland was asking for, its proposal was much more radical. It was proposing that a national entity, the Confederation Congress, assert sovereignty over the states in order to change state boundaries. This was clearly out of line with the limitations imposed in the Articles. Congress would not even have the power to tax let alone move or limit state boundaries.

Although Maryland could no longer get their proposal into the Articles, it persisted in the ultimate objective. In instructions to their delegation in December 1778, Maryland first acknowledged the reasons it was worried.

> Virginia, by selling on the most moderate terms a small portion of the lands in question, would draw into her treasury vast sums of money, and in proportion to the sums arising from such sales, would be enabled to lessen her taxes: lands comparatively cheap and taxes comparatively low, with the lands taxes of an adjacent state [Maryland], would quickly drain the state thus disadvantageously circumstanced of its most useful inhabitants, its wealth; and its consequence in the scale of the confederated states would sink of course.[12]

In other words, Virginia would become much too large compared to Maryland and have the significant advantages of size.

The instructions to the Maryland delegates then went on to state the main objective.

> We are convinced policy and justice require that a country unsettled at the commencement of this war, claimed by the British crown, and ceded to it by the treaty of Paris, if wrested from the common enemy by the blood and treasure of the thirteen states, should be considered as common property, subject to be parceled out by Congress into free, convenient and independent governments, in such manner and at such times as the wisdom of that assembly shall hereafter direct.[13]

The delegates were instructed to read these instructions before Congress. This was done on May 21, 1779, just sixteen days after Delaware was the twelfth state to ratify the Articles. Maryland would not move to ratify until the question on the western lands was settled. Also, in May 1779 the Virginia legislature passed legislation setting up a Land Office to determine terms for issuing land grants, presumably for the Ohio country.[14]

Maryland's determination not to ratify the Articles until the land issue was settled was firm. Under the Articles the states now could not be forced by Congress to turn over their western lands so the discussion switched to a request that the states cede these lands. A motion was made in Congress on September 6, 1780, by Virginia delegates Joseph Jones and James Madison:

> respecting the lands that may be ceded in pursuance of the foregoing report and resolve.
> That in case the recommendation of Congress to the States of Virginia, North Carolina and Georgia to cede to the United States a portion of their unappropriated Western Territory shall be complied with in such a manner as to be approved by Congress, the Territory so ceded shall be laid out in separate and distinct States at such time and in such manner as Congress shall hereafter direct.[15]

These Virginia delegates were acknowledging the Maryland proposal to have the Congress make states out of the western lands through state cession of the land rather than by annexation by Congress. The fact that this resolution was made by Virginians is interesting. Most Virginians, most notably Thomas Jefferson revered their Virginia home, as a sovereign state beholden to no one else. The Virginia resolution would allow a national body, the Congress, to lay out the new states using land Virginia had been claiming for over one hundred years.

Virginia was doing this under pressure; they were getting anxious. All the states were prosecuting a war as best they could under the Articles of Confederation, adopted in 1777, but not yet ratified. The Articles required unanimous consent for ratification and Maryland was still holding out.[16] It is significant that Madison was one of the delegates who proposed this resolution. Later he, along with Washington and others, would be one of the prime movers of a new Constitution with strong central government powers. This resolution may have been an early sign he was already becoming frustrated with operating under the Articles and beginning to see a need for a stronger central government. In Federalist Paper number thirty-eight Madison cited this example of creating western states that could be constructively done by a national body, the Confederation Congress.

It finally happened. In January 1781, Virginia, "offered to cede to the Confederation complete jurisdiction over all lands north-west of the Ohio." The wording of the Virginia act was taken almost verbatim from the Congressional resolution. Everyone acknowledged that this cession was primarily a final effort to achieve ratification of the Articles. New York and Connecticut also ceded the land in question. Maryland had won and it ratified the Articles of Confederation on March 1, 1781.[17]

The war ended eight months later, in October, with the victory at Yorktown. It had taken almost the entire length of the war to get the Articles ratified, an indication of the troubles the states would have operating under those Articles in the next few years. It took a while to work out the terms of some conditions Virginia had put on this cession, but this was finalized by October 1783 and the Virginia land cession was completed on March 1, 1784, three years after the ratification of the Articles of Confederation and six months after the Treaty of Paris.[18]

The Americans now knew what they were going to do with the land that eventually became Ohio.

Land Ordinances of 1784 and 1785

Cession of the lands, however, was only the first step. The states knew they had to act quickly to take charge of these lands to preclude problems and make them useful for the Confederation. Eventually the states saw the sale of these lands as a way to reduce or eliminate the war debt. There were three problems they had to deal with immediately or they wouldn't even be able to keep the land. Action wasn't taken by the states individually but by the Confederation Congress, which was decisive on the western lands issue although it was weak concerning control of the states. The Confederation Congress enacted the Land Ordinances of 1784, 1785, and 1787.

The first problem was the presence of the British in these northwestern territories. The British operated a series of forts in the area, controlled out of Detroit, and were in no hurry to leave even after the Treaty of Paris was signed in 1783. They urged the Indians to resist the Americans, claiming the Treaty of Fort Stanwix was still in force.[19] The Indian determination to stay in and control all the area northwest of the Ohio was the second problem the Confederation had to face. The Indians were clearly willing to fight to hold onto this last section of land after they had been driven out of all land east of it. The third issue, and probably the most troubling, was the influx of settlers moving into Ohio and beyond. Many of these people were squatters who took the position that they could take any land they wanted as long as they could hold it.[20] They didn't care for the rules of the governments back east. If these people moved far enough west they would be subject to control by the British, still in the territory in violation of the treaty, or even of the Spanish at the Mississippi. By settling in the far western territories of the United States these people would essentially be independent of the eastern state governments and could drift toward the British or Spanish. Should this happen the Confederation would lose any control of the land.[21]

George Washington, always interested in the west, saw these problems. In a letter to James Duane on September 7, 1783, just four days after the Treaty of Paris was signed, he said,

> Unless some such measures as I have been taken the liberty of suggesting are speedily adopted one of two capital evils, in my opinion, will inevitably result, and is near at hand; either that the settling, or rather overspreading the Western Country will take place, by a parcel of Banditti, who will bid defiance to all Authority while they are skimming and disposing of the Cream of the Country at the expence of many suffering Officers and Soldiers who have fought and bled to obtain it ... or a renewal of Hostilities with the Indians, brought about more than probably, by this very means.[22]

In the same letter Washington proposed two states for northwest of the Ohio. Interestingly they were very close to the present States of Ohio and Michigan.

Congress acted fairly rapidly. In early 1784 they established a committee of three headed by Thomas Jefferson to come up with a framework for these lands. The committee reported on March 1 and on April 23, 1784, Congress voted 22–2 to approve the Ordinance of 1784.[23]

The Ordinance was not specific as to the number of states that were to be established, stating only that they were to be bound by latitude and longitude, some of which were specified. In other words, the new states were to be laid out in a rectilinear pattern without regards to natural boundaries. There have been claims that ten states were envisioned but the specific number is not mentioned. The Ordinance did declare these states would be part of the Confederacy with the same rights and obligations as the original thirteen. When a territory reached twenty thousand residents, these residents would call a constitutional convention and establish a republican government for themselves. When they had as many free inhabitants as the least of the original states had, they could apply for statehood. Although not specific on the formation there was the acknowledgment of ultimate statehood for these western lands.

No states were admitted based on the ordinance of 1784, but Congress kept working. There were two issues that had to be addressed, how the land would be divided and laid out, and how it would be governed.

The first issue was addressed by the Land Ordinance of 1785, enacted by Congress on May 20, 1785. Although Thomas Jefferson was now minister to France and no longer in Congress, his approach of laying out the land on a rectangular grid was adopted. The Ordinance was very detailed in the way it specified the land to be laid out. Once the Indian title had been purchased (the subject of another section), the land was to be surveyed in a grid pattern. The starting point for both the north-south line and the east-west line of the grid was at the Ohio River where it crossed the western boundary of Pennsylvania. The east-west line was called the Geographer's Line or Baseline. The surveyors were to divide the land into townships of six-miles square using the north-south lines and perpendicular east-west lines. These townships were to be in vertical strips called ranges.[24]

The Pennsylvania dispute with Virginia over their common boundary was still ongoing in 1784. During the war the other states lost patience with them and urged a compromise so they would cooperate in prosecuting the war without distraction. Pennsylvania and Virginia finally created a commission to extend the Mason-Dixon Line (1767) west to the agreed longitude, five degrees west of the Delaware River to mark the western boundary of Pennsylvania.[25] The actual survey of Ohio land was started by Geographer Thomas Hutchins and geographers from eight other states on September 30, 1785, only a month after the Pennsylvania border had been established. Because that border was the starting point for the survey, the geographers had to wait until it was officially established. Hutchins recorded the mark of the Geographers line at 40°38'02".[26]

The first survey line by Hutchins was laid out forty-two miles to the west along the Geographer's Line. The starting point for the Geographer's line was the Pennsylvania border where the Ohio River crosses into Ohio, near the present-day East Liverpool, Ohio. They ran the lines south from the Geographer's Line to the Ohio River every six miles. This made seven ranges at six miles wide each. They then laid out the six-mile square townships south of this line in each of the ranges. This survey became known as the Seven Ranges and was the first methodical survey of land in the Ohio country. Most six-mile square townships were to be divided into thirty-six one-mile square sections. A section of one square mile or, 640 acres, was to be the minimum lot for sale. The minimum sale price was to be one dollar per acre. This made the land very expensive for any individual. Congress didn't want to deal in lot sales to individual settlers, but expected sales to large landowners who would then subdivide the sections for resale. All sales were to be in cash; no credit.[27]

They specified the numbering for the sections starting at one in the lower southeast corner and moving up along the range. They also reserved some sections for special purposes. Section sixteen in each township was reserved for the support of public schools. Sections eight, eleven, twenty-six, and twenty-nine were reserved for sale later by the Confederation government. They hoped these would bring higher prices because of the development around them.[28]

The Seven Ranges were laid out in this pattern, which would become the pattern for almost all of the new states that would enter the Union later. However, the Ordinance was careful to set aside some land specifically for public purposes or for sale to private groups. Some land was set aside as a military district for distribution to veterans of the Continental Army as compensation for their service as they were paid little or nothing during the war. Similarly, as part of its land cession deal, Virginia had negotiated some Ohio land for a Virginia Military District to be used, along with Kentucky land, for Virginia veterans of the war. Most of the Ohio land was laid out in the rectangular sections described but some sections were irregular. The Virginia Military District, for example, was laid out as land in Virginia was, in a "metes and bounds" system.[29]

According to Hurt, Washington had thought the Pennsylvania border would be the best place to start, because one could easily reach Pittsburgh from there and it would be a good place for the bounty claims of the Revolutionary War veterans, a group Washington was always concerned about. "This is the tract which, from local position and peculiar advantages, ought to be the first settled in preference to any other whatsoever." He was overly optimistic.[30]

The survey was not easy, and it took a long time. There were three obstacles they faced as they were surveying. One was the continuing Indian threat that caused at least one interruption of the survey. The Ohio Indians still claimed the Ohio country north of the Ohio River and would fight for it. Another problem was the influx of settlers who saw no need of official surveys and felt they could take any land they wished, continuing to move across the river as squatters. Finally, the land itself was rugged, located on the Allegheny Plateau where it was rocky, hilly, and covered with trees. This made a survey difficult to conduct, especially with the other two obstacles.

Only eight days into the survey Hutchins received word of an Indian attack about fifty miles west. His team had only surveyed four miles west of the starting point, but he reacted to the report and sent everyone back to Pennsylvania ending the survey for 1785. Surveying didn't restart until August 9, 1786, and on August 11 they marked their first line south from the six-mile point, the start of the first range. When they reached the seventh range on September 13, they again stopped because of Indian trouble. They restarted in October, this time with military protection. Weather caused them to stop at the end of the year with the completion of four ranges but with seven ranges laid out along the Geographer's line.[31] "In February 1787, Hutchins completed the plats and descriptions of four ranges and seven townships in range five, totaling 800,000 acres, and 'flattered himself that he had performed his duties to the entire satisfaction of Congress.'"[32] He hadn't. They were unhappy that only four ranges were done. They wanted the work done as quickly as possible so they could start selling the land. The work was completed by mid-summer 1788.[33]

Congress couldn't wait for all seven ranges to be complete so they started selling the land when four ranges were complete. The auction in New York was from September 21 to October 7, 1787. "The lands bordering the river sold quickly, but the rough interior lured few settlers, and Congress closed the auction after only 108,431 acres had been sold for $176,090. With the minimum bid of $1 per acre, one-third paid down and the remainder due in three months for a section of land, the terms proved prohibitive."[34] The expense and surveying problems caused Congress to end work during the Confederation period. Coincidently, there was a Constitutional Convention being held in Philadelphia in the summer of 1787, which may also have influenced the cessation of work on the surveying at the time.

Despite these early difficulties, Congress had established a system for laying out the lands in all the new states, except some (Vermont, Texas) which were part of other states at the time or were independent republics when they were admitted. This was a monumental precedent instrumental in the westward expansion of the nascent country, a plan which became known as the United States Public Lands Survey System (PLSS).

Northwest Land Ordinance of 1787

Even though the survey of the Seven Ranges wasn't complete until 1788 Congress could not wait to address the second issue, governance and statehood. While the survey was going on, and even after it was completed, the land was not part of a state; there was no western boundary of a state later known as Ohio. The survey was just the first step in the process. By this time the designation of Northwest Territory had been given to all the remaining area ceded by Great Britain, consisting of lands north of the Ohio River, west to the Mississippi, and northwest to the Great Lakes and Canada. The Northwest Territory included area that ultimately became Ohio, Indiana, Illinois, Michigan, Wisconsin, and part of Minnesota. The original states, acting through the Confederation Congress, knew that area was to be divided into an, as yet, undetermined number of states.

The Northwest Ordinance of 1787 was the action taken by Congress to establish a method of governance and to outline the process by which regions in the Northwest Territory could apply for statehood. This year, 1787, was an important year for another reason,

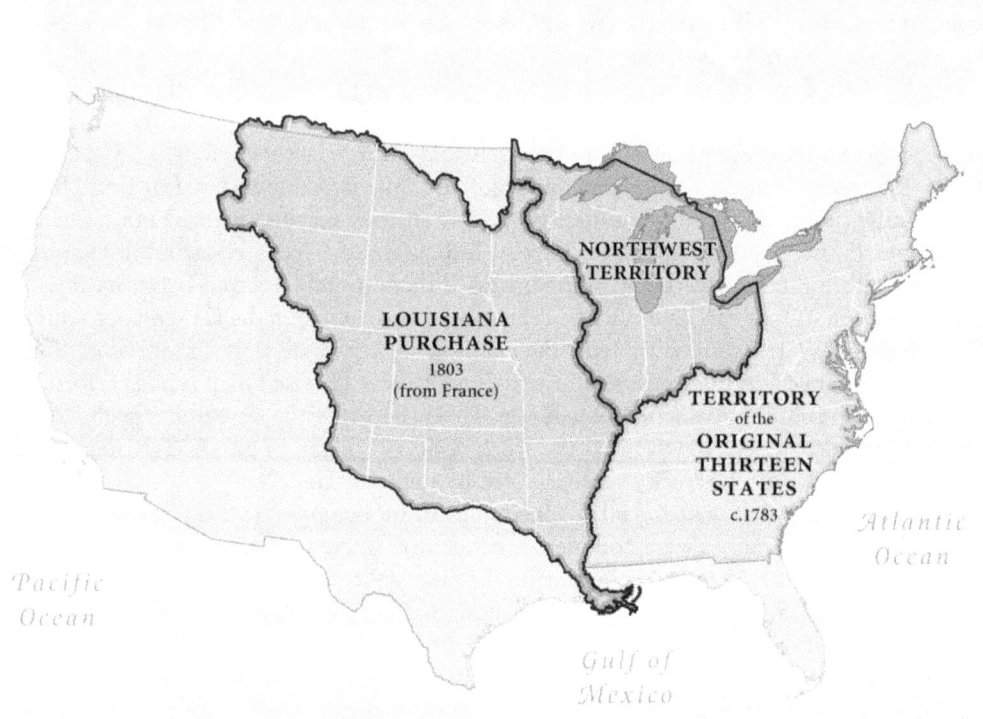

Map 12: Northwest Territory and Louisiana Purchase. The Northwest Territory extended west of Pennsylvania, north of Kentucky, and to the Mississippi. It was an area that would eventually include more than five new states.

the Constitutional Convention was being conducted in Philadelphia at the same time.[35] As Reginald Horsman points out, "Without the writing of a new constitution in the summer of 1787, the Northwest Ordinance might well have been a futile effort of a disintegrating nation rather than the keystone of a continental federal republic."[36] The word "nation" in this quote should be construed loosely. Almost nothing accomplished by the Confederation Congress during its existence, from 1781 to 1789, was done as a nation. The individual states were very concerned about maintaining their sovereignty and the Confederation was purposely kept weak. The only examples of national action came through the enactment of the Land Ordinances of 1784, 1785, and 1787, making these Ordinances all the more remarkable. Considering the jealousy each state felt for maintaining its own independence, it is almost stunning that they would invite future states, first into the Confederacy, and then into the Union, as equals to the original thirteen in all respects.

Men, such as Thomas Jefferson, who believed in the most basic form of grassroots democracy would have allowed settlers to move into the Northwest Territory and organize their own state governments believing that was the most natural approach. There was a real concern though that the formation of new constitutional governments would not take place, that there would be an unorganized rush for land farther and farther west. Congress felt it was necessary to include in the Ordinance a provision that a territorial governor and secretary would be appointed by Congress for three and four years respectively. A legislature would be elected but the governor would have veto power over any laws it enacted. It was acknowledged that these measures were temporary because states would be formed from the territory, but Congress would have control of the territory until that happened.

Even as the Constitutional Convention was meeting in Philadelphia that summer the Confederation Congress was meeting in New York to enact this Ordinance. Although the former was held with sessions in secret many of the same issues were being discussed at both gatherings. The Ordinance explicitly included many personal rights such as writ of habeas corpus, freedom of religious worship, trial by jury, no cruel and unusual punishment, and others. Ironically these rights were not included in the original Constitution of 1787, but eventually emerged in the Bill of Rights. These concepts were clearly on the minds of many, including the delegates at both of these meetings.

The key issue of governance was in Article 4 of the Northwest Ordinance which stated, "The said territory, and the states which may be formed therein, shall forever remain a part of this Confederacy of the United States of America, subject to the Articles of Confederation." There were also responsibilities as the new states "shall be subject to pay part of the federal debts contracted or to be contracted."[37] The Constitution superseded the Articles of Confederation, and during the first session starting on March 4, 1789, in New York, the First Congress reenacted the Ordinance of 1787.[38]

Article 5 got down to the specifics. It stated at least three but no more than five states were to be formed out of the Northwest Territory. The boundaries were not fixed exactly, partly because Virginia had not yet fixed the boundaries of the part of Ohio which they negotiated to keep for their military district, although they had ceded their land in Ohio country in 1784. Congress did identify three state areas generally, with an eastern state, middle state, and western state, corresponding roughly to Ohio, Indiana and the states west of Indiana. Congress also indicated that one or two more states could be carved out of the territory north and west of these. Congress would have the final approval of all the boundaries.

The final stipulation for statehood was,

> And whenever any of the said States shall have sixty thousand free inhabitants therein, such State shall be admitted, by its delegates, into the Congress of the United States, on an equal footing with the original states in all respects whatever, and shall be at liberty to form a permanent constitution and State government: Provided, the constitution and government so to be formed, shall be republican, and in conformity to the principles contained in these articles.[39]

They specifically repealed the Ordinance of 1784 to avoid confusion, it had a different method of determining the number and size of states.

It would not be possible for individuals or states to set up their own governments outside the Confederation and rule them as private domains. The size stipulation assured any new state would not overwhelm any of the original ones. Control by a Congressional Governor and then by a state government had the intended effect of tying the people in the new states closely to the original thirteen. The new states would not be allowed to stray, to become independent countries or to align with Great Britain or Spain. This was the main concern for the Confederation Congress for their relatively quick and unified action. They recognized the land west of the mountains would be hard to govern from the east. Settlers could move west rather easily but government control across the mountains would be difficult. One reason Virginia was willing to cede the Ohio country was they couldn't control it from Richmond.[40] In the previous thirty years two wars had caused the land in the Northwest Territories to change hands twice, first to the British and then to the Americans. Because of those rapid changes involving thousands of square miles, the states acting through Congress knew they had to move quickly to maintain control over the inevitable rapid changes in the future.

The area that was to become the State of Ohio was now established and the rules were in place allowing it to become a state. The surveying of the first lands, the Seven Ranges, was continuing and would be completed the next year. As far as the Confederation Congress was concerned there was now an orderly procedure for settlers to buy land, move in, and when the numbers were sufficient, to become a state.

However, this was not the scenario accepted by the Native Americans who inhabited the Northwest Territory.

Ohio

The Northwest Ordinance of 1787 established the possibility of a State of Ohio by enabling development but not assuring it. The land, beyond the Seven Ranges, had to be distributed, surveyed and sold. Most important, it had to be secured. The Americans wanted to treat the Native Americans fairly, by paying them for the land, but like the British before them they assumed they could take the land, pay for it, and that the natives would just move on. Many viewed the situation the same way that George Washington did. His logic was simple. The Indians had sided with the British, the British lost the war, therefore the Indians lost the war and, given proper compensation, they would have to move out. It wasn't that easy. The Native Americans conceded the land south of the Ohio but still saw the northwest as theirs through the validity of the Treaty of Fort Stanwix. The British, who still held forts in the northwest, encouraged the Native Americans to cling to that treaty.

Ohio Indian Wars

Once again, another treaty had been made, the 1783 Treaty of Paris, in which the British and American adversaries made peace and divided up land without any participation of the Native Americans living on that land. The Ohio Indians, mostly Miami, Wyandot, Ottawa, Ojibwa, and Shawnee, saw the last of their land being forfeited felt they had one last chance to keep the land north of the Ohio. For almost ten years a series of battles between the Indians and Americans took place, they paused before continuing early in the nineteenth century. Before, during, and after the War for Independence settlers were moving to Ohio ignoring the violence of the war. The Indians resisted this migration, resulting in a great deal of bloodshed that was independent of the War itself.

Early in 1785, Congress sent a party, including Richard Butler and George Rogers Clark to meet at Fort McIntosh on the Ohio River in Pennsylvania with the Wyandot, Delaware, Ottawa, and Ojibwa in order to negotiate a treaty. Under duress, these tribes relinquished their lands in southeast Ohio and agreed to a reserved area in northwest Ohio, west of the Cuyahoga River at present-day Cleveland. The Treaty of Fort McIntosh was signed January 21, 1785, but was immediately repudiated by the Shawnee who claimed they had not given authority for the agreement. Their lands in southern Ohio were the most affected.[41]

In retaliation, the Shawnee instituted numerous raids across the river into Kentucky. George Rogers Clark, a successful Indian fighter in the Ohio country during the War for Independence, led raids into Ohio from Kentucky to punish the Shawnee. This did not lead to peace but further inflamed tensions leading to the prolonged war. The states had little military strength, prompting the Secretary of War, Henry Knox, to ask Arthur St. Clair, Governor of the Northwest Territory, to meet with the Indians at Fort Harmer (Marietta) in an attempt to stop the fighting with another agreement. On December 13, 1788, St. Clair met with representatives of the Wyandot, Ottawa, Ojibwa, Potawatomi, and Sauk, absent the Shawnee. This group of Native Americans hoped to get an agreement which would reserve lands for them west of the Muskingum and south to the Ohio. If this had been done, it would have been a partial reversal of the Treaty of Fort McIntosh. On January 9, 1789, in the Treaty of Fort Harmer, St. Clair refused Indian demands and coerced them to accept the boundaries of the Treaty of Fort McIntosh. These terms were still unacceptable to the Native Americans and there was still no peace after two treaties. The Shawnee rejected the Treaty of Fort Harmer, once again claiming the other tribes did not represent them. The Indians had tried to trade some land for peace but not enough of it.[42] The bloodshed continued.

Over the next three years there were two weak American attempts to force peace on the Ohio country. In 1790 Secretary Knox (by now George Washington's Secretary of War in the new republic) ordered General Harmer to move north from Fort Washington (Cincinnati) with about 300 regular troops and 1,100 untrained and unmotivated militia. An Indian confederacy had been established under Little Turtle, a Miami, and Blue Jacket, a Shawnee. In late 1790, Harmer had marched north into a trap set by Little Turtle and the American force was decimated, retreating back toward the Ohio. The Indian attacks now increased and they continued to win battles, maintaining control of Ohio.[43]

In the early days of the new republic, Washington had many issues to resolve in his first presidential term, including how the new republic was to operate. Years had passed since the Northwest Ordinance and it was time for settlers to be moving into Ohio under new rules. That could not happen in any significant way unless and until the violence stopped. Protective measures were now taken to allow safe movement, including protection for boats floating down the Ohio.

> the settlers tried to make the best of a dangerous frontier. When packet boats began a regular schedule between Pittsburgh and Cincinnati with departures spaced two weeks apart, the owner repeatedly took "great pains to render the accommodation agreeable and convenient" by keeping passengers "under cover" from rifle and musket fire and provided "convenient port holes for firing out of." Each boat had six one-pound cannon and "a number of good muskets amply supplied with plenty of ammunition, strongly manned with choice hands."[44]

Knox ordered the formation of an army under the command of General Arthur St. Clair, Governor of the Northwest Territory. In March 1791, he was ordered to establish a series of forts in the Indian country, western Ohio, and garrison them with 1,200 men. Another regiment of 2,000 would be raised to form the attack force. St. Clair quickly realized that once again the force would not achieve the intended size and would include some very unqualified militia. Nevertheless, On August 7 he started north.[45] Undermanned, and with poor morale, they also ran into weather problems, yet St. Clair was confidant the Indians could not stand up to his regular force.

They met Little Turtle at dawn on November 4. "Little Turtle sent the Wyandots and Iroquois ... against St. Clair's right, the Shawanees, Miamis, and Delawares into the center, and the Ottawas, Objibwas, and Potawatomis along the left, deployed in a half-moon formation that would encircle the camp.... Although a reconnaissance party had warned that an attack was imminent, everyone was unprepared."[46] An unprepared and overconfident American army was once again defeated by Native Americans fighting for their homeland. This was the worst defeat for the Americans yet and the worst defeat ever at the hands of Native Americans, worse than any battle of the War for Independence. There were 623 killed out of 918 soldiers, and 69 of 124 officers killed or wounded as well as many civilians. St. Clair and his army fought their way back toward Cincinnati to lick their wounds.[47]

Washington was furious. He accused St. Clair of incompetence and removed him from the army, although St. Clair remained as Governor of the Northwest Territory. The area was not under American control and was still dangerous, it could not remain that way. In 1792 Washington assigned a new commander of the United States Army to the Northwest, General Anthony Wayne, later known as "Mad Anthony Wayne." He had a reputation from the War for Independence as a tenacious, aggressive and disciplined commander. Wayne's job continued to be the protection of Ohio settlers. He arrived at Fort Washington in May 1793 but a series of illnesses in camp prevented him from moving aggressively. He left Fort Washington in October and moved six miles north of Fort Jefferson where he constructed Fort Greenville, near the southwest Ohio border. He also built Fort Recovery on the site of St. Clair's defeat. He remained at Fort Greenville over the winter of 1793–1794. The situation had not improved when, in early to mid-1794, a band from Little Turtle's confederacy attacked a supply train going from Fort Recovery to Fort Greenville.[48]

Little Turtle was facing his own problems other than Wayne. For years, the British in northwest Ohio had been encouraging and supplying the Indians in their fight against the Americans, even helping to build fortifications. It had been over ten years since the Treaty of Paris had required the British to move out. They had not done so, but the pressure was building on them to make the move. The British now became more worried about their support for the Little Turtle confederacy as they wanted to avoid another war with the Americans. Little Turtle realized that without British support he would not be able to resist Wayne's army.

On August 20, 1794, Wayne's army, much larger and better prepared than previous American forces, overran the Indian confederacy under Little Turtle and Blue Jacket in the "Battle of Fallen Timbers," which took its name from an area recently hit by a tornado which felled trees in this part of far northwest Ohio. Although not a large battle it was decisive and the tribes involved knew they could no longer fight to retain the whole of Ohio. A series of meetings began in January 1795 and eight months later, on August 3, 1795, the Treaty of Greenville was signed. The treaty line was similar to that of the Treaty of Fort McIntosh.[49] It reserved northwest Ohio for the Native Americans, but allowed them to hunt on the land they had ceded to the east and south. The settlers agreed to relinquish their claims north and west of the line.[50] This agreement also would not last.

Although the Battle of Fallen Timbers was decisive in ending the northwest Indian wars, the attacks did not end. The Shawnee chief Tecumseh formed another confederacy in the early nineteenth century with many tribes east of the Appalachians. Their new attempt to expel the settlers resulted in troubles with them, which lasted another twenty years after the Treaty of Greenville. Nonetheless, Wayne's victory did provide enough stability for many settlers to move to Ohio.[51]

The existential battle for Ohio was over but it had lingering effects. For over half a century settlers had been interested in moving into this rich, fertile land, but they had been deterred by Ohio wars with the French, the British, and the Indians. Areas south of the Ohio, which were controlled by Virginia and North Carolina were pacified earlier Kentucky (1792) and Tennessee (1796) became states before Ohio, which entered the Union in 1803.

Land Companies and Grants, Pre-War

Ohio was now pacified and a plan to sell and occupy the Ohio lands had been approved in the Ordinance of 1787. In light of this new plan what had happened to all the previous attempts to move into and settle across the mountains and into the Ohio country in particular?

The Ohio Company of Virginia and the Greenbrier Company were devastated by the French and Indian War and never recovered. The Greenbrier Company actually predated the Ohio Company, in 1745, it received a grant of one hundred thousand acres in the Greenbrier Valley, along the present-day West Virginia-Virginia border. The surveyor, Andrew Lewis, had laid out about fifty thousand acres by 1754. The settlers who had moved there by then were subsequently chased out by the Indian allies of the French during the war, as had most others on the frontier.[52]

The Loyal Land Company was the other land company established prior to the French and Indian War. This company's grant, like that of the Greenbrier Company, was in western Virginia, across the mountains but below the Ohio River. (The Ohio Company of Virginia was the only company to try to enter the Ohio country above the Ohio River.) After the war the Loyal Land Company had to wait until the Treaty of Fort Stanwix freed Virginia lands below the Ohio before they could restart settlement.[53]

In summary, all the attempts by private companies to acquire and settle land in the Ohio country from mid-century through the end of the War for Independence were unsuccessful. After the Treaty of Fort Stanwix in 1768 settlers were successful in populating western Virginia, in what became the states of Kentucky and Tennessee. The Ohio country above the Ohio River, struggling through Indian wars, was still sparsely populated. That started to change after the war ended in 1783 when some companies started to apply for land in Ohio.

Land Companies and Grants, Post-War

Ohio was a hostile area between wars and even after the War for Independence; it was reserved for the Indians and they were fighting to hold it. Despite the hostilities pioneers were moving into Ohio because of the attractive land. The Confederation Congress moved rapidly with a series of land ordinances to lay out the lands and set up a governance policy. The ordinances provided organization for some of the Ohio land but there were also private grants and sales.

One of these private sales started even before the War was over. In 1783, General Rufus Putnam, originally from Massachusetts, and along with almost three hundred army officers stationed at Newburgh, New York wrote a petition to Congress asking for grants of land in the Ohio country. They reminded the Confederation Congress of its promise of land grants in recognition of service in the Continental Army. They submitted the petition to George Washington who sent it on to Congress with his recommendation. This petition was not acted upon but Putnam did not give up on Ohio.[54]

Putnam, along with General Benjamin Tupper, started looking for "adventurers" and investors to settle in the Ohio country. Meeting at the Bunch of Grapes Tavern in Boston on March 1, 1786, with potential investors from all over Massachusetts, they formed the Ohio Company of Associates. (No relation to the earlier Ohio Company of Virginia.) Within a year, they had 250 investors, including five surveyors who had worked on the Seven Ranges who probably eagerly extoled the virtues of having land in Ohio. This meeting was unique as this group of potential investors was from New England. Up to this time most of the interest in the Ohio country was from the east and south. Previously the only ones interested were Virginians from the Ohio Company of Virginia, and unauthorized settlers from Pennsylvania, Maryland, and Virginia. This New England group, and others from New England, were to put their stamp on the Ohio culture in the coming years.[55]

On March 8, 1786, the Ohio Company of Associates appointed three men, including Putnam, Samuel Parsons, and the Rev. Manasseh Cutler, to apply to Congress for land in Ohio. Parson requested six hundred thousand acres northwest of the Ohio River to be paid for in Continental currency or military rights. The request was unsuccessful. Whether Congress turned them down because the Continental currency was greatly depreciated after the war or for another reason is hard to say. Cutler had many contacts and went to the meeting of the Confederation Congress in New York in July 1787. This was at the same time the Constitutional Convention was meeting in Philadelphia. A skillful lobbyist, he managed to convince Congress of the advantages of settling the Ohio country, perhaps for less than they wanted to charge. He arranged a contract between the Board of the Treasury and the Ohio Company to obtain 1.5 million acres of land in southeast Ohio for one million dollars. The land would have the southern boundary at the Ohio River, eastern boundary at the western edge of the Seven Ranges, western boundary east of the not yet surveyed sixteenth range, and as far north as necessary to complete the sale. One-half the purchase price was paid at the time of the sale and the second half was due on completion of the survey. The private survey would use the pattern established by the 1785 Land Ordinance of six-mile square townships. At about sixty-seven cents per acre, this was already below the price Congress was asking for land in the Seven Ranges. Since the first payment was paid in severely depreciated Continental securities the actual price was closer to twelve and one-half cents per acre.[56]

This became one of the more orderly settlements in Ohio.

> The associates proceeded to take up their lands in an orderly fashion. Early in 1788, company boat builders moved to Sumrill's Ferry on the Youghiogheny where they prepared an ark, first called the *Union Galley* and later renamed the *Mayflower,* a flatboat named *Adelphia* and three canoes (pirogues). In these craft forty-eight men of the advance parties embarked on April 2, 1788. Five days later, they landed at the mouth of the Muskingum River, on the east bank, across from Fort Harmer.[57]

They could not move much farther inland at the time because of the Indian trouble. They built a town at the Muskingum and Ohio and named it Marietta in honor of Queen Marie Antoinette of France, clearly out of respect for the help France had provided during the recent War for Independence. These associates were officers who had served in that war and were appreciative. On July 9, 1788, the townspeople and Fort Harmer soldiers welcomed Arthur St. Clair to Marietta as the first governor of the Northwest Territory.[58]

Why this group from New England, the Ohio Company of Associates, started their journey on the Youghiogheny floating up to the Monongahela and down the Ohio, is not clear. It was a ferry point, Sumrill's Ferry, and perhaps a boat building center for these float trips on the Ohio which were already common. It is ironic because the Ohio Company of Virginia had pioneered that southern route, from the south following the Monongahela to the Ohio River, almost forty years previously. As noted previously, and as noted by Knepper (*Ohio and Its People*),

> The New Englanders who settled Marietta, and those who came in succeeding years, transferred to this new land their classical education, their sense of community order, their organizational skills, their energy and determination. Their culture was little modified by the wilderness. They shaped the wilderness to a much greater extent than it shaped them. While this was true of the Ohio Company settlers, it was not always equally true of others who made homes in the Ohio country.[59]

Map 13: Ohio Land Subdivisions. This traces the subdivisions of land laid out in Ohio as the land was up for sale. The Seven Ranges was the first section surveyed (by David Deis, Dreamline Cartography, based on a map from George W. Knepper, *Ohio and Its People, Bicentennial Edition*, Kent, OH: Kent State University Press, 2008, with permission from Kent State University Press).

This was the first group of settlers from New England. There would be many more but most of them moved into northeastern Ohio, into an area originally claimed by Connecticut.

Even at the depreciated price the Ohio Company could not make its second payment and settled for what they had paid for, 750,000 acres. Congress had already broken its own rule about cash purchases only so they were not earning what they had expected by selling the land. The Indian situation worsened, this led to a grant called the Donation Tract, a buffer zone of 100,000 acres north of the Ohio Company lands. This zone was inserted by Congress in 1792 because of the Indian problems the Ohio Company was having on its property. One hundred acres were given to any male who would settle the land and provide a buffer between the Ohio Company lands and the Indians. This was the first-time land would be *given* away, but it wouldn't be the last.[60]

The Ohio Company Purchase was a sale to a private company, not a public sale of publicly surveyed lands such as the Seven Ranges. There was another private sale of land in the southwest corner of Ohio. In 1787, Judge John Cleves Symmes of New Jersey, a member of Congress, persuaded that body to sell him one million acres between the Miami Rivers. This purchase did not go as smoothly as the Ohio Company Purchase. Symmes mishandled the transaction and was eventually limited by Congress to much less than the original one million acres. He also sold land haphazardly sometimes selling the same land twice and he mishandled the reservation of land for a university. Ultimately Miami University of Ohio was located at Oxford, west of the Symmes tract, much to the dismay of settlers in that tract who felt they lost their university.[61] In 1788 three land speculators, Israel Ludlow, Matthias Denman, and Robert Patterson, purchased eight hundred acres of Symmes' land on the Ohio River across from the mouth of the Licking River of Kentucky. They used a fanciful name for their settlement, Losantiville, a convoluted contraction meaning "*across from the mouth of the Licking River.*" When Governor St. Clair arrived in 1790 he made the city the county seat of Hamilton County, renaming it Cincinnati in in honor of the Society of the Cincinnati, of which he was a member from the time of the Revolutionary War.[62]

Besides the Seven Ranges and the private sales of land Congress set aside two areas as military districts. These were meant to reward soldiers for their service or, more accurately, serve as back pay for compensation they never received during the wars. When Virginia ceded the Ohio land to Congress for the benefit of all, it reserved a section in Ohio to be used to repay the Virginia soldiers of both the French and Indian War and its troops in the War for Independence. They reserved about four million acres in southern Ohio between the Scioto and Little Miami River, extending about 141 miles north of the Ohio and just east of the Symmes Purchase. It had set aside land in Kentucky for the same purpose and would use the Ohio land when the Kentucky grants were exhausted. Although this Virginia land was in Ohio where the rectangular survey system was introduced, the Virginia Military District surveyed the land as it was done in Virginia, in metes and bounds. Not unexpectedly, this resulted in many claims and counterclaims and a great deal of litigation.[63]

Although the land was intended for veterans,

> Most of this land, however, went to someone besides a soldier. Indeed only 35.1 percent of those men who received warrants for their military service had their lands surveyed. And only 15.4 percent received a payment, that is, title to all of their lands that had been warranted. For the most part, these patents went to single owners who claimed lots ranging from 100 to 1,000 acres, with the smallest patent for 5 and the largest for 5,333 acres, Speculators bought up most of the land warrants for the Virginia Military District.[64]

This was not uncommon. Speculators did a lot of the land business in Ohio. They made the earlier efforts by the Ohio Company of Virginia look very small.

George Washington, Virginia veteran of two wars, was entitled to 23,333 acres. He never claimed them but instead purchased two warrants of 3,100 acres surveyed in 1787.

Congress nullified these surveys in 1788, "and Washington never filed for a U. S. patent under the congressional acts of 1790 and 1794. He mistakenly believed he owned the surveyed land." His heirs never received this benefit. Even someone as savvy as Washington concerning western lands could be confused about land speculation in Ohio.[65]

As early as 1776, and again in 1780, the Continental Congress authorized land for the veterans of the War for Independence. The Confederation Congress (1781–1789) provided lands for the veterans in the Seven Ranges under the Articles of Confederation. That did not meet the need. Finally, in 1796 the United States Congress passed the legislation that established the United States Military District. It was located just west of the Seven Ranges; the survey started in 1797. The land was to be surveyed in five-mile square townships instead of the six-mile square townships used in the Seven Ranges. These did not conform easily to the military land warrants, there were practical problems subdividing the land into a finer grid, five miles instead of six. This may be the reason land speculators once again got into the mix: "many veterans sold their warrants to speculators or jobbers at a fraction of their true value. Of the 1,043,460 acres claimed by land warrant, 569,542 acres were patented to just 22 persons."[66]

When Connecticut received its charter from Charles II in 1662, it was, like the Virginia charter, from "sea to sea." What is now northern Ohio was included in that strip of land. As with the Virginia claim, it also was whittled back by various treaties and cessions. The 1763 Treaty of Paris limited the Connecticut claim to land east of the Mississippi. In 1786 Connecticut ceded most of its western lands but maintained a reserve in the northwest of present-day Ohio called the Western Reserve or "New Connecticut." It lay above the forty-first parallel and extended west from the Pennsylvania line for 120 miles. Connecticut sold all but the westernmost part of the Reserve to the Connecticut Land Company in 1796 for 1.2 million dollars. The money was to be used to fund education in Connecticut.[67]

In 1796 the Connecticut Land Company sent one of its founders, a lawyer and War for Independence veteran named Moses Cleaveland, to survey lands in the Western Reserve. On his way there his party stopped in Buffalo to meet with the Indians, including Red Jacket and Joseph Brant. He had to convince them that the Indians had indeed ceded the Western Reserve in the Treaty of Greenville just the year before. Bribing the Indians with trinkets and liquor, Cleaveland obtained safe passage to the Ohio Western Reserve. At the mouth of the Cuyahoga River, he found what he termed an ideal location for the capital of the Western Reserve. He laid out land around the area, including a ten acre "Public Square" at the center of the city they named Cleaveland in October 1796. The Public Square was a touch of New England that he imparted to northern Ohio. Interestingly, the Public Square was laid out just to the *east* of the Cuyahoga River which itself was the eastern boundary of the Indian land in the Greenville Treaty. The Western Reserve was to become a final destination of many New Englanders. Cleaveland returned to New England and never returned to Ohio.[68] The land of the Western Reserve was laid out in the rectangular grid pattern, but in five-mile squares instead of six-mile squares.

During the time it was allotting these public and private land grants Congress also set aside some smaller grants to specific groups for specific purposes. They also set aside large areas, called Congress Lands, for the future. Most of the Congress Land was in western Ohio, where the most intense Indian wars took place through the 1780s and 1790s, and therefore was unattractive for early settlement.[69]

After the ratification of the Constitution, the United States grew into a large republic which many of the Founding Founders were concerned could not be sustained. The accepted wisdom up to that time was that only small states could sustain a republic.[70] They all agreed that a well-educated public was very important for the United States to survive, a belief confirmed in their insistence that section sixteen of each township was to be reserved for education.

Congress went farther than this for some universities, reserving two townships, forty-six thousand acres, in the first Ohio Company survey for universities. These townships were Athens and Alexandria, in Athens County. Ohio University in Athens opened modestly in 1806 but was providing college level courses by 1820. "Ohio University was the first collegiate institution in the Northwest Territory, and the first publicly assisted institution of its kind in America."[71] As noted previously, Symmes mishandled many of the lands he was supposed to develop and lost the university that was supposed to be within his grant. Congress did not let this pass and set out 23,000 acres *west* of the Symmes Purchase for educational purposes in 1803. In 1809, Ohio chartered Miami University on that land and classes started in 1824. The Ohio State University started later after Congress passed the Morrill Act in 1862 which authorized public land for education in the agricultural and mechanical arts. Ohio received a grant in 1862 and established the Ohio Agricultural and Mechanical College. Later it expanded the curriculum and changed the name to Ohio State University. Shortly after, to emphasize the state sponsorship, it changed the name to "The Ohio State University."[72] (The article "The" is often emphasized by proud athletes in identification of their university during athletic events on television.)

These public universities, the first supported by public funds, led the way in Ohio education. Ohio education became much richer in later years when many religious institutions established their own colleges and universities there, which became well-known for various activities. Among these were Marietta, Oberlin, Western Reserve, Baldwin (later Baldwin-Wallace), Xavier, Dayton, and many others. The foresight of the Founding Fathers led to a rich educational environment in Ohio that continued in other states.

By the turn of the century there would be an enormous influx of people into Ohio.

Ohio Settlers

After the wars, Congress facilitated land sales and encouraged settlement in the Ohio country. In the 1780s and 1790s settlers were rapidly settling on Ohio land although the Indian wars were still going on. Many of these settlers used the Maryland to Ohio route but they also came from New England in the north and from Kentucky in the south. The newcomers were a diverse lot, but it was not a melting pot in the modern sense, not quite as diverse as we use that term today.

The United States today is thought of as a diverse nation with a mixture of people from hundreds of countries, of different races, cultures, and religions. The demographics are still changing today even after the major immigration waves have subsided. It was not always that way. Aside from the French, who could neither settle nor hold the land they claimed, there were only two world powers that had a lasting presence in the area of the present United States, Spain and England. Early in the sixteenth century, the Spanish entered South and Central America and moved up to the southwest and west coast of this country. The Spanish colonization effort was run top-down from Spain and the culture was more or less uniform across all their colonies.

The English settlement of the East Coast was different. It was not centrally run from London, but was a collection of colonies founded for different reasons, religious and commercial, up and down the East Coast from Massachusetts to Georgia. As the colonies grew and developed, they also developed their own governments and cultures. How and why did this come about? David Hackett Fischer describes four British immigration movements in his classic *Albion's Seed: Four British Folkways in America*. Briefly these are the exodus of the Puritans to Massachusetts, the Cavaliers to Virginia, the Friends migration to the Delaware River, and the Borderlanders from North Britain to the American backcountry. These constituted British North America and eventually led to the thirteen colonies and then states. These cultures often clashed, but finally came together to form one republic.

Since the Northwest Territory, including Ohio, was no longer the province of one or two states but belonged to all it was an inviting place for people from all the eastern states. The proximity of the New England States, Mid-Atlantic States of Pennsylvania, Maryland, and Virginia, and of Kentucky made them primary sources of settlers. Many thousands came through the original route first traced by Christopher Gist, and later by Braddock over the Alleghenies. Now that Ohio was open settlers also came down from New England following Lake Erie, and up from Kentucky to southern Ohio.

The early diversity of Ohio can be roughly categorized by three of the four migrations Fischer discusses, New Englanders whose forbearers were Puritans, Mid-landers from Pennsylvania and the middle states, and Borderlanders.

The Borderlanders, as the name suggest, came from the border areas between England and Scotland, and some from Northern Ireland (Scots-Irish), in a migration from roughly 1717 to 1775, most in the latter part of that period. Their reason for leaving was purely personal, to live a better life. They had been caught for hundreds of years in battles between English and Scottish kings. They had to scrape an existence from a hard landscape. The unreliability of the government, as exemplified by the continuing warfare, taught them not to trust government. They depended on themselves through blood relationships, and would not be controlled by outside forces, "valued individual liberty and personal honor above all else."[73] The border was a lawless area. "On the ... 'debatable land' that was claimed by both kingdoms powerful clans called Taylor, Bell, Graham and Bankhead lived outside the law, and were said to be 'Scottish when they will, and English at their pleasure.'"[74] Most of the Borderlanders entered through Philadelphia. These were people the Quakers could not abide so they shunted them to the backcountry of western Pennsylvania, hoping they would be a buffer between the easterners and the Indians. This suited these immigrants very well. They were used to the hardscrabble existence of mountain farmers. They were outside the law there, and saw the Indians as a group to be eliminated. Unlike other immigrants they did not come to a particular colony so they were stateless. They soon moved down the Great Valley Road to occupy other southern Appalachian areas. They founded and occupied what Colin Woodard (*American Nations*) would call Greater Appalachia. They spread far south and far west, though by the 1790 census they were mostly concentrated in southwestern Pennsylvania, western Maryland, western Virginia, North and South Carolina, Georgia, Kentucky and Tennessee.[75]

These were the people who seeped over the mountains during, between, and after the wars, grabbing land for themselves on the Monongahela and Ohio because they thought they had a right to any land they could hold. These were the squatters, the ones Washington and others called "Banditti." They could not be easily routed from their lands even by the army after the wars. The Borderlanders, now Appalachian Mountain people, also moved into southern Ohio. They came via the Braddock Road, but also up from Kentucky where many had settled in the 1770s. For this reason, Woodward includes southern Ohio as part of Greater Appalachia.

New Englanders started moving out of their states late in the eighteenth century when there was a shortage of land for the growing population of young people, especially in Vermont, New Hampshire, and Maine. The land they had in those states was not always ideal farmland. They started moving west and south, first to New York, on into Pennsylvania, and then into Ohio. The first serious settlement by the Ohio Company was at Marietta in 1788, after which New Englanders started moving into the Western Reserve in northeastern Ohio. After Moses Cleaveland surveyed the land around the Cuyahoga River in 1796, (present-day Cleveland) the Connecticut Land Company surveyed the rest of the Western Reserve from the Pennsylvania border to Cleveland in five-mile square townships. New Englanders started moving in, taking the natural route along the south shore of Lake Erie. As they came the towns started to resemble those of New England with town squares and churches with white steeples. They also took New England town names such as, Bristol, Danbury, Fairfield, and others. The Western Reserve was called "New Connecticut" by some.[76]

The cultures of northern Ohio and southern Ohio couldn't be more different. The prim, pious, neat New Englanders with a Puritan heritage, were a totally different culture from the laid-back libertarian people of the south, of Greater Appalachia. When the National Road was later completed as an extension of the Cumberland Road across the mountains, it went straight through the middle of Ohio. Travelers along that road would notice the difference between the well-maintained houses and farms with well-fed livestock north of the road and the shabbier, unpainted dwellings south of the road. Even before that it was noticeable, "In September 1790, a traveler who passed through Marietta noted the 'industry, sobriety and good order of the Newenglanders.' But in the Virginia Military District and Miami Purchase, moccasins were perfectly acceptable forms of attire, while settlers in Gallipolis and Mount Pleasant gave spoken English a peculiar sound that marked their heritage."[77] Between these two cultural strata the third general migration was from the middle states such as Pennsylvania, New Jersey, Delaware, Maryland, and Virginia straight across the Cumberland Road, later National Road, which went from Cumberland, Maryland, to Wheeling, Virginia, and west to mid-Ohio and beyond. Many in this migration were German settlers, either from those who settled previously in Pennsylvania, Maryland, and Virginia or immigrants from Germany. Many Quakers from Pennsylvania also made the migration. The religious Quakers, Moravians, Mennonites, and others did not have the rigidity of the Congregationalists of New England but were more moderate, willing to live side by side with others. They also did not have the libertarian views of the Greater Appalachia people in the south. As the Germans moved into Ohio those who stayed tended to live in the middle of the state, between the New Englanders in the north and the Greater Appalachian people in the south and fit well between these groups. Many of the Germans found their way to Cincinnati, the largest city in the Northwest Territory.[78]

Woodward's analysis shows that Ohio is the only state with three distinct cultures in its heritage; all others have two or less.[79] Later, the state mixed in a more recognizably diverse manner as other immigrants came into it, but these three cultures remain evident today.

Six

The Waterway West

The establishment of the Ohio Company headquarters and storehouse at Wills Creek on the Potomac at present-day Cumberland, Maryland, was an act of faith. Wills Creek was in the middle of nowhere. There wasn't a good road from Winchester, Virginia, which had been settled only a few years earlier by settlers coming down from Pennsylvania, or from Alexandria, Virginia, which was founded at the same time as the Ohio Company and is located on the tidal Potomac. By looking at a map and identifying two rivers, the Potomac and the Monongahela, which ran in opposite directions, and were very close to one another at Wills Creek, it was decided this was the ideal place to cross the mountains using waterways. The Atlantic could be connected with the Mississippi by using these two rivers, going up one (Potomac) and down the other (Monongahela). This was the logic that John Hanbury used to convince the King to grant the Ohio Company their land. Unfortunately, maps were misleading and it was not quite that simple.

When one crosses the mountains and reaches the Monongahela it is possible to float quite a distance down the Monongahela and then the Ohio. The river is not rough because it is far from its source and in a relatively flat plateau. On the other hand, the Potomac starts in the Alleghenies and drops hundreds of feet before it reaches Chesapeake Bay. Much of it flows gently over long stretches, but there are at least four places where the Potomac falls rapidly over a short distance. In addition, the river is still shallow near its source in the North Branch of the Potomac. These falls and shallows along the four-hundred-mile river length make it difficult for anyone who wants to travel upriver from Alexandria to Wills Creek.

Ohio Company members met on February 6, 1753, to answer the question of why German immigrants should come to settle in Ohio Company grant lands; they were essentially writing a real estate brochure. After pointing out the tax advantages they addressed the travel to the land.

> As no Countrey in the world is better or more conveniently watered than Virginia the most convenient Passage will be into the Potomack River which is navigable by the largest ships within ten Miles of the Falls. The Companys Store house at Rock creek where they may land and have their goods secured is sixty miles from Connococheege a fine road from whence they may go by Water in the Companys Boat to their Store house at Wills Creek about forty miles and from thence the Company have cleared a Waggon Road about sixty miles to one of the head branches of the Ohio.[1]

Rock Creek enters the Potomac at Georgetown, Maryland, across the river from Alexandria, one of the farthest places inland reachable by ocean-going ships. Georgetown was founded in 1751 on the Maryland side of the Potomac, just two years after Alexandria was founded on the Virginia side. There was a road, which is still in existence from Georgetown to Frederick,

Maryland. From there one could take the Monocacy Road to Conococheague Creek and the Potomac, near present-day Williamsport, Maryland. The company was proposing the immigrants leave Georgetown by road to Conococheague and then take a company boat from there to Wills Creek. The claim of the wagon road to the Ohio was an exaggeration because there was not yet a "Waggon Road" from Wills Creek to the Monongahela, only a trail that had been blazed by Christopher Gist. They were acknowledging that immigrants could *not* take the Potomac all the way to Wills Creek, even if they started above Great Falls, which is very near Georgetown. This is because of all the rough water between Great Falls and Wills Creek.

When they made their grant proposal, the Ohio Company founders assumed that the route up the Potomac would be a good way to get to Wills Creek, the jumping-off point to Ohio. Upham ("Washington's Canoe Trip Down the Potomac") claims that Ohio Company people had made a trip from Great Falls to Wills Creek in 1749, the year they had received the grant. Although that would seem to be a logical step for the company, there is no record of such a trip in the histories of the Ohio Company to ascertain if the Potomac route to Wills Creek was feasible.[2] However by this time, and even by the time of the grant in 1749, it would have been well-known that there were impediments to river travel in addition to Great Falls. Thomas Cresap and Christopher Gist would certainly have known that, as would the German immigrant settlers in western Maryland. The water route from Conococheague Creek to Wills Creek, however, was feasible by canoe most of the time and by flat boat some of the time since low water could be a problem in the dry months. Nevertheless, despite low water and rough water, at least part of the Potomac was seen as a waterway west.

The events of 1754, including Washington's foray toward the Forks of the Ohio, would heat up the frontier and lead to war the next year. These events would ignite in George Washington an idea about using the Potomac as a transportation corridor for the looming war. As he lived on the Potomac and had undoubtedly been thinking about it for a long time he acted on his idea when he returned to Williamsburg after the Battle of Fort Necessity in 1754.

Washington's Waterway West

In early 1754, Virginia Governor Dinwiddie originally thought of appointing Colonel James Innes to head the force to challenge the French at the Forks of the Ohio. He instead settled on Colonel Joshua Fry and appointed George Washington Lieutenant Colonel to serve as second in command. Washington was in Alexandria in early April when he started to Wills Creek, reaching it on April 20. Fry reached Wills Creek in May, but suffered a fatal accident when he fell off his horse and died a short while later. Governor Dinwiddie then commissioned Colonel Innes to that leadership position on June 4. Innes was still in Virginia at the time and Washington decided not to wait for Innes but to lead the force that eventually was defeated at Fort Necessity on July 3. Innes was in Winchester on July 5 and probably made it to the fort at Wills Creek in mid–July, which he promptly renamed Fort Cumberland, according to some accounts. Washington was there still licking his wounds from the Fort Necessity battle. Washington had yet to give his version of the events at Fort Necessity to Governor Dinwiddie at Williamsburg.[3]

Washington decided to return to Virginia by taking a canoe trip down the Potomac from Fort Cumberland to Great Falls; he had a tactical objective in mind, and this venture was possibly suggested by Innes. He wrote a letter to Innes on August 12, 1754, reporting on the trip down the river. This might have been the earliest recorded trip about Potomac River travel by anyone interested in moving west to settle, such as the Ohio Company, and Washington himself.[4]

The canoe trip that Washington made with a few men had the dual purpose of returning himself to Williamsburg and of exploring the Potomac.[5] Innes and Washington certainly reviewed the recent battle and anticipated more fighting on this western frontier. Fort Cumberland and Nemacolin's Path, which was also called Washington's Road after his recent expedition to the Forks, could be expected to figure prominently in future battles with the French, because they were in a key location on the frontier. The problem was the route to get to Fort Cumberland, as roads to the Fort were nonexistent and one had to travel over paths on foot or by horseback. An obvious potential solution was a water route via the Potomac from Alexandria to Fort Cumberland. After discussions with Innes, Washington and his men made the canoe trip down the Potomac to Great Falls, exploring the possibility of using it as a means to get supplies to the Fort. The route around Great Falls had to be by foot, there was no way to go down the Falls by canoe.

It is unknown how many men traveled with Washington, but they probably all traveled in one canoe, or possibly two. The romanticized version of Native Americans traveling by canoe on placid waters was not the norm in the middle colonies. Those picturesque canoes were birch bark, which was plentiful in the north but not available around the Potomac. The canoes in the middle colonies were dugout canoes, made from a whole tree. They were not easy to make and were generally made large enough to hold perhaps twenty men. They were made from hardwood trees found close to the river because they could weigh several tons and couldn't be easily moved over land. The early Native American builders felled a tree using fire, because they did not have metal axes. They would make a wattle mixture of mud and straw around the tree at head height to protect the tree above, then burn the tree below this band to fell it. The top part of the fallen tree, above the fire, would be made into the canoe. They immediately stripped the bark from the tree and carefully started to dig out the trunk with fire and hand tools. The canoe had to be made light enough to handle but with sides high enough to keep out the water. They molded the front and rear so it could travel in either direction, and to save weight they shaped the bottom. Finally, the canoe was coated in bear grease to stop the wood from drying out; this coating had to be repeated periodically. Canoes were made to be durable because they were difficult to make and had to last a long time.[6]

Washington's expedition had to be careful because the Potomac was rugged and hostile and the war he helped start a few weeks earlier was ongoing. They probably stopped at Oldtown, about seventeen miles downstream from Fort Cumberland, where his friend Thomas Cresap had built his fortified house and trading post; the river was smooth to this point. In the next one hundred miles, the river remained calm but shallow at points. They might have had to float an empty canoe through the shallow areas. They passed sites of future forts and towns, including Fort Tonoloway (1755) on the Maryland Tonoloway Creek, present-day Hancock, Maryland, and Fort Frederick, a permanent stone fort built by Governor Horatio Sharpe in 1756 to replace Fort Tonoloway. These would be built during the war to help protect settlers from the Indian allies of the French.[7]

The river became rougher when they got nearer the confluence of the Potomac and Shenandoah rivers. In his letter, Washington notes the rapids,

> From the mouth of Paterson's Creek to the beg[inning] of Shenandoah Falls there is no other obstacle other than the shallowness of the Water to prevent craft from passing—The first of those Falls is also even and shallow but swift and continues so with interruptions of Rocks to what is known by

the Spout w[hich] is a mile & half—from this there is Rocky swift and very uneven water for near 6 miles, in which distant there are 4 Falls.[8]

As he continues to describe the rapids he begins to have ideas on how they can improve the river at that point to make it more hospitable for travel, by taking out some of the rocks, for example. His canoe took on a lot of water in these rapids:

> water being confined shoots with great Rapidity & what adds much to the difficulty is the bottom being exceeding Rocky occasions a Rippling so prodigious that none but boats or large canoes can pass—The canoe I was in w[hich] was not new had near sunk having received much water on both sides.... Their may be a passage also got round this also upon the Maryland shoar that Vessels may be hald up after removing some Rocks which a moderate expence may accomplish.[9]

His letter perhaps written in haste, had many lineouts and insertions and is not typical of his usual well-constructed prose. He continued to Seneca Falls and then to Great Falls, which are about twenty miles apart. "From this to Seneca Falls the Water is as smooth & even as can be desired, with scarcely any perceptible Fall—The Seneca Fall is easily pass'd in two places and canoes may continue within two Miles of the G[reat] Falls but further is not possible."[10] The Great Falls of the Potomac, the magnificent cataract just a few miles north of present-day Washington, D.C., was not passable in canoes or boats of the day. Only the most experienced kayaker braves the Falls today. Great Falls, about 170 miles downstream of Fort Cumberland, drops the river seventy-six feet in a very short distance. Eleven miles farther downstream is Little Falls with a drop of thirty-seven feet. The river then gives way to the smooth waters of the tidal Potomac, an estuary of the Chesapeake Bay. Here were the two new cities, Alexandra, Virginia (1749), and Georgetown, Maryland (1751), founded as ports to allow ocean-going ships as far up the Potomac as possible. It is believed Washington wrote his letter from Alexandria.[11]

Having given his description of the trip through the various rapids and the impossibility of traveling over Great Falls Washington still remained optimistic about using the river above Great Falls: "but you will readily concur with me in judging it more convenient least expensive and I may further say by much the most expeditious way to the country. There is but one objection that can obviate this Carriage & that is y[e] scarcity of water in the best season of y[e] year for this kind of conveyance."[12] The only thing that concerned him when he made his journey was the low water at the driest time of the year. He never mentions traveling upstream which, even aside from Great Falls, would have been a formidable trip considering all the rapids he experienced in going downstream. He maintained his optimism over the next several years, although interrupted by two wars and a presidency. He actively worked on navigating the Potomac and building a canal, to bypass rapids and falls, and ultimately reach across the mountains to the Monongahela in the Ohio Valley.

The Potomac in the War Years

Washington's trip down the Potomac just after the Battle of Fort Necessity was an early exploration, but he was not the only one thinking of the river route to the fort after that battle. Both Virginia Governor Dinwiddie and Maryland Governor Horatio Sharpe were very interested in these recent events. Dinwiddie had started the push to clear the French from the Forks of the Ohio and had appointed Fry, Washington, and Innes to their posts. As a British citizen, he believed this was his duty, as a Virginian because he considered that land as part of Virginia, and therefore as part of Great Britain. Less than a year earlier, in August 1753, Sharpe had come from England with great fanfare and as an activist who wanted to cooperate with Dinwiddie.[13] Wills Creek was in his province and he wanted to support any action from there. Dinwiddie and Sharpe conducted a lively correspondence at the time.

On July 31, 1754, only a few weeks after Washington's defeat at Fort Necessity Dinwiddie wrote to Sharpe about his plan: "Colonel, Innes the Commander in Chief will have my orders to march all the Forces he can collect together over the Allegany Mountains; & if he cannot dispossess the Enemy of the Fort, he is to build a Fort at Red Stone Creek."[14] He went on in the same letter to thank Sharpe for a new road that Sharpe had proposed: "The road you are pleased to mention from Rock Creek to Wills's Creek will be of very-great use & Advantage & therefore desire you will please give your orders to execute it immediately."[15] In a second letter on September 5 Dinwiddie thanked Sharpe for opening the new road.[16]

The July letter was written about the same time that Washington was making his canoe trip down the Potomac. Dinwiddie and Sharpe assumed a road would be necessary to get to Wills Creek because the river was not considered suitable for travel at this time. The main objective was to get troops and supplies to Wills Creek so they could move to the Forks over the road Washington had just cleared.

There was an existing road on the Maryland side of the Potomac for a good portion of the distance. As early as 1720, Prince George's County, Maryland, had extended a road to Rock Creek and the Potomac from the east. As settlers moved up the river from there they extended the roads parallel to the river. By 1728 there was a road paralleling the river all the way to what would become Frederick, Maryland, on the Monocacy. By 1750 this was a thriving road, even including an inn at Clarksburg, Maryland, known as Dowdens' Ordinary, half-way between Rock Creek and Frederick.[17]

The road that Sharpe built to Fort Cumberland followed this road, passing Dowden's to Frederick. The road continued from Frederick about thirty-five miles to Congogee (Conococheague) Creek at present-day Williamsport, Maryland. The latter part of the route, from Frederick probably followed the Monocacy Road which was well traveled by that time. From there the road traced through a number of private settlements to the Cacapon River confluence with the Potomac, on to Cresap's place at Oldtown, and then to Wills Creek, a total distance of about 174 miles. The only new part of the road was between Conococheague Creek and Oldtown.[18] This was the route taken by one of Braddock's regiments in 1755. This road, in all its varied sections, led northwest, generally parallel to the river but not always close to it. There was now a road from Rock Creek near Georgetown all the way to Wills Creek.

Events began to move quickly once hostilities had started in July. In early fall of 1754 Governor Sharpe received a commission from the Baron of Baltimore appointing him, "Lieutenant-Colonel of the forces intended to be sent against the Forces which have invaded his Majesty's Dominions.... Almost at the same time Sharpe received a commission as commander-in-chief from his Majesty George II."[19] This was a temporary expedient, because on September 24 the Duke of Cumberland had appointed General Edward Braddock to be the commander in America. Braddock was in Europe at the time and it would be several months before he arrived in America.[20]

Sharpe, delighted at his appointment, was very active in getting ready to lead forces to the Forks; he hadn't yet heard of Braddock's appointment. He made his first inspection trip to Fort Cumberland in November. He was greeted there by the officers one of whom observed Sharpe and remarked in a November 21 letter, "He appears to be a stirring active gentleman, and by his method of proceeding I believe a very good soldier; cheerful and free, of good conduct, and one who won't be trifled with."[21] Sharpe returned from Wills Creek in early December 1754, and sent a long letter to Dinwiddie conveying his estimate of the provisions that would be needed for the march to the Forks. These two colonial governors were doing their best to rid the Ohio country of the French. In this December 10 letter Sharpe did his best to dissuade Dinwiddie from going to Wills Creek on the south (Virginia) side of the Potomac. His recommendation was to use the Maryland road to Conococheague Creek and float the supplies to Wills Creek by bateau. Interestingly, Sharpe didn't recommend using the road he recently had constructed all the way to Wills Creek. The last part of the road must have been poor and it being December, the Potomac water was higher and more able to carry flat-bottomed boats (bateaux) from Conococheague to Wills Creek.

> I cannot but think that the several Rivers & waters that occur & intersect the Road from Bellhaven [Alexandria] to Wills-Creek on the South Side of the Potowmack will render the Conveyance of Stores that way expensive & very uncertain wherefore I apprehend it will be the best & easiest way to land every thing that shall be sent up Potowmack for the Troops at Rock Creek whence our wagons will carry them to Conegocheek where Battoes may be made to convey every thing hence by water.[22]

Braddock wouldn't arrive in America until the spring of 1755, but he sent his Deputy Quartermaster General, Lieutenant Colonel Sir John St. Clair, ahead to look over the situation. St. Clair arrived in Virginia in early January 1755, met with Dinwiddie, and on January 26 he arrived at Fort Cumberland for a tour of inspection. He was not very impressed with the fort. Nevertheless, he found Sharpe at the Fort and they tarried for two days at Wills Creek before setting off on a canoe trip down the Potomac, similar to the trip Washington had taken about six months before. Their objective was the same, to see if the river could be used for transportation to the fort. They canoed down to Great Falls. Sargent (*The History of an Expedition against Fort Du Quesne*) makes a comment about Great Falls that is very unlikely, fanciful even, if one has ever seen Great Falls. He claims, "[they] had no doubt that, by the aid of gunpowder, the rocks in the channel at that point might be removed to an extant sufficient to permit the passage of the flat-bottomed boats or bateaux." The river falls seventy or more feet in a few hundred yards and his suggestion would prove difficult even today, but totally impractical at the time. George Washington had a similar idea about removing rocks much farther up the river in much more advantageous circumstances, but not at Great Falls. Possibly Sargent confused the area of the river being addressed.[23]

Both St. Clair and Sharpe wrote about their assessment of the river as a viable means to supply Fort Cumberland. St. Clair wrote to Braddock on February 9, 1755,

> In my last letter to you, I acquainted you that Governor Dinwiddie told me that the Navigation of the Pattommack is impracticable, this I can affirm from Experience, for Governour Sharp and I found it so for all other Vessels but Canoes cut out of a Single Tree; We attempted to go down the River in this Sort of Boat, but were obliged to get on Shore and walk on foot especially at the Shannondeau Falls; So that the getting Batteaus or Floats made for the transport of the Artillery and the Baggage of the Regiments, cou'd serve for no other thing, but to throw away the Governments Money to no purpose, and loose a great deal of time.[24]

Governor Sharpe, having made the trip with St. Clair came to the same conclusion in a letter to Lord Baltimore on March 12, 1755: "in order to examine the Channel of that River we came down Potowmack by water for the Distance of about 250 Miles, the many Falls & Shoals in that River will we find render the conveyance of Artillery & other Stores to the Camp by water impracticable."[25] These were essentially the final words on the use of the

Potomac to supply Fort Cumberland during the looming war with the French. The original thought was a good one. Both Alexandria, Virginia, and Georgetown, Maryland, were accessible by ocean-going ships. If one could get the supplies from those ships just past Great Falls, only a few miles upstream from either city, the river would then be a good way to move supplies to Wills Creek. The reality was different. It was bad enough coming down the river by canoe, but going up would have been almost impossible, at least to a point, because of rough water or low water. Sharpe indicated that taking the Maryland road from Georgetown through present-day Montgomery County, Maryland, to Frederick, then to Conococheague Creek, followed by a bateau trip to Wills Creek was a viable option. This road was apparently good by standards of the day; Braddock traveled by coach on it for part of his trip to Wills Creek. The road through Virginia to Wills Creek was not an option. St. Clair traveled from Fredericksburg, Virginia, through Winchester, Virginia, on his way to Wills Creek and wrote to Braddock, "I was from the 19th to the 22nd in getting to Winchester which is 93 Miles of very bad Road.... From the 23rd to the 26th I was on the Road to Wills's Creek, this is 85 Miles of the worst Road I ever traveled."[26] Since the major part of the Potomac was unusable to supply Fort Cumberland, the road and water transport through Maryland was the way to move these supplies; northern Virginia roads were not.

The Potomac Canal, the Way West

The two canoe trips down the Potomac from Fort Cumberland early in the hostilities of the French and Indian War were not very encouraging. The consensus was that the river could not be easily used to transport military supplies up the river, even if one started above Great Falls. As everyone was focused on prosecuting the war, nothing was done about Potomac River navigation during the conflict. Although access was not easy, the river undoubtedly was used to move people and supplies over the smoother parts of the river above the Shenandoah River to Fort Cumberland. Parts of the river became too shallow even for canoes during the dry season.

Things began to change even before the end of the war. The Potomac was still seen as a gateway to the west. Considering all the obstacles in the river from low water to rocks to falls, it might seem to be an unpromising way to travel. It was, except for all the other possibilities were even more unattractive. For centuries movement by water had been seen as the best way to travel long distances, whether by sail or oar or both. If there was water between the points you wanted to connect, that is what you used. It is not coincidental that major cities grew up on oceans or lakes or rivers as those locations provided for trade and intercourse between distant peoples. Alexandria and Georgetown, accessible to ocean going vessels, grew in stature for that reason. From these cities people moved to the interior to settle or trade with those already there. It was logical that the Potomac was seen as a waterway to parts of inland Maryland and Virginia, and by Washington as a gateway to all of the west despite the known obstacles.

Washington always saw the Potomac as the first step in "going all the way" to the west. The river would get him to Cumberland, and then the road he helped clear would get him, and others, across the mountains to the Monongahela and Ohio rivers. Others also saw possibilities in navigating certain sections of the Potomac even without using the entire river.

An advertisement was published in the *Maryland Gazette* on February 4, 1762, a year before the peace treaty, offering a subscription to shares in a company.

> The opening of the River *Potowmack* and making it passable for Small Craft, from Fort *Cumberland*, at *Wills's-Creek*, to the *Great-Falls*, will be of the greatest Advantage to *Virginia* and *Maryland*, by facilitating Commerce with the Back Inhabitants, who will not then have more than 20 Miles Land-Carriage to a Harbour, where Ships of great Burthen load annually; whereas at present many have 150; and what will perhaps be considered of still greater Importance, is, the easy Communication it will afford the Inhabitants of these Colonies with the Waters of the Ohio.[27]

Here was a group that was going to put into practice what many had dreamed of for years—a navigable Potomac—with a water link to the Ohio country. The people authorized to take subscriptions included names we have seen with settlement in the Shenandoah Valley and western Maryland, including George Mercer, Jacob Hite, Thomas Cresap, and Jonathan Hager.

They wanted to develop the river so anyone living along the river or its tributaries would be able to ship goods to Great Falls. There were twenty miles of land carriage available to move the goods around Great Falls to Georgetown where they could be loaded onto ocean-going ships. By this time of course, the Shenandoah Valley was settled and the Shenandoah River gave access to the Potomac. Similarly, Frederick and Hagerstown in Maryland had access to this trade. Hagerstown is very near the river and Frederick is accessible via the Monocacy River. Agricultural goods from Virginia and Maryland could thus be easily shipped all over the world. Farther up the river, in the mountains, coal could be shipped down-river.

As Kapsch (*The Potomac Canal*) points out there is no record of subscriptions to this proposal.[28] The idea, however, was too good to totally abandon, especially as still water canals were then proving to be very successful.

The ease of water travel had been recognized for millennia making smooth flowing rivers a valuable asset for any economy. Even rougher rivers could be improved and used to transport goods. Man-made canals linking bodies of water would improve the system of transportation, making it possible to move goods over very long distances by water. This was an early discovery; the history of canals goes back to at least 500 BCE when the Persian emperor Darius improved the economy of the newly conquered Egypt by building a canal linking the Nile to the Red Sea. Canal building developed independently around the world including in China in the third century BCE. In the tenth-century CE the Chinese engineer Chiao Wei-yo invented the pound lock for changing the level of the water in a canal or river, making it possible to raise or lower a boat to accommodate the changing level of the river. In a pound lock water was "impounded" between two guillotine-like gates that were opened and closed to allow the boat between them to raise or lower to the canal or river level. The Chinese were said to have hundreds of miles of rivers linked by canals. Canals were used in Europe in the twelfth to fifteenth century, especially in the Netherlands. The more modern miter lock canal gate was invented by Leonardo da Vinci (1452–1519) and is still used. The two doors of the gate are slightly over-sized so the "mitered" joint is kept tightly closed by water pressure.[29]

The modern canal era started in Great Britain in 1759 when the Duke of Bridgewater wanted a cheaper way than horse cart to move coal and asked engineer James Brindley (1716–1772) to build a canal for moving coal from his mine in Worsley to the River Irwell near Manchester. Brindley exceeded that by building a flat canal, without locks, all the way to Manchester using an aqueduct over the Irwell River. The first load of coal was pulled over the canal on July 17, 1761. It was the first canal to be independent of any river and started the inland waterway system in England.[30] The canal was a huge economic success and encouraged similar innovation, including in America.

Men like John Semple and John Ballendine were encouraged and took steps in the mid to late 1760s to improve navigation on parts of the Potomac for commerce. Semple was an entrepreneurial Scotsman who dealt first in tobacco and later in iron ore. In 1763 he purchased several thousand acres of land, including an iron ore bank, on both sides of the Potomac above the confluence of the Shenandoah and Potomac rivers. He named the tract Keep Triste which was derived from his family's motto. He built a furnace to process the iron ore approximately two miles above the Shenandoah on the Potomac. He shipped the output of this furnace approximately seven miles upriver to the Frederick Forge at Antietam Creek. Although he also wanted to ship ore to another facility he owned at the Occoquan River, which enters the Potomac downstream of Alexandria it was impossible at that time because of the Great Falls. By 1769, Semple was proposing improvements in Potomac navigation from his furnace above the Shenandoah to the head of Great Falls. There were many smaller rapids and falls in this stretch including Shenandoah Falls and Seneca Falls and he proposed canals with locks around some of these obstacles. He ignored Great Falls and Little Falls as impractical for river navigation and would use land carriage around them.[31]

The two known ways to make a river navigable were with a sluice canal or with a bypass canal using lift locks. A sluice is, "An artificial channel for conducting water, with a valve or gate to regulate the flow."[32] The sluice is a chute built in or next to the river, cleared of rocks. When the gate is open, a boat can slide down the sluice to change levels in the river thus bypassing the falls or rough water. Going upriver would be more difficult as the boat would have to be pulled up the sluice with great effort. A canal using a lift lock which parallels the river rapids is more difficult to build, but is much less hazardous for the boat. The lock in the canal is a section of the canal with two gates on either side, upriver and downriver. The upriver part of the canal is at the upriver level and the downriver part of the canal is at the downriver level. Going upstream, the boat enters the lock at the downstream level of the river, the downstream gate is closed, and the lock is allowed to fill with water. When the water reaches the upstream level of the canal and river, the upstream gate is opened, and the boat moves back into the river from the canal. The process is reversed for moving downstream. Lift locks were common in Europe at this time but not in America. Clearly the lift lock requires more engineering skill, more workers to build it, and more time for construction. Some of Semple's ideas were ahead of their time for America, but Semple didn't live to carry them out.

John Ballendine was another iron manufacturer who was interested in Potomac navigation. He interested number of prominent Virginians, including George Washington, in investing in a company for river navigation in the early 1770s. His plans were more ambitious than Semple's because he also wanted to include locks around Great Falls and Little Falls. He visited England to see the Bridgewater canal engineered by James Brindley, and later had Brindley visit Virginia to consult on a Potomac canal. Washington, who never lost interest in a Potomac canal, encouraged Ballendine and helped pass legislation in Virginia enabling navigation on the Potomac. Despite calling for investors and possibly starting on parts of the bypass canals, Ballendine never had the resources to finish.[33]

The War for Independence that started in 1775 not only put a halt to all Potomac navigation schemes but it took Washington away from his beloved Potomac canal ideas for several years. He didn't return to these ideas until his western canoe trip in 1784 after the war.

Washington settled back at Mount Vernon after the war working to improve his lands. Before long, he returned to two of his favorite subjects, his land in the west and the possibility of linking the west with the Atlantic via the Potomac and the Ohio rivers. He started on a canoe trip on September 1, 1784, accompanied by his nephew Bushrod Washington and friend Dr. Craik. The two objectives for this trip are clearly stated in his journal on the first and fourth days of his trip: "Having found it indispensably necessary to visit my Landed property West of the Apalacheon Mountains ... & one objective of my journey being to obtain information of the nearest and best communications between the Eastern & Western Waters & to facilitate as much as in me lay the Inland Navigation of the Potomac."[34] This 1784, trip, which he computed as 680 miles in total distance, took him northwest generally along the Potomac, but not on it. He stopped again at Cresap's, followed the road to Fort Cumberland, and then traveled through Great Meadows following the Braddock Road over the mountains. Apparently, he went as far as Miller's Run in southwest Pennsylvania visiting his land there which was occupied by some tenants. Miller's Run flows into Chartier's Creek which in turn empties into the Ohio just below the Forks. He planned to visit his lands on the Kanawha River but was warned by an officer from Fort Pitt of the danger of Indian trouble in the area; he took that advice and traveled no farther. His return trip took him farther southeast than the trip out, through middle Virginia, returning to Mount Vernon on October 4, 1784.[35]

He had mixed feelings about the success of the trip. On the one hand,

> I was disappointed in one of the objects which induced me to undertake this journey namely to examine into the situation quality and advantages of the Land which I hold upon the Ohio and Great Kanhawa—and to take measures for rescuing them from the hands of Land Jobbers and Speculators—who I had been informed regardless of my legal & equitable rights, Patents, & e[tc.]; had enclosed them within other Surveys & were offering them for Sale at Philadelphia and in Europe.[36]

On the other hand,

> I say not withstanding this disappointment I am well pleased with my journey, as it has been the means of my obtaining a knowledge of facts—coming at the temper & disposition of the Western Inhabitants—and making reflections thereon, which, otherwise, must have been as wild, incoher[ent], or perhaps as foreign from the truth, as the inconsistency, of the reports which I had received even from those to whom most credit seemed due, generally were.[37]

In the latter paragraph, he referred to the first-hand knowledge he received by actually seeing the area and talking to the people who lived there. He devoted a great deal of space in his journal talking about possible water routes from the Potomac to the Ohio. He talked about the Potomac North Branch, the Cheat, Youghiogheny, Kanawha, and other rivers as possible links, using portage at places, to set up a connection between the Atlantic and Ohio. He talked to many people, sometimes getting good news and sometimes bad, about the possible routes.

After he returned from the trip he considered and summarized all the combinations of rivers and portages that could close the link between the east and west. He was more optimistic than ever,

> The more then the Navigation of Potomack is investigated, & duly considered, the greater the advantages arising from them appear.... These then are the ways by which the Produce of that Country; & the peltry and fur trade of the Lakes may be introduced into this State; & into Maryl[and]; which stands upon similar ground.[38]

Washington always thought large when it came to the west. His summary of the 1784 trip was no different; he started by thinking of going by water to Detroit interrupted only by small portages. He did some remarkable calculations, many of which were based on his actual travels. He calculated the distance from Detroit to Alexandria using three different routes. One route, for example, was from Detroit to the Cuyahoga River (present-day Cleveland), up the river to a short eight-mile portage to Beaver Creek, down that creek to the Ohio and to Fort Pitt. That distance he calculated to be 303 miles. He calculated alternate routes from there to Alexandria. One route was down the Monongahela to the Youghiogheny to its falls, a one-mile portage to Turkey Foot, thirty miles overland to Fort Cumberland (portage along the Braddock road) and then 200 miles down the Potomac to Alexandria. This segment was 304 miles making the total distance from Detroit to Alexandria 607 miles. Most of this, except for about forty or fifty miles of portage, was by water. Developing this route would have required a major improvement to the Braddock Road. The road was later improved to become the Cumberland Road but not as part of Washington's route. Washington calculated alternate routes, including one from Detroit to Philadelphia across Pennsylvania to show that the route to the port city of Philadelphia, at 741 miles, was much longer than the route to the port city of Alexandria.[39]

Optimistic by what he saw on the trip he acted with great dispatch when he arrived back home in Virginia. On October 10, 1784, Washington wrote to Governor Harrison suggesting the Potomac and James rivers be surveyed for inland navigation. He wrote to other friends in the following weeks for he was in a hurry. The British and Spanish were not the immediate threats; it was the westward movement of the New Yorkers and Pennsylvanians, and the squatters he had seen on his land that worried him. As the federal union had not yet been born, individual states were still in competition. He had made a previous visit to the Mohawk Valley in New York and had seen how that river cut a clear path through the mountains that would make it easy for New Yorkers to move west. New York took advantage of that path in 1825 with the Erie Canal.[40]

Undoubtedly at his insistence, a large number of Washington's friends and neighbors met in Alexandria on November 14, 1784, to draft plans for a company to open the Potomac. He wanted legislation from both Maryland and Virginia sanctioning such a company, so he personally visited Annapolis where he received a warm welcome and support.[41] He approached James Madison in Virginia and suggested saving time by having both legislatures pass a bill with the same wording. When Maryland passed the bill on December 28 Washington advised Madison that "to alter the Act ... will not do." Madison ushered the act through the Virginia legislature ten days later, unaltered from the Maryland version. Washington was proud of his achievement and wrote his friend the Marquis De Lafayette on February 15, 1785: "for improving and extending the navigation of the river Potomac as far as it should be found practicable, and for opening a road of communication therefrom, to the nearest navigable water to the westward. In both I happily succeeded ... advantages of extending the inland navigation of our river, and opening free and easy communications with the Western Territory (thereby binding them to us by interest, the only knot which hold)."[42] Washington was already acting like a canny chief executive. He was also undoubtedly trading on the high esteem of his countrymen following the war that had just ended the previous year.[43] The compact that Maryland and Virginia promulgated about joint navigation of the Potomac was a very important agreement between two independent states, uncommon at the time. It was also illegal under Article VI of the Articles of Confederation which required that any compact between states had to be approved by the Confederation Congress. Madison and others later considered this an important step toward the national convention in 1787 and the drafting of the Constitution. It was also a popular step. By the May 1785, meeting they had sold 403 shares at a capitalization of £40,300.[44]

On May 17, 1785, Washington became president of the Potomac Company, a post he held until he became President of the United States in 1789. It was an important milestone in Washington's life and for the soon-to-be new nation. As Abbot ("George Washington, the West, and the Union") points out, "The evidence presented does suggest, however, that Washington's long experience with the West and his strongly held views about its importance, leading in 1784 to his active participation in measures to bind it to the newly confederated states, more than anything else, except the war itself, served to prepare him for the role of nation builder."[45] The Potomac Company had a number of design decisions to make and George Washington was right in the middle of all of them. They had already decided upon a river canal, not a separate still water canal. They also decided that most of the river would use sluice channels around the rapids and small falls which were less expensive than locks and would be faster to build. Washington also envisioned, correctly, that most of the early traffic would be downstream with loads of flour from the farmlands for export, and therefore sluices would work well. Because bypasses around Great Falls and Little Falls were too steep for sluice navigation, the plan was to use a lock system at these points. In order to size the locks, they decided on a boat size of six to ten tons, drawing three feet of water and no longer than sixty feet. They purchased four work boats, thirty-five feet long and eight feet or more wide, from Captain Abraham Sheppard of present-day Shepherdstown, West Virginia. When they set out to hire one hundred workers they had trouble, as they could never find as many workers as they needed. This problem continued for the duration of the construction and it included both supervisors and laborers. The work was difficult and isolated from any towns; there was ample work around, and in, eastern towns to absorb the labor available.[46]

They started quickly, but they had a shortage of expertise in key roles. In a letter to Lord Fairfax on June 30 Washington laid out the near-term plan,

> The subscriptions for improving and extending the inland navigation of Potomac, have filled very fast … and the work will begin about the first of August. We still want a skillful Engineer, a man of practical knowledge to conduct the business; but where to find him we know not at present: In the meanwhile the less difficult parts of the river will be attempted, that no time may be lost in effecting so important and salutary an undertaking.[47]

The sluices around Seneca and Shenandoah Falls could be started without much technical support. Washington believed the engineering expertise needed for the dam and locks around Great Falls and Little Falls existed only in Europe at that time. Washington was well-connected and well-respected so his inability to find an acceptable American mechanical or civil engineer probably indicated the needed skill was not yet available in this country. He believed the most capable person was James Brindley from England, the nephew of the James Brindley who had constructed the Bridgewater canal to Manchester only a few years before. Brindley was working with another American canal company, the Susquehanna Canal Company, and was therefore unavailable. Nevertheless, Washington convinced Brindley to visit in 1786, to provide some advice, but he did not become the chief engineer.[48]

Only forty-four workmen started clearing the river at Seneca Falls on August 1, 1785, not the one hundred Washington originally planned. This was indicative of the labor problems they faced throughout the project; they could not find and keep good workers. The very next day, August 2, Washington and the board took a canoe trip up the river to Seneca Falls and Shenandoah Falls to inspect the work being done and to validate their initial decision to use sluice navigation for most of the river. Near the Shenandoah Falls he records a rough but, in his mind, reasonable ride, which could be improved. On Sunday, August 7 he wrote, the Water is deep with rocks here and there, near the surface, then a ripple; the Water betwn. which, and the Spout, as before. The Spout takes its name from the rapidity of the Water, and its dashings, occasioned by a gradual, but considerable fall, over a rocky bottom which makes and uneven surface & considerable swell. The Water however, is of sufficient depth through it, but the Channel not being perfectly straight; skilfull hands are necessary to navigate and conduct Vessels through this rapid. From hence, there is pretty smooth & even Water with loose stone, & some rocks, for the best part of a Mile.... But the passage which seemed most likely to answer our purpose of Navigation was on the Maryland side being freest from rocks but Shallow. From hence to what are called Pains [Paynes] falls the Water is tolerably smooth, with Rocks here and there. These are best passed on the Maryland side. They are pretty Swift—shallow—and foul at bottom but the difficulties may be removed. From the bottom of these Falls, leaving an Island on the right, & the Maryland Shore on the left the easy & good Navigation below is entered.[49]

Labor, weather, and river problems made the work slow over the following years. Washington dealt with all the problems, including the loans for the funding, the labor problems, and the legislatures, until his resignation in 1789 after he had been elected President of the United States. Thomas Johnson was elected president of the Potomac Company in September 1789, and work continued. In 1792 Johnson reported, "A canal at the Little Falls is cut on the Maryland side of the river nearly the whole distance necessary."[50]

In other words, the river was usable at least up to Great Falls, but they would still have to build the locks at the Falls.

The work on the Little Falls bypass canal started in 1791. The locks were made from wood which meant they would require replacement sooner than if they were made of stone. The work continued slowly because they were having their usual labor problems. In 1794, they had hired, from an owner, only sixty slaves, well below the authorization they had for two hundred. The labor shortage remained as one of their major problems. They had no qualified engineer to guide the lock building project, which called for more expertise than ever. Poor design was the result. For example, they did not build a guard lock upstream of the bypass canal this allowed floodwaters and debris to enter the lock, creating a blockage which then had to be removed. The Little Falls bypass canal was finally complete in 1794, allowing the company to start serious work on the Great Falls locks.[51]

The construction of the locks around Great Falls started in 1794 and took several years to complete. It was clearly the major engineering challenge in the country at the time. Lift-lock canals had been built in Europe for many years but it is unlikely any of those projects had the challenge of this effort. The Great Falls locks had to be built to cover a vertical distance of seventy-six feet over a river distance of approximately one-half mile. The fact that much of the work had to be done by cutting through solid rock added to the difficulty. Washington maintained interest in the canal and would contribute ideas even from his new position as President of the United States. Concerned about the expense of locks, he speculated about the use of inclined planes that could possibly be built to bypass the Falls. These planes would be wooden ramps by which the boats could be lowered around the Falls or pulled above the Falls. Obviously very hefty ropes and mechanisms would be needed to accomplish this over the height of the Falls. Washington was persuaded not to use planes for the boats. However, by 1797 a plane was built, not for boats but for transferring cargo in barrels, mostly flour, from the top of the Falls to the lower river. Land transportation was used to move the cargo around the Falls while the locks were being built.[52]

In addition to the ever-present river problem of high or low water, the company continued to struggle with an inadequate labor force. They were always seeking competent engineering help especially during the lock building. The labor problems continued, "the year 1798 began with only eleven employees, mostly slave, at work at Great Falls under overseer John Panton. By the following month, February 1798, this workforce was increased to twenty-four men, mostly slaves owned by John Templeman." Financial problems were somewhat alleviated by a loan from the State of Maryland in 1800. In spite of all obstacles, they persisted.[53]

Finally, on February 2, 1802, seventeen years after construction began, the first boat went through the locks at Great Falls. Now a boat loaded with coal could float down the river from coal country at George's Creek, past Cumberland, Oldtown, Williamsport, and Harper's Ferry to the locks at Great Falls, then down to Alexandria or Georgetown. It was a difficult trip and there were not many return trips upstream. Most owners dismantled the boats at the eastern end and started over back upstream. The Potomac Company's first and only dividend was paid in 1802.[54]

> Three hundred five boats paid tolls in 1802, carrying 1,952 tons of flour, whiskey, tobacco, iron, and other cargo. This was a fairly impressive haul considering the lack of rain in the summer, the low water levels, and a recurring problem with mill dams and fish weirs ... imperiling the flatboats. By 1803 the number of boats had risen to 493, carrying 5,549 tons. But in keeping with company tradition, revenues never matched expenditures.... In 1805, for example, it would manage to collect $5,213 in tolls against $19,447 in expenses. Such was the norm, year after year. Technological success refused to translate into commercial riches.[55]

Despite good years in 1802 and 1803, the company continued to struggle. It made progress but was always behind in meeting its objective, a profitable operation. In an 1813 report to the Virginia legislature it touted its progress ("have long since removed the great obstacles to the navigation of the Potomac river from tide water to about thirty miles above Cumberland") but acknowledged their objective of profitable commerce on the Potomac was not yet accomplished, and requested five more years to complete the project. The peak years of canal building were behind them and they were now competing in a new technological world.[56]

The entire enterprise was summarized in 1819 as follows,

> In round numbers the whole sum actually expended on the works from the commencement of the operations of the Company in 1784 may be stated as $670,000.00
> And the debt due from the Company including the $30,000 and interest due the State of Maryland, at 150,000.00
> The tolls received since the existence of the Company and re-invested in carrying on the works ... —amount to 185,202.78
> An average amount of tolls now received may be fairly put at rather more than less than 15,000.00[57]

This dismal report suggested something must be done as these losses could not be sustained. By 1824 there was talk of a new canal,

> acts were passed during the past winter, by the legislatures of both Virginia and Maryland, for incorporating a new company to make a navigable canal from the tide water of the Potomac in the District of Columbia to the mouth of Savage Creek, on the north branch of said river, and extending thence across the Alleghany mountains to some convenient point on the navigable waters of the Ohio or some of its tributary streams.[58]

Since the canal work had started in 1785 there had been dramatic changes in technology and national governance. The Constitution was written in 1787, ratified in 1788, and resulted in a new republic in 1789. By 1800 there was a new seat of government on the Potomac, the District of Columbia, or Washington D. C. The District incorporated Georgetown within its new borders. As the American Industrial Revolution blossomed in the early part of the century new technologies, including steam power became common. The Potomac Canal was still operating under the old rules.

It had been seventy years since Washington first canoed down the Potomac with the idea of turning it into a westward transportation artery. It had been almost forty years since the Potomac Company had been formed to turn his dream into a reality. First under Washington and then under others, the Potomac Company struggled to improve the river, pay off debts and hopefully make a profit for the shareholders. On a map this seemed like an ideal approach, using a river stretched from the tidewater to the mountains. A short road over the mountains would reach other rivers such as the Youghiogheny or Cheat, which would, in turn, get travelers to the Ohio River.

The Potomac Company didn't succeed for at least two reasons. The first was that the difficulties of dealing with the river were vastly underrated. It dropped hundreds of feet from its source to the tidal waters meaning many falls, shoals, rapids had to be navigated. Either high water or low water made the river difficult to navigate at any time especially during the wet or dry seasons. The obstacles at Great Falls and Little Falls were especially challenging. The Potomac is not a natural waterway for travel; it had to be pushed and shoved to make it useable, and the problems they had with the labor force made it even more difficult. The Mississippi, which drains the middle of the country, and its tributaries, such as the Ohio, are much different. For hundreds of miles those rivers are wide, deep, and slowly flowing making them ideal waterways for migration and commerce. The Potomac Company founders, including Washington, wanted to imagine the Potomac in the same mold, but their imagination could not make it so.

The other factor that caught up with the company was technology. When the Potomac Company started its ambitious enterprise in 1785, nothing like it existed in this country; there were no canals and they were truly breaking new ground, both literally and figuratively. It is true the project was not a true canal, but a river improvement with canal-like locks.[59] Depending on the definition of canals they have been around for centuries. The "modern" canal age dates to the 1760s in Europe although those canals used locks over less challenging terrain, were shorter, and usually connected a coalfield to a nearby city. The first canal in this country is claimed to be the Schuylkill and Susquehanna Canal, started in 1791 and, in part, completed in 1797.[60]

Although the lock technology chosen for the Potomac River bypasses was state-of-the-art when begun, it was difficult to apply. One drawback was the lack of experienced designers as most were working on other projects. It also took a long time, ten years, to build the locks around the falls. By that time both technologies and modes of transportation were changing. These changes included both inland still water canals and steamboats.

The problem for the Potomac Canal was not that steamboats could use the river, they could not, but that easy travel on inland waterways by steamboat would increase the competition from others on the East Coast to get to those waterways. The in-landers would then no longer be isolated, as they could travel the Ohio and Mississippi for migration and commerce. Suddenly the struggle to keep the Potomac open, mostly to one-way traffic, seemed an anachronism. The need to move across the mountains became more urgent, causing more competition in modes of transportation.

Washington died in 1799 without seeing his dream of a waterway from the Potomac to Ohio realized. Even after his death the company struggled, having it best year in 1802. They never came close to making the portages from the upper part of the river to the Cheat or Youghiogheny rivers which would have connected the Potomac and Ohio rivers. The Potomac Company did, however, lay the groundwork for the next attempt to bridge the mountains by water. Its effort merged into the new still water canal that would parallel the Potomac up to Cumberland, and hopefully beyond. That was the Chesapeake and Ohio Canal.

The Chesapeake and Ohio Canal

The Potomac Canal was conceived during the Confederation period, four years prior to the birth of the new republic in1789. The country had changed dramatically by 1824 when there was discussion of a new canal to replace it. The United States spent the 1790s consolidating itself, resisting wars with Great Britain and France, and growing modestly from about 3.9 million in 1790 to about 5.3 million in 1800. By 1800 growth became dramatic in area, population, wealth and confidence. In 1820 the population exceeded 9.6 million, more than double the 1790 population. In Ohio population growth was even more dramatic; not even measured in the 1790 census, population was about 45,000 in 1800 when Ohio was still a territory, and was about 580,000 in 1820. West Virginia, still a part of Virginia at that time, grew just as rapidly, from 55,000 in 1790 to 136,000 in 1820. These examples demonstrate that the west was growing much faster than the nation as a whole; the frontier was moving into Ohio.[61] As Turner (*The Frontier in American History*) described it, "American development has exhibited not merely advance along a single line, but a return to primitive conditions on a continually advancing frontier line."[62]

In 1790 Ohio was on the cusp of settlement, but it was delayed because of conflicts with the Native American population, a situation that was about to change. Otterstrom and Earle ("The Settlement of the United States from 1790 to 1990") analyze the spread of settlement using population density, or persons per square mile. In Figure 4 they show that one of the highest population densities on the frontier in 1790 was along the Ohio-Pennsylvania border that is along the Monongahela and Ohio rivers.[63] Not surprisingly this was at the western terminus of the Braddock Road, soon to become the Cumberland Road, which provided the land bridge across the mountains into Ohio. Settlers were about to forge out along that path from Maryland, Pennsylvania, and Virginia into Ohio. The Braddock Road was the point of the population spear to the west. Its eastern terminus at Cumberland, Maryland, was also near the headwaters of the Potomac, the water pathway from the mountains to the Atlantic. Although the Potomac Company was struggling, having its best year in 1802, the corridor from the Atlantic, up the Potomac, then across the mountains via the Braddock Road to the Ohio country, was still seen as very important. When the 1824 discussions took place about a new canal to replace the Potomac River Canal, that corridor was naturally considered.

The explosive growth in the early nineteenth century was also fueled by the Louisiana Purchase and the War of 1812. Transportation to move people and goods was becoming more important. Moving west meant moving into a wilderness without a road system; development of roads such as the Cumberland Road take time. Water highways, such as rivers and canals, have always been attractive as means of moving people and goods long distances. The early nineteenth century could be considered the age of canals in America as a number were constructed, especially in the mid–Atlantic, northeast, and finally in Ohio. The Erie Canal, proposed in 1808, delayed by the War of 1812, started in 1817, and completed in 1825, was a notable example. It was a huge success, cutting travel time between Lake Erie and Albany from weeks to nine days. Freight rates dropped over ninety percent. (The route from Albany to the Great lakes would have been shorter and easier if the canal terminated on Lake Ontario instead of Lake Erie. The choice of Lake Erie was made due to a concern that if the Ontario route was used, the trade would go up to Montreal instead of to the American west.) Because of the success of the Erie Canal, major East Coast cities such as New York, Philadelphia, and Baltimore started to devise ways on how they could get their goods across the mountains. The competition for the western trade was so intense it helped determine the route of the new canal being considered.[64]

The Erie Canal would have been George Washington's worst nightmare, had he lived to see it. It was the opening to the west he wanted, but he wanted it closer to home in Virginia. He had visited the Mohawk Valley and had seen that the Mohawk River cut a natural opening across the mountains, therefore making an easy route to the west. The struggles of the Potomac Company, the population ready to take the Maryland-to-Ohio corridor, and the anticipated success of the Erie Canal, convinced many that the ideal waterway west would be a still water canal paralleling the Potomac then extending across the mountains to the Youghiogheny. The Youghiogheny enters the Monongahela, which meets the Allegheny River at the Forks. This canal would be the direct water route to the west that Washington and others imagined decades earlier.

Albert Gallatin (1761–1849) was an immigrant from Switzerland who arrived in America in 1780. He became active in politics in Pennsylvania and served in the House of Representatives from 1795 to 1801. A very able master of finances while in Congress, he often clashed with Alexander Hamilton, the first Secretary of the Treasury; unsurprisingly, since Hamilton would clash with anyone not an arch-Federalist like himself. Both Hamilton and Gallatin matured politically in the 1790s when the American political parties initially formed. Federalists, led mostly by Hamilton, were opposed by Thomas Jefferson's Anti-Federalists or Democratic-Republicans. The United States financial system, ably set up by Hamilton, was strongly opposed by Jefferson's followers who envisioned more of an agrarian society rather than a financial and manufacturing society promoted by Hamilton. When Jefferson was elected President in 1800 he chose Gallatin as his Secretary of the Treasury. "Although Jefferson asked Gallatin to revolutionize Hamilton's Federalist money machine, in fact Gallatin had no dissatisfaction and only minor differences with Hamilton's approach."[65] The country was well-served by the financial system set up by Hamilton and refined by Gallatin.

Jefferson, a supporter of the small yeoman farmer and of limited government, became president just as the country was about to expand dramatically into western land. He was an enabler of that expansion. Despite his small government philosophy, Jefferson convinced himself of the propriety of the Louisiana Purchase in 1803, which doubled the land area of the United States. See Map 12. The population, mostly bottled up on the East Coast, wanted to expand westward but there was no internal infrastructure to enable massive moves. Rivers did not go everywhere people wanted to locate, and the road system varied from very bad to nonexistent. Congress was aware of this and with an eye to improving transportation infrastructure, commissioned a report from the Secretary of the Treasury on the subject of roads and canals. Gallatin was happy to oblige because he believed an adequate infrastructure was necessary for a sound economy.[66]

In the first sentence of his April 12, 1808, report to Congress, entitled *Public Roads and Canals,* Albert Gallatin optimistically stated, "The general utility of artificial roads and canals, is at this time so universally admitted, as hardly to require any additional proofs." In the report, he described various local canals up and down the East Coast. However, when he addressed the subject of the communication between the Atlantic and the western waters, he started with a detailed description of the mountains, especially the Alleghenies where he emphasized their height, two thousand to three thousand feet above sea level. He then became more pessimistic about crossing the mountains with a canal: "This description has been introduced for the double purpose of pointing out all the rivers which can afford the means of communication, and of shewing the impracticality, in the present state of science, of effecting a canal navigation across the mountains."[67] His numbers were convincing; in no other country had there been a canal greater than 430 feet in elevation between its terminal waters. That would compare with an elevation of 2,000 to 3,000 feet across the Alleghenies. Talking about the local canals, "there is none which is not of an elevation much beyond what has ever been overcome by canals in any other country."[68] He was also concerned about supplying water to the canal at these high elevations.

Less than ten years after this report, almost in defiance of Gallatin's prediction, work on the Erie Canal started. But the canal, very long at 363 miles, rose only 560 feet along its length, fairly close to the European canals to which he referred. It was nothing like the minimum 2,000-foot elevation that would be required for the Chesapeake and Ohio (C&O) Canal.[69] This would make a significant difference in the final leg of the proposed C&O Canal; Gallatin's prediction would ultimately prove accurate.

The origin of the C&O Canal was founded in the slow demise of the Potomac Company as it struggled, mostly unsuccessfully, to make the river canal a paying proposition. In 1816, the Virginia Assembly created the Board of Public Works to oversee all public works that involved the state. Virginia was, of course, invested in the Potomac Canal, and soon after the Board was founded it requested a review of connecting the Potomac and Ohio waters "by a navigable canal." Until the Potomac Company itself requested help in determining the future course of Potomac navigation, in 1819, nothing was done. The following January the Board commissioned Thomas Moore (1760–1822), Chief Engineer of the Board, to investigate the best way to connect these two rivers by conducting a survey of the rivers. Moore started his survey on June 30, 1820, and submitted his report in December 1820.[70] Moore went into exquisite detail in the report, noting for example, "the fall from the last mentioned point to the mouth of Savage River, is 1366.71 feet."[71] About three-quarters of the report covered the link from the upper Potomac to the Ohio country rivers via the Cheat and Youghiogheny rivers. The engineering detail and the reasoning behind it is very well done; he was a well-respected engineer. He devoted the last quarter of the report to an independent canal. He avoided making a solid recommendation between the existing river canal that must be improved, and an independent still water canal, saying that was not his job. However, his preference was clearly stated.

> But when the powers of art have been exerted to the utmost extent, to produce an easy navigation in the bed of a stream, still it must hold a very inferior grade to that of an independent canal; because the natural fall of the river must be overcome by the labor of men; and if the whole fall of a river is great in proportion to its length, it will require a great number, in proportion to the tonnage; and therefore must be very expensive compared with a canal furnished with locks, where the boats are on level water by the labor of horses.... The transportation, however, on such a canal, is so much cheaper than by any other means of internal improvement.[72]

This report, plus the troubles the Potomac Company was having, probably were the deciding factors in the decision to go with a new canal, a still water canal with locks and a towpath for horses or mules to pull loaded canal boats.

In February 1823, the Virginia Assembly passed a bill for the incorporation of the Potomac Canal Company. That would not be enough as it would be necessary for Maryland to do the same, especially since the canal would be on the Maryland side of the river.[73] Maryland hesitated, as the merchants of Baltimore were concerned about losing the western trade that was becoming a reality. For twenty-five years prior to 1812, Baltimore had been the leading exporter of flour from the United States. Most of the flour had come down the Susquehanna, placing them in competition with Philadelphia. The cities reached a compromise and the status quo was maintained for years but by the early 1820s, things were changing. The Erie Canal threatened the western trade for both Philadelphia and Baltimore. Philadelphia started to look for its own route across the mountains, worrying Baltimore. When the canal route was proposed from Georgetown to Cumberland, Baltimoreans felt they would lose on that trade. As a result, in February 1823, the Maryland legislature commissioned a study of the practicality of a canal from Baltimore to the Potomac River, perhaps to the Monocacy. This would be a way to connect Baltimore to the proposed canal along the Potomac. The results of the study were disappointing and that cross-country canal was not pursued.[74]

There was still strong interest in a canal along the Potomac and therefore in attempts to bring Maryland into the mix. At the first public meeting on the subject in Leesburg, Virginia, on August 25, 1823, the participants passed a resolution recommending the canal. They proposed another meeting to be held later in the year in Washington, D. C. with representatives from all the neighboring states. At the meeting in November there were representatives from all the nearby states except Ohio, although a few private citizens from Ohio attended. About a third of the representatives were from Maryland, but tellingly Baltimore was not represented. Although Virginia had taken the legislative lead Maryland had signed up for more shares in the project. The meeting in Washington produced a resolution.

> "Whereas, A connection of the Atlantic and Western waters by a canal, leading from the seat of the National Government to the river Ohio ... is one of the highest importance to the states immediately interested therein, and considered in a national view, is of inestimable consequence to the future union, security and happiness of the United States,
>
> "*Resolved,* That it is expedient to substitute for the present defective navigation of the Potomac River, above, a navigable canal from Cumberland to the Coal Banks at the eastern base of the Allegheny, and to extend such a canal as soon thereafter as practicable to the highest constant steamboat navigation of the Monongahela or Ohio River."
>
> It was further brought out that the canal was to extend ultimately to Lake Erie, thus connecting the seat of Government and the Great Lakes. If this idea was not new it was the earliest complete statement of the Chesapeake and Ohio Canal project.[75]

The movement to construct the canal was strong and gaining support. This would be a major undertaking and involve several states and the Federal government. Despite the popularity of the canal with the public, the participation of the Federal government was still problematic. The interstate public Cumberland Road had been approved by the Federal government early in the century, but that was a special circumstance. See the next chapter. There was still a constitutional question at the time on whether or not the Federal government could fund internal improvement projects or if they had to be done by the states or private parties. When Gallatin issued his report in 1808, even though he was in favor of internal development, he thought that a constitutional amendment might be necessary to allow Federal participation; it was not forthcoming. There was no problem with the Erie Canal because it was sponsored by the State of New York and was entirely within New York. Gallatin's recommended plan for internal improvements was postponed during the War of 1812. In 1817, Senator John C. Calhoun of South Carolina introduced a bill in Congress to revive the plan for internal improvements. It barely passed as states' rights emerged as an issue and some states were not anxious to have the Federal government involved in state matters. President Madison vetoed the bill in March 1817, saying in his message he thought it to be unconstitutional.[76]

The path that did lead to Federal participation started about a year previous to the 1823 Washington convention on the canal.

Congress was still willing to fund internal improvements and in late spring, 1822, passed an appropriation for the repair of the Cumberland Road. President Monroe vetoed the bill on the grounds that it was unconstitutional. The pressure continued, Congress was clearly behind the canal and by December Monroe had changed his mind. This is covered in more detail in Chapter Seven.

After altering his position, Monroe summed up the reasons to support the C&O Canal, if not all internal improvements.

> First, "A great portion of the produce of the very fertile country through it would pass would find a market through that channel."
> Second, "Troops might be moved with great facility in war, with cannon and every kind of munition, and in either direction."
> Third, "Connecting the Atlantic with the western country in a line passing through the seat of the National Government, it would contribute essentially to strengthen the bond of union itself."[77]

The door barring the Federal government from participating in internal improvement projects had been cracked open earlier with the Cumberland Road. Now it had been opened much wider although ostensibly only for this canal. It would be hard to close in the future.

President Monroe's second reason is very similar to the reasoning President Eisenhower used in the 1950s to develop the Interstate Highway System, national defense. His last reason to support the canal, connecting the Atlantic with the west pointed to the heart of the matter, opening the routes to the west, and strengthening the bonds between east and west. The canal would be in two parts, one from Georgetown through Cumberland and across the mountains all the way to Pittsburgh, and the second part from Pittsburgh through one of various routes to Lake Erie. Only the first part would be known as the Chesapeake and Ohio (C&O) Canal. The canal was to be built in sections, with the eastern section from the tidewater of the Potomac to the mouth of the Savage River, the middle section from the mouth of the Savage River to the Youghiogheny River at the mouth of Bear Creek, and the western section from the mouth of Bear Creek through the Youghiogheny to Pittsburgh. Later the eastern section was to terminate at Cumberland and the middle section was to go from Cumberland through Wills Creek to the Casselman River and then to the Youghiogheny River. The middle section would be the most difficult; it was to be the one that would get the canal over the mountains.[78]

A government survey was commissioned to provide a more detailed estimate of the total cost of the C&O Canal. As might be expected the detailed cost estimate was much higher than the costs estimated by the proposers while they were selling it. For the eastern section from Georgetown to Cumberland the cost was 8.085 million dollars compared to the earlier estimate of 2.75 million dollars, an enormous sum for the day. This necessitated another meeting in Washington in 1826 to consider the cost and the fact they did not have enough money subscribed to do the job. The 1826 meeting decided on another survey after which they convinced themselves the cost could be reduced to less than five million dollars.[79]

The struggle to fund and start the canal continued for another two years. Finally, in 1828 it all came together.

> The Chesapeake and Ohio Canal Company was formally organized June 20, 1828, when the stockholders met in Washington and elected Mr. Charles Fenton Mercer of Virginia as President. The

Potomac Company gave its final consent on July 10, 1828, and the conveyance of the C & O Canal Company was made by a deed on August 15, 1828. Thus the Potomac Company passed into legal oblivion, though in spirit it remained as the pioneer forerunner of the C & O Canal Company.[80]

The official construction started on July 4, 1828, when President John Quincy Adams turned the first spade of dirt in Georgetown for the canal. The official ceremony was moved to coincide with the national holiday even though the official conveyance by the Potomac Company wasn't completed until days later. This was upholding a tradition, "All the major canals ... in the nation had been started on Independence Day—the Erie on July 4, 1817, the Ohio and Erie on July 4, 1825, and the Pennsylvania Grand Canal on July 4, 1826." Coincidently and ominously for the canal, another opening ceremony was taking place about forty miles away in Baltimore. The sole surviving signer of the Declaration of Independence, Charles Carroll of Carrollton, was turning over a spade of dirt on the western edge of Baltimore, on the estate of his relative James Carroll, to start work on the Baltimore and Ohio (B&O) Railroad.[81]

With the Chesapeake and Ohio Canal and the Baltimore and Ohio Railroad starting on the same day, and the Erie Canal in operation, the race to the west was on. Although George Washington had not lived to see the west opened to this extent, his vision had been shared and implemented by others; he would have been proud of his legacy.

The canal promised a smoother, almost year-round, trip from Georgetown to Cumberland. Its early advocates also claimed it would be easier to build compared to making the Potomac navigable for its entire route, one would not be fighting the river, and the river was open only part of the year. The reality, as is often the case, was different. The charter of the canal required that one hundred miles of the canal be open within three years. On July 4, 1828, there was good reason to be optimistic about that goal, but the difficulties started almost immediately. The first omen might be considered the moment President Adams tried to overturn a spade full of earth and was unable to do so because he struck a root and could not fill the spade with dirt,

> whereupon the last of the dignified, old-school Presidents, threw off his coat and amidst the applause of the assembled thousands, with music by the band thrown in, proceeded with that determination which, he declared, should characterize the efforts of the company to begin the excavation of the eastern section of the canal. The work was completed twenty-two years later.[82]

The root typified the early construction problems. They ran into hardpan (clay under soil), slate, and gravel which made it difficult to excavate. Building supplies such as lumber, building stone, and lime for cement were hard to acquire and were expensive. They also faced the problem that had plagued the Potomac Company for years—lack of labor. Unlike urban, bustling Baltimore this was still an agricultural area and was therefore short of labor.[83]

Anticipating this would be a problem Mercer left for Europe immediately after the groundbreaking to put advertisements in papers in Dublin, Cork, Belfast, and even in Holland, appealing for workers. He knew he was appealing to low-income workers so he increased the pool of applicants through a broad appeal, therefore keeping wages low. "Prospective employees were offered meat three times a day, plenty of bread and vegetables, "a reasonable allowance of whiskey," and from $8 to $12 a month in wages, $20 for masons."[84] These workers were brought to America as indentured servants with specific contracts. The workforce was comprised mostly of Irish and German immigrants who had to be assigned to separate crews because they did not get along. There was not only fighting between groups but also within groups. The Irish workers, for example, often had fights among those who had come from different Irish towns. The whiskey ration didn't help, whether it was spread throughout the day or kept for evenings. Some workers would get drunk and were unable to work the next day. An attempt to cut off the ration made things worse so it had to be reinstated. These immigrant workers did backbreaking work using primitive tools such as axes, stump-pullers, wheelbarrows, and plows and scrapers. They also experienced a lack of respect from their employers. In addition, there was a cholera epidemic that struck in 1832. Highly contagious and lethal, cholera killed so many workers that a cemetery in Hagerstown resisted taking more bodies and a special cemetery was constructed near the canal for workers who died on or near the job.[85]

Soon groundbreaking contracts were granted for all sections with the section from Seneca to Georgetown, about twenty miles, the first to be started. It was a little late but in November 1830, "the section from Seneca to the old locks of the Potomac Company at Little Falls through which it was possible to reach tide-water, was opened to navigation.... Early in the spring of 1831 the canal was opened a mile below Little Falls, and with the further extension of a mile a little later, the work was brought in sight of Georgetown."[86] The first section was complete.

The canal company took a rather leisurely approach in the purchase of the right-of-way along the river. It assumed the legacy of the Potomac Company would be enough to guarantee the appropriate path. They ran into problems only forty-eight miles above Georgetown at Point of Rocks, Maryland. Here the river cuts through a very narrow gap in Catoctin Mountain leaving steep sides along the river and a very narrow area between the river and the mountain, apparently not large enough for both the canal and the B&O Railroad. The B&O was very aggressive and obtained an injunction against the canal for the right-of-way at that gap. Work on that part of the canal stopped for years while the court battle raged. The court battle for the right-of-way was a metaphor for the new, aggressive, industrial age which challenged the more leisurely approach of the old way of doing business. Originally the court ruled in favor of the railroad, but in 1832 the court of appeals ruled for the canal, and then ruled favorably on the entire right-of-way to Cumberland for the canal.[87]

After the court battles the company ran out of money. The Federal government was no longer contributing, but the farmers in western Maryland were still pushing for the canal, which would enable them to transport their goods to the east. The state, to protect its previous investment, lent the company two million dollars but it was not enough and in 1836 they appealed to the state for more. Maryland responded by buying three million dollars' worth of stock that put the state in tacit control of the canal.[88]

Progress was slow but steady and each section opened as it was complete. The C&O Canal opened to Seneca in 1831, was completed to Harpers Ferry in 1834, a twelve-mile section from Point of Rocks. It reached Williamsport in 1834, eighty-six miles from Georgetown, then reached Hancock, 134 miles from the start at Georgetown, in 1839. It took another eleven years, until 1850, to cut the remaining 50.5 miles and reached the supposed halfway point at Cumberland, Maryland, eight years after the railroad.[89]

The canal was the engineering masterpiece of the day because of the topographical challenges it had to overcome. It used seventy-four lift locks to lift the boats 610 feet from Georgetown to Cumberland, eleven stone aqueducts to carry the canal over various Potomac tributaries, seven dams to supply water, plus various lock houses and other support buildings. It was fifty to sixty feet wide at the towpath level and carried a minimum depth of six feet of water compared to a depth in the Erie Canal of four feet of water. The locks were fifteen feet wide and ninety feet long, the same as the Erie Canal, and the boats were typically 14.5 feet wide and ninety-two feet long. (The rudder was put at the side so the boat could fit into the ninety-foot long lock.) The boats drew about 4.5 feet of water and could carry a load of 135 tons. A typical load of coal would be 120 tons.[90]

One of the solid engineering feats of the canal was the Paw Paw tunnel, approximately twenty-five miles downriver from Cumberland. Paw Paw is actually across the river in West Virginia but it is the closest town to the tunnel. At this point the river makes a number of loops, resembling a series of S-curves strung together, with steep cliffs on either side of the river. Although the plan was to keep the canal close to the river at all places it made sense to cut a tunnel through one of the loops near Paw Paw to save at least five miles of digging around steep cliffs. The tunnel site was chosen in December 1835 and construction started in 1836. It was all hand work done by unskilled labor using black powder to blast out certain areas. The lack of experience meant much was trial and error; for example, they sometimes blasted out more than necessary and would refill the area after the tunnel brickwork had been done. Brickwork lined the arched ceiling, usually thirteen layers of brick deep but as much as thirty-three layers at some points. Multiple crews worked from both ends on both the tunnel above and the canal below. The completed tunnel was 3,118 feet long, almost two-thirds of a mile.[91]

The tunnel was scheduled for completion in 1838. After labor riots, workers leaving, and money running out the contractor closed shop in 1846, abandoning both the tunnel and the canal. Another contractor took on the job and through great effort and expense, completed the canal almost to Cumberland in the spring of 1850. It took one last contractor, Michael Byrne of Frederick County, Maryland, to put on the finishing touches and by fall the canal was completed to Cumberland; it was the last gasp. It had taken twenty-two years to reach Cumberland, 184.5 miles, when the plan was to get to Ohio in twelve years. "It had cost $14 million, not counting repairs and interest—nine and a half million more than estimated. As a proportion of Gross National Product, this was as much as the country would spend 150 years later to put a man on the moon."[92] The C&O Canal was moderately successful, especially for western Marylanders. Its best year was in 1875 when "over 500 boats carried 973,805 tons of cargo: 904,898 tons of coal; 1,000 of flour, 8,894 of wheat; 1,270 of lumber; 3,573 of corn; and the remainder, miscellaneous cargo." As is evident, coal from western Maryland was the principal cargo. In the last years of its operational life from 1892 to 1924, the major cargo consisted of coal, lime, building materials, and flour. These are all exports from the west; there is no mention in the literature of goods or people moving west from Georgetown to Cumberland and if it had happened, it was too small to mention. Over the years there were labor and weather problems, a boatman's strike and flood in 1877, and a miner's strike and drought in 1879. It suffered severe damage in the Johnstown Flood of 1889, after which the company filed for bankruptcy. The canal was revived after being taken over by the B&O Railroad. It was back in operation in 1892 but it never fully recovered. A final flood in 1924 closed the canal for good. It was taken over by the National Park Service in 1938 and by January 8, 1972, the lower part of the canal was restored and the entire canal was designated the Chesapeake and Ohio National Historical Park.[93]

The Waterway West Is Not Possible

In 1754 George Washington made a canoe trip down the Potomac specifically to assess its potential as a waterway to the west. This was just five years after the Ohio Company of Virginia was established to settle the Ohio country. The Ohio Company was founded to enable the dream English colonists had for a century—to move west over the mountains.

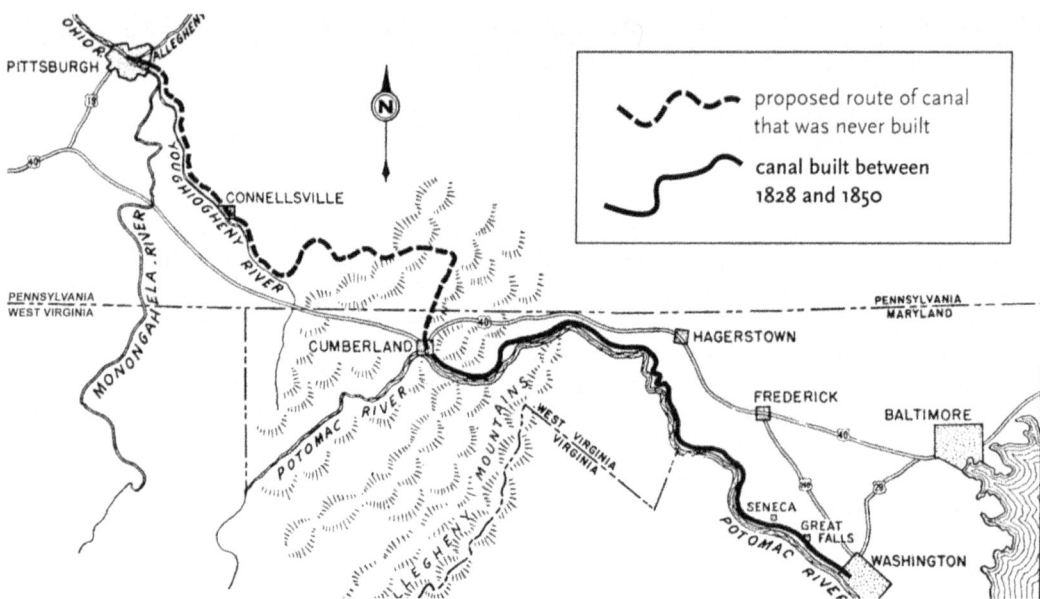

Map 14: Chesapeake and Ohio Canal National Park Service. The canal was built from Washington, D.C., to Cumberland, Maryland; the proposed route to Pittsburgh was abandoned as impractical. Also shown is the road over the mountains, the Baltimore Pike from Baltimore to Cumberland, followed by the Cumberland Road through to Wheeling, Virginia (off the map) (National Park Service).

Washington's 1754 dream of using the Potomac to move west was immediately put on hold by the French and Indian War, but it never left his mind. He continued to purchase land in the west, in Ohio country, and dreamed of moving there eventually. Throughout the two following wars he was consumed with national priorities. In 1785, very shortly after the Peace Treaty of Paris in 1783, he was the driving force behind the Potomac Company, which was established for the purpose of using the Potomac to link the tidal waters of the East Coast with the rivers of the Ohio country. He was determined to make the dream come true and would maintain that interest for the rest of his life, even throughout his presidency.

The company constructed sluices and locks and made the river moderately successful for navigation, but only for moving goods from west to east; it was unsuccessful in moving people or goods westward, the original concept. It struggled for a few decades but could not continue beyond the 1820s when it closed shop in favor of the Chesapeake and Ohio Canal, a still water canal. Remarkably, as the name suggests, the goal remained the same, to achieve a water crossing of the mountains. Various surveys were conducted over the years for mountain crossing points, places where one could cut a canal from an eastern flowing river to a western flowing river. They considered the Cheat, Youghiogheny, and other rivers. The plan for the C&O Canal, started in 1828, was to continue to the Ohio. The grand dream was still alive.

The grand dream did not survive as the C&O Canal stopped at Cumberland and never made it to Ohio. Although it was moderately successful in its own right the water link from the Potomac to the Ohio never was achieved. It was just not possible to cross the two thousand to three thousand foot Alleghenies by canal.

However, the route that Christopher Gist had blazed from Wills Creek in Maryland, across to the Monongahela in Ohio country in 1751, was still the preferred route from the mid–Atlantic to Ohio even though the canal was unsuccessful in exploiting it. His trail became Nemacolin's Path, Washington's Road, Braddock's Road, the Cumberland Road and eventually part of the National Road; a railroad was to follow. As the American Industrial Revolution took root in the early nineteenth century, methods of transportation other than water transportation were developed.

Seven

Maryland as the Gateway to Ohio

It seemed the only way across the mountains was by walking or by horseback. The Ohio Company of Virginia recognized early, in 1750, that it would not be possible to move large numbers of people to the west this way so they attempted to open the gate between Maryland and Ohio with a road, but all the wars of the late eighteenth century precluded that opening. By the beginning of the nineteenth century Ohio was ready for settlement and the new republic made it a high priority to breach the Alleghenies with a real road to open the west. A road across the mountains became a necessity if the east and west were to be united.

Moving to Ohio

The Ohio country was blessed with a great deal of fertile, arable land, and many rivers, mostly flowing north-south. Although these rivers facilitated commerce within Ohio they did nothing to help settlers reach Ohio. As a result, most travel into the frontier was by foot and horseback. Carts, wagons, and coaches moved in, and between, the East Coast cities but not in the west. A road was not built just for its own sake, but to allow travel back and forth to a settlement someone had hacked out in the wilderness. In other words, roads followed the people, not the other way around. The people started to move to Ohio in greater numbers, coming by foot and by horseback, most often using the Braddock-Burd Road, the path originally blazed by Christopher Gist.

The real turning point in the migration to Ohio was the Treaty of Greenville, signed on August 3, 1795. The Treaty reserved only the northwest corner of Ohio for the Indians; the remainder was open for settlement. With the Indian wars settled for the time being, the whole eastern part of the Northwest Territory, what would become Ohio, saw major movements of people and new population centers. These usually grew upstream of the many rivers in Ohio.

The Ohio rivers were numerous and long and they provided channels for settlement within the future state. In the east the Hocking River is 102 miles long, and the Muskingum 111 miles long. In the middle of Ohio is the Scioto, through present-day Columbus, at 231 miles in length. In the west is the Miami, 170 miles long. All these, and others, drained into the Ohio River so once one reached the Ohio it was easy to follow one of these tributaries inland to fertile farming areas, and many did. They started on the Ohio itself: "in 1797 Virginian Bezeleel Wells established Steubenville on the abandoned site of Fort Steuben." Many poor families from western Virginia became either legal settlers or squatters in the area. Farther down the Ohio settlers pushed up the Hocking (then known as the

Hockhocking) and Muskingum rivers using the fertile river valleys for farming. A college, which later became Ohio University, was founded on the Hocking at Athens, laid out in 1797. Nathaniel Massie was the driver for a new town on the Scioto River. Many lots were laid out and sold at modest prices and some were offered free to new settlers, to encourage more immigration. The town known as Chillicothe drew many from Kentucky and Virginia, those who wanted to avoid the slave society, and it became a center of politics in the Territory. More town building also took place farther up the Scioto. Settlement expanded in the valleys of the Miami Rivers, in and near the Symnes Purchase. Israel Ludlow laid out a town he called Hamilton in 1795, which became a prosperous trading center, just north of present-day Cincinnati. In northeast Ohio, the area originally known as the Connecticut Western Reserve, and later just as the Western Reserve when Connecticut relinquished its control, was settled by New Englanders. These New Englanders were the first ones to enter Ohio without using the Ohio River. By the end of the eighteenth century the search for land in Ohio was in full swing.[1]

After a slow start Ohio was now booming. Early migration started even before 1795 when the Ohio Company of Associates established its settlement on the Ohio River at Marietta in 1788. Cincinnati was founded in 1788 and Cleveland in 1796. Soon after Zane's Trace was cut in 1797 population centers, places such as Zanesville, Lancaster, and Chillicothe grew along the Trace. The settlers came mostly from the east although some came through Kentucky. Many of the earliest settlers, the Scots-Irish, came well before this Zane's Trace wave and settled in southern Ohio often as squatters. The settlers in the Symnes Purchase, between the Great and Little Miami rivers, came from New Jersey. Virginians predominated in the Virginia Military district, as did Pennsylvanians in the upper part of the Seven Ranges. After the Harrison Land Act of 1800 when the minimum amounts of land sold was cut in half to 320 acres instead of full sections of 640 acres, and it was sold on credit for the first time, the immigration picked up even more rapidly.[2]

Immigrants from abroad, as well as settlers from the eastern seaboard, moved over the mountains to settle in Ohio. In 1790, when the United States was less than a year old the first European immigrants came from France. Six hundred emigrants left Havre de Grace, France in February and arrived in Alexandria, Virginia, after the first leg of their journey. They had purchased land in the Northwest Territory from the Society of the Scioto in Paris, a company associated with the Scioto Company in America. The company had sold land it did not own so the new immigrants in Alexandria were left with worthless titles. Some returned to France but others set out for Ohio. They traveled northwest from Alexandria, through Winchester, Virginia, to Brownsville, Pennsylvania, probably over the Braddock-Burd Road. They reached the Ohio River and settled in southeast Ohio on the Ohio River just south of its confluence with the Kanawha River. As city dwellers, they struggled in the wilderness, but received help from their American neighbors. A Monsieur Mentelle who arrived in 1791 observed, "To migrate from the eastern States to the 'far west' is painful enough now-a-days, but how much more so must it be for a citizen of a large European town! Even the farmer of the old countries would find it very hard, if not impossible, to clear land in the wilderness."[3] The French immigrants eventually settled the land ownership issue and established a settlement which they later named Gallipolis. These were the first of millions of European immigrants to claim land in the new republic, work hard, and successfully establish themselves as Americans. Like the millions that followed they found that the streets were not "paved with gold," but hard work in a new land would provide the new life they were looking for.

The country was going through rapid change politically also, and was finding its footing during the two terms of the Washington presidency. This was challenging because everything had to be done for the first time. The 1790s saw the threat of two wars, the formation of political parties, and the foundation of a financial system designed by Alexander Hamilton, among other things. The frenetic activity of the period left little time for formulating or implementing western policy.

All this changed around the turn of the century, beginning in 1800 with the election of Thomas Jefferson over John Adams, an election decided in the House of Representatives. The political shift in Washington was not the only change. Around that time the Industrial Revolution, which had started in Great Britain a few years earlier, reached America. These factors, and the 1803 purchase of the Louisiana Territory, forced the issues of a national economy and a national system of transportation into the political arena. Prior to the construction of any national road system the settler had to deal with these transportation issues as best they could.

Ohio Roads

The settlers moved west into Ohio along the various footpaths and trails, but they couldn't easily move back and forth between Ohio and the east. They were reasonably self-sufficient on their farms but they still needed some goods such as salt and iron and steel that they could not produce themselves. They had to travel back over the mountains, usually at least once a year, to barter for these goods. The lack of roads required them to use the packhorse trails back to the east. Once they reached the Ohio River there were some rudimentary roads, such as the Forbes Road in Pennsylvania, and the Braddock-Burd Road in Maryland and Pennsylvania, to allow them to return to Philadelphia or Baltimore for supplies. They could also use the Ohio River to travel east, but it was much more difficult traveling upstream to the east than floating downstream to the west.

Dr. Joseph Doddridge published some notes on his experiences living on the frontier between 1763 and 1783 (*Notes on the Settlement and Indian Wars of the Western Parts of Virginia and Pennsylvania from 1763 to 1783*) in which he described the travel back and forth over the mountains.

> The acquisition of the indispensable articles of salt, iron, steel, and castings presented great difficulties to the first settlers of the western country. They had no stores of any kind ... nor had they money to make purchases.... Peltry and furs were their only resources.... Every family collected what peltry and fur they could obtain throughout the year for the purpose of sending them over the mountains for barter. In the fall of the year ... every family formed an association with some of their neighbors for starting the little caravan. A master driver was selected from among them.... The horses were fitted out with pack-saddles, to the hinder part of which was fastened a pair of hobbles made of hickory withes; a bell and collar ornamented his neck. The bags provided for the conveyance of the salt were filled with feed for the horses; on the journey a part of this feed was left at convenient stages on the way down to support the return of the caravan; large wallets well filled with bread, jerk, boiled ham and cheese furnished provisions for the drivers. The barter for salt was made first at Baltimore.... Each horse carried two bushels of alum salt weighing eighty-four pounds to the bushel. This ... was not a heavy load for the horses but it was enough, considering the scanty subsistence allowed to them on the journey.[4]

He did not say how long this annual journey from the Monongahela to Baltimore and back took, but it had to be weeks, and it was not an easy trip. The paths over the mountains were originally Indian trails, and perhaps animal trails before that; the Indians walked single file and had no need to widen the paths.

The process of widening the paths began with the pack-horse of the early settler, whose burden on each side broke off and brushed aside the overhanging brush and branches. As the important trails became thus widened, minor ones were discontinued and became wholly overgrown with brush. Even the military roads of Braddock, Washington, and Forbes soon became impassable on account of fallen trees and underwood, so that the narrow pack-horse paths continued for many years to be the only routes for travel.[5]

James Veech's (*The Monongahela of Old*) account about the packhorses was similar. He observed that up to 1800 there were two major emigrant routes over the mountains heading to Ohio. The Pennsylvania Road was the old Forbes Road, and the Virginia Road was the old Braddock Road. He had seen as many as thirty packhorse caravans a day passing near Uniontown (Virginia Road). Each horse carried two to three hundred pounds of goods besides provisions and feed, everything from salt, sugar, kettles, iron, dry goods, glass, rum, powder and lead. The provisions consisted of poen, cheese and dried venison.[6] Citing a James L. Bowden, Veech claimed John Hayden brought the first wagon load of goods over the mountains on the Braddock Road from Hagerstown, Maryland, to Brownsville, Pennsylvania, near Redstone Creek in 1789. "With four horses he brought over two thousand pounds at $3 per hundred, making the trip in about a month." The Braddock Road was badly overgrown by this time and this had to have been a grueling journey by wagon.[7]

Veech points out some other facts that cried out for better land routes over the mountains, something that especially worried the easterners. The cost of goods was very high for those living on the western side of the mountains if they had to make the trip back and forth over the mountains to obtain them. For example, coffee in the west sold at thirty-three cents per pound, sugar at twenty-five cents, and Jamaica spirits at $2.33 per gallon. In 1784 wheat was selling at sixty-seven cents per bushel, corn at twenty-two cents, and rye at fifty cents. "But flour at Natchez—if you could get it there was worth $25 per barrel!"[8] One could reach Natchez by floating down the Ohio and then down the Mississippi. Agricultural goods grown in the Ohio country would fetch much more on the Mississippi than if they were transported back across the mountains. The worry in the eastern states was real. The western settlers would be tempted to look farther west for trade rather than back east. It was important to bind any new states that would come out of the Northwest Territory to the east by carving out real roads over the mountains.

The use of footpaths and packhorses was common in the last quarter of the eighteenth century for travel to Ohio from Maryland or Virginia, despite the fact that a road had already been cut from Wills Creek and the Potomac through to the Monongahela—the Braddock-Burd Road. Following Braddock's defeat on the Monongahela, the Braddock Road was closed for the duration of the French and Indian War. The fierce fighting on that frontier precluded even the hardiest settlers from using that road during the war. Shortly after the war, in 1768, the Treaty of Fort Stanwix set the Ohio River as the dividing line between Indian territory to the north of it from colonial territory to the south of it. Kentucky and Tennessee were now open to settlement by colonials from the east, but Ohio was isolated and guarded by the Native Americans as their last viable land possession. Colonial population of Ohio was discouraged, removing any incentive to improve travel to the Ohio Valley. So when the settlers started moving to Ohio late in the century they had no good roads.

The War for Independence, which started only seven years after the Treaty of Fort Stanwix, kept the frontier unsettled. Undoubtedly the Braddock Road was used by the combatants in this war, but not by major armies, so the maintenance of the road was not a priority. From the time it was improved by Braddock in 1755 until the turn of the century there were only two times the road was used by a military force. In 1774 Lord Dunmore led his force across the Braddock Road into Ohio to fight the Shawnee Chief Cornstalk in what became known as Dunmore's War. In 1794 Washington used the road when he called out the militia to put down the Whiskey Rebellion or Whiskey Insurrection. His force of about fifteen thousand was composed of militia from Pennsylvania, New Jersey, Virginia and Maryland. General Daniel Morgan, leader of the Virginia Division, rendezvoused his troops at Fort Cumberland and marched up the Braddock Road toward Pittsburgh. Fortunately, the rebellion ended with little bloodshed.[9] These two military forays did not carry the baggage of a large army as they traveled lightly and their horses would not need much more than a path over the old Braddock Road.

The underbrush in the mountains grew rapidly when not cleared regularly so over the decades the original Braddock Road became overgrown. As Hulbert (*The Cumberland Road*) notes, "Braddock's Road was for three score years the only route westward through southwestern Pennsylvania, and it grew worse and worse with each years travel."[10] Despite the lack of roads and the danger from Indians the pioneers continued to move over the mountains attracted by land. As Doddridge notes,

> The settlements on this side of the mountains commenced along the Monongahela, and between that river and the Laurel Ridge, in the year 1772. In the succeeding year they reached the Ohio river. The greater number of the first settlers came from the upper parts of the then colonies of Maryland and Virginia. Braddock's trail, as it was called, was the route by which the greater number of them crossed the mountains.[11]

The land was filling up between the mountains and the Ohio River and except for the relatively peaceful Kentucky, it had the highest population density on the frontier. The area was like a bubble ready to burst. The land was rich, but across the Ohio there was more abundant land with even more fertile plains. Although there were war and Indian troubles throughout the time that Doddridge recounts (1763–1783) the settlers still came, drawn by the land. The land companies, such as the Ohio Company of Virginia, had folded, overtaken by the wars, leaving no formal process for allocation and purchase of the land in the years before the Land Ordinances. The settlers moving over the mountains were squatters grabbing any land they could claim by tomahawk.[12]

There were three main gateways into the territory, from the east: along the Forbes Road through Pittsburgh and down the Ohio, from Virginia and Maryland from the southeast across the old Braddock-Burd Road, and from the south through Kentucky. The Kentucky immigrants often had come previously from Pennsylvania or Virginia during the earlier migration to Kentucky after the Treaty of Fort Stanwix. None of these gateways could be called roads as they could take wagons only to a point but not into Ohio where there were only trails.

Immigration from New England was also beginning to increase, but there were no roads from the northeast into Ohio. It was so difficult for wagons that as late as 1818 wagon travel into Ohio from New England was perilous. On August 19, 1818, the extended Fenn family, totaling twenty-three with friends, left Milford, Connecticut on Long Island Sound and headed for Tallmadge, Ohio, near present-day Akron in the Western Reserve. They had three wagons, one drawn by two horses, another by a yoke of oxen and a horse, and the third, with goods, was drawn by oxen. The family was not poor. They had china dishware in the wagons, and leather-backed seats that could be folded for easier access to the back of the wagon. They hired another person to take some of their goods to Albany and another to transport them from there to Buffalo. From Buffalo the goods were shipped to Cleveland.

The Fenns went through New York to Albany where they crossed the river, and probably followed the Mohawk River west through the Mohawk Valley to Buffalo.

Buffalo was still recovering from the British raid in the War of 1812, and the Fenns saw only one street with a few houses. They traveled south along Lake Erie, heading from Buffalo to Cleveland. There were many Indian trails but no wagon roads. They had to travel literally on the shore of the lake.

> After we left Buffalo there were no good roads, and much of the way the path was marked by blazed trees, and we often had to cut underbrush and saplings to get along with our big wagons.
> There were not many towns along the lake shore.
> When we came along by the lake it was rough. Some of the way the road lay by the lake, but mostly we left it quite a ways one side. Sometimes the sand would look very dry and we would be walking quite a distance from the water, when all at once we would see the big waves coming and would have to run to get out of the way of them. Part of the way was dangerous on account of quicksand. One afternoon one of the wagons began to sink. Father propped it up as well as he could and went for help. He found some men, but they said it was so near night he would better leave it till morning. Father was not willing to risk it, so they came with him, and when they reached the wagon the hubs were covered and they had a hard time getting it out. He went back there the next morning and found the place covered with water, and he was sure that if he had waited much longer he would have lost his wagon. We heard that a great many wagons had been lost along the lake shore.[13]

Thus, no matter how comfortable the wagons, the trip was perilous because of the lack of roads into Ohio. There were poor roads *to* Ohio through Pennsylvania, Maryland, and Kentucky, but none *in* Ohio. The first organized effort to correct this problem was initiated by Ebenezer Zane in 1796.

Zane's Trace

Commerce on the Ohio River and other rivers in the Ohio country was well established by the mid–1780s. There were some obstructions, such as the Falls of the Ohio, that had to be avoided, but as Kentucky historian John Filson said, "Excepting this place there is not a finer river in the world for the navigation of boats."[14] The potential business was so lucrative that in 1784 the Virginia Assembly passed an act for the collection of customs at both Louisville and Limestone another important shipping point on the Ohio River. Limestone, which became Maysville, was established at the mouth of Limestone Creek by the Virginia Assembly in 1787. It was described by the early settlers as "without current" and from the beginning was a popular landing place for immigrants. One traveler said, "Maysville is the greatest shipping port on the Ohio below Pittsburgh." It is 193 miles above Louisville and sixty-five miles by road from Lexington, in Bluegrass Country in northeast Kentucky.[15] Between 1787 and 1790, trading facilities and warehouses were established at places such as Boonesborough and Limestone. Boonesborough had been established on the Kentucky River in 1779 by the Virginia Assembly a few years after Daniel Boone had opened the Wilderness Trail into Kentucky. Sometime between 1783 and 1787 Daniel Boone and his family moved to Limestone and opened an inn and trading house; the area hosted a lot of travelers along the Ohio. In Kentucky, Louisville, Boonesborough, and Limestone were soon engaged in trading items such as fur and salt. The products were shipped across the mountains to the East Coast, via the Ohio River from Limestone to Pittsburgh.[16] Limestone was a thriving trading center on the Ohio River.

The family of Ebenezer Zane (1747–1812) and his two brothers, Silas and Jonathan, originally resided on the South Branch of the Potomac, near present-day Moorefield, West Virginia. Although we do not know how they made their wealth, they were not poor and they owned slaves. In 1769, when Ebenezer was twenty-two, the three brothers and their slaves, as well as several neighbors with names that became prominent in West Virginia history—Wetzel, Caldwell, Shepherd, and McColloch—moved to the area near the mouth of Wheeling Creek on the east bank of the Ohio. The same area had been explored previously by Christopher Gist, George Washington, and Celeron de Blainville. A year after the Treaty of Fort Stanwix which opened settlement up to the eastern shore of the Ohio, they established the first white settlement in the area, known as Zanesburg. Many were moving over the mountains to at least the east side of the Ohio River. Zane made two four-hundred-acre claims on the site of present Wheeling, West Virginia. Zane fought in Lord Dunmore's War (1774), helped build Fort Fincastle at Wheeling Creek, which was renamed Fort Henry in 1776, and then fought in the War for Independence, withstanding attacks at Fort Henry in 1777 and 1782. In 1793 he laid out the town of Wheeling.[17]

In 1796 Ebenezer Zane either saw an opportunity or decided to make an opportunity. Ohio was still part of the Northwest Territory but many people were anxious to move there. The Indian problem had subsided, but there were no roads to speak of only a few trails. Zane probably noticed the commercial activity around Limestone, Kentucky and decided to build a road from Wheeling to Limestone.[18] The ultimate objective was Fort Washington, present-day Cincinnati, only about fifty miles from Maysville (Limestone). Since Ohio was not yet a State he had to petition Congress for permission to cut the trail. He also asked for financial help, surveying costs, and land at the river crossings. He knew he had to cross three rivers with ferries, the Muskingum, the Hockhocking, and the Scioto.[19]

Congress was impressed with his proposal, especially "that his proposed all-weather road would enable the government to send mail for $1,000 or less per year from Wheeling to Frankfort, Kentucky, a savings of $3,000 from the fee charged by the boatman who floated at the mercy of the sometimes flooded and ice-filled Ohio River."[20] On May 17, 1796, Congress authorized the road and provided the land at the river crossings, with the stipulation that the road and ferries were to be operating by January 1, 1797. This was a very challenging schedule especially for a road through wilderness areas, but it indicated how important Congress thought this road would be to help populate Ohio and encourage trade with the west. With his brother Jonathan, Ebenezer started building the road immediately. They didn't pursue the straightest path but tried to use existing Indian and military trails avoiding terrain obstacles such as marshland. At first, they headed west to the present-day Zanesville, Ohio, and then southwest through the present-day locations of Lancaster and Chillicothe, then to Limestone. The trail wasn't completely blazed until the summer of 1797, still a remarkable feat, and it wasn't operational with the ferries until that autumn.[21]

Map 16 shows the general route of Zane's Trace from Wheeling, Virginia, southwest to Maysville (Limestone), Kentucky. Zanesville and Chillicothe came later. The section of Zane's Trace from Wheeling to Zanesville was incorporated into the National Road.

Zane's Trace, as it was called, was not a road but a trail, passable only by foot or horseback. It was not wide enough for wagons until 1800, when it was widened from Wheeling to Zanesville. The trace was steep, rutted, and had high stumps in the roadway. There is a story that sometimes wagons would get caught on these high stumps and travelers called that "getting stumped," which led to the phrase we use now when we say we are stuck on something.[22] Zane's Trace was not improved until a few years later when Ohio became a State. Nevertheless, it became a popular route into Ohio. It was the shortest distance between Wheeling and Limestone and included ferry service across the intervening rivers, and until after the War of 1812 was the only major road in Ohio.²³ Limestone was also easily accessible from other parts of Kentucky. It was only about sixty-five miles northeast of Lexington and nearby Boonesborough, all through the easily traveled Bluegrass Country. The fairly large population of Kentucky now had as easy an access to southern Ohio as others had from the east. The first settlers in the small town of Columbia, now part of Cincinnati, came from Limestone, Kentucky, in 1788. The area including Columbia was renamed Losantiville in 1788. To counter the Indian threat in the area, Fort Washington was built in Losantiville in 1789. In 1790 General Arthur St. Clair renamed Losantiville Cincinnati after the Roman General Cincinnatus.²⁴ It is likely these Columbia or Losantiville settlers were Limestone inhabitants who originally arrived at Limestone from the east over Zane's Trace or via the Ohio River, or from other parts of Kentucky. The region along Zane's Trace from Wheeling to Limestone was soon settled.²⁵

Ohio Statehood

Midway through Washington's second administration Ohio was finally at peace and serious immigration could begin. Land, however, was still expensive, too expensive to be purchased directly from the government, which sold it in 640-acre sections. This precluded a large influx of small farmers who could not afford the terms. When the Northwest Territorial Assembly meeting in Philadelphia chose William Henry Harrison to be the Territory Representative in Congress in 1799, this began to change. Harrison was a native Virginian, an Indian fighter who took part in the Greenville Treaty negotiations, a son-in-law of John Symmes, and was well connected politically. He wanted to make it easier for more settlers to come to Ohio so he sponsored the Harrison Land Act of 1800. This Act made it possible for people to purchase half-sections—340 acres—directly from the government and pay one-half of the price up front and the rest on credit in four installments over four years. Although it was still expensive, the direct purchase from the government was attractive and a great deal of land was sold through four land offices around the state (Marietta, Chillicothe, Steubenville, and Cincinnati). By the time of statehood in 1803 almost 940,000 acres had been sold this way.²⁶

When the first Jefferson administration, began in 1801, it faced issues in foreign affairs such as war with the Barbary Pirates, but most of its focus was internal, dealing with the westward expansion of the new nation. During his two administrations, the population of the states and territories beyond the Appalachian Mountains increased from about 456,000 to about 1,000,000. Only Ohio entered the Union while Jefferson was president but by 1820 Louisiana, Indiana, Mississippi, Illinois, Alabama, and Maine had joined the Union and the transmontane population had increased to about two million. In 1803, Jefferson had basically doubled the land-mass of the United States by purchasing the Louisiana Territory. Managing this population and territorial expansion was the central challenge for Jefferson and his immediate successors.²⁷

Although the population of the transmontane region more than doubled during Jefferson's terms, the population of Ohio more than quintupled, from 45,000 in 1800 to 231,000 in 1810. Clearly this eastern section of the Northwest Territory was ready for the statehood originally planned when the Northwest Territory was established. The process, however, was not easy.²⁸

The contentious push for Ohio statehood began around 1800. Eventually aided by Jefferson's election later that year, the statehood struggle within the future state took place along the same political lines that defined the national election. There was no disagreement about statehood as everyone agreed that the next state would be carved out of the Northwest Territory. The disagreement concerned the borders, which would affect political control of the new state.

The "eastern state" of the Northwest Territory as defined by the Northwest Ordinance, roughly the Ohio of today, was divided politically along the same lines as the nation, that is, Federalist and Democratic-Republican; John Adams versus Thomas Jefferson. Arthur St. Clair, territorial governor, was a strong Federalist who didn't believe the people of Ohio were yet qualified to vote, and therefore believed an appointed governor was still necessary. His power base was located in Marietta in the east and Cincinnati in the west. The Democratic-Republicans, led by William Henry Harrison, Thomas Worthington, and Nathaniel Massie, favored a government more broadly elected rather than that of an appointed governor. Their political base was in Chillicothe on the Scioto River. In 1800 Ohio did not have the sixty thousand people required to petition for statehood, but St. Clair knew that population figure would soon be reached, so he made a move to consolidate his power and postpone statehood. He proposed dividing the "eastern state" in half by a line that ran from the mouth of the Scioto River (in mid-state) north to Lake Erie. The eastern half of this division would be dominated by Marietta and the western half would be dominated by Cincinnati, thus neutralizing the opposition base in Chillicothe. This would have the additional advantage of having each half wait longer to achieve the required population for statehood, thus maintaining his status as governor. Both divisions would still be part of the Northwest Territory. Harrison, the Northwest Territory delegate in the House of Representatives, was joined by Worthington to lobby Congress to keep the original boundaries. They were successful and on May 7, 1780, Congress passed the bill that defined the Northwest Territory to be roughly the present Ohio, and the territory west of Ohio to be the new Indiana Territory. Cincinnati was to be the temporary capital of this new Northwest Territory.[29]

St. Clair did not give up. His term as Governor was to expire in December of 1800 but the lame-duck President John Adams appointed him for another term, thus disappointing the Territory's Democratic-Republicans who rightly saw him as an opponent to statehood. Throughout 1801 the statehood issue remained the major topic of the legislature, although the almost evenly divide territorial legislature managed to pass some other meaningful long-term legislation. When the new territorial legislature met in November 1801, St. Clair convinced them to once again divide the territory into two halves at the Scioto pending Congressional approval. This was too much for the Chillicothe clique and they sent two representatives to appeal to Congress against the bill. Thomas Worthington and Michael Baldwin easily convinced the Democratic-Republican House, in January 1802, to overwhelmingly overturn the division bill.[30]

The House was clearly disposed toward statehood also. Although the census of 1800 showed the Territory to be short of the required sixty thousand inhabitants, they assumed there would be the required number by this time of their action or at least by the time of statehood, so they introduced legislation for statehood. It easily passed Congress and on April 30, 1802, Thomas Jefferson signed the Enabling Act that would allow Ohioans to apply for statehood. In Section 1 it stated "That the inhabitants of the eastern division of the territory northwest of the river Ohio, be, and they are hereby, authorized to form for themselves a constitution and State government, and to assume such name as they shall deem proper, and the said State, when formed, shall be admitted into the Union upon the same footing with the original States in all respects whatever."[31] The boundaries were to be

Pennsylvania on the east, the Ohio River on the south to the Great Miami River and then north to a line that would run into Lake Erie. Lake Erie would be the most prominent part of the northern border. There have been some border changes over the years but these are essentially the borders of present-day Ohio.

Events proceed rather rapidly after that. A constitutional convention opened in Chillicothe on November 1, with a large majority of Democratic-Republican delegates. They allowed St. Clair, still an opponent, to speak. He gave a rather intemperate speech in which he claimed Congress had no authority to enact the Enabling Act. St. Clair's political opponents made sure Jefferson heard about the speech which angered Jefferson and cost St. Clair his position as Governor. The convention completed the constitution by November 29. The vote to establish Ohio as a free state was passed by a large majority, and even the right to grant the voting franchise to blacks was only defeated by a small margin. They did not submit the constitution to a referendum, afraid of roadblocks by the Federalists. "The document was entrusted to Thomas Worthington, who crossed the mountain trails on horseback, arriving in Washington on December 19. The next day he called on President Jefferson, and on December 19 he delivered the constitution to Congress."[32] The process continued its rapid progress. Both houses of Congress considered the request and acted quickly. The Senate approved the constitution, the House adopted it and on February 19, 1803, President Jefferson signed it. The officially adopted date was assigned to be March 1, 1803. By the standards of the day this was a whirlwind romance, taking only about three years from the early stirrings of statehood until Ohio became a member of the Union as the seventeenth state.

It was also rapid if one considers the time it takes for people to form nation-states. It had only been fifty years since colonial Englishmen took steps to extend their reach over the mountains to take advantage of the very fertile Ohio country. In that relatively short time they fought two wars, one to capture that land, and another to separate from the mother country and establish a new republic. A lot had been accomplished in fifty years.

The Louisiana Purchase

The territory beyond the Mississippi River, known as Louisiana, was foreign to the United States, claimed at various times by France or Spain. It was never part of the land ceded to the United States by Great Britain in the Treaty of Paris in 1783, and therefore was never part of the Ohio country or Northwest Territory. The Mississippi was the border with a foreign country. Why then should the acquisition of Louisiana be considered as part of this story? When considering the history and geography of a region it is instructive to look at a wider picture to ascertain the impact of the broader scope. The Louisiana Purchase of 1803 had an impact on the migration to the Ohio country. The Purchase made it appear that the west was boundless and enticed even more settlers from the east and it assured control of the Mississippi. Ohio now became the middle of the country not the frontier and, therefore, more hospitable to settlement. It can be argued that "manifest destiny," a term not really used until a few years later, was actually born with the Louisiana Purchase. The expansion beyond Louisiana to the west coast was now seen as inevitable. Louisiana was admitted as a state in 1812, only nine years after Ohio.

Throughout the seventeenth century France had explored and claimed the vast majority of the inland area of North America from the St. Lawrence Valley down through the Ohio and Mississippi Valleys to the mouth of the Mississippi River as described in Chapter

One. Prior to that, Spain had claimed most of the west coast back to the Rocky Mountains. Following its claim, New France had exploited the territory known as Louisiana for its resources, but made no great effort to settle it in any density; it was sparsely populated. However, following the Seven Years War, the French and Indian War in America, the territory changed ownership multiple times. Spain had entered the war late on the side of France and as a result when France lost its North American empire Spain also suffered. In 1762, France had transferred to Spain all the territory west of the Mississippi, including the River and the city of New Orleans, and ceded the territory east of the Mississippi to Great Britain.[33]

Spanish officials did not want to encourage trade and shipping on the river so they kept it closed to American commerce. This was restrictive to those in the southern states and those on the frontier; they wanted to use the river. The Americans managed to negotiate a treaty with Spain to allow them (Americans) free navigation of the Mississippi and duty-free passage through New Orleans. The Treaty of San Lorenzo, or Pinckney's Treaty, was signed in October 1795. This gave the United States confidence that westward expansion could proceed unhindered by Spanish control of the Mississippi.[34]

Pinckney's treaty did not last very long before it was overtaken by events in Europe again, more fallout of the French Revolution. When Napoleon came to power he wanted both Louisiana and St. Domingue (Haiti, lost to a slave rebellion) back, and he intended to invade them for that purpose. Prior to any invasion, Charles IV of Spain quietly ceded Louisiana back to France in 1800 and France took possession in 1802. American access to the New Orleans warehouses was immediately revoked which endangered American use of the Mississippi and caused concern about a much more powerful owner in the neighborhood; it prompted outrage in the United States.[35]

Jefferson was concerned about the loss of New Orleans, which he considered a key hub for American trade in the west. He struggled with the constitutionality of the action but in 1803 he sent James Monroe to Paris as a minister extraordinary, to join Ambassador Livingston in attempting to purchase New Orleans and all or part of Florida for as much as ten million dollars.[36]

In a surprise move France offered to sell all of Louisiana to the United States including New Orleans for fifteen million dollars. Monroe and Livingston reached agreement with France on April 30, 1803. The official announcement was made on July 4, 1803, after Monroe had returned from France. The 827,000 square-mile area would double the United States land area.[37]

The extent of the Louisiana Purchase is shown in Map 12.

Although Jefferson was concerned about the constitutionality, the Senate was apparently not ambivalent; on October 20, they ratified the treaty twenty-four to seven. Jefferson had gambled and won; he had set a precedent and he knew it.

The next challenge would come with the establishment of the Cumberland Road. At first this was easier to enact, but it still required new ways of thinking. The challenge would be the issue of internal improvements to land already part of the United States. Who was responsible for any improvements and how would they be funded? Were there any constitutional issues?

The Cumberland Road

Ohio statehood and the Louisiana Purchase occurred only weeks apart in 1803, increasing the pressure to improve the east-west link that George Washington had envisioned twenty years earlier when he had taken a trip in the fall of 1784 to inspect his western lands and look for a water way to the west. Washington had traveled over the mountains on a familiar route, one he helped open in 1754. He knew there was a land route across the mountains but in 1784 he was looking for the water route. Although his diary for the trip and his subsequent letter to Virginia Governor Benjamin Harrison do not mention the land route, his ultimate objective was to link the east and the west in any way he could. Both his diary and his letter to Governor Harrison ultimately summarized his concern and his proposed solution, using almost the same words in each.

> The Western settlers, (I speak now from my own observation) stand as it were upon a pivot—the touch of a feather would turn them any way—They have look'd down the Mississippi ... for no other reason, than because they could glide gently down the stream ... & because they have no other means of coming to us but by a long Land transportation & unimproved roads.... But smooth the road once, & make easy the way for them, & then see what an influx of articles will be poured in upon us—how amazingly our exports will be increased by them, & how amply we shall be compensated for any trouble & expence we may encounter to effect it.[38]

He first proposed the water route to the west because he thought it could be done easily, but here talked about smoothing a road also; anything to link east and west. He made it clear what the consequences could be if opening a route to the west was not done:

> greatest advantage by this State; if she would open her avenues to the trade of that Country, & embrace the present moment to establish it—It only wants a beginning—the Western inhabitants wou'd do their part towards its execution ... rather than be *driven* into the arms of, or be made dependent upon foreigners; which would, eventually, either bring on a separation of them from us, or a War between the United States & one or the other of those powers—most probably with the Spaniards.[39]

Washington's exhortation to "smooth the road" did not happen via the water route as canals over the mountains were unsuccessful. The final chapter on using canals to cross the mountain had yet to be written, but by 1803 it was clear this was not the panacea originally thought. East-west travel by water proved to be impractical and the land route was still an adventure. As Hulbert pointed out "travelers spoke of "going into" and "coming out of" the West as though it were a Mammoth Cave."[40] If the promise of Ohio, and even more recently, of Louisiana, was to be fulfilled there had to be a better way to travel between east and west or Washington's fear of loss of the west would be realized.

Legislation for the Road

All the land in Ohio was originally part of the Northwest Territory and belonged to the federal government, which divided it into sections. The intent was to sell the land to pay for the war debt. The Congressional framers of the Enabling Act (April 30, 1802) foresaw another use for those funds, the building of roads to and in Ohio. Congress had provided a very small amount of land to Ebenezer Zane when he built his Trace a few years earlier but it was a small fraction of what would be needed to open the land route to Ohio. Also, Zane's Trace started at Wheeling, on the Ohio River and went west; it did not go back east. In Section Seven of the Enabling Act Congress offered the new state three propositions to encourage road building. The relevant proposition was the third one, which stated,

> That one-twentieth part of the net proceeds of the lands lying within the said State sold by Congress, from and after the thirtieth day of June next, after deducting all expenses incident to the same, shall be applied to the laying out and making public roads, leading from the navigable waters emptying

into the Atlantic, to the Ohio, to the said State, and through the same, such roads to be laid out under the authority of Congress, with the consent of the several States through which the road shall pass.[41]

Much of this wording in the Enabling Act was originally that of Treasury Secretary Albert Gallatin. Gallatin was a visionary who was able to look ahead and see the need for the road and to propose a unique way to pay for it. A member of Jefferson's cabinet he held views on internal improvements that were closer to Hamilton's than to Jefferson's. Hamilton's capitalist ideas were anathema to Jefferson, but much to the Jefferson's credit he was able to see the need for western expansion and was amenable to Gallatin's idea for the road and his proposed method of financing it.

Prior to the act enabling Ohio to enter the Union, Gallatin wrote to Congressman William Giles and proposed that ten percent of the sale of federal lands in Ohio should be used for roads leading to and through Ohio. Congress reduced the ten percent to five percent but passed the measure. They also put a stipulation in the act that Ohio could not tax Congressional land sales in the state for five years. Considering the amount of land in Ohio, five percent was still a large amount. Now a means to fund roads for national purposes existed. Similar measures were later passed to fund roads in Indiana and Illinois from the sale of federal lands in those states. In Ohio, the funding was used for the relatively short road from Cumberland to Wheeling. Eventually the Cumberland Road was the first stage of what became the National road.[42]

Surprisingly, Jefferson did not question the Enabling Act, but signed it. This federal money, from the sale of federal lands, was to be used to build roads within a state (Ohio), as well as in states between Ohio and the Atlantic. Without calling it such, it was the federal funding of internal improvements later a constitutional issue for some opponents. Hamilton was convinced the federal government had the right to make internal improvements under the general welfare clause of the Constitution and Washington tacitly accepted Hamilton's premise by not challenging him. The Act required that the consent of the states through which the road would pass, but this did not diminish the fact that federal funds would be used to build roads in the states.

One year later on March 3, 1803, just two days after Ohio became a state and on the last day of the session, Congress passed a number of bills, one of which modified the Enabling Act of 1802 by specifically allocating three of the five percent to be "applied to the laying out, opening, and making roads within the said State, and to no other purpose whatever,"[43] This implied, and was later acknowledged, that the other two percent would be for roads between Ohio and the Atlantic.

The Senate appointed Connecticut Senator Uriah Tracy to chair a committee to determine the best way to carry out the road building project. The committee looked over possible routes to compare distances from the Atlantic to the Ohio River. They considered Philadelphia, Baltimore, Washington, and even Richmond as the eastern terminus. They made no direct measurements but used available information, probably contemporary maps, and found problems with all the routes; they settled on Maryland for two reasons. One was that the distance to Cumberland was about the same for Baltimore, a major port, and Washington, D. C., the Capital. The second reason was probably more compelling: "The State of Maryland, with no less spirit and perseverance, are engaged in making roads from Baltimore, and from the western boundary of the District of Columbia through Fredericktown to Williamsport."[44] In other words, Maryland was already building roads west from Baltimore, at least to Williamsport so the federal government would not have to do so, besides Congress did not believe they had enough money for a road across Maryland.

The Maryland road would essentially cross the entire state. Maryland would be making a major contribution to linking the Atlantic coast with the western lands across the mountains with the road it was building. Another reason for originating at Cumberland may have been the sensitivity of the constitutional question. One of the objections to the federal government financing internal improvements was that the road or canal would only benefit the small portion of the population which could take advantage of it. Funding a federal road all the way across Maryland would have been a glaring example of that concern. The Senate committee calculated only about twelve thousand dollars was available for the project. They also concluded that Maryland had no incentive to build across the mountains, so the committee

> have thought it expedient to recommend the laying out and making a road from Cumberland on the northerly bank of the Potomac, and within the State of Maryland, to the river Ohio, at the most convenient place between a point on the easterly bank of said river, opposite to Steubenville and the mouth of Grave Creek, which empties into said river Ohio, a little below Wheeling, in Virginia. This route will meet and accommodate the roads leading from Baltimore and the District of Columbia; it will cross the Monongahela river, at or near Brownsville, sometimes called Redstone, where the advantage of boating can be taken, and from the point where it will probably intersect the river Ohio, there are now roads, or they can easily be made over feasible and proper ground, to and through the principal population of the State of Ohio.[45]

They estimated the distance from Williamsport to Cumberland at about eighty miles "by the usual route which is circuitous." They assumed that Maryland would open the road from Williamsport to Cumberland. The committee estimated the distance from Cumberland to the western extremity of Laurel Hill, "by the route now traveled," to be about sixty-six miles, and the distance from Laurel Hill to the Ohio River, "by the usual route," to be about seventy miles. Using their estimates, the length of the Cumberland Road route they were proposing would be about 136 miles. Grave Creek is about eleven miles south of Wheeling and Steubenville is about twenty-two miles north of Wheeling, so the target area on the Ohio River was about thirty-three miles long.[46]

Senator Tracy's committee concluded their report with their optimistic assessment of the impact of the road. It recognized the importance of binding the east and the west.

> Politicians have generally agreed that rivers unite the interests and promote the friendship of those who inhabit their banks; while mountains, on the contrary, tend to the disunion and estrangement of those who are separated by their intervention. In the present case, to make the crooked way straight, and the rough ways smooth, will, in effect, remove the intervening mountains, and by facilitating the intercourse of our Western brethren with those on the Atlantic, substantially unite them *in interest*, which the committee believe, is the most effectual cement of union applicable to the human race.[47]

This choice was not accidental or haphazard. They knew the most difficult section of the road would be over the mountains so when they said "by the usual route" or "by the route now traveled" they knew there were rudimentary roads there already. They also knew Maryland was building roads toward Cumberland from Baltimore and Washington, D.C. The committee had chosen the route Christopher Gist had blazed fifty years previously when he went from Wills Creek to Redstone Creek near Brownsville, Pennsylvania. Nemacolin, Cresap, Washington, and Braddock had all improved the road over the mountains, although it had deteriorated after the wars in the region. The Burd's Road spur from the Braddock Road was on that route to the Monongahela. Colloquially when one talked about using the Braddock Road to go to Ohio this is the route that was meant—directly to the Monongahela; the Burd Road was not mentioned. Wheeling was almost due west of Brownsville so that extension was an obvious choice, especially since Zane's Trace started at Wheeling and went into Ohio. When the Tracy committee submitted their report to Congress in December 1805 it became known as the Cumberland Road, from Cumberland, Maryland, to Wheeling, Virginia, through Brownsville, Pennsylvania.

On March 24, 1806, the House took up the bill on the Cumberland Road that the Senate had passed previously, and approved it by a vote of sixty-six yeas and fifty nays. Members from New England, Maryland, Kentucky, and Ohio supported it, with opposition of members from Virginia and Pennsylvania. That opposition was presumably because the proposed road passed through little of Pennsylvania or Virginia and did not include a terminus at either Philadelphia or Richmond.[48] It passed both houses "of Congress assembled" on March 29, 1806. The act called for the President to appoint "three discrete and disinterested citizens" to lay out the road. When they made their report, the President was authorized to accept or reject the plan, and if it was accepted he had the authority to create the road. The law was very specific about the construction. The road was to be four rods wide (sixty-six feet) and marked every quarter of a mile. "the road shall be raised in the middle of the carriage way with stone, earth or gravel and sand ... leaving or making ... a ditch or water-course on each side, and contiguous; to said carriage way." Probably the most stringent requirement was to limit the maximum grade to five degrees, a challenge throughout the path across the mountains but necessary to allow normal wagon traffic. The sixty-six-foot width was by far the widest of any road previously built along this path. Clearly, they wanted a permanent road that would accommodate a lot of traffic.[49]

The question again arises concerning Jefferson's decision to sign the act. He was of two minds. He strongly approved of western expansion, clearly revealed by his purchase of Louisiana and his concern for the security of the United States in the west. In his message to Congress in December 1806, although a budget surplus was anticipated, Jefferson wanted to keep the impost taxes on luxury goods to acquire money for "public education, roads, rivers, canals.... By these operations new channels of communication will be opened between the States; the lines of separation will disappear, their interests will be identified, and their union cemented by new and indissoluble ties."[50] In this his thinking was in concert with Washington's. However, he disagreed vehemently with Hamilton's expansive view of the general welfare clause for justifying internal improvements. Later in the same message to Congress Jefferson claimed a constitutional amendment would be necessary to permit federally funded internal improvements and he expected Congress to initiate one. "I suppose an amendment to the constitution, by consent of the States, necessary, because the objects now recommended are not among those enumerated in the constitution, and to which it permits the public moneys to be applied."[51] More than six months had passed since he signed the act and Congress had not taken any action on an amendment. No one knows exactly why Jefferson hesitated to veto the bill especially since he was on record as believing a constitutional amendment would be necessary to implement any internal improvements by the government. He never raised an objection to private sponsorship of these improvements or ones implemented by the states within their own borders. Federal sponsorship though was not specifically enumerated in the Constitution, and was therefore opposed by Jefferson.

The responsibility for starting the amendment process rests with Congress in Article 5, but the lack of action by this Congress on an amendment caused the proponents to use what Jeremiah Young (*A Political and Constitutional Study of the Cumberland Road*) calls the fiction of "compacts" to circumvent the issue of eminent domain. When Congress set the terminals of the road in Maryland and Virginia, the issue was how to build this federal road in the states without the federal government claiming eminent domain and taking over the land for the road. At the time, eminent domain was seen as an infringement on the sovereignty of the states because there was nothing in the Constitution enumerating such Congressional powers. The answer for both Young and Theodore Sky (*The National Road and the Difficult Path to Sustainable National Investment*) was the "compact" between the federal government and the state which provided that the proceeds from the sale of federal lands in the new state of Ohio would be used for roads but would not be taxed for at least five years. Along with the requirement in the Enabling act "that consent of the several States through which the road shall pass" this formed a compact, an agreement, between the federal government and the state.

> Congress was merely carrying out the agreement with the state that had been written into the admission law with the consent of both parties. It was not using its appropriation power contrary to state wishes but rather to carry out the terms of a compact with the state in which the state had given up its right to tax the proceeds of land sales in the state.[52]

Possibly Jefferson became convinced that the combination of the land sales agreement and the consent of the states made the need for a constitutional amendment unnecessary.

Sky points out that although the "compact" might have resolved the eminent domain issue, it did not address appropriation of federal funds for the Cumberland Road. Moreover, as Sky points out, "...it is doubtful that a state's consent would confer upon Congress the power to appropriate funds for a purpose for which appropriation was not authorized under the Constitution." Jefferson's silent acquiescence may have been because he felt he had done his duty and done all he could by twice asking for a constitutional amendment, once in his second inaugural address, and again in his December 1806 message to Congress only months after the road bill became law. He favored of the road linking east and west and wanted it built. If a constitutional amendment was necessary, it was the duty of Congress under Article 5 to start that process. Congress saw no need for the amendment so work on the road started.[53]

Jefferson may have been influenced to sign the bill because of the age-old worry of losing the west, and because of the threat created by the Burr conspiracy, which predated the bill but ended after the bill was signed. While serving as Vice President, Burr killed Alexander Hamilton in a duel in 1804 and then was dropped from the ticket for Jefferson's second term. He later fled New York as a fugitive. As early as 1805 he was reported to be in the Mississippi Valley plotting against the United States hoping to separate the American West, from Ohio to Louisiana, and to seize some Spanish territory in the west. Burr's conspiracy was unsuccessful, he was arrested in late 1806, then acquitted in an 1807 trial. Although the plots, arrest and acquittal, occurred *after* the bill signing, Jefferson may have had unofficial knowledge of the conspiracy in 1805 or early 1806. This would have rekindled the fear, around since the birth of the republic, that the transmontane west was vulnerable to separation unless it was bound tightly to the east.[54]

The Enabling Act was the major step in opening the Ohio country from Maryland. Fifty years after the first steps toward that goal the force of the state and the force of law were finally behind it. This would be the first solid land link between the East Coast and the transmontane areas north of the Ohio River. The Cumberland Road would be the critical link allowing commerce between the Mid-Atlantic States and Ohio in the west, finally binding these two parts together and reducing the fear of many that they would drift apart because of lack of communication and commerce.

Laying Out the Road

The law passed by Congress in 1806 providing for the Cumberland Road called for Jefferson to appoint "three disinterested citizens" to lay out the road, but Thomas Moore and Eli Williams, were from Maryland and Joseph Kerr was from Ohio, so their level of "disinterest" might be questioned. Congress had already chosen the two terminal points of the road as being in Maryland and on the Ohio River, so these men were reasonable choices. They certainly took their commission seriously, especially the parts requiring the shortest distances. In the commissioners' first report, which they presented to Jefferson and he presented to Congress on January 31, 1807, there were four objectives in laying out the road.

> 1st. Shortness of distance between navigable points on the eastern and western waters.
> 2d. A point on the Monongahela best calculated to equalize the advantages of this portage in the country within reach of it.
> 3d. A point on the Ohio river most capable of combining certainty of navigation with road accommodation…
> 4th. Best mode of diffusing benefits with the least distance of road.[55]

All of the objectives aimed at reducing expenses by making the road as short as possible. The commissioners had started work in September and worked until December when winter set in, forcing them to stop. They acknowledged the job was bigger than they thought it would be and they had to hire a surveyor to help plot the route because the maps of the day were incomplete. The surveys were done in the fall because the foliage was off the trees, allowing a clear line of sight over the route they were surveying. Even though they had not completed their work, they provided the President with an interim report in January 1807.

They had a few miles leeway concerning where to start the road, but to them the obvious choice was Cumberland.[56] They started "From a stone of lot No. 1, in Cumberland, near the confluence of Will's Creek and the north branch of the Potomac River." From there they could have gone north on Wills Creek to Jennings run and taken that west. However, that line appeared perpendicular to the westerly route and therefore not the shortest way so they chose to go west over Wills Mountain, a somewhat curious route. Years before, Braddock had originally chosen to go over the mountain but found it very difficult. Instead one of his men found the way *around* the mountain by following Wills Creek north through what is now named the Cumberland Narrows and then back west around the mountain. The Cumberland Narrows is a gash in Wills Mountain cut by Wills Creek. This is a slightly longer route but much more level. Years later the Cumberland Road, then the National road, made that detour around the mountain. The commissioners certainly knew of Braddock's detour but stubbornly held to the shortest route objective.[57]

Because of the time of year, and the need to complete a survey beforehand, they only had time in their first trip to outline an approximate route. From Wills Mountain they basically followed the Braddock Road to the crossing of the Youghiogheny River, in fact they mentioned they crossed between the Braddock Road and the confluence at Turkey Foot. From there they headed slightly northwest for about twenty miles, parallel to the river and slightly north of the Braddock Road, which also paralleled the river. This route brought them over the crest of what they called Laurel Hill, but was more likely Chestnut Ridge, about five miles southwest of Connellsville or very close to Gist's Plantation. From there the commissioners went to Redstone Creek near Brownsville, Pennsylvania, which was the closest point on the Monongahela.[58]

In spite of their objective of the shortest route, they were not oblivious of the importance of the route they did choose; they were reminded of it constantly by the importunities of the inhabitants of every part of the district, who severally conceived their grounds entitled to a preference.... Not unmindful of the claims of towns, and their capacity of reciprocating advantages on public roads, the commissioners were not insensible of the disadvantages which Uniontown must feel from the want of that accommodation which a more southwardly direction of the route would have afforded; but as that could not take place without a relinquishment of the shortest passage, considerations of public benefit could not yield to feelings of minor importance.[59]

They were only about five miles northeast of Uniontown but regarded that town as off the shortest route. These were three tough civil servants!

They recognized the strong desire townspeople felt about having the road come through the town or very near it. It could be the difference between a town thriving or withering once the road was in place. Favor seekers emerged to promote the importance of having the road in their area. John Sloane, a local politician in Jefferson County, Ohio, wrote to Ohio Senator Worthington proposing that Steubenville be named the terminus on the Ohio River, because "Steubenville was a pleasant and flourishing town." Although he was a representative from Jefferson County "he was not writing from self-interest," he said.[60]

There were similar stories about Wheeling. Two of the leading citizens and landowners in Wheeling were Colonel Moses Shepherd and his wife Lydia Boggs Shepherd Cruger, among the area's first settlers. She was also prominent in the nation's capital, visiting there often to act as a hostess for the leading statesmen of the day. She often met Henry Clay, supposedly captivated by her dark eyes, and her ability to discuss national affairs, apparently to him an uncommon skill among beautiful hostesses. Wheeling was chosen and the credit given to the Shepherds although there was some resentment when two additional bridges were built, bringing the road past their front door. The Shepherds had a statue erected to honor Clay, visible from the road for all to see.[61]

Wheeling was chosen by the commissioners, not due to that pressure but because of singleness of purpose toward the shortest route. They chose it because it was almost due west from Brownsville. Also, the Ohio River above Wheeling was not as conducive to water travel as it was downstream. One of their objectives was to be "most capable of combining certainty of navigation with road accommodation." In other words, once one reached the Ohio one should be able to use water transportation as well as road transportation. Their plan was to head straight west to Wheeling from Brownsville, or as they said "to give such a direction to the road as would best secure certainty of navigation on the Ohio at all seasons, combining, as far as possible, the inland accommodation of remote points westwardly."[62]

Once they got over the mountains to the Allegheny Plateau they found the going would continue to be difficult. The route from the Monongahela to the Ohio had many hills and hollows but did not have the abundance of stone present in the mountains, an important material in the construction of the road. The commissioners concluded their report by estimating the cost of the road by using the cost of other roads in Pennsylvania and Maryland as a guide. They claimed the other roads would cost more because they did not have an abundance of stone necessary for a firm road, which the mountain road had. The stone for those roads would have to be brought in. They estimated the cost of the Cumberland Road to be about six thousand dollars per mile. Even though it was through mountains, there was plenty of stone available persuading them the cost would be less than that of the other roads. They were proud of their work and looked forward to the new road. "As to the policy of incurring this expense, it is not the province of the commissioners to declare; but they cannot, however, withhold assurances of a firm belief that the purse of the nation cannot be more seasonably opened, or more happily applied, than in promoting the speedy and effectual establishment of a great and easy road on the way contemplated."[63] The 1806 act establishing the road required the President to obtain the consent of the states through which it would pass. Jefferson quickly received the consent of Maryland and Virginia, but Pennsylvania hesitated. The proposed road in Pennsylvania was short and would go through a sparsely populated part of the state, nowhere near a population center such as Pittsburgh. The Pennsylvanians thought Wheeling was too far from Pittsburgh, and, besides, Philadelphia was not on the route either. When Jefferson sent the commissioner's first report to Congress in January 1807, he said he could neither approve nor disapprove the road because he hadn't heard from Pennsylvania. A few weeks later, Pennsylvania approved with the stipulation that the road had to go through the county seats of both Fayette and Washington (Uniontown and Washington).[64]

A series of changes in the route began, especially from Brownsville to Wheeling, with some interesting comments from Jefferson along the way. In an April 1807 letter to Gallatin he acceded to the deviation of the road through Uniontown, but did not mention Washington; he gave these instructions to the commissioners. In the fall of 1807 the commissioners rerouted the road slightly south of their original route, identifying the various mountains and elevations along the route but stopping at the courthouse in Uniontown. This is the route that exists today from Cumberland to Uniontown. In the introductory paragraph to Congress for the commissioners' second report, Jefferson made what was probably the first public announcement of the ultimate destination of the road: "which is to lead from the Indian[a] boundary near Cincinnati by Vincennes to the Mississippi at St. Louis.... In this way we may accomplish a continued and advantageous line of communication from the seat of the General Government to St. Louis, passing through several very interesting points of the Western country."[65] Jefferson was thinking great distances, he was thinking Louisiana Territory, he was thinking far west. Although this was the first public statement of intent of where he expected the road to go, it was not the first time he thought of this goal. In a July 14, 1806, letter to Gallatin he said, "The road from Cumberland to Ohio will be an important link in the line to St. Louis." Ohio was the first objective once over the mountains, but then the land appeared almost endless and fertile. So thinking to St. Louis would be an easy dream.[66]

The final route was not yet determined. Jefferson had not approved the road through Washington, but Pennsylvania pushed the issue proposing legal opposition if Washington was not on the route. Jefferson showed some irritation on the subject when he wrote to Gallatin on April 22, 1808.

> I know my determination was not to yield to the example of a State's prescribing the direction of the road; and I understood the law as leaving the route ultimately to me. If I have misconstrued the law, I shall be sorry for the money spent on misconstruction, but that loss will be a lesser evil to the United States than a single example of yielding to a State; the direction of a road made at national expense and for national purposes.[67]

Jefferson even considered adopting another route that did not include Pennsylvania. From a strong advocate of states' rights, this was a remarkable statement, almost exactly the opposite of what one might expect. He was complaining that a state was getting in the way of a national project. Was he changing his position on states' rights? A more likely explanation was that Jefferson was now seeing things on a national scale, especially since the Louisiana Purchase. He saw the wide-open west and was irritated with anything that did not provide quick access.

He wrote that letter in a fit of pique, but Gallatin, who once represented that Pennsylvania district in Congress, was more practical. After several weeks, on July 27, 1808, Gallatin wrote Jefferson in almost scolding tones reminding him that he had originally recommended that both Uniontown and Washington should be included on the route, stating "It was my impression that you had acquiesced, and would instruct the commissioners to that effect. I find, however, that it has not been done." The savvy politician quickly gets to the point in the election year.

> Permit me, however, to state that the county of Washington, with which I am well acquainted, having represented it six years in Congress, gives a uniform majority of about 2000 votes in our favor, and that if this be thrown, by reason of this road, in a wrong scale, we will infallibly lose the State of Pennsylvania at the next election; for the imprudent steps taken there seem unavoidably to lead to three distinct *electoral* tickets.[68]

Shortly thereafter, August 6, Jefferson wrote to the commissioners to "make as good an examination ... of the best route through Washington to Wheeling." He also gave them some choices other than Wheeling that they could consider as the Ohio River terminus. When they reported back to the President on August 30, the two commissioners (Kerr was absent because of family problems) considered other routes but stayed with the terminus at Wheeling; they reiterated their reasons for this choice from their first report. They also indicated that the Wheeling location would be the start of the road in a straight line west beyond Ohio. In fact, even though the Cumberland Road was not yet built everyone was looking to extend west. They also observed in the report that although the law specified the road width to be sixty-six feet, they thought that forty feet would suffice, and that the middle twenty feet should be a particular stone base, which they described. They suggested designs and estimated costs for some of the bridges, and finally noted that the route through Washington would be three miles longer than the straight route. They never forgot the original charge that the road was to be the shortest possible route. Jefferson submitted the report to Congress on December 13, 1808, after the election of James Madison.[69]

In February 1809 funding for the Cumberland to Brownsville part of the road was approved in an appropriations bill, but funding for the roads within Uniontown and Brownsville was specifically excluded. The federal government would fund the road west but it would not fund the roads internal to existing towns. The Washington inclusion was finally settled by legislation in 1811.[70] The route for the Cumberland Road, officially designated to go from Cumberland, Maryland, to the Ohio River, was finally settled in 1811, five years after the initial legislation. The road followed previous, more primitive roads in many places but was not exactly congruent with them.

After the commissioners crossed the mountains at Chestnut Ridge they were near Gist's place, a trivial five miles or so northeast of Uniontown, making it easy for Jefferson to include Uniontown in the route. Map 15 shows the slight northern arc in the road from Uniontown through Washington to Wheeling, not quite a straight line so it took longer to settle on this route. That does not seem to be of consequence considering the importance of including two county seats in the route. Uniontown and Washington undoubtedly contributed significantly to the success of the road in later years.

The Cumberland Road was short, less than 150 miles long from Maryland to Ohio. It went through three states, Maryland, Pennsylvania, and Virginia, but none of them had an incentive to build it themselves. It took an overriding national interest in a link across the mountains, and therefore the national government, to get it started and built. This short road by itself would not be enough to link the east and the west it would take other roads

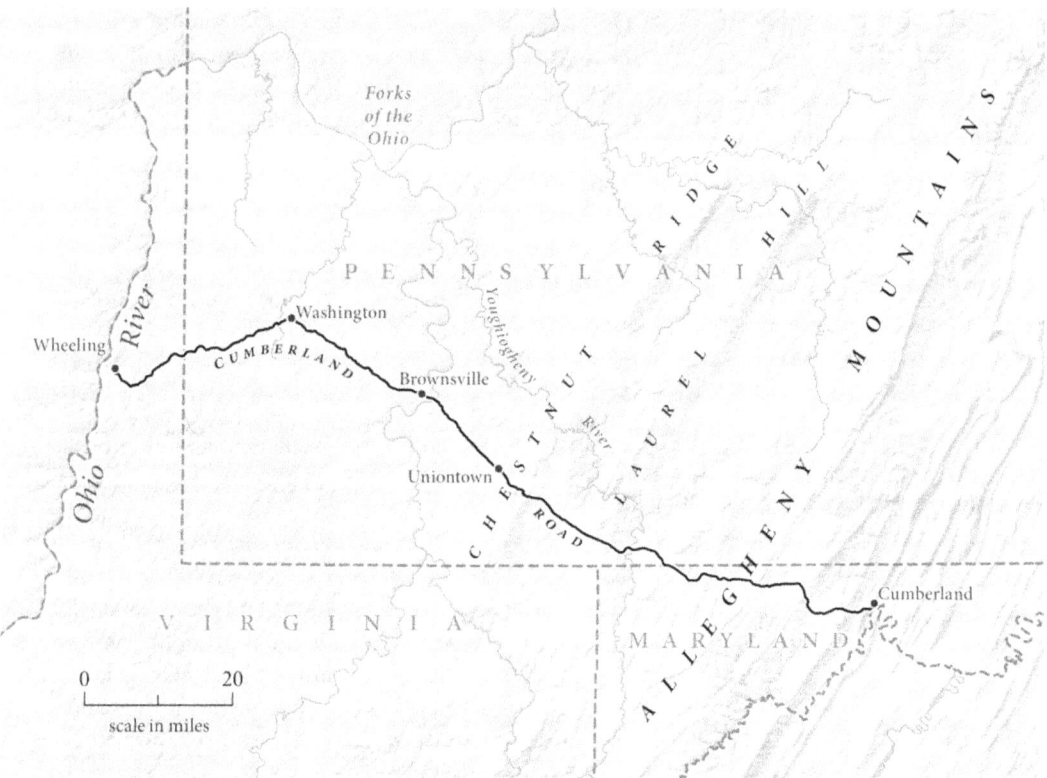

Map 15: Cumberland Road. The Cumberland Road ran from Cumberland, Maryland, through the county seats of Uniontown and Washington, Pennsylvania, to Wheeling, Virginia, on the Ohio River. The route from Cumberland to Uniontown was the same route opened by Christopher Gist and followed by Cresap, Nemacolin, Washington, and Braddock. The route from Uniontown to Brownsville was the same one originally blazed by Gist and then reopened by Colonel Burd during the French and Indian War. See Maps 6 and 9. The Braddock road appellation, in use for many years, was no longer applicable.

linking to the Cumberland Road to make a difference. Before the road was even built, people like Jefferson were looking forward to the road being continued to St. Louis.[71] Only then would the full potential of the Louisiana Purchase become a reality. The Cumberland Road was extended to Vandalia, Illinois and eventually became known as the National Road. In the east Maryland completed the Baltimore Pike from Baltimore to Cumberland. It was not officially part of the National Road but traditionally was seen as part of it.

> In the contest of Jeffersonian republicanism and the economic and political tensions of the Jeffersonian era, the National Road must be viewed as a device for western development—potentially a generator of profits as well as a tool for managing and defending territory beyond the Appalachians. A road would enable land sales and settlement, and it would enable troops to move west to quell any uprising that might occur there. A road, in short, would extend the reach of central authority at the same time it pointed the direction that settlement ... might follow.[72]

Building the Road

In 1811, Secretary of the Treasury Albert Gallatin signed the contracts for the first ten miles of the road, including specifications for the amount of stone each contractor was to supply. Mr. Henry McKinley was to build the first two miles of the road, supplying 246 perches of stone at $21.25 per perch. A perch is about twenty-four cubic feet of stone. McKinley's contract was signed on May 8, 1811.[73]

The contract was clear on the specifications. The width to be cleared was to be sixty-feet, and the bed of the road was to be thirty feet wide. Hills were to be cut down, the trees removed and the stumps grubbed (uprooted) and "The road to be covered twenty feet in width, with stone eighteen inches in depth in the middle, and diminishing to twelve inches at the sides: the upper six inches; thereof, to be broken to such a size that each particle thereof will pass through a ring of three inches in diameter, and the remaining or lower stratum to be broken so as to pass through a seven inch ring."[74] This design was a variation of the road developed by French engineer Pierre Tresaguet in the 1770s. The Tresaguet road had a seven-inch lower layer but this road would have a twelve-inch lower layer. Assuming the bottom layer was a constant twelve inches the top layer of small stone would slope to almost nothing at the sides. Initially the road was not macadamized as Scotland's. John McAdam did not develop his system until after this road was started. In the late 1820s it was macadamized.[75] The contractor was to fill four additional feet in breadth to make the road thirty-four feet wide. It is not clear if this was of the stone construction or just graded earth. There were to be water ditches on each side for run-off and the slopes off the sides were to be no more than thirty degrees. McKinley's was the "first section, beginning at Cumberland, in Maryland, and ending at a place on said road two miles and two hundred and forty-six perches distant from Cumberland." This was the first stage of the major and permanent road to the west over the mountains, and it was expected to bear a lot of traffic so the specifications were for a wide, sturdy road.[76]

Considering the terrain, the construction was slow. First the sixty-six-foot width had to be cleared by cutting down trees and extracting stumps by hand and by horse. The stone, easily available in the mountains, had to be collected, broken by hand-held hammers to fit through seven and three inch rings, and then laid in the roadbed. The hills had to be leveled to meet the five-degree (8.75 percent) grade requirement. The sides had to be sloped and the water ditches dug, all by hand. As always, there was a labor shortage because the cities back east were booming and this road was in a remote area. Each of the several contractors used his own crews. Most of the laborers were English and Irish immigrants living in nearby Virginia or Pennsylvania. Nevertheless, because of the labor shortage they considered, but did not use, slave labor.[77] "For those living along the way, it was a not-to-be-forgotten sight: 'a thousand strong' they came, wrote a farmer near Uniontown, 'with their carts, wheelbarrows, picks, shovels, and blasting tools, grading those commons and climbing the mountainside, leaving behind them a roadway good enough for an emperor to travel over.'"[78] They struggled to make progress. By December 31, 1813, David Shriver, the Superintendent of the project, was able to report that the first ten miles were complete. Undoubtedly some miles in advance of that had been cleared. He also reported that the first four miles were now being used by travelers, an indication of how the public had looked forward to the road. There wasn't actually much in the way of a destination ten miles from Cumberland so these travelers were using what they could and then using the part that had been surveyed and cleared to move toward Ohio. A year later Shriver reported that travelers were now using the eleven miles of the next four sections. Contracts were let to the Youghiogheny River, thirty-nine miles away, with an estimate of about $7,500 per mile. Shriver reported in December 1815, that construction was complete, or nearly so, up to the Youghiogheny and construction had started on the bridge. He also reported he had already spent $1,200 on repairs on the road. He didn't specify if this was due to poor construction or because of wear due to the travelers. The Secretary of the Treasury sent Shriver's report to Congress with the following summary of appropriations so far:

1806, by the act of March 3	$30,000
1810, by the act of February 14	60,000
1811, by the act of March 3	50,000
1812, by the act of May 6	30,000
1813, by the act of March 3	140,000
1815, by the act of February 14	100,000
TOTAL	$410,000

He then estimated it would take another $300,000 to complete the road, costing $3,000 to complete the survey, $117,000 to reach Uniontown, $90,000 to reach Brownsville, and $90,000 to reach Wheeling. It was expensive and the debates in Congress were heated but both the public and Congress were looking forward to the completion.[79]

Despite the heated debates in Congress the needed support was forthcoming. Representative Jackson, a member of the House committee that received the President's report, strongly supported the request for the new $300,000 appropriation for the road. He reiterated the thoughts of many: "If Congress persevere with becoming spirit in this great public work, we shall soon see one of the best roads in the world over the chains of mountains which separate the western from the Atlantic waters, and which, but a few years since were supposed to present insurmountable obstacles to a safe and easy intercourse."[80] He then had an answer for those who thought the west held its own lures to those in the Atlantic states and it would be "impolitic to contribute to their increase," let alone making it easier for them to get there.

> The emigrant removes with intention to reside for life in his new habitation; and when he determines upon such removal, he bestows but little attention upon the inquiry whether the road on which he has to travel is a very good one, or in the condition of the principal State roads now used. This policy, therefore, although it cannot prevent him from going to the West, may, and, if persisted in, soon will, materially affect his future connexions with the eastern country in all the ramifications of a mutually profitable trade and intercourse.[81]

To bolster the last argument, Jackson cited recent trade with Louisiana in which sugar and cotton were shipped upriver to Pittsburgh and sold at a profit even though Pittsburgh was west of the mountains. He argued that with steam navigation on the rivers, if the roads to the west weren't improved, trade would diminish, New York, Philadelphia, and Baltimore would suffer, and all the commerce would go to New Orleans. He concluded with additional reasons to finish the road.

> But the advantages of an intimate commercial connexion ... are not the most important. Good roads have an influence over physical impossibilities. By diminishing the natural impediments, they bring places and their inhabitants nearer to each other. They increase the value of lands and fruits of the earth in remote situations.... They promote a free intercourse among the citizens of remote places, by which unfounded prejudices and animosities are dissipated, local and sectional feelings are destroyed, and a nationality of character ... is universally inculcated.
> The road ... has additional recommendations. It leads as far as Washington a direct line from the seat of Government to the important frontier of the United States on the upper lakes; and if, ... it be the true policy of the nation to have a direct military communication for the entire distance, a road can be extended from Washington, and, passing as it will through a large extent of public lands, inducements will be held out to the western settlers to purchase them, and by a rapid increase of the population, the necessity of keeping up a considerable military force in that quarter will be diminished, if not entirely superseded.[82]

The need for the road Jackson supported had been explicitly recognized for over thirty years and implicitly for over sixty years. A road would bind those in the east and the west in one nation and would improve trade with the eastern cities instead of sending it all through New Orleans. There was also a military argument to support the importance of the link between Washington and the west. Despite the increasing cost, these arguments are the ones that supported the continued funding needed to complete the road.

The chopping of trees, grubbing of the stumps, reduction of the grades, grading of the roadbed, breaking of the rocks, and laying of the stone all continued as the road progressed. At some point the road finally reached Wheeling. It may have been August 1, 1818, but that date is somewhat in doubt, because in February 1819, a Treasury Department report said, "I am now authorized to state that contracts can be made for that part of the road between Uniontown and Washington [PA] at the rate of $9,500 per mile."[83] Other reports said "In 1818, United States Mail coaches were running between Washington, D. C. and Wheeling, Virginia."[84] Still others,

> Hillsboro was laid out in the year 1819, a date coincident with the completion of the road.[85]
> In the year 1822, shortly after the completion of the road.[86]

All these might have been correct at some time because the road was built in sections and some were finished before others. The mail coaches going to Wheeling may have been traveling over an incomplete road.

There had been an uneasy truce since the Jefferson-Gallatin era concerning the constitutional arguments about the federal government's authority to fund internal improvements, including roads. In his discourse in 1816 Representative Jackson had referred to the state "compacts" that had allowed the federal funding to support the road. However, this was challenged by President James Monroe when he received an appropriations bill for repairs on the road. The road had been in need of almost continual repair from the beginning as it was difficult to construct through very rugged terrain, and some contactors did poor work. When Monroe received the bill in the spring of 1822, he vetoed it and sent it back to the House with his message of May 4. He acknowledged but rejected the states "compact" argument by which funding had been provided so far. He said, "I am of the opinion that Congress do not possess this power.... This power can be granted only by an amendment to the Constitution."[87] Congress did not have enough votes to override the veto.

Although Monroe maintained his position that an amendment was needed, he made a remarkable, pragmatic turnaround by December when he gave Congress his Sixth Annual Message. He acknowledged the incalculable value of the road and its need of repair. He reiterated his constitutional objection but then said,

> Should Congress, however, deem it improper to recommend such an amendment, they have, according to my judgment, the right to keep the road in repair by providing for the superintendence of it and appropriating the money necessary for repairs. Surely if they had the right to appropriate money to make the road they have a right to appropriate it to preserve it from ruin. From the exercise of this power no danger is to be apprehended. Under our happy system the people are the sole and exclusive fountain of power. Each government originates from them, and to them alone, each to its proper constituents, are they respectively and solely responsible for the faithful discharge of their duties within their constitutional limits.[88]

At the end of that same paragraph he made an attempt to justify his apparently opposing positions by making a distinction between "the right of appropriation" and the "right of jurisdiction and sovereignty over the territory." The pressure must have been intense on both Monroe and the Congress to finish and repair the road. It sounds like he had heard from "some of the people" between May and December. He alluded to that when he said the people are the sole fountain of power. Monroe did essentially the same thing Jefferson had done previously when he suggested a constitutional amendment, but then went along with Congressional appropriations to fund the road.

The Cumberland Road started with a bill enacted in 1806, was initiated in 1811, and constructed to Wheeling, Virginia, around 1819, was now complete. This was the route across the mountains from Maryland to Ohio that had been dreamed about for decades as the link between east and west. It was a great success although it alone it did not connect major centers of commerce; other roads had to connect to the Cumberland Road to obtain the benefits it promised. Even before the road was completed to Wheeling there were plans to extend it all the way to St. Louis. In the east, Maryland was already building roads to link it to Baltimore and Washington, D.C.

Maryland Roads: Baltimore to Cumberland

By the end of the eighteenth-century Maryland had a rather extensive network of roads, but unfortunately most were very poor. Governor Sharpe had built a road from Georgetown to Cumberland for Braddock's march to the Forks of the Ohio. Another road completed in the 1760s from Fort Frederick to Cumberland covered the gap in the army road to Cumberland and then there was Braddock's road from Cumberland to the Forks. These were roads for specific military purposes and weren't intended to be permanent. A map of Maryland in 1776 would show other roads, including Georgetown to Frederick, Baltimore to Frederick, and Frederick to Hagerstown.[89] Many of these were established to fill the expanding need for communication and commerce with western Maryland in the latter half of the century. These roads were in poor shape, deeply rutted and muddy much of the time.

> Even on the most important roads, stagecoach passengers were often compelled to get out and help the driver pull the vehicle from the mud. It was not uncommon to see horses in mud up to their haunches. Sticks or rails were often stuck in the road to warn travelers of mudholes or quicksand. Fences were sometimes pulled down so vehicles could bypass the road in favor of adjacent fields. One stretch of road in Maryland ... was so uneven and rutted that stagecoach passengers frequently were asked by the drive[r] to lean out the side of the coach to prevent its overturning. "Now gentlemen," he would say, "to the right; "now gentlemen, to the left."[90]

The state attempted to do something about the poor roads, partly to help improve commerce with the west. In May 1787, the legislature passed "An ACT to lay out several turnpike roads in Baltimore county." These roads would fan out from Baltimore to various towns such as Frederick, Reister's-town, and others. The specific definition of a turnpike at that time meant it had to have (1) an improved road surface, (2) a system of toll-gates at certain intervals, and (3) an incorporated company with shares of stock.[91] The key part of this definition was the improved road surface as recognized in the preamble to the act.

> Whereas the public roads leading from Baltimore-town to the western parts of this state, by manes of the great number of waggons, that use the same, are rendered almost impassable during the winter season, and the ordinary method of repairing the said roads is not only insufficient, but exceedingly burthensome; and the establishment of several turnpike roads in the said county would greatly reduce the price of land-carriage of produce and merchandise, and raise the value of the land in the said county, and considerably increase the commerce of the state.[92]

This was just a start which covered Baltimore County and did not go as far west as Cumberland. The improved roadbed specified by the act was a major step in improving the poor road system. The road had to be cleared to fifty-two feet wide and grubbed and stoned to forty feet wide; the bed was to be raised in the middle to not less than eighteen inches and covered with small stones or coarse gravel. Although not quite as good as the Cumberland Road specification, this was almost twenty years prior to it. The act also specified toll gates, but lacked the third attribute of a turnpike, an incorporated company; instead, state commissioners were appointed to oversee the projects.[93] Unfortunately this plan to have the county create these roads was unsuccessful and the act was amended no less than ten times in fourteen years. Since the county apparently couldn't build the roads, there were attempts to draw in private capital to build the turnpikes. A company established in 1796 to build a road from Baltimore to Washington was unsuccessful.[94]

Prospects started to improve for Maryland roads through legislation in the November 1804, session which passed "An ACT to incorporate companies to make several turnpike roads through Baltimore County, and for other purposes." The act was similar to the 1787 law, but this act had a better result. The environment had changed considerably with statehood for Ohio and the imminent prospect of trade with the west. The Maryland act established three turnpike companies to build turnpikes from Baltimore; one was to Frederick and then to Boonesborough, Maryland. As usual the act specified the construction of the road which was to be twenty feet wide and bedded with "wood, stone or gravel, or any other hard substance ... and the road is to be faced with gravel or stone pounded ... in such a manner to secure a firm ... and even surface." Inclines of four degrees were specified except over the Catoctin Mountains where six degrees was allowed.[95] These specifications were not quite as rigid as those for similar roads. This sixty-two-mile turnpike, from Baltimore through Frederick to Boonesborough, was built and the first tollgate was opened in April 1807. Maryland was the first of the Mid-Atlantic States to finance its roads using this turnpike system; others followed.[96]

In the same session, a supplementary act was passed, which authorized extending the road to Hagerstown and to Williamsport. This part of the road was not built as quickly. A supplementary act to extend the road from Williamsport to Cumberland took even longer. Why the delay and how did the road to Cumberland get finished?

The act authorizing the Cumberland Road was enacted in 1806. In 1807, Secretary Gallatin asked the states affected to report on their progress. The Maryland report on the turnpike to Frederick said that contracts had been let on July 4, 1805, for the first twenty miles and that section had cost about nine thousand dollars per mile; tollgates were open on April 24, 1807. Contracts were let for the next seventeen miles and were expected to cost seven thousand dollars per mile. However, the next paragraph indicated that the last section from Boonesborough to Cumberland, would be a problem.

> It may be observed that, from Boonesborough to Cumberland, a distance of seventy four and a half miles, as the road now runs, is as yet without any provision by law for its improvement, further than as common country roads in other part of the State, and not laid out on the best ground, in many places which it is capable of; and, to bring into full operation the benefits contemplated by the General Government by the road leading from Fort Cumberland to the Ohio, it becomes necessary that the State of Maryland should either take this matter upon her own account, or put it in the power of Congress to promote a design which is in the interest of the Union to carry into effect.[97]

In other words, Maryland did not have a plan to use private turnpikes to complete the road from Boonesborough to Cumberland and the Federal government might want to help. On the next page the report showed a table with the plan for the new road compared with the present, unimproved roads, even including a straight-line sketch of the route.

From Baltimore to Fredericktown	49.25 miles	The road as will be made	43.5 miles
From Fredericktown to Williamsport	24.5 miles	The road as now runs	27.25 miles
From Williamsport to Hancock	21.5 miles	The road as now runs	23.75 miles
From Hancock to Cumberland	31.75 miles	The road as now runs	40.25 miles
TOTAL	120 miles		135 miles

If and when completed, this would be the route from Baltimore to the Maryland terminus of the Cumberland Road. The table and sketch showed the route skirting Boonesborough and skipping Hagerstown, but it ultimately went through those towns and skirted Williamsport.

The fast start of the Baltimore to Frederick turnpike in 1805 had some in Congress predicting that the road to Cumberland would be complete before the Cumberland Road was even started. This fast start, and the plan laid out to complete the road to Cumberland, was one of the reasons the commissioners planned to begin the Cumberland Road at Cumberland instead of farther east. The fast start was illusory with respect to completing the Maryland road in the west. In fact, the federal road over the mountains was completed to Wheeling in 1818 before some sections of the Baltimore turnpike were even started. "The plain fact was that no Maryland capital wanted to tackle the mountains of Western Maryland." The logical candidate, the company doing the front end from Baltimore to Frederick, declined to tackle the western half of the road. The turnpike came to a dead end in Boonesborough for a number of years while the Marylanders haggled about whether the road would go through Hagerstown or Williamsport.[98]

Maryland was embarrassed as the state still did not have a company to finish the road from Boonesborough to Cumberland, and the Cumberland Road construction was well underway. The mountain crossing for the Maryland road was expected to cost about $400,000 and no investors wanted to risk it. Finally, in 1812 a Senator asked the question, "Who in Maryland besides the banks has that kind of money?" The question was not mere rhetoric; he had an answer which was encapsulated in the title of the act of the Maryland General Assembly on December 17, 1812, "An act to incorporate a company to make a turnpike road leading to Cumberland, and for the extension of the charters of the several Banks in this State, and for other purposes." Maryland banks depended on the legislature for the periodic renewal of their charters. This act would make extension of the charters conditional on their incorporation of a turnpike company to build the road to Cumberland. In other words, it was coercion, hardball. If the banks acquiesced, and they had little choice, their charters would be extended through 1835. They were to subscribe for stock proportional to their capitalization.[99]

The commissioners decided the Cumberland Turnpike Road would start at a point on the west bank of the Big Conococheague Creek, near both Williamsport and Hagerstown. The specifications were "That this road shall be cleared out, stoned, and made in the same manner as is the Baltimore and Frederick-town turnpike road...." They were given the option of not stoning the road provided the road be kept in good repair. Perhaps that relaxed specification was a tacit recognition that the banks were being forced into this and the General Assembly didn't want to make it any harder than necessary.[100] The road was planned, surveyed, and bids let in 1815, with construction starting in 1816. Completed in 1821, the fifty-eight-mile road from Conococheague Creek to Cumberland became known as the infamous Bank Road.[101]

The Cumberland Turnpike and the Baltimore to Boonesborough Turnpike constituted the two ends of a road across Maryland that linked Baltimore to the Cumberland Road and Wheeling. However, there was an embarrassing gap between the end of the Boonesborough Turnpike, and the beginning of the Cumberland Turnpike at Conococheague Creek. This gap of about fifteen miles consisted of a very poor road. Around the time the Cumberland Turnpike construction was started in January 1816, the General Assembly passed another bill to incorporate companies to extend the road from Boonesborough to the road starting on the Conococheague Creek.[102] This act apparently failed because three years later the governor was still proposing some alternatives for closing the gap.[103] The gap was finally closed after more time passed. Some of the alternatives would have bypassed Hagerstown because it was not on the direct path between Boonesborough and the Conococheague terminus of the Cumberland Turnpike. Interested parties in Hagerstown did not want to miss the road so they formed the Hagerstown and Conococheague Turnpike Company and built a toll road from the center of the town to the road at the Conococheague Creek. This road, completed in 1819, closed five miles of the gap, but still left the bad ten-mile gap between Boonesborough and Hagerstown. "Travelers told of taking five to seven hours to cover the ten miles in bad weather over this only unpaved stretch of the whole 268 miles from Baltimore to Wheeling."[104]

The bickering continued, but finally in 1821 the legislature again prevailed on the banks to incorporate the Boonesborough Turnpike Company in exchange for extending the bank charters ten more years to 1845. The only benefit to this long delay was that the road surface technique developed by Scotsman John Loudon McAdam was introduced to this country and the Boonesborough Turnpike was the first road in America that was "macadamized." This superior pavement method was eventually applied to the entire Cumberland Road. The Baltimore Pike was finally finished in 1824.[105]

The Cumberland Road from Cumberland to the Ohio River at Wheeling opened in 1818 and the Baltimore Pike was completed in 1824. There was now a legitimate, stone-paved road across the mountains, from Maryland to Ohio, which fulfilled a century old dream. Ohio was opened to the east to Baltimore. Traffic and mail were running on these roads even before they were complete. The extension of the road west of Wheeling was a foregone conclusion. Jefferson had envisioned a road all the way to St. Louis years earlier, and by 1820 Congress was authorizing the layout of the westward extension.

In the late eighteenth-century the goal of crossing the mountains was modest—to connect the eastward flowing waters such as the Potomac, with the westward flowing waters of the Ohio River by means of a road over the mountains. The implicit assumption was that one could use the Potomac to get to Cumberland, use the road over the mountains to get to the Ohio, and use that river to go farther west. Over the years, it became obvious the Potomac could not be used effectively to travel upriver to Cumberland, and a road was needed from Baltimore to get to Cumberland. The road from Cumberland to Wheeling was only a means to get over the mountains to the Ohio River. It became just as obvious that the Ohio River, limited by its route, could not answer all the communications and commercial needs in the west so Congress authorized extending the Cumberland Road due west from Wheeling all the way to the seat of government in Missouri. The Cumberland Road plus that extension became the National Road.

The National Road

For 150 years after the first settlements in America the west was considered to be the Ohio country, the Ohio Valley; if one crossed the mountains one was in the west. This perception changed dramatically after the 1783 Treaty of Paris ended the War for Independence and the United States land mass was extended all the way to the Mississippi. Twenty years later the west increased even more dramatically with the Louisiana Purchase in 1803. In an historical blink of an eye the American West became almost unimaginably large. Ohio, the easternmost state of the original Northwest Territory no longer defined "the west," as it was now much larger than Ohio. Ohio joined the Union in 1803 and by 1821 seven other states had joined—Louisiana (1812), Indiana (1816), Mississippi (1817), Illinois (1818), Alabama (1819), Maine (1820), and Missouri (1821). Indiana, Illinois of the Northwest Territory, and Missouri of the Louisiana Purchase, were directly west of Ohio and north of the Ohio River, so "the west" now included four states as well as the remainder of the Northwest and Louisiana Territories, not yet ready for statehood.

In retrospect, the Congressional act in 1806 which authorized the road from Cumberland to the Ohio River was a tepid response for connecting the Atlantic to the Mississippi through this vast northern territory on the verge of statehood. A larger response of a national road from the Atlantic to the Mississippi would have been more appropriate. Indiana and Illinois were not yet states, but as part of the Northwest Territory they were destined to join the Union, and the United States now had territory well beyond the Mississippi. The seemingly tentative response in 1806 could be attributed to a lack of imagination in envisioning a project of that scope. Considering the rapid expansion of the west this is somewhat understandable. Jefferson did envision a road to St. Louis although he did not act on it and probably saw it as a dream for the distant future. A combination of factors explains the limited response—the single-minded purpose of the colonies, and then states, of building over the mountains to link east and west, the real constitutional concerns early in the new republic of whether or not this road could be funded through the federal government, and the concerns about paying for any internal improvements while still paying off the war debts.

Once there were states on both sides of the Appalachians the intense interest in a road over the mountains could now be realized. Defining endpoints on either side of the mountains would focus the effort to complete that link, the Cumberland Road. Anticipating that Maryland would complete the road link from Baltimore to Cumberland was a bonus. The constitutional issue was a real concern and various constructs, such as the idea of "state compacts" were used to get around it These constitutional concerns continued for a couple of decades and were the basis of some vetoes. The Cumberland Road only passed for small distances through three states and care was taken to obtain the permission of those states for the road. The difficulty of that modest undertaking would have made the feasibility of broad federal construction through entire states problematic. Inevitably though, once they started to build the road everyone wanted it to go through their town. The funding issue had actually been solved four years earlier by the act of Congress that enabled Ohio's entrance into the Union.

Building the Road

It is not clear when the term National Road was first used, nor what it referred to. The phrase, "Origin of National Road," was handwritten by Gallatin on top of the letter he had sent to Giles in 1802 suggesting his proposed funding plan; it could have been added years later.[106] In all the legislation to fund the road all the way through Illinois, there was no mention of a name—it was "laying out the road," or "for continuation of the road," or "construction of the road." This was a reference to the road from Cumberland to Ohio.

Colloquially, the term Cumberland Road caught on early, and the term National Road probably caught on by 1818 when the Cumberland Road was being completed and they were thinking about extending it west.

The decision to build the Cumberland Road seemed an obvious project since, a road across the mountains had been envisioned for decades. The extension of the road west from Wheeling should have been obvious, a natural way to connect the far west with the east, but it took years to actually start this project. Congress funded the road for twenty years after the Enabling Act for Ohio until Monroe vetoed the bill for repairs of the road in 1822. After his veto, there was uncertainty for several years over the constitutional question and the fear was that the road west from Wheeling would not be built. The road to Wheeling from Cumberland was usable in 1818, and the nation was growing rapidly, yet it took seven years before the authorization of funds for the extension of the road west. By the time the road reached Wheeling there was already universal acceptance that it could not stop there but needed to be continued. The National Road realization can be considered to have taken place in three stages. First, the Ohio Enabling Act provided funding for the Cumberland Road from Cumberland, Maryland, to Wheeling, Virginia. Second, Maryland completed the Baltimore Pike from Baltimore to Cumberland, Maryland. It was started prior to the start of the Cumberland Road but completed after the Cumberland Road. Technically the Baltimore Pike is not part of the National Road, it was strictly a Maryland endeavor, but traditionally it is considered part of the National Road. The third phase started with the funding of the road beyond Wheeling.

The National Road dates from May 15, 1820, when Congress appropriated ten thousand dollars to "examine the country, between Wheeling, in the state of Virginia, and a point on the left bank of the Mississippi river, to be chosen by said commissioners, between St. Louis and the mouth of the Illinois River, and to lay out a road from Wheeling aforesaid ... to be on a straight line."[107] This was the birth of the National Road, an extension of the Cumberland Road and Baltimore Pike, which would extend across the nation from the Atlantic coast to the Mississippi River. Appropriations to build the road started on March 3, 1825, when Congress passed "An Act for the continuation of the Cumberland road," and appropriated 150,000 dollars for its construction.

> for the purpose of opening and making a road from the town of Canton, in the State of Ohio, on the right bank of the Ohio river, opposite the town of Wheeling, to the Muskingum river at Zanesville ... to extend the same to the permanent seat of government of the state of Missouri; the said road to conform, in all respects, to the provisions of the said recited act, except that it shall pass by the seat of government of the states of Ohio, Indiana, and Illinois.... That the said road shall commence at Zanesville.[108]

James Monroe signed this bill the day before he left office, apparently not concerned about the constitutionality of a new road although he had previously vetoed repairs to the original road.

The road would essentially be a straight line west to Zanesville then all the way to Missouri, it would pass through the state capitals of Ohio (Columbus), Indiana (Indianapolis), and Illinois (Vandalia). There apparently was a geographical mix-up in writing the bill as Canton is *neither* on the Ohio River across from Wheeling, *nor* is it near Zanesville. The starting location was clarified, and on July 4 the road was started east and west from St. Clairsville, Ohio, located slightly west of Wheeling. The road originally went west over Zane's Trace up to Zanesville, then west to Columbus rather than following the southwest direction of Zane's Trace. See Map 16.

The construction west of Wheeling was still on the Allegheny Plateau and the road was still difficult to build. Farther west in Ohio it became much easier when it entered the fertile Till Plains. The 1825 act did not specify the dimensions of the road as previous acts had done, but

> All along its course, specifications required that the Road be cleared to width of sixty-six feet, graded to slopes no more than 5 percent, drained, and macadamized, but the requirements and the reality often did not match, especially in the West: as one author put it, "that part of the National road between Cumberland and Wheeling was much more substantially built than those portions of it lying between the Ohio river and its western terminus."[109]

The specifications were not always uniform. A later contract specification for the road around Springfield, Ohio, in 1837 required that trees and growth were to be cleared to forty feet on either side from the centerline of the road, and stumps and roots cleared to twenty feet on each side.[110]

Despite one claim by a Baltimore editor in October, "The National Road now extending through Ohio, westward, goes on rapidly," progress was slow. Congress appropriated money in 1827 to complete the road to Zanesville, and again in 1828 and 1829 to complete the road to Indiana. The road reached Zanesville around 1828 or 1829 and bids were let for the fifty-two miles between Zanesville and Columbus. The Army Corps of Engineers was now in charge of the road building and apparently doing a good job of supervision. Nevertheless, the slow pace continued. The *Zanesville Ohio Republican* noted,

> "Five years now have nearly elapsed since the present retrenching, economical administration came into power and the road between here and Columbus, 52 miles, not half done ... and we venture to say the cost already of these 52 miles equal, if not exceed, the cost of the road, 73 miles, between here and Wheeling. But so we go under the economical reign of Mr. Andrew Jackson, Esq."[111]

The Congressional approach of funding the road year-by-year doubtless had a retarding effect as no one was sure when the next appropriation would be passed. A single appropriation funding the entire road would have promoted better planning and therefore a faster completion. Because the nation was becoming more divided and sectionalism was rampant, there was reluctance to give one section an advantage and the appropriations limped along. There was also a hint of the future as railways were being considered in the east. Would this have an impact on the road system?

The road finally reached Columbus in 1833 and the road from Baltimore was now totally open. Construction continued through all two hundred miles of Ohio. Congressional appropriations continued almost yearly until the final one in 1838 which continued the road through Indiana, Illinois, and into Missouri. Interest in the road waned as the years passed and Congressional appropriations became more restrictive. For example, in the 1836 bill it stated, "that the appropriation for Illinois shall be limited to grading and bridging, and shall not be construed as pledging Congress to future appropriations for the purpose of macadamizing the road."[112] As Hulbert observed, "The Cumberland Road was not to Indiana and Illinois what it was to Ohio, for somewhat similar reasons that it was less to Ohio than to Pennsylvania, for the further west it was built the older the century grew, and the newer the means of transportation which were coming rapidly to the front."[113] He was referring to railroads in general, but by the mid–1820s there was a railroad beginning construction to link Maryland and Ohio, a competitor to the National Road. In 1832 the House Committee on Roads and Canals began to consider funding a railroad instead of the remainder of the National Road. By 1836, the committee proposed to do just that and substitute a railroad for the National Road between Columbus and the Mississippi. The measure did not pass because a study showed the railroad would be more expensive at the time, but this did reveal some exasperation with the slow pace of road construction.

The construction of the road did not progress smoothly from east to west. After it reached Columbus in 1833 there was some controversy about the route for the rest of Ohio and it didn't reach Springfield, Ohio, until 1838. In the meantime, contracts were let in Indiana in 1830 for building the road east and west from Indianapolis. "The eastern leg arrived in Richmond, Indiana, sometime between 1835 and 1841 ... the western leg was open to Terre Haute by 1835 and completed by 1838." Being completed did not mean macadamized. The road was open to Vandalia, Illinois, the capital at the time, by 1839, but it was incomplete, surfaced only with clay. The federal government did not fund the part of the road which was finished to Vandalia in 1850. The National Road never reached the original objective, the capital of Missouri.[114]

Although a means of funding the construction of the road was found after the Monroe veto of 1822, the ban remained through the Jackson presidency on the federal government funding repairs through tolls. After a decade of hard use the road fell into disrepair with no federal solution in sight. A resort to state control was the only option for maintaining the road. Ohio was the first to act when the legislature passed an 1831 act to preserve and repair the road within Ohio, provided Congress gave its assent, and provide toll houses for the collection of tolls after the road repairs were made.[115] Over the next few years the other states, Virginia, Pennsylvania, and Maryland passed similar measures. Congress accepted these proposals on June 24, 1834, when it passed appropriations for "300,000 for the entire completion of repairs east of Ohio to meet provisions of the Acts of Pennsylvania (April 4, 1831), Maryland (January 23, 1832), and Virginia (February 7, 1832), accepting the road surrendered to the States, the United States not thereafter to be subject for any expense for repairs."[116] The federal government surrendered the road to the states and allowed them to collect tolls for repairs although no tolls could be levied on federal goods passing over the road, such as mail. Many appropriations for the National Road were passed in following years ceasing in 1844 at a total of almost seven million dollars.[117]

Traveling the Road

The name National Road meant many different things to the people of the day and it still is not uniquely defined. When the road over the mountains was first created in 1806 it was the road from Cumberland to the Ohio River and was known as the Cumberland Road. Until the completion of the road to Wheeling in 1818, reference was always to the Cumberland Road and Congressional appropriations in this period referred to "making the road from Cumberland." Even the March 1831 act appropriating funds for the road was entitled "an Act for the continuation of the Cumberland road in the states of Ohio, Indiana, and Illinois." Although the Congressional language was consistent, the term National Road came into use in reference to the Cumberland Road sometime prior to 1818. This name became even more prevalent after 1820 when plans were made for the road to extend from Wheeling to Missouri.[118]

The terms National Road and Cumberland Road came to be used interchangeably, most often in reference to the road from Cumberland west across Ohio, Indiana, and Illinois. Crossing several states and built by the federal government, they were national roads. However, the road from Baltimore to Cumberland, the road that truly completed the link from the Atlantic to the west, the Baltimore Pike, was built by, and within, Maryland, without federal funding. Nevertheless, when looking at a map connecting Baltimore with the

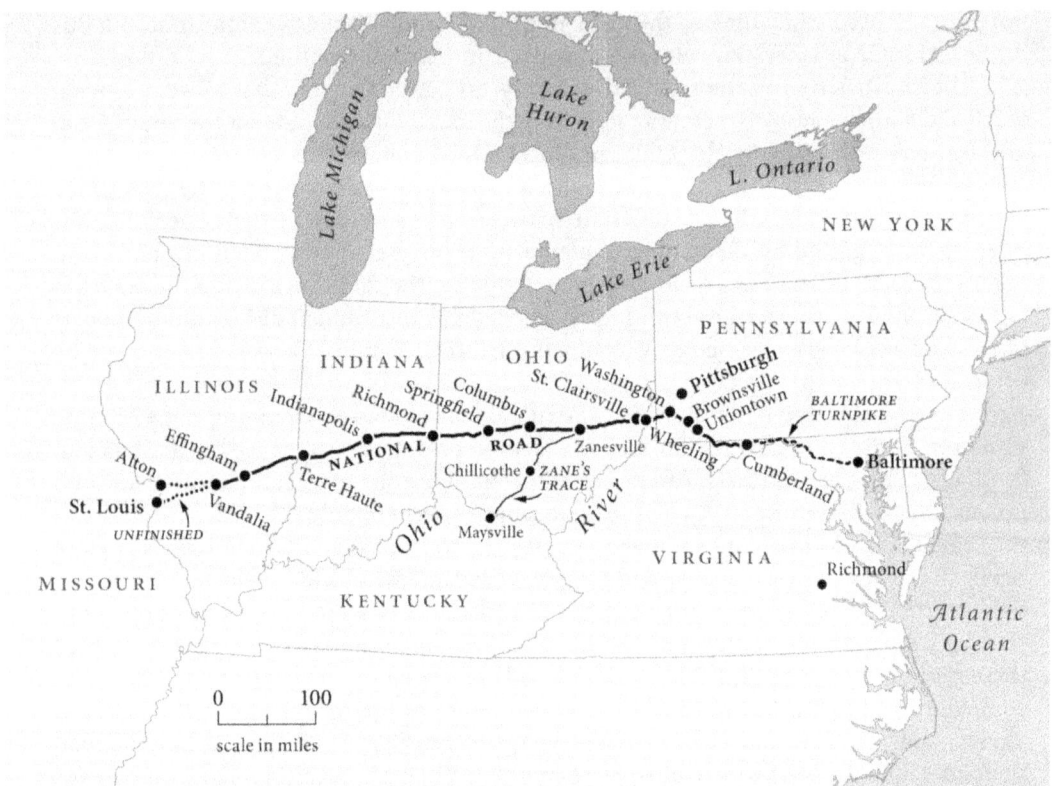

Map 16: A simplified map of the National Road. It extended from Cumberland, Maryland, to Vandalia, Illinois, beyond which it was never completed. The original Cumberland Road, from Cumberland to Wheeling, was traditionally assumed to be part of the National Road once the road was extended past Wheeling.

west, it seemed natural to include the Baltimore Pike as part of the National Road, and traditionally this designation has been used since early in the nineteenth century. The National Road was sometimes referred to as The Old Pike (Searight, *The Old Pike: A History of the National Road*).

Depending on the definition of the road and the completion date used, it was under construction and in operation for fifty years. The Cumberland Road was started in 1811 and was complete by 1818. Although there were gaps in it, the road from Baltimore to Cumberland was also nearly complete by 1818. Even as it was being extended in the west in the 1820s and 1830s, the National Road was being used. The heyday of the road lasted from 1818 until 1852 when the B&O Railroad reached Wheeling.

The purpose of the National Road was to link the west tightly with the eastern United States, first to assure the integrity of the Union, and second to foster trade and communications between east and west. There could be no doubt of the road's utility in facilitating commerce between east and west as it was a major factor in linking Maryland, especially Baltimore, with Ohio. Was the tight link binding east and west also achieved by means other than trade? A key measure of this would be the extent of permanent migration of easterners pulling up stakes and moving west to inhabit the relatively empty western lands. There is no question that there was a massive migration to the west, first to Ohio and then to the other states of the Old Northwest Territory.

Migration

After the Cumberland Road was complete to Wheeling on the Ohio River the population of Ohio exploded from over 580,000 in 1820 to almost 2,000,000 in 1850, an increase of almost 350 percent. The road reached Indiana about 1835 when the population of the state was about 500,000; it doubled to about 1,000,000 in 1850. The Road didn't reach Illinois until around 1838 and its population almost doubled from 1840 to 1850 from 480,000 to 850,000.[119] These are large population increases with an inference that the National Road was the major thoroughfare facilitating them. Many historians have described,

> the horde of emigrants hurrying westward.... Their covered wagons had been forming an endless procession ever since the Cumberland Road was opened ... they clung to the National Road like a mosquito to a denizen of the Swampy Bottoms. It was the people's highway, and the people crowded it from rim to edge until their carts, wagons, stages and carriages challenged one another for the right of way.[120]
>
> Thousands now began pouring into the state by wagon from the more thickly populated districts of the east. Many settled in the more remote sections of the state and many more passed to the fertile prairies beyond.[121]
>
> Indiana and Ohio received more than ninety thousand inhabitants a year for a generation and at least ninety per cent of them came by way of the Pike ... the average number traversing the Cumberland Road every year was close to two hundred thousand.[122]

However, Gregory Rose (*Extending the Road West*) presents a good case that most of the migration took place prior to the construction of the road and that the road followed the migration rather than preceded it. This is consistent with the claim made above that roads followed the settlers, not the other way around. This explanation is especially persuasive since it took twenty years to complete the road after it had reached Wheeling and many people moved during that time. Rose also provides evidence that after many Virginians and Pennsylvanians moved to Ohio they continued to move farther west into Indiana and Illinois along with Ohioans. Once they started moving these migrants would often move again, farther west. If they didn't have much invested in the land, if the crop was poor, or for many other reasons, it was common to move farther west. Even if the early population of Ohio, Indiana, and Illinois did not enter Ohio on the National Road, it was used for further migrations west. This is especially true in Ohio where building roads, north and south, to link up to the National Road was a priority.[123]

Even if Rose is correct there was still plenty of migrant traffic on the road.

> A company of Middle States families, well equipped with Conestoga wagons and family possessions, leading and driving extra horses, neat cattle and hogs, might be followed by a single couple in an old-fashioned, high-wheeled carriage which could straddle the stumps and ford the streams. Virginia and Carolina travelers of the better-to-do class favored lighter wagons of the Conestoga type, with single teams. Poorer folk from the Upland South used the little carts and wagons made of tough young oak without nail or iron tires, pulled by unshod, scraggly little southern ponies. There were two-wheeled Philadelphia carts, four-wheeled New Jersey carts, and push carts. And some people walked.[124]

One example of a family that moved a lot in this area is the Lewman family, originally probably from Germany. Moses Lewman and his brother Caleb were born in Allegheny County, Maryland, c.1735. By 1778 Moses was living near Williamsport, Maryland. The 1790 census listed several of Moses's sons in Bedford, Pennsylvania. By 1800 Moses, his son Reason, and Moses's brother Caleb were living in Cumberland, Maryland, not far from Williamsport. Moses's grandson, James Aaron, was born in Mason County Kentucky, which is Bluegrass Country, on the Ohio River. Reason Lewman lived in Allegheny County,

Maryland, in 1810, but by 1820 he had also moved to Lewis County, Kentucky on the Ohio River, abutting Mason County and the location of Maysville, the southern terminus of Zane's Trace. Many people moved from Kentucky to Ohio, especially near Cincinnati, from the Maysville region. Later Lewman descendants moved west to Illinois. It is not known if this family ever used any part of the National Road, but their constant movement west was a common trait of early western settlers and their use of the road at some time was quite possible.[125]

There is just no way to ascertain how many migrants used the National Road. There were no official records, only family records which are still preserved, and genealogical records which reveal many of these migrations. Undoubtedly there were thousands on the road using their own wagons, renting rides on commercial wagons, riding by horseback, and walking. Whether in the original migrations to the west or in subsequent moves, many families moved from the east to the west using this National Road.

COMMERCIAL TRAFFIC

There are numerous stories related by Archer Butler Hulbert (*The Cumberland Road*), and Thomas Searight, about the people and traffic on the road. They include migrant wagons, freight wagons, stagecoaches, droves of animals (especially swine), and mail coaches. The people of the road were migrants, wagoners, stage drivers, herders, tavern owners, toll collectors, and mail drivers. Although the data for family migration is almost nonexistent there is better data on the commercial traffic, especially after tolls were collected. Even before tolls were collected, an idea of the heavy use of the road is available from the observations and stories of its travelers.

The heaviest users of the road, both by weight and numbers, were the freight wagons. They carried supplies from Baltimore to Ohio and beyond, returning with western products to the East Coast. The most common design of the freight wagon, by far, was the Conestoga wagon. This wagon was developed around 1750 near Lancaster, Pennsylvania, and named for an Indian tribe located near the area. It was particularly used for freight in Pennsylvania, Maryland, Ohio, and Virginia, and was used extensively on the National Road. Made of White Oak and Poplar, the bed measured sixteen feet in length, four feet in width and was four feet deep; the total length was close to twenty-six feet. The front and back sloped down to help keep the load centered in the lower middle of the wagon. Wooden hoops were used to hold a canvas cover that was sometime treated with oil to make it water resistant. The cover stretched about twenty feet from stem to stern. The finished wagon, usually painted Prussian blue, would weigh between 3,000 and 3,500 pounds and would be pulled by four or six Conestoga horses. A Conestoga wagon with a six-horse team is shown in the photo.[126]

The teams of horses, at $170 to $200 per horse, were more expensive than the wagons themselves which sold for about $250. These horses were specially bred and very sturdy because they often pulled weights over five tons. The front wheels were three and a half feet in diameter and the rear ones four to four and a half feet. The steel rims around the wooden wheels were two to six inches wide, four inches being very common. Wide wheels were preferable for the road because they put less pressure on the road and therefore did less damage. Later the wheel width could be a factor in the toll charge; wider wheels would reduce the toll.[127]

The Conestoga wagons were not the wagons later used to move families across the plains to Oregon or California. Those wagons were called Prairie Schooners and were much smaller and lighter.[128] The Conestoga wagon was the source of another term in American culture. Tobacco was expensive but in demand among the wagon drivers. A manufacturer

A Conestoga wagon (Library of Congress).

in Washington, Pennsylvania, came up with a cheap way to wrap small cigars and sold them four for a cent. These little cigars were very popular with the drivers and became known as Conestoga cigars; the name eventually shortened to "stogies."[129]

Thomas Searight, who worked on the road with his father, described the constant use of the National Road, day and night, by family wagons, stage coaches, and freight wagons.

> As many as twenty-four-horse coaches have been counted in line at one time on the road, and large, broad wheeled wagons, covered with white canvass stretched over bows, laden with merchandise and drawn by six Conestoga horses, were visible all the day long at every point, and many times until late in the evening, besides enumerable caravans of horses, mules, cattle, hogs and sheep. It looked more like the leading avenue of a great city than a road through rural districts.[130]

Wagons were not the only thing Searight had seen on the road. He had also seen slaves driven over the road in pairs, fastened with rope or cable, and driven like horses.[131]

Hulbert made similar observations about life on the road.

> "wagoners," and tens of thousands of passengers and immigrants who composed the public which patronized the great highway. This was the real life of the road—coaches numbering as many as twenty traveling in a single line; wagonhouse yards where a hundred tired horses rested overnight besides their great loads; hotels where seventy transient guests have been served breakfast in a single morning; a life made cheery by the echoing horns of hurrying stages; blinded by the dust of droves of cattle numbering in the thousands; a life noisy with the satisfactory creak and crunch of the wheels of great wagons carrying six and eight thousand pounds of freight east or west.[132]
>
> As early as the year 1822 it is recorded that a single one of the five commission houses at Wheeling unloaded one thousand and eighty-one wagons, averaging three thousand five hundred pounds, and paid for the freightage of goods the sum of ninety thousand dollars.[133]

All the men and boys associated with the road were called "pike boys," whether drivers, drovers, tavern owners or any other occupation that had to do with the road. The "regular" freight drivers worked year-round hauling freight; they usually covered about fifteen miles a day on average compared to the "sharpshooters" who could log as much as twenty miles a day. The "sharpshooters" were usually full-time farmers who would sometimes use their lighter farm wagons to haul freight when prices were high. At night, the freighters would stop at wagon houses or taverns. The horses would be outside, covered with blankets in winter, and the wagoners would spread their bedrolls inside on the tavern floor around the fire. Often, they tried to stop at a tavern where the landlord was a fiddler and they would enjoy some hoedown music before bedding down.[134]

By present standards the trips took a long time and the wagons were lightly loaded, but in comparison to the time prior to the road, the trips were fast indeed. In 1838, Daniel Barcus contracted to haul a load of general merchandise weighing 3,800 pounds from Baltimore to Mt. Vernon, Ohio. He delivered the goods in good condition thirty days after he left Baltimore. He traveled by way of Wheeling, Zanesville, and Jacktown, Ohio, then thirty miles to his destination, 397 miles total. He returned to Baltimore with 7,200 pounds of Ohio tobacco. He received $4.25 per hundredweight for hauling out to Ohio and $2.75 per hundredweight for hauling back east. The $4.25 per hundredweight was comparatively high for the time, perhaps because of the long distance and the thirty miles off the road to the destination. More common and still considered very good, was $1.25 to $2.25 per hundredweight between Brownsville or Wheeling to Cumberland.[135] "Before the era of the Cumberland Road the price for hauling goods of emigrants over Braddock's Road was very high. One emigrant paid $5.33 per hundred for hauling "women and goods" from Alexandria, Virginia, to the Monongahela. Six dollars per hundred-weight was charged one emigrant from Hagerstown, Maryland to Terre Haute, Indiana."[136] One wagoner named Lucas, using only five horses on his team, was said to have carried twelve thousand pounds, the heaviest load to that date (1844).[137]

Stagecoach lines had less income than freighters but they moved people and mail quickly, and on a regular schedule. There were a few large lines such as National Road Stage Company and Good Intent, but there were also many smaller lines, which were often gobbled up by the larger lines. The exteriors of the coaches were gaily painted and decorated, and the coaches were lined with soft plush silk inside. These coaches were named, as later trains would be, with honorifics such as "Ivanhoe," "Sultana," and "Loch Lomond." Most had three seats inside accommodating three passengers each. The coaches did not have springs and the bodies were hung on leather straps, so the ride was very uncomfortable, especially since they moved rapidly to speed the journey to the next town. Their regular schedule was legendary.[138]

> Their arrival in town was the leading event of each day, and they were so regular in transit that farmers along the road knew the exact hour by their coming, without the aid of watch or clock. They ran night and day alike. Relays of fresh horses were placed at intervals of twelve miles, as nearly as practicable. Ordinarily a driver had charge of one team only, which he drove and cared for.... During the prosperous era of the road it was not uncommon to see as many as fifteen coaches in continuous procession, and both ways, east and west there would be thirty each day.[139]

The regularity and speed of the coaches were attributes that made them ideal for the delivery of mail. At first the mail went in a long wooden box behind the passenger compartment, which the drivers called the "monkey box." These early mail coaches carried only three passengers. That coach design was soon abandoned and regular passenger coaches were used for the mail. The ordinary passenger coaches, including the mail, could take several days to reach the western cities on the road. For example, in 1837, the time from Washington, D.C., to Wheeling was two days and eleven hours, to Columbus it was three days and sixteen hours, and to Vandalia it was nine days and ten hours. Compared to previous travel days, these trips were all quite rapid. However, the Post Office also had an express mail coach service in 1837 which specified much shorter times, including from Washington, D.C., to Wheeling in thirty hours, to Columbus in forty-five and one-half hours, and to Vandalia in eighty-five and one-half hours. In the days before the telegraph reached the west these were extremely fast delivery times.[140] In fact, these are probably comparable to present-day schedules for regular mail.

Prior to the telegraph, fast coaches were used to send Presidential messages west. For example, in 1846 a driver named Redding Bunting delivered President Polk's message about the war with Mexico. He left Cumberland at two in the morning, arrived at Uniontown at eight o'clock, Washington (Pennsylvania) at eleven, and Wheeling at two in the afternoon—a distance of one hundred and thirty-one miles in twelve hours. Although this was unusually fast it did demonstrate the speed made possible by a paved road across the mountains.[141]

The stagecoaches, either regularly scheduled or special, served mostly locals, business people, and tourists, including Europeans. The fares, modest (low) by our standards, were probably high for an ordinary farmer of the time.[142]

Baltimore to Frederick	$2.00
Frederick to Hagerstown	2.00
Hagerstown to Cumberland	5.00
Cumberland to Uniontown	4.00
Uniontown to Washington	2.25
Washington to Wheeling	2.00
Through fare	$17.25

It was possible to run into some prominent people of the time when riding the stage, including presidents and future presidents. Some famous people known to have traveled at least part of the National Road included Andrew Jackson and James Polk, both of whom took the road to their respective inaugurations, James Monroe, John Quincy Adams, Martin Van Buren, William Henry Harrison, Zachary Taylor, Millard Fillmore, James Buchanan, and Abraham Lincoln. Henry Clay, a champion of the National Road, was a regular. Other notable names included Sam Houston, John C. Calhoun, Daniel Webster, John C. Fremont, James G. Blaine, and Davy Crockett. Jenny Lind traveled it, but probably in the ten-horse entourage of P. T. Barnum.[143]

The lengthy journeys meant the travelers, whether wagoners or stage riders, had to be accommodated and there were taverns and wagonhouses every few miles along the road. In some towns, such as Cumberland, the traveler had his or her choice of more than one tavern. Both Searight and Hulbert cover tavern life in detail, including the food, accommodations, and sometimes, the entertainment available.

The freight wagons and stagecoaches had to share the road with another group—drovers. The fertile plains of Ohio, Indiana, and Illinois soon gave rise to livestock breeding, especially swine, sheep, cattle, and horses. William Blane, traveling from Cumberland to Wheeling in October 1822 observed the following:

> On the road I met vast droves of hogs, four or five thousand in a drove, going from the State of Ohio across the mountains to the Eastern States. Afterwards, when in Kentucky, I was informed that upwards of 100,000 hogs had been driven from that State alone. Owing to the quantity of nuts, acorns, and mast, throughout the Western states, a great number of these animals are allowed to run at large in the woods, are bred at little or no expense, and when fat are sold in the eastern States for about five dollars apiece.[144]

Vast numbers of swine were produced in Ohio and the west to satisfy the easterner's desire for meat. Cincinnati became a major pork-processing center even gaining the nickname

"Porkopolis." Because of the lack of salt for preserving the meat, a great many hogs had to be driven east over the road for processing at the eastern destination. One Pennsylvania innkeeper noted more than two thousand head in a single month, and another that one hundred droves passed his door within a year. The drover did not always end up at a tavern or wagonhouse at night and had to settle outside, allowing his charges to roam the woods for feed. He would round up as many as he could the next morning, often not one hundred percent, and continue east. Despite these difficulties, it was profitable to get the meat to the East Coast cities of Baltimore, Philadelphia, and New York. "One drover testified crisply that sows' ears make silk purses."[145]

The story was the same for sheep, cattle, and horses. Thousands of sheep were driven east not only for the meat but for the Merino wool. "One farmer estimated that more than 6,000 passed his door within five weeks, and a Pennsylvania general storekeeper said that almost 50,000 had filed by...." Cattle moved at seven to nine miles per day and were little trouble in Ohio, but that changed when they got to the mountains; then all the livestock drivers had problems. Animals could drown fording streams, or stampede in thunderstorms. The drovers didn't always stick to the road either, sometimes bypassing tollgates to avoid the tolls. The horses that moved east on the road were generally of two types, with Ohio producing many of the large draft horses, such as, Clydesdales and Percherons, which were bred to haul the Conestoga wagons. However, there were also horses that came from Kentucky, bred for racing.[146]

The impact of the National Road was transformative,

> The National Road cut the travel time for passengers between Baltimore and Wheeling from eight days to three and the wagon time for freight from five weeks to two. Rates were reduced proportionally. Before there was a turnpike, moving a ton of merchandise 265 miles from Baltimore to Wheeling cost about $120, which was more than ten times as much as it cost to ship the same cargo 3,000 miles across the Atlantic from Liverpool. After the National Road was finished, freight charges fell to $48 a ton in the 1820's to $35 a ton a decade later.[147]

The Gateway to Ohio Is Open

The Cumberland Road, or National Road, had accomplished a great deal just by reaching Wheeling, but it still had hundreds of miles to cross before reaching Illinois. In reaching Ohio from Maryland, the road had bridged the distinct cultures of the east and west. It was natural that the road and its purpose were viewed through different lenses. Two of its early chroniclers, Searight and Hulbert, had variant views on the relative importance of the eastern and western sections of the road. Searight claims,

> It is estimated that two-fifths of the trade and travel of the road were diverted at Brownsville, and fell into the channel furnished at that point by the slack water improvement of the Monongahela river, and a like proportion descended the Ohio from Wheeling, and the remaining fifth continued on the road to Columbus, Ohio, and points further west. The travel west of Wheeling was chiefly local, and the road presented scarcely a tithe of the thrift, push, whirl and excitement which characterized it east of that point; and there was corresponding lack of incident, accident and anecdote on the extreme western division.[148]

In other words, eighty percent of all the western traffic on the National Road stopped at or before Wheeling, and all the excitement happened in that section! Searight spent his life working on the road east of Wheeling, which probably colored his view. Hulbert disputes Searight's traffic premise by showing the tolls collected in the west exceeded those in the east. Hulbert points out this is true although, "the Cumberland Road in Pennsylvania was almost the only road across the portion of the state through which it ran, while in Ohio other roads were used, especially clay roads running parallel with the Cumberland Road."[149] Hulbert concedes many travelers west did leave the road at Brownsville and Wheeling and floated west from there, and that most of the travel on the road west of Wheeling was probably local, but that did not alter his view of the importance of the western section of the road.

These differing viewpoints actually highlight the impact of the National Road in opening Ohio from Maryland. For about two hundred years the mountains had acted as a barrier, precluding any mass migration from east to west. The National Road became a gateway opening the route to Ohio from Maryland, crossing the Ohio River at Wheeling. Migrants and traders poured through that gateway and spread out through the states of the Old Northwest Territory. Significant as it was for middle Ohio, once through the gate the National Road was of less importance than the opening of the gate itself; travelers from the East Coast could disperse in any direction, north and south and down the Ohio, and they did.

> By expending travel, the road quickly became the principal artery for westbound commercial traffic. James Flint reported that some 4,000 wagons were engaged in in the trade between Pittsburgh and the two seaboard cities of Philadelphia and Baltimore in 1818. In 1822, 5,000 wagons reached Wheeling, and many more unloaded their supplies at Pittsburgh or other towns along the way. In large measure, travelers were settlers seeking new homes in the west or teamsters transporting some of the 10 million pounds of cargo shipped annually to Wheeling and other Ohio Valley communities. One estimate placed the volume of traffic at 200,000 individuals a year along the initial stretch of completed road.[150]

Baltimore became a major port and a world trading center, surpassing Philadelphia in population for a short time in the 1820s, ranking it second only to New York. The argument can be made that the road opened, not just the East Coast, but world markets to trade with the American west.[151]

The National Road was the first major overland route across the mountains and, as such, it had a major impact on travel and trade between east and west. However, the Erie Canal which opened in 1825, about the same time as the National Road, may have had an even more transformational economic impact because it was easier to use the canal to transport large amounts of goods, east to west, from central New York to the Great Lakes. The ease of water transportation was the reason so many people, from George Washington on, tried to develop a water route from the Potomac to the Ohio. That water route failed because there was no natural water passage through the mountains, unlike the Mohawk Valley, a gift of nature, which allowed the construction of the Erie Canal.

The National Road, which still exists today, had its heyday for only about three decades. The road, and the canal, would be eclipsed by another new technology—the railroad—whose invention had preceded the building of the road. The Baltimore and Ohio Railroad, which also went from Baltimore to Wheeling and beyond, would lead other railroads to the west. The railroads would provide the ultimate vehicle for mass migration from the east to the Ohio country and beyond.

Eight

The Iron Link Between Maryland and Ohio

The Cumberland Road was completed to Wheeling in 1818 and an extension was authorized to continue it all the way to Missouri, but the extension wasn't started until 1825 and by 1838 had only been completed to Illinois. The road, especially the Cumberland-to-Wheeling section, was heavily used by thousands of migrants, freighters, and livestock drovers going both east and west, and achieved the purpose of a tight communication and commercial link between east and west. The road took a long time to build because of construction problems, perceived constitutional concerns, and opposition from some people who did not want to see it built. Some opposition was based on sectional concerns that became national issues during the heyday of the road from the 1820s to 1840s. Despite the obstacles, the road was successful and achieved the objectives for which it was built. However, the rapidly growing nation and technological changes limited its impact after only a few decades.

The period from 1800 to 1850 was an era of explosive growth in the United States. The population grew from just over five million to just over twenty-three million, and fifteen new states were added to the Union. Trade and the movement of people was facilitated by the Erie Canal in New York, steamboats on the Ohio and Mississippi rivers, and the National Road, but there was more coming. The blossoming of the Industrial Revolution in America was founded upon two important inventions: the railroad early in the century, and the telegraph in 1837. Both of these inventions had an impact on the ultimate success of the National Road. The National Road had a major positive impact on opening Ohio from Maryland and the Mid-Atlantic States, but it would have had an even greater value had it been completed shortly after its authorization in 1806. As it was, the telegraph and, more importantly, the railroad, ultimately had a greater impact on communication and trade between east and west.

The Baltimore and Ohio Railroad

The intensity of the competition between New York, Philadelphia, and Baltimore escalated dramatically when Ohio, Indiana, Illinois and other states entered the Union between 1803 and 1818. These major cities, directly east of Ohio, benefited from trade with the newly opened west. All modes of transportation would be tried in the attempt to be the first, then the most productive, route, to the west. The two oldest technologies, water and road, would be tried first. George Washington's unsuccessful Potomac Canal was started even before

Ohio entered the Union. The Cumberland Road was the first successful route over the mountains and carried a great deal of traffic during its peak years from the 1820s through the 1840s, but that was only the beginning.

In a span of about ten years there were several major projects to link east and west.

- 1817 The Erie Canal was started.
- 1818 The Cumberland Road was open to Wheeling.
- 1820 Extension of the Cumberland Road from Wheeling to Illinois was approved.
- 1825 Erie Canal was completed; construction on the Cumberland (National) Road extension west from Wheeling started.
- 1826 The Pennsylvania Main Line of Public Works Company was established.
- 1827 The first railroad in the United States, the Baltimore and Ohio Railroad, was formed.
- 1828 July 4th ground breaking for the Chesapeake and Ohio Canal, *and* the Baltimore and Ohio Railroad. Pennsylvania Main Line of Public Works construction started.

The Erie Canal was the New York entry in the race to the west. It took advantage of the Mohawk Valley, a natural breach in the Appalachians that allowed a waterway from Albany through to Lake Erie. The Hudson River was the link from Albany to New York City. The canal was very successful and spurred the development plans of other canals and railroads.

Maryland was the first of the eastern states to link Baltimore with the west using the Baltimore Pike and Cumberland Road. The second link through Maryland was the Chesapeake and Ohio (C&O) Canal that started in 1820s. It had some local success but was unsuccessful in breaching the mountain barrier. The third passage from Maryland would be the Baltimore and Ohio (B&O) Railroad, which coincidently had its groundbreaking the same day as the C&O Canal. It was not by coincidence that both the railroad and the canal had the name "Ohio" in their company titles; this was the ultimate destination of both.

The Pennsylvania entry in this race to the west was the Pennsylvania Main Line of Public Works, an odd combination of railroads, canals, and inclined planes. The Main Line Company was a Pennsylvania state project. The intention was to link Philadelphia on the East Coast with Pittsburgh. The problem with this route was the lack of a natural crossing point over the Allegheny Mountains. Years before, around 1750, Maryland and Virginia had found a relatively narrow gap in the mountains from Cumberland to the Monongahela, and used the relatively flat Maryland countryside, and the Potomac Valley to exploit that gap and develop the passage that became the Cumberland Road. Pennsylvania had no such gap and as a result the Main Line became a hybrid of railroads, canals, and inclined planes that eventually crossed the Alleghenies.

The first leg of this route was the Philadelphia and Columbia Railroad which spanned eighty-two miles from Philadelphia to Columbia on the Susquehanna River. Opened in 1832, at first the wooden cars were pulled by horses. The second leg was forty-three miles from Columbia to Hollidaysburg, Pennsylvania, via the Eastern Division Canal. The third leg, thirty-six miles, was by inclined plane over the mountains from Hollidaysburg to Johnstown, Pennsylvania. On the inclined planes the passengers rode in special railcars which were kept horizontal, maintaining an angle with their wheels on the railroad tracks as they moved uphill and then downhill. At first, they were pulled up the mountain by rope or cable using horses and mules but later steam power was used. There were five inclined planes up the mountain and five down. The cars were similar to today's cog railroads up mountains but did not use cogs. The last part of the trip, 103 miles from Johnstown to Pittsburgh was by the Western Division Canal.[1]

Clearly this grueling, awkward trip was inefficient. The inefficiency was demonstrated by comparing the Erie Canal with the Main Line in 1844: The Canal carried 350,000 tons of goods whereas the Main Line carried only 75,000 tons. Years later the Pennsylvania Main Line of Public Works route was replaced by the all-rail Pennsylvania Railroad from Philadelphia. New York also started to build a network of railroads toward the west, but competition was between the Erie Canal and the Cumberland Road in the early years.[2]

Railroads

For centuries, some carts had been forced to run in rutted roadways or on wooden tracks. These guides kept the carts moving in a fixed direction making them easier to control. In the sixteenth and seventeenth centuries, especially in England, these carts and tracks or rails were used to move coal or ore from mines to a distribution point, perhaps a river, from which they were moved to their final destination. The railways were either man-powered or horse-powered and their use was entirely industrial. An example was the Mumbles Railway, established in England in 1804, "authorizing the removal and carriage of limestone from the quarries at Mumbles to the docks of nearby Swansea." Children hitched rides on these cars for fun, inspiring one entrepreneur, and by 1807 the world's first horse-drawn railway to carry passengers was born as the Swansea and Mumbles Railway. Taking place right in the middle of the Industrial Revolution in England, this seems late for the introduction of rail travel. However, the Industrial Revolution was more about applying power to industry than about personal travel. Although Cornishman Richard Trevithick demonstrated a steam locomotive for a railway car in 1804, it was not successful so any use of rails necessarily involved horse power. Trevithick's invention and similar ones, however, were meant for industrial purposes, not passengers.[3]

The age of steam started about a century earlier when Thomas Savery had invented a steam engine to remove water from mines, a problem that had always plagued mining. His machine worked only at shallow depths and by 1711 Thomas Newcomen had developed a much more efficient steam engine to operate at deeper levels in the mines. The Newcomen engine became the mine workhorse for about sixty years but it also was inefficient. In 1776 James Watt developed a more efficient, high-pressure, steam engine that would ultimately power the Industrial Revolution. Although these were all stationary engines used to power stationary machinery, there were always men looking for a way to use steam power for locomotion. Richard Trevithick was one, but credit for the first practical steam locomotive belongs to George Stephenson.[4]

The process of inventing a truly effective steam locomotive was to be a long one. Although Trevithick demonstrated his engine in 1804, real progress was not made until 1814 when Stephenson and his son Robert developed his "Blucher" locomotive to haul coal at the Killingworth colliery. He made several engines for the colliery, and in 1821, when he heard of a projected horse-drawn railway from Darlington to Stockton, Stephenson convinced the owner to allow him to build a steam locomotive to pull those trains. He was given the commission and on September 27, 1825, the first passenger railway using steam locomotion made its first run using an engine called Active but later renamed Locomotion. In an 1829 competition, the Rocket locomotive, also developed by Stephenson and his son, won the prize with a speed of thirty-five miles per hour. It had taken over twenty years, from 1804 to 1825, to develop steam locomotives capable of hauling passengers and freight by rail.[5]

By the time Stephenson's locomotive was successful the Cumberland Road was being extended west, the Erie Canal was operational, the Chesapeake and Ohio Canal was starting construction, and the Pennsylvania Main Line was about to start; all were creating openings to the west with more to come.

Baltimoreans were in a quandary by the mid–1820s as there was a canal in New York to the north and one about to be built from Washington to Cumberland south of Baltimore. It was recognized that canals, although slow, were very efficient at carrying large loads the length of the canal. There would be a line in Pennsylvania using both railroads and canals to connect Philadelphia and Pittsburgh. Baltimore, the fourth largest city in the country, had no direct link to the west other than the Baltimore Pike and the National Road. Baltimore had prospered because it was the first major coastal city to benefit from the National Road, the major artery west, but now it faced stronger competition. If Baltimore was to remain a competitor for western trade it would have to make a move to gain a more robust link to the west. The Baltimore Pike and National Road, although in place before the Erie Canal, would not be able to compete with the canal in the amount of goods moved. There were many ideas about linking the city to the west by canal either through Pennsylvania or through the C&O Canal but none of these were practical.

England was using advanced railroads but this country possessed only the three-mile railway from the quarries at Quincy, Massachusetts to the Neponset River, and the short railroad at Mauch Chunk, Pennsylvania, to transport coal nine miles to the Lehigh River. Clearly, neither was a model for a long-distance railroad. Despite the novelty of railroads in this country, just eighteen months after the opening of the Stockton and Darlington Railroad in England, Baltimore decided to build a railroad.[6]

> In 1827, Baltimore, then the nation's fourth largest city after New York, Philadelphia, and Boston, adopted the railroad. When operations began three years later, it became, as it turned out, the first planned, long-distance, general-purpose railroad in the world. The Baltimore and Ohio Railroad was in its own way quite as audacious as the Erie Canal…. The projectors of the Baltimore and Ohio were planning to build a railroad far longer than those [Quincy and Mauch Chunk]—ten times longer than any in existence—over mountains 3,000 feet high. Their decision represented the rejection of the dominant canal technology, which they considered outmoded, and the application of a primitive form of mine transportation to a long-distance internal improvement to the west. It was an amazing intellectual step, no less daring because it was desperate.[7]

A group of Baltimore businessmen started discussing a possible railroad in 1826 turning more serious in February 1827 when they appointed a committee to submit proposals on whether or not to build the railroad, and what route it should take. One calculation they made was based on the transportation of flour, a valuable commodity produced in Ohio. They calculated that transporting flour from Ohio to Baltimore by rail would increase its value by three hundred percent because of the speed and capacity of rail transport. Flour would then be a valuable export commodity from the port of Baltimore.[8]

The frontier was moving west at about thirty miles per year, having reached the Osage and Missouri rivers already without any change in the rate of expansion: "if not checked by some unforeseen circumstances, it will, within the next thirty years, reach the Rocky Mountains, or even to the Pacific Ocean. We have therefore, no reason to look for any falling off in this trade, but to the contrary, for an increase of it."[9] Just a nine years earlier the first road across the Alleghenies had been completed and now these Baltimore businessmen were considering trade across the Rockies! The upcoming Chesapeake and Ohio

Canal at Georgetown in Washington, D.C., was also a potential western route if Baltimore could connect to it. The committee only took about a week, before they made some recommendations. They knew two destinations they definitely wanted to reach. "The committee concluded its report with a call to connect Baltimore and the western states "by intersecting the contemplated Chesapeake and Ohio Canal within the District of Columbia, and by A DIRECT RAIL ROAD FROM BALTIMORE TO SOME ELIGIBLE POINT ON THE OHIO RIVER" [Emphasis in the original]."[10] The Baltimore and Ohio (B&O) Railroad was born.

The B&O Route

Wheeling was a logical place to consider as the terminus on the Ohio River because the National Road passed through that city. Similarly, a route that paralleled the Baltimore Pike and Cumberland Road was seen as a natural route but following the route of that road would not be as easy as it would have been years earlier; circumstances had changed. For one thing Pennsylvania now was starting its Main Line to connect Philadelphia with Pittsburgh and the west and was not interested in a competing railroad from Baltimore. Philadelphia was determined not to be cut out of the western trade as it had been with the National Road. However, some in Pittsburgh thought it might be advantageous to have two railroads available in the city and thought the B&O could also reach the Ohio at Pittsburgh as well as the Main Line.[11]

Virginia was a different story, as it lacked one of the major East Coast cities found in New York, Pennsylvania, and Maryland, but was still interested in increasing its western trade. The obvious place for this, especially since Baltimore was about to build a railroad, was through the Potomac corridor. Maryland and Virginia saw an advantage in building the railroad to the Ohio River through both states. James Dilts (*The Great Road: The Building of the Baltimore & Ohio, the Nation's First Railroad, 1828–1853*) quotes Philip E. Thomas, the first president of the B&O,

> Thomas was confident that the railroad was the best means by which Virginia and Maryland, in a united effort, could "turn the tide of the immense western trade along the Road, to be divided between the ports of the two states and afford ample means of enriching both." The major eastern cities wanted to retain their political influence as much as revive their commerce, and there is no doubt that sectional jealousy was a great influence on the B&O's determination to succeed. Pennsylvania had rejected the railroad's charter because of conflict with its own canal plans and the route restriction stayed in Virginia law for the same reason.[12]

The March 8, 1828, law incorporating the railroad in Virginia included a requirement that the railroad had to reach the Ohio River at a point no lower "than the mouth of the Little Kenhawa" at Parkersburg, Virginia.[13] The intention of this restriction is not clear unless it was to make sure the railroad struck the river far enough upstream to assure it reached the Ohio River where the commerce was active because of the National Road. Later the engineers enlarged the area under consideration to seven thousand square miles in the shape of a triangle from Baltimore to Wheeling to Point Pleasant (at the Kanawha) on the Ohio. Somewhere within this triangle they would have to go over the peaks of the Alleghenies.[14]

The "sectional jealousy" that Dilts refers to was in full flower between the free states and the slave states. There must have been some interesting discussions in the Maryland and Virginia legislatures about the route. They wanted to keep the railroad within their states for commercial reasons, but because they were both slave states there was also a sectional rivalry in play. It must have galled many legislators that the railroad would head into the free state of Ohio. During the Civil War Maryland remained a slave state but did not try to secede. The Union made good use of the B&O during the Civil War even though the South attacked the railroad many times.

On the traditional day for such ceremonies, July 4, ground was broken in Baltimore in 1828 by Charles Carroll of Carrollton, the last living signer of the Declaration of Independence. Ironically, near Washington, President John Quincy Adams was breaking ground for the Chesapeake and Ohio Canal on the very same day. The race from Maryland to Ohio by rail and water had begun; both ventures were trying to catch the Erie Canal and the National Road in competition for the western trade.

B&O Construction

Construction of the B&O started soon after the groundbreaking even though the final route and destination had not yet been chosen. Originating in England just a few years earlier railways were a new technology and the B&O was literally breaking new ground for railroads worldwide. This would be the first long-distance, general purpose railroad in the world. They had very little precedence on which to base the design; everything was new. They first determined the track gage, the inside distance between the tracks, would be four feet eight and one-half inches. This was recommended by an engineering team that had toured England and it was the standard English gage. Later railroads used a variety of gages, depending on where the road was built, until ultimately the U.S. Standard Gage was set at four feet eight and one-half inches. Railroad cars were originally horse-drawn so the gage is roughly the width of two horses' rumps.[15] The tracks were originally of three types, a wrought iron strap laid directly on longitudinal stone sills, a strap rail attached to wooden stringers on stone blocks, and a rail strap on wooden stringers attached to sleepers or crossties. The ties were laid in a ballast of crushed stone sloped to keep water off the tracks. Eventually it was found that the rail strap on wooden stringers laid on crossties was the least costly way to build.

> The strap rail used in all three methods consisted of wrought iron ⅝ inches thick, 2½ inches in width, and 15 feet in length. Such rail weighed no more than fifteen pounds per yard, and was imported from England at a cost of $55 to $60 per ton. Such rail produced in the United States cost up to $90 per ton. All track, whether laid on wood or stone, was provided with sufficient earth cover between the rails for a horse path.[16]

The strap rail could be dangerous. If it was peeled up by one car it could pierce the following car killing or injuring the passengers or crew. This strap rail wasn't replaced until the modern "T"-rail, invented by Robert Stevens, president of the Camden Railroad, became readily available in the 1840s.[17]

The B&O had to build west from Baltimore toward the Ohio River. The first interim destination was Ellicotts Mills thirteen miles west of Baltimore's Pratt Street, the starting location. Construction was very slow at first although it started soon after groundbreaking. It took eighteen months, to the end of 1829, to lay three miles of track heading out of Baltimore. Work sped up after that and by the third week of May 1830 the track was complete to Ellicotts Mills, allowing the B&O to start passenger service between the two stations. "The cars, still hauled by horses, made the thirteen-mile trip in about an hour and a half." The demand was heavy so "Four trips a day each way were started on July 5, 1830. This horse-powered limited operation was the first regular passenger service in the United States."[18] Construction continued west toward Frederick, a natural destination and eastward shipping point for western Maryland produce. The main road didn't go into Frederick but swung in an arc past the town heading for the Potomac with a spur into Frederick. The road completed the sixty-one miles to Frederick in December 1831. The horse-drawn trains were on a schedule that allowed eight hours to reach Frederick from Baltimore, including meal stops and twelve changes of teams. A significant transportation change took place when this rail line was open and the Great Western Stages, one of the stagecoach lines that operated on the National Road, at this point the Baltimore Pike, announced that it would deposit its eastward bound passengers at Frederick to make the remainder of the trip by rail. The rail line from Frederick to Baltimore was not only much smoother it was faster. The new railroad technology, even though still horse-drawn, was having an impact by replacing the overland road for long distances.[19]

The plan had been to use the Potomac Valley for most of the route west. This would, not only take advantage of the relatively level valley, but satisfy the agreement that a substantial portion of the railroad would be located in Virginia after it crossed the Potomac River at Harpers Ferry. So at Frederick the railroad took a left turn toward the Potomac to Point of Rocks, Maryland, about twelve miles downstream from Harper's Ferry. Catoctin Mountain was very close to the north bank of the river at this point, the right-of-way along the river being a strip of land barely one hundred feet wide between the mountain and the river. It didn't appear to be wide enough for a canal or railroad let alone both. This was the spot discussed in Chapter Six over which the C&O Canal and B&O Railroad had the legal disputes about the right-of-way along the river.

The case dragged on for years, with the canal winning the early court battles and delaying railroad construction. The Maryland legislature had an interest in both projects and finally intervened in the spring of 1833, forcing a compromise in which the narrow ledge between the mountain and river would be shared with the canal allocated a fifty-foot width and the railroad confined to a single-track width of twenty feet. The same agreement also provided the right-of-way along the river north of Harpers Ferry for the canal. This presented no problem because the B&O intended to cross the Potomac River into Virginia at Harpers Ferry.[20] The railroad line was open to Point of Rocks on April 1, 1832, and on April 20, three to four hundred barrels of Potomac flour arrived in Baltimore; three days later fifty passengers on the *Columbus* made the first trip to Point of Rocks from Baltimore.[21]

Even as the railroad was under construction, and before the final route was determined, the technology for motive power was improving. The Liverpool and Manchester Railroad in England began operation in 1830, the same year the B&O started, but it used steam locomotives developed by George Stephenson whereas the B&O operated with horses. England was still the leader in the new railroad technology. Earlier an English locomotive had been tried in America but was too heavy for the track system of the time. The use of English locomotives would have been more difficult to use because of the steeper grades and tighter curves on the B&O route compared to the flatter and straighter layout of the Liverpool and Manchester.[22]

Nevertheless, the B&O was always attempting to improve the capacity and speed of their system and was open to Peter Cooper's proposal of a steam locomotive which came in 1830. Peter Cooper was from New York and had made a modest fortune in glue manufacturing. He was also an inventor who went to Baltimore in 1828 to invest in land and specifically to be associated with the railroad in which he had developed an interest. Using B&O facilities, he used scrap metal and spare parts to build an experimental locomotive that somehow was given the name *Tom Thumb*. In 1830 it was successfully used for a demonstration ride to transport B&O executives on a thirteen-mile run in a time of fifty-seven minutes. This demonstration was enough to convince the B&O Directors that they should bet on the future of steam. In January 1831, they offered a prize for the best coal-burning, one and one-half ton locomotive that could be ready by June 1, 1831, only five months away. The prize was won by Phineas Davis whose design had vertical rods moving up and down suggested the movements of a grasshopper. These Grasshopper steam engines were light enough and nimble enough to work on the B&O grades and curves and by the mid–1830s they were the standard locomotives. The new technology was now developing as fast as the tracks could be laid.[23]

It may seem obvious that a railroad from Baltimore to the Ohio River would head west and first link Baltimore to Frederick, but that was the only obvious part of the route. Soon after the formation of the railroad survey and map teams were sent out to locate and plan the route. This was a continuous process some parts of which occurred not long before construction. The route was determined by a combination of terrain (crossing the Alleghenies using minimum slopes), finances, legal issues (C&O Canal dispute) and politics, many of these caused delays. After the railroad passed Frederick, a terrain decision was made to move directly south to take advantage of the route along the Potomac, passing Catoctin Mountain where it encountered the legal troubles with the C&O Canal that caused delays. Even after it reached Point of Rocks in early 1832 it took over two years to reach Harpers Ferry even using the Potomac Valley. There are at least three places in Maryland on the river between Point of Rocks and Harpers Ferry where the mountains pinch the river as they do at Point of Rocks, making this a difficult stretch for construction. The construction didn't reach Harpers Ferry until December 1, 1834, where it crossed the river.[24] At Harpers Ferry the alternatives included going farther into Virginia or following the Potomac Valley to Cumberland.

The original Virginia charter had required construction in the state to be complete by 1838. This could not be accomplished, so more legislation was required causing new delays. Legislation passed in 1838 gave the railroad another five years for completion, but required that the route from Harpers Ferry, Virginia, to Cumberland, Maryland, had to remain in Virginia to a point only five or six miles below Cumberland. More money was provided, but with a further stipulation that the western terminus *had* to be Wheeling, a more specific destination than heretofore provided, and farther north than the original stipulation of the Little Kanawha. Pittsburgh had expressed an interest in being the terminus, but that idea was squashed by the State of Pennsylvania, at that time building their Main Line across the state. Despite this, there was still consideration of keeping the road in Maryland and going through Hagerstown to Cumberland. As a result, even as late as 1838 the final route was still undetermined.[25]

The decision was made to go straight through Virginia's Shenandoah Valley and Martinsburg, Virginia, and then back north into the Potomac Valley close to Fort Frederick, near present-day Big Pool, Maryland, but staying on the Virginia side of the Potomac. From there the railroad was to follow the Potomac Valley in Virginia until it was about six miles below Cumberland, where it would cross the Potomac River to reach Cumberland. Crossing the flat Shenandoah Valley was relatively easy and following the Potomac River Valley had the advantage that proximity to the river allowed them to avoid cutting through many mountains. Staying on the south side of the river in Virginia also precluded any conflict with the C&O Canal being constructed on the north side of the river. The cost of this one-hundred-mile segment from Harpers Ferry to Cumberland was estimated at about three million dollars. Compared to other sections, it was constructed fairly rapidly. The B&O

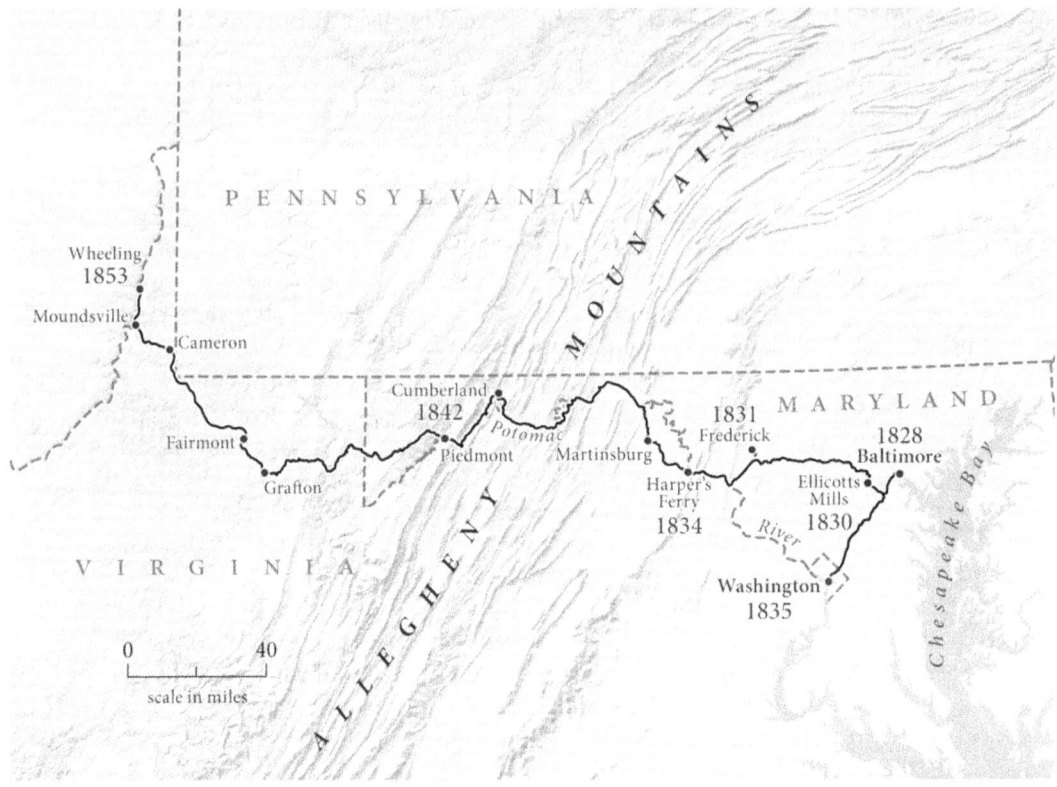

Map 17: Baltimore and Ohio Railroad. The route from Baltimore crossed the Potomac at Harpers Ferry, went back into Maryland before Cumberland, crossed the Alleghenies in Virginia, and ended at Wheeling in late 1852.

reached Martinsburg in May 1842, Hancock, Maryland, in June 1842, and Cumberland in November 1842, well before the C&O Canal reached Cumberland in 1850.[26]

Intersection with the National Road

The Baltimore Pike, the Maryland connection to the National Road between Baltimore and Cumberland, was in its heyday in 1842. The taverns and wagon houses serving the passengers and freighters traveling the road were very busy. Long lines of Conestoga wagons and stagecoaches could be seen moving both west and east. The National Road and Baltimore Pike had achieved a decade's long dream of linking east and west across the mountains, and it was paying off. Everything changed on November 3, 1842, when the first B&O train left the Pratt station in Baltimore bound for Cumberland. James Dilts uses several paragraphs to describe the trip that started at 7 A.M. He describes a scenic journey through mountain gashes and a few tunnels, over bridges and viaducts, and crossing the river into Virginia.

> Proceeding over Sleepy Creek on a 240-foot viaduct, the train passed Hancock and entered a singular landscape of alternating high, steep, curving ridges, dotted with pine groves and waterfalls that pushed the tracks close to the river's shore.... There was one final bridge to cross, of 100 feet over Evitt's Creek. About 5:00 p.m., the train pulled through the crowd of spectators and musicians to the Cumberland depot at the National Road. All day business had been suspended awaiting the train.[27]

The use of the National Road depot in Cumberland was ironic because this trip changed everything between the road and the railroad. Cumberland and Baltimore were now connected with two thoroughfares, the Baltimore Pike and the B&O Railroad. Although slightly longer in distance because of the need to go through Virginia the railroad offered advantages in speed, capacity, and comfort. This started to make a difference immediately. The number of stage lines between Cumberland and Baltimore diminished because train travel was more convenient. Since the railroad had not yet reached Wheeling arrangements were made between the railroad and coach lines for passengers traveling from Baltimore on to Wheeling.

> The passenger trains ran from Baltimore to Cumberland in a scheduled ten hours and Stockton's six-horse stages could get over the Alleghenies from there to Pittsburgh and Wheeling in about sixteen. By taking the railroad to Cumberland, a passenger going from Baltimore to Wheeling could cut the former all-turnpike travel time from 72 hours to about 24. The through ticket price had fallen from $18.75 (in the 1820's) to $11 (in 1844).[28]

Many passengers arrived at the depot by stagecoach and 150,000 of them rode the rails in 1843. Between 1841 and 1844 railroad passenger receipts tripled. The railroad contributed to another American cultural phenomenon, the immigration wave. In 1840 the B&O received a letter from some German immigrants saying they would be willing to ride in freight cars for a reduced price. The company accommodated them at a two-dollar fare for adults and half price for children. Second class travel had arrived. By 1843 the railroad was accommodating immigrant groups of twenty or more in second class coaches for $2.50 each.[29]

The railroad had a similar impact on the movement of freight. Freight trains from Baltimore to Cumberland could make the trip in about thirty hours at the rate of six dollars per ton. The freight could be moved onward by wagon to Wheeling at ten dollars per ton. The former two-week time frame was cut in half and the freight rate was less than half the rate of thirty-five dollars per ton in the 1830s. The B&O moved fifty-two thousand tons of freight from Cumberland to Baltimore in 1843 and freight receipts tripled between 1841 and 1844.[30]

These were dramatic changes. It was clear even before the railroad reached its final destination that railroads would change long distance travel forever.

Although Cumberland was not intended to be the final destination, it looked like it might be. A route west had not even been chosen and there were legislative difficulties. By the mid–1840s the B&O railroad was considering three routes to finally achieve a railhead on the Ohio. The shortest was northwest through Pennsylvania to Pittsburgh, closely following the National Road route over the mountains. The second route was more directly west in Virginia, then northwest to Wheeling. Many with the B&O favored the third route, directly west to Parkersburg, Virginia, on the Ohio which would be in a straight line to the growing cities of Cincinnati and St. Louis. Legislative actions, influenced by railroad technology, helped determine that the Wheeling option would be selected. By this time, except for the wildly successful Erie Canal, most states regarded canals as old technology compared to railroads. There was a rush to build new railroads, especially in New York, Pennsylvania, Maryland, and Virginia, most heading west.[31]

The Push to Wheeling

In 1828, about a year after Maryland and Virginia, Pennsylvania confirmed a B&O charter which required that any construction in the state would have to be completed within fifteen years, by 1843. Pennsylvania had by now acquiesced in a Maryland railroad presence in Pennsylvania that would compete with the Main Line. However, by the time the railroad was ready to move into Pennsylvania the charter had expired. In the spring of 1846 the Pennsylvania legislature passed two railroad bills, granting a charter to the Pennsylvania Railroad to go across the state on April 13 and a week later, on April 21, to the B&O to go from Cumberland to Pittsburgh. The Pennsylvania Main Line was operating between Philadelphia and Pittsburgh but it was slow, clumsy, and inefficient because of its use of a combination of canals, railroads, and inclined planes. The Pennsylvania Railroad was to replace the Main Line with an all-rail system. The state would prefer the option of the all-Pennsylvania railroad but they were hedging their bets by also chartering the existing B&O Railroad for a route to Pittsburgh. Some of the legislative conditions placed on the B&O charter actually were incentives for the Pennsylvania Railroad.

> The B&O act was not to be effective until July 30, 1847. Also, if within those fifteen months, should the Pennsylvania Railroad obtain $3 million in stock subscriptions, with $1 million paid into the company treasury and have fifteen miles of road at the Pittsburgh end of the line under contract, then the entire B&O act would be null and void.... Pennsylvania Railroad met all these conditions.... Thus twenty years after Baltimore had chosen to build a railroad, the Quaker city of Philadelphia followed suit.[32]

Pennsylvania was now no longer a B&O option as the route from Philadelphia to Pittsburgh, and beyond to Wheeling was exclusively the Pennsylvania Railroad's. In the spring of 1847, the Virginia legislature gave the B&O twelve more years to complete the road through Virginia, once again requiring the terminus to be Wheeling. The desired route to Parkersburg was ruled out and the road through Virginia would be a longer one but this was still better than terminating the road at Cumberland. The competition had begun between the Pennsylvania Railroad and the B&O to get to see who could reach the Ohio River first, the B&O to Wheeling and the Pennsylvania to Pittsburgh.[33]

The B&O was slow in selecting a final route and it wasn't until 1849 that the new president, Thomas Swann, sped things up. Along the North Branch of the Potomac River, construction started southwest from Cumberland to Piedmont, Maryland. From there it continued northwest along the Savage River, which flowed into the Potomac, up to Backbone Mountain. The B&O next traveled south west along Backbone Mountain to its peak at Altamont, Maryland, the continental divide. The railroad headed west, crossing into Virginia at Corinth and reaching Grafton, Virginia, the inflection point. If the Parkersburg route had been chosen, the road then would have moved directly west to the Ohio River. Instead the route veered northwest, crossed the Monongahela at Fairmont, Virginia, continued to New Martinsville, Virginia, on the Ohio River, and then along the river past Fish Creek and Grave Creek to Wheeling.[34]

In an article published in the *American Railroad Journal* in the spring of 1850, the *Baltimore American* acknowledged the competition and was optimistic:

> we are assured that the work cannot be greatly delayed thereby, and if the line heretofore adopted by the Company be sustained, the whole road will be opened in the summer of 1852.... We see Philadelphia hurrying forward to reach Pittsburg, and New York to reach Dunkirk, if they can, before we get to Wheeling; and we see Ohio and the states north and west of her, and indeed the whole Mississippi valley, stimulated to the highest enthusiasm in the railway race by that which is now running between the Atlantic cities.[35]

This route, essentially forced on the railroad, was a difficult one. Swann had to press the issue negotiating with bankers, and pressuring the contractors to keep moving. The terrain was challenging. The roughly two hundred miles from Cumberland to Wheeling required eleven tunnels with a total length of 11,156 feet. The most difficult tunnel was at Kingwood, Virginia, elevation 1,800 feet, which took two years to build. By the summer of 1850, 3,500 men and 700 horses were working the tracks. Piedmont was reached on July 18, 1851; by the fall of 1851, 5,000 men and 1,250 horses were working the road. The western part of the system, from Cumberland to Wheeling, required about 22,000 tons of iron rail, mostly imported from England at forty dollars per ton. It required 113 bridges with spans from twelve to 215 feet. The line reached Fairmont, only seventy-seven miles from Wheeling, on June 22, 1852, and regular trains were started between Fairmont and Baltimore at once. Swann promised Wheeling the B&O would arrive at the city by the end of the year. About eighteen miles southeast of Wheeling the last spike on the line was driven on Christmas Eve 1852. The first scheduled train from Baltimore to Wheeling was on January 1, 1853. "Some 500 citizens of Baltimore made the 379 mile trip in eighteen hours."[36]

Although the B&O was the first railroad to start west to Ohio, it was not the first to reach the Ohio country or the Ohio River. The Pennsylvania Railroad had a train reach Pittsburgh and the Ohio River, on November 29, 1852, just weeks before the B&O reached Wheeling. However, the Pennsylvania Railroad was still using some inclined plains at that time and the B&O people correctly claimed the B&O was the first to reach the Ohio River "without the aid of stationary engines," an important qualification. It was also the first to the river coming all the way from the East Coast. The Erie Railroad, chartered in 1832 to go from the Hudson River to Dunkirk, New York on Lake Erie was the first into Ohio country, reaching Dunkirk in May 1851. At about the same time, J. H. Sullivan president of the Central Ohio Railroad announced that his road would complete its fifty-eight-mile segment from Columbus to Zanesville. The railroad wars which would last the rest of the century and beyond, were now on; not only the eastern states but the Midwestern states as well, were building railroads.[37]

From the East Coast to the Ohio River, the west was now open, and this was just the beginning. The expansion west now proceeded unabated until the country was linked coast-to-coast. The expansion of the B&O was just a small example of this trend. The line from Grafton to Parkersburg was eventually built as the B&O moved west toward Cincinnati, reaching St. Louis in 1857. There was now a rail link from the Atlantic to the Mississippi.[38] "The B&O finally reached Chicago in November of 1874 after completing 811 miles of track…. By the end of the 19th century the B&O had achieved almost 5,800 miles of track and connected Chicago and St. Louis to Baltimore, Washington, Philadelphia, and New York City."[39]

Years earlier the B&O had constructed the rail link between Baltimore and Washington, D.C. Samuel Morse, receiving a grant from Congress, had constructed a line of telegraph poles twenty-four feet high and two hundred feet apart along this right-of-way. During the Whig convention in Baltimore early in 1844, he tested his invention. At Annapolis Junction, Maryland, about half-way between Baltimore and Washington, a colleague received news from a train bound for Washington with the results of the convention, the nomination of Henry Clay. He telegraphed it to Morse in the Capitol. The telegraph message reached the Capitol about an hour before the train with the news, which was news no longer. May 24, 1844, just after the convention, was the historic day when Morse, from the Supreme Court chamber in the Capitol, telegraphed his famous "What hath God wrought" message to the B&O depot in Baltimore. The railroads were slow in grasping the significance of this form of communication, but eventually all did and the telegraph became imbedded in railroad operations for scheduling among other uses.[40]

Maryland and Ohio: Linked by Road and Rail, 1853

By 1853, the National Road was joined by another link between Maryland and Ohio, a railroad with much more capacity. It was the final link between these states, one that could not have been envisioned one hundred years earlier when the first trail from Wills Creek to the Monongahela was blazed by a Marylander to gain access to the Ohio country. Maryland and Ohio had little in common. Ohio was large, fertile, and provided an opening to an almost unbounded west. Maryland, although possessing fertile farmland, was small in size and bounded in the west by the mountains.

What they shared was proximity between the eastern flowing Potomac River of Maryland and the western flowing Monongahela River of the Ohio country. Where rivers were close, a reasonably short path led across the mountains from the mountain-bounded east to the unbounded west of Ohio. This possibility was quickly recognized and for one hundred years, interrupted by several wars, attempts were made to develop the link from Cumberland, Maryland, to the Monongahela and Ohio rivers in Ohio country. No technology eased the early efforts of Christopher Gist as he walked and rode by horseback. The path progressed to a crude wagon trail, and finally to a stone-paved Cumberland Road. The B&O Railroad completed the link using a technology that did not exist in this country even as the Cumberland Road reached Wheeling in 1818. It is significant that the effort to open and then improve this route lasted as long as it did. It lasted because a path west was always seen as necessary to complete a tight link between east and west, not only for commercial reasons, but for reasons of national cohesion.

The population of Ohio increased from about forty-five thousand in 1800, around the time of statehood (1803), to about two million in 1850. The decade with the largest percentage increase, four hundred percent, was from1800 to 1810; the percentage was large because of the low initial population. It shows that upon statehood families started moving over the border into lands now open for settlement. The largest increase in numbers though came in the following decades.[41]

Decade	Population increase	Total Population
1810–1820	350,000	581,000
1820–1830	357,000	938,000
1830–1840	552,000	1,519,000
1840–1850	461,000	1,980,000

From 1800 to 1820 many entered Ohio from the Wheeling area and onto Zane's Trace which took them into mid–Ohio or southwest Ohio. Many probably reached Wheeling via the Braddock-Burd Road, which was being replaced by the Cumberland Road by 1811. The Cumberland Road reached Wheeling in 1818, and in 1825 the extension to Illinois was started.

The gateway to Ohio was originally opened through Maryland, but it did not take long for other pathways to open to the state. As Wilhelm and Noble (*Ohio's Settlement Landscape*), and others, point out there were three major settlement patterns in the state in this time period. The northeast part of Ohio, the Western Reserve, was settled by new Englanders from Connecticut, Massachusetts, Vermont, and upper New York. They came along the edge of Lake Erie, as we traced one family earlier, and through the Erie Canal. A small contingent settled on the Ohio River near Marietta. Another cultural contingent came from the Upland South. They entered the state from near Limestone, Kentucky, and from near the Kanawha River in the southeast and settled in southern Ohio, many in the Virginia Military District. Many of these were Scots-Irish, the original settlers of the Ohio

Valley. However, the largest number of settlers were from the Mid-Atlantic States of Pennsylvania, Maryland, Virginia, New Jersey, and New York. They arrived at the center of Ohio from the Wheeling area. They either took Zane's Trace to the southwest or went straight across the state. Most of these took the Cumberland Road or the Baltimore and Ohio Railroad to enter the state.[42]

By 1850 about sixty-two percent of Ohioans had been born in Ohio, presumably the children of those immigrating in the previous five decades. The third or so of Ohio residents in 1850 born outside of Ohio were, as Wilhelm and Noble claim, distributed by state of origin as follows.

State	Number	Percent
Pennsylvania	190,396	38
Virginia	83,300	17
New York	75,442	15
Maryland	34,775	7
New Jersey	21,768	4
Connecticut	20,478	4
Massachusetts	16,437	3
Vermont	13,672	3
Kentucky	11,549	2
Indiana	5,059	1
TOTAL	472,876	94

Presuming the native-born Ohio population in 1850 was similar to that of the non–Ohio born residents in 1850 it is clear that the Mid-Atlantic States of Pennsylvania, Virginia, New York, Maryland, and New Jersey were by far the greatest contributors to Ohio's population, and most of them came through Wheeling on the Cumberland Road or the B&O Railroad. Regarding Pennsylvania, another source claims, "Migrants from this border state were mainly German and Scotch-Irish and constituted 43% of all migrants during the first half of the 19th century." These people, mainly farmers, settled in central Ohio between the New Englanders in the north and the Upland Southerners in the south.[43]

Many of these migrants, or their offspring, did not stop but kept moving west. Again, as Wilhelm and Noble put it, "Ohio functioned as the smaller end of a huge funnel through which America's migrating masses were channeled on their way to the broader interior." Colin Woodard (*American Nations*) names the immigrants from central Pennsylvania as Midlanders and shows their westward movement through Indiana and Illinois all the way to Nebraska and Kansas. Similarly, Fischer and Kelly (*Bound Away: Virginia and the Westward Movement*) trace the westward movement of Virginians through 1850. As would be expected, some Virginians moved to southern states such as Kentucky, Tennessee, and North Carolina, but by far most moved into Ohio country and then west toward Indiana, Illinois, and Missouri. Ohio had by far the greatest number of former Virginians, almost eighty-six thousand, compared to Virginia's closest western neighbor, Kentucky, with fifty-five thousand. Once Ohio was open the migration through the Ohio corridor virtually exploded into the west. The northern states were growing rapidly in the decade before the Civil War and the growing northern population would make a difference during the war.[44]

Conclusion

For eons Maryland and Ohio had been divided by mountains, ever since the movement of tectonic plates had caused continents to collide and result in the uplifting of the

Appalachian Mountains in accordion shaped ridges. The names "Maryland" and "Ohio" didn't exist at the time. The areas remained divided for millennia after that, even as what became the Native American people migrated from Asia twelve thousand or more years ago. Over time the original Americans occupied all of North America including both sides of the mountains. The mountains were no barrier to the Native Americans who moved across them for trade or war on well-traveled paths. By the tradition of the Native American Iroquois the river that drained the large valley west of the mountains was known as the Ohio.

It was only when the Europeans settled in North America that these mountains took on any significance as they automatically became a barrier. In less than 150 years from the first settlements early in the seventeenth century, the English colonists occupied the East Coast and settled from the sea to the mountains, which were now a barrier to further movement west. In the same time period, the French settled the St. Lawrence River Valley and claimed all the land west of the mountains. They also saw the mountains as a barrier and as a natural border between them and the English. What had been a natural geographical feature had now become a barrier and a border.

It was not an official border though, and around 1750 an English company decided to test the boundary and claim land in the Ohio Valley. This effort was interrupted by the French and Indian War (1755–1763) in which the British victory resulted in the cession to Great Britain of all the land west of the mountains to the Mississippi River; the border was gone but the barrier was still there. These mountains could not be allowed to remain as a barrier; they had to be breached to provide a stable link between east and west. Even before the new republic was formed plans were made to occupy and settle the west. By the turn of the nineteenth century thousands had moved west legally and illegally to settle in Ohio.

Very early (1806) a real road, a stone-paved road, was proposed to cross the mountains. The route chosen was the one blazed by Christopher Gist over fifty years earlier and later recut by Thomas Cresap and Nemacolin, George Washington, and General Edward Braddock. The Cumberland Road went from Cumberland, Maryland, to Wheeling, Virginia, on the Ohio River. This technologically advanced road was overtaken by a new technology in 1828 when the B&O Railroad was founded. Although the traffic on both routes peaked and then subsided they were very successful in opening the west; Maryland had become the gateway to Ohio and the mountain barrier was breached.

Ironically, as the migration and population increase was strengthening the bonds between the northeast and northwest could it have contributed to dividing the north and the south? From 1803 through 1821, four northern states were admitted to the Union—Ohio, Indiana, Illinois, and Maine—and three of them were west of the Ohio River. In the same time period the three southern states of Louisiana, Mississippi, and Alabama, and the border state of Missouri were admitted. Missouri was admitted as a slave state and Maine as a free state in the famous Missouri Compromise of 1820.

The country seemed to be moving west in two layers stratified by two different cultures; the Cumberland Road and B&O Railroad basically followed the Mason-Dixon Line separating north and south. This was no accident as the north had a free, vigorous agriculture and manufacturing society which depended on good transportation. Chicago, for example, was founded in 1833 and grew rapidly. A strong link, even across difficult mountains, was demanded and provided. The slavery-based southern economy depended on one crop, cotton, and had virtually no industry. The southern railroad system was designed to transport cotton to ports where it was shipped north or abroad. In the north, the road and railroad developed east to west despite the difficult mountains because there was no reason to go south. Except for cotton, controlled by a few people, it was an economic wasteland. Since a major driver of the Cumberland Road and B&O Railroad was commerce, if the culture of the south been similar to that of the north there would certainly have been roads and railroads going north and south. It would have been easier to go in those directions, parallel to the mountains rather across them. The road direction was a *result* of the cultural differences *not a cause* of them.[45]

The age of canals was over long before 1850 when the C&O Canal reached Cumberland, which turned out to be its terminus. The C&O Canal decided to stop in Cumberland, because of the realization that it would be unable to cross the mountains to the Ohio rivers. The B&O Railroad reached Cumberland first, eight years before the C&O, even though both had broken ground on the same day, July 4, 1828. Canals were difficult to build and were limited in speed, and terminal destinations compared to railroads, and compared to the versatility of overland roads. It is not surprising that roads and railroads quickly replaced canal construction. Somewhat more surprising is the decline of the National Road after the railroad was completed. Of course, there would always be roads within and between towns and cities, but the railroad advantages in capacity and speed seemed to doom the long-distance road; the National Road fell into disrepair.

This all changed in the twentieth century when the latest technological transportation marvel, the automobile, exploded on the scene in the late nineteenth and early twentieth centuries. All of a sudden, the motorist regained control over his schedule and specific destination when he drove his own automobile. Intercity road transportation was now possible by personal vehicle and was much more convenient. The road system was restored, old roads were repaired and new ones built. At first the new roads had names, such as the Lincoln Highway that went from New York to San Francisco, but the proliferation of the automobile and its road system soon caused named roads to be unworkable. In the early twentieth century highways received numbers according to a national system. The National Road became U.S. Route 40. This route starts in Baltimore and crosses most of the country. In the Maryland-Pennsylvania area it closely follows the Baltimore Pike and the old National Road. If you travel the route from Cumberland, Maryland, to Brownsville, Pennsylvania, you are essentially traveling the route Christopher Gist took in 1751, and will go over the same Savage Mountain and cross the same Youghiogheny River. As you pass through Uniontown, Pennsylvania "Gist's Place" will be just a few miles north.[46]

It is now possible to travel to all four corners of the lower forty-eight states on a modern Interstate Highway system initiated by President Eisenhower in the 1950s. When he was a young soldier in the early twentieth century he traveled across the country on a road system he found to be very inadequate. When he became president, and after seeing the autobahns in Germany, he was determined to improve the system. His rationale for an entirely new and modern road system: national defense, the same justification used by many in proposing the National Road. What used to be an arduous journey, taking days, from Baltimore, across the mountains, can now be accomplished in a few hours on Interstate 70 (I-70) or Interstate 68 (I-68). One can also take other, parallel, interstates farther north including the Pennsylvania Turnpike, the nation's oldest superhighway, which runs past Pittsburgh.

Interstate 70 which runs through southern Pennsylvania meets U.S. 40, the old National Road at Washington, Pennsylvania, and continues west through Wheeling, West Virginia, Zanesville, Ohio, and on to the far west. Interstate 68 starts at Hancock, Maryland, and travels west in Maryland along U.S. 40, passing through Cumberland and Frostburg, Maryland, before stopping at Morgantown, West Virginia. These two routes are scenic in their own way but do not have the intimate scenery or historic feel of U.S. 40. However, they do achieve the objective the first trailblazers wanted to obtain over 250 years ago, travel between east and west with speed and comfort.

The story of the push across the Allegheny Mountains to open the Ohio country appears to be a fairly small episode in the history of America, and even less in the scope of world history. However, the people who made it happen acted in the same way, and for the same reasons, as their predecessors in more famous adventures, the ones that pushed the boundaries they felt constrained them. Ever since humans left Africa fifty thousand years ago there have always been adventurers willing to push the boundary for personal gain and for a better life.

The opportunity to utilize the rich land in Ohio was the initial motivation for moving into Ohio country. In addition to the entrepreneurs who financed it, the Ohio Company of Virginia, there were also the adventurers, such as Christopher Gist, Thomas Cresap, and George Washington, who actually blazed the trails. They were all dreamers who wanted to demolish a boundary, no less so than Columbus. They had to breach a mountain barrier with a road that never previously existed. Over the next one hundred years this process continued, interrupted by momentous events such as wars and the founding of a new republic. The dream for the path across the mountains never died but became more important as the need to build this road was critical to binding a new nation. As time went on the task switched from the dreamers to the doers, the engineers and workmen who actually built the road, and then to the migrants who moved west on it.

This gateway into Ohio, which breached the Appalachians, helped bind the nation together and its opening ranks as a significant accomplishment in American history.

Chapter Notes

Introduction

1. Morse, Jedidiah, *The American Geography*. London: Printed for John Stockdale, Piccadilly, 1794, p. 463.
2. Raitz, Karl, ed., *The National Road,* Chapter Three: "The Idea of a National Road by Joseph Wood." Baltimore: The Johns Hopkins University Press, 1996, p. 96.
3. The Ohio country originally referred to land west of the mountains above the Ohio River. Later as the Pennsylvania border was settled Ohio was the eastern section of the Northwest Territory.

Chapter One

1. Clark, Sandra H. B., *Birth of the Mountains: The Geologic Story of the Southern Appalachian Mountains*. U.S. Geological Survey, Department of the Interior [no date], http://www.usgs.gov.
2. Clark.
3. Not to be confused with the Cumberland River Valley in Kentucky and Tennessee.
4. The Appalachian Plateau includes the Allegheny Plateau on the northern end and the Cumberland Plateau which goes as far south as Alabama.
5. Knepper, George W., *Ohio and Its People*. Kent and London: Kent State University Press, 2003, pp. 3–5.
6. Knepper, p. 9.
7. Fort Ancient, "Ohio Prehistory," 2016, http://fortancient.org/archaeology/ohio-pre-history?showall=&start=1.
8. Knepper, p. 14.
9. Walden, Carl, and Braun, Molly, *Atlas of the North American Indian*. New York: Facts on File Publications, 1985, p. 21.
10. Language here refers to the language unique to the cultures. Many archeologists believe human language was necessary of cooperation and art and therefore it evolved prior to humans leaving Africa, that is, prior to fifty thousand years ago. *See* Wade, Nicholas, *Before the Dawn: Recovering the Lost History of Our Ancestors*. New York: Penguin, 2006, pp. 45–46.
11. Donehoo, George P., D.D., "The Indians of the Past and of the Present," *Pennsylvania Magazine of History and Biography* 46, no. 3 (1922), p. 186.
12. Donehoo, p. 187.
13. "The Walam Olum: Its Origin and Authenticity," 2016, http://abob.libs.uga.edu/bobk/walamc.html.
14. Walden and Braun, p. 67.
15. The Lennapi creation myth described has the Iroquois moving from the Mississippi area, which is also plausible.
16. Answers.com, 2016, http://www.answers.com/Q/What_does_Iroquois_mean_in_Mohawk?#slide=2.
17. "Hurons," 2016, http://geo.msu.edu/extra/geogmich/Hurons.html.
18. Walden and Braun, p. 32.
19. Clark, Jerry E., *The Shawnee*. Lexington: University Press of Kentucky, 1993, p. 5.
20. Clark, pp. 5–6.
21. Clark, pp. 8–9.
22. Mayre, William, "Patowmeck Above Ye Inhabitants." *Maryland Historical Magazine* 30, no. 2 (June 1935), p. 126. Cites: *Handbook of Americans Indians,* Bureau of American Ethnology, Bulletin 30, part 2, p. 533.
23. Hanna, Charles Augustus, *The Wilderness Trail, Volume One*. New York and London: G. P. Putnam's Sons/Knickerbocker Press, 1911, p. 152. It is unknown what the town was named before it became Opessa's Town. Opessa must have been an impressive figure to have a town named after him *after* he arrived.
24. Mayre, pp. 131–132.
25. Hanna, p. 156.
26. Lowensteyn, Peter, "The Role of the Dutch in the Iroquois Wars, 2014, http://www.lowensteyn.com/iroquois/.
27. Baker, Peggy M., "The Pilgrims and the Fur Trade," *Pilgrim Hall Museum,* 2014, http://www.pilgrimhallmuseum.org/pdf/The_Pilgrims_Fur_Trade.pdf.
28. Volwiler, A. T., "George Croghan and the Westward Movement, 1741–1782," *Pennsylvania Magazine of History and Biography* 46, no. 4 (1922), pp. 273–274.
29. Lowensteyn, Peter, "The Role of the Dutch in the Iroquois Wars, 2014, http://www.lowensteyn.com/iroquois/.

30. Jennings, Francis, *The Ambiguous Iroquois Empire*. New York, London: W. W. Norton, 1984, p. 89.
31. Jennings, p. 85.
32. Wallace, Anthony F. C., "Origins of Iroquois Neutrality: The Grand Settlement of 1701," *Pennsylvania History* 24, no. 3 (July 1957), p. 224.
33. Jennings, p. 95.
34. The Canadian Encyclopedia, "Iroquois Wars," 2016, http://www.thecanadianencyclopedia.ca/en/article/iroquois-wars/.
35. The Patriot Files, "Beaver Wars (1642–1698)," 2016, http://www.patriotfiles.com/index.php?name=Sections&req=viewarticle&artid=8531&page=1.
36. Wallace, Anthony F. C., p. 234.
37. Wallace, Anthony F. C., pp. 234–235.
38. Iroquois Indians: A Documentary History, pgs. 908–911, Reel 6, Newberry Library, Chicago, Illinois: "July 19, 1701 Deed or Nanfan Treaty: Deed from the Five Nations to the King of Their Beaver Hunting Ground," http://www.sixnations.ca/LandsResources/NanFanTreaty.pdf.
39. This treaty was ratified again by three of the five Nations in Albany on September 14, 1726. Early Ratified Treaties with the American Indian Nations, "Deed in Trust from three of the Five Nations of Indians to the King," 2015, http://earlytreaties.unl.edu/treaty.00002.html.
40. Jennings, p. 212.
41. Jennings, p. 11.
42. Hurt, Douglas R., *The Ohio Frontier: Crucible of the Old Northwest, 1720–1830*, Bloomington & Indianapolis: Indiana University Press, 1996, p. 4.
43. Gist, Christopher, *George Mercer Papers: Relating to the Ohio Company of Virginia*, compiled and edited by Lois Mulkearn. University of Pittsburgh Press, 1954, p. 18.
44. Knepper, pp. 14–17.
45. The Mingo Indians, 2016, http://www.cynthiaswope.com/withinthevines/penna/native/Mingo.html.
46. The Delaware River was named for Thomas West, Lord De La Warr, the first governor of Virginia. Apparently he returned to England without ever having seen the bay and river named for him. The Nanticoke Lenni-lenape: An American Indian Tribe, "Our Tribal History," 2015, http://www.nanticoke-lenape.info/history.htm.
47. Wallace, Paul A.W., *Indian Paths of Pennsylvania*. Harrisburg: Commonwealth of Pennsylvania, Pennsylvania Historical and Museum Commission, 1965, p. 2. All the other paths in this section are described by Wallace in this paper also. The range of the white birch used for these canoes starts well above the Great Lakes so bark from these trees was not available to the tribes in most of the Appalachian Mountains.
48. Wallace, Paul A.W. p. 72.
49. Hanna, Charles Augustus, *The Wilderness Trail*, Vol. 1. New York and London: G. P. Putnam's Sons/Knickerbocker, 1911, p. 182.
50. Yale Law School Lillian Goldman Law Library, "Avalon Project: The First Charter of Virginia; April 10, 1606," 2014, http://avalon.law.yale.edu/17th_century/va01.asp.
51. National Park Service, Historic Jamestowne, "The Virginia Company of London," 2016, https://www.nps.gov/jame/learn/historyculture/the-virginia-company-of-london.htm.
52. Yale Law School Lillian Goldman Law Library, "Avalon Project: The Second Charter of Virginia; May 23, 1609," 2014, http://avalon.law.yale.edu/17th_century/va02.asp.
53. Yale Law School Lillian Goldman Law Library, "Avalon Project: The Charter of New England: 1620," 2014, http://avalon.law.yale.edu/17th_century/mass01.asp.
54. Caleb Johnson's MayflowerHistory.com, "Voyage of the Mayflower," http://mayflowerhistory.com/voyage/.
55. Yale Law School Lillian Goldman Law Library, "Avalon Project: The Charter of Massachusetts Bay: 1629," 2014, http://avalon.law.yale.edu/17th_century/mass03.asp.
56. United States History, "Massachusetts Bay Colony," 2016, http://www.u-s-history.com/pages/h572.html; Zeichner, Oscar, Scholastic Magazines, Teachers, "Massachusetts Bay Company," 2016, http://www.scholastic.com/teachers/article/massachusetts-bay-company.
57. Alvord, Clarence W., and Bidgood, Lee, *The First Explorations of the Trans-Alleghany Region by the Virginians, 1650–1674*. Cleveland: Arthur H. Clark, 1912, pp. 29–31.
58. Alvord and Bidgood, p. 45.
59. Alvord and Bidgood, p. 71.
60. The sources do not speculate on the meaning of these letters, but they might have represented the names or initials of the persons who previously blazed that trail.
61. Alvord and Bidgood, p. 73.
62. GeoFacts, No. 10, Ohio Department of Natural Resources, Division of Geological Survey, "The Teays River," 2014, http://geosurvey.ohiodnr.gov/portals/geosurvey/PDFs/GeoFacts/geof10.pdf.
63. E-Encyclopedia Virginia, "Thomas Batte (fl. 1630s-1690s)," contributed by Alan Vance Briceland and *The Dictionary of Virginia Biography*, 2016, http://www.encyclopediavirginia.org/Batte_Thomas_fl_1630s-1690s.
64. Campbell, Charles, *History of the Colony and Ancient Dominion of Virginia*, Philadelphia: J.B. Lippincott, 1860, pp. 387–388.
65. Miles, H. H., Canada History, "1534 Cartier Explores Canada, French Attempts at Colonization," 2016, http://www.canadahistory.com/sections/documents/explorers/jacquescartier.htm; New France, "Fur Trade 1500s to 1700s," http://www.canadahistoryproject.ca/1663/1663-05-fur-trade.html.
66. The name Acadia derives from the early Verrazano voyages. He used a similar name for the area around Delaware Bay but others later named the area of present day New Brunswick and Nova Scotia, Acadia.
67. Yale Law School Lillian Goldman Law Library, "Avalon Project: Charter of Acadia Granted by Henry IV of France to Pierre du Gast, Sieur de Monts; December 18, 1603," 2014, http://avalon.law.yale.edu/17th_century/charter_001.asp.

68. Fischer, David Hackett, *Champlain's Dream*, New York: Simon & Schuster, 2008, p. 221.
69. Fischer, p. 235.
70. Virtual Museum of New France, The Explorers. "Samuel de Champlain," 2016, http://www.historymuseum.ca/virtual-museum-of-new-france/the-explorers/samuel-de-champlain-1604–1616/; biography.com, "Samuel de Champlain-Diplomat, Explorer." http://www.biography.com/people/samuel-de-champlain-9243971.
71. Canada's First People, "The Fur Trade," http://firstpeoplesofcanada.com/fp_furtrade/fp_furtrade2.html.
72. Fischer, p. 405.
73. Statistics Canada, "Estimated Population of Canada, 1605 to Present," 2014, http://www.statcan.gc.ca/pub/98-187-x/4151287-eng.htm.
74. Lucas, Charles Prestwood, Sir, *A Historical Geography of the British Colonies, Vol. V, Canada-Part I (New France)*, London, Edinburgh, New York: Oxford at the Clarendon Press, 1901, p. 338.
75. U.S. Census Bureau, "Chapter Z-Colonial and Pre-Federal Statistics," 2014, http://www2.census.gov/prod2/statcomp/documents/CT1970p2-13.pdf, page 1168.
76. Quebec History, Marianopolis College, "Company of New France (1627)," 2016, http://faculty.marianopolis.edu/c.belanger/quebechistory/encyclopedia/CompanyofNewFrance-QuebecHistory.htm.
77. Quebec History, "Company of New France"; Statistics Canada, U.S. Census Bureau.
78. The Canadian Encyclopedia, "Filles du Roi," 2016, http://www.thecanadianencyclopedia.ca/en/article/filles-du-roi/.
79. Statistics Canada, U.S. Census Bureau.
80. Statistics Canada.
81. Vachon, André, "Talon, Jean," in *Dictionary of Canadian Biography*, 2015, http://www.biographi.ca/en/bio/talon_jean_1E.html.
82. Parkman, Francis, *La Salle and the Discovery of the Great West: France and England in North America, Part Third*, Boston: Little, Brown, 1908, p. 53, http://www.gutenberg.org/files/40143/40143-h/40143-h.htm.
83. Parkman indicates that La Salle received permission and encouragement from both the governor and the intendant Talon. However, this was in 1669 and Talon did not return to New France as intendant until August 1670.
84. Parkman, Francis, pp. 17–18.
85. Dupré, Céline, "Cavelier De La Salle, Rene-Robert," in Dictionary of Canadian Biography, 2017, http://www.biographi.ca/en/bio/cavelier_de_la_salle_rene_robert_1E.html.
86. Parkman, Francis, pp. 30–32.
87. Canadian Museum of History, "Virtual Museum of New France: The Explorers, Rene-Robert Cavelier de La Salle," 2014, http://www.historymuseum.ca/virtual-museum-of-new-france/the-explorers/rene-robert-cavelier-de-la-salle-1670–1687/.
88. Hanna, Charles A., *The Wilderness Trail Or The Ventures and Adventures of the Pennsylvania Traders on the Allegheny Path*, Volume Two, New York and London: G. P. Putnam's Sons, 1911, pp. xxii, 143.
89. Fleming, George Thornton, *History of Pittsburgh and Environs: From Prehistoric Days to the Beginning of the American Revolution*, Volume One, New York and Chicago: American Historical Society, 1922, p. 157.
90. Fleming, p. 158.
91. Vachon., André
92. Dictionary of Canadian Biography, "Jolliet, Louis," 2016, http://www.biographi.ca/en/bio/jolliet_louis_1E.html; Vachon, André.
93. Canadian Heritage, "Origin of the Name Canada," 2014, http://canadaonline.about.com/od/history/a/namecanada.htm.
94. Statistics Canada, U.S. Census Bureau.

Chapter Two

1. New Hampshire, carved out of the Council of New England grant, was first settled in 1623. However, it was a collection of small, independent towns that didn't unite until 1639. They united under Massachusetts, which laid claim to the territory. All this led to a slow population increase. See: History of the USA, "New Hampshire," 2015, http://www.usahistory.info/New-England/New-Hampshire.html.
2. Land, Aubrey C., *Colonial Maryland: A History*, Millwood, NY: KTO, 1981, p. 59; Walsh, Richard, and Fox, William Lloyd, eds., *Maryland: A History 1632–1974*. Baltimore: Maryland Historical Society, 1974, p. 39.
3. Land, *Colonial Maryland: A History.* p. 4; Andrews, Matthew Page, *History of Maryland: Province and State*. Hatboro, PA: Tradition, 1965, p. 2.
4. Andrews, p. 2.
5. Andrews, p. 7.
6. Walsh and Fox, p. 2.
7. Andrews, p. 5. The Oath of Supremacy claimed the king as head of the Church of England.
8. Land, Aubrey C., *Colonial Maryland: A History*, p. 5.
9. Walsh and Fox, pp. 2, 3; Land, *Colonial Maryland: A History*, pp. 6–8.
10. Yale Law School Lillian Goldman Law Library, "Avalon Project: The Charter of Maryland: 1632," 2015, http://avalon.law.yale.edu/17th_century/ma01.asp.
11. In other words, the eastern boundary was the ocean on the south, and the west side of Delaware Bay in the north. It was actually the Delaware River by this point.
12. Andrews, p. 21.
13. Russell, William, T., *Maryland: The Land of Sanctuary. A History of Religious Toleration in Maryland from the First Settlements Until the American Revolution*, Baltimore: J. H. Furst, 1907, p. 61.
14. Walsh and Fox, p. 4.
15. Walsh and Fox, pp. 25, 29; Land, *Colonial Maryland: A History*, p. 89.
16. Land, *Colonial Maryland: A History.* p. 8.
17. Russell, p. 55.

18. Andrews, pp. 19–20
19. Bayliff, William H. *The Maryland-Pennsylvania and the Maryland-Delaware Boundaries, Bulletin 4, Second Addition.* Annapolis: Maryland Board of Natural resources, July 1959, pp. 4, 6.
20. Land, *Colonial Maryland: A History,* p. 81; Bayliff, p. 6.
21. Bayliff, pp. 1–9, *passim.*
22. Bayliff, p. 5.
23. The Penn family also claimed some land below what is the present northern border of Maryland so the disputed strip was over twenty miles wide.
24. Bayliff, p. 7.
25. Bailey, Kenneth P., *Thomas Cresap, Maryland Frontiersman,* Boston: Christopher, 1944, p. 32.
26. Bayliff, p. 9.
27. Land, *Colonial Maryland: A History,* p. 81.
28. One part of the Maryland panhandle is less than two miles wide between Pennsylvania and West Virginia.
29. Land, *Colonial Maryland: A History,* p. 19.
30. Walsh and Fox, p. 5; Andrews, pp. 28–31, *passim.*
31. Quitrent was a land rent paid to a feudal superior, now outdated and considered a tax.
32. Walsh and Fox, pp. 9–10.
33. Andrews, p. 36.
34. Land, *Colonial Maryland: A History,* pp. 34–36.
35. Land, *Colonial Maryland: A History,* pp, 217–223, *passim.*
36. Paper currency wasn't introduced into Maryland until one hundred years later.
37. Walsh and Fox, pp. 16–17; Land, *Colonial Maryland: A History,* p. 28.
38. Land, *Colonial Maryland: A History,* p. 58; Walsh and Fox, p. 15.
39. Walsh and Fox, p. 15.
40. Wallace, Paul A. W. *Indian Paths of Pennsylvania.* Harrisburg: Pennsylvania Historical and Museum Commission, 1965, p. 2.
41. Clearly Cresaptown did not have that name at the time. It was probably an Indian village. Obviously it was later named for the Cresap family.
42. Wallace, p. 180.
43. Wallace, p. 184.
44. Sioussat, St. George Leakin, "Highway Legislation in Maryland and Its Influence on the Economic Development of the State," *Maryland Geological Survey,* Volume Three. Baltimore: John Hopkins Press, 1899, pp. 127–128.
45. It was at York that the Monocacy Road branched off to go toward Frederick.
46. Dollarhide, William, *Map Guide to American Migration Routes, 1735–1815.* Bountiful, UT: HeritageQuest, 2000, pp. 5, 12. The city names are contemporary, not yet named at the time.
47. Gould, Clarence P., *Money and Transportation in Maryland, 1720–1765.* Johns Hopkins University Studies in Historical and Political Science, Series 33, No. 1, Baltimore: Johns Hopkins Press, 1915, p. 126.
48. Gould, p. 126.
49. Gould, p. 127; Bell, Carl, D., *The Development of Western Maryland 1715–1753,* University of Maryland Master of Arts Thesis, 1948, p. 22.
50. Sioussat, p. 109.
51. Porter, Frank W. III, "From Backcountry to County: The Delayed Settlement of Western Maryland," *Maryland Historical Magazine* 70, no. 4 (winter 1975), p. 339; Bailey, *Thomas Cresap, Maryland Frontiersman,* p. 64.
52. Porter, "From Backcountry to County," pp. 336–337.
53. Sioussat, "Highway Legislation in Maryland," p. 114.
54. Sioussat, "Highway Legislation in Maryland," p. 125.
55. A land warrant was a certificate that authorized a person to take possession of some government owned land. It was like a reservation for that land. A land patent conveyed the title to the patentee. He now owned it.
56. Porter, "From Backcountry to County: The Delayed Settlement of Western Maryland," p. 338
57. Porter, "From Backcountry to County," p. 338.
58. Porter, "From Backcountry to County," p. 334.
59. The Anglican Church became the established church after the revolution of 1688.
60. Porter, "From Backcountry to County," p. 336; Bell, pp. 27, 28.
61. Bell, p. 29.
62. Porter, Frank W. III, "Expanding the Domain: William Gooch and the Northern Neck Boundary Dispute." *Maryland Historian* 5 (Spring 1974).
63. "The Fairfax Grant," 2015, http://www.virginiaplaces.org/settleland/fairfaxgrant.html.
64. Kemper, Charles E. ed., "The Early Westward Movement of Virginia, 1722–1734: As Shown by the Proceedings of the Colonial Council," *The Virginia Magazine of history and Biography* 13, no. 2 (October 1905), pp. 115–117.
65. Nead, Daniel Wunderlich, M.D., *The Pennsylvania-German in the Settlement of Maryland.* Lancaster: Pennsylvania-German Society, 1914, p. 42.
66. Nead, pp. 32–39, *passim.*
67. Kemper, pp. 129–131
68. Kemper, p. 137. The different spellings of the river names are in the original.
69. Porter, "From Backcountry to County," pp. 27–60.
70. Bailey, *Thomas Cresap, Maryland Frontiersman,* pp. 26–28; Wroth, Lawrence C., "The Story of Thomas Cresap, A Maryland Pioneer." *Maryland Historical Magazine* 9, no. 1 (March 1914), p. 2.
71. Bailey, *Thomas Cresap, Maryland Frontiersman,* pp. 28–29.
72. Wroth, p. 3.
73. Wroth, p. 8.
74. Bailey, *Thomas Cresap, Maryland Frontiersman,* pp. 31–48.
75. Bailey, *Thomas Cresap, Maryland Frontiersman,* p. 52.
76. Bailey, *Thomas Cresap, Maryland Frontiersman,* p. 54.
77. Bailey, *Thomas Cresap, Maryland Frontiersman,* p. 59; Wroth, p. 15; Land, Aubrey C. "A Land Speculator in the Opening of Western Maryland."

Maryland Historical Magazine 48, no. 3 (September 1953), p. 195.
78. Porter, "From Back Country to County," p. 83.
79. Wroth, p. 15.
80. Bailey, *Thomas Cresap, Maryland Frontiersman*, pp. 61–63.
81. Bailey, *Thomas Cresap, Maryland Frontiersman*, pp. 62–63; Wroth, p. 16.
82. Wroth, p. 17.
83. Land, "A Land Speculator in the Opening of Western Maryland, pp. 191–203; Walsh and Fox, p. 41.
84. Mayre, William B., "'Patowmeck Above Ye Inhabitants,' a Commentary on the Subject of an Old Map." *Maryland Historical Magazine* 30, no. 2 (June 1935), p. 114.
85. Land, "A Land Speculator in the Opening of Western Maryland," pp. 193–194.
86. Bailey, *Thomas Cresap, Maryland Frontiersman*, p. 52.
87. Land, "A Land Speculator in the Opening of Western Maryland," p. 195.
88. Land, "A Land Speculator in the Opening of Western Maryland," p. 196.
89. Land, "A Land Speculator in the Opening of Western Maryland," pp. 196-198.
90. Land, *Colonial Maryland: A History*, p. 200.
91. Porter, "From Backcountry to County," p. 343.
92. Land, "A Land Speculator in the Opening of Western Maryland," p. 197.
93. The Edict of Nantes was promulgated by Henry IV of France in 1598 to allow more rights for the Calvinist Protestants of France, the Huguenots.
94. Nead, pp. 28, 29.
95. Nead, pp. 29–32.
96. Nead, p. 33.
97. Porter, "From Backcountry to County," p. 345.
98. Porter, "From Backcountry to County," p. 345.
99. Porter, "From Backcountry to County," p. 345.
100. Land, *Colonial Maryland: A History*, p. 202; Porter, "From Backcountry to County," pp. 345–346.
101. Porter, "From Backcountry to County," p. 346.
102. Nead, p. 55.

Chapter Three

1. Hildreth, S. F., *Pioneer History: Being an Account of the First Examinations of the Ohio Valley, and the Early Settlement of the Northwest Territory*, Cincinnati: H. W. Derby & Co., Publishers, 1848, pp. 23–24. The claim ("the preceding Kings of France") was based on La Salle's supposed discovery of the Ohio in 1669-1670.
2. Bailey, Kenneth P., *The Ohio Company of Virginia and the Westward Movement, 1748-1792: A Chapter In the History of the Colonial Frontier*, Glendale, CA: Arthur H. Clark, 1939, p. 17. (Reprinted in India by Isha, New Delhi, 2013.)
3. Bailey, Kenneth P., *Thomas Cresap: Maryland Frontiersman*, Boston: Christopher, 1944, pp. 28–29.
4. Bailey, *The Ohio Company of Virginia*, p. 25. Bailey cites: Osgood, Herbert L. *The American Colonies in the Eighteenth Century*. Vol. 4, p. 78.
5. Some claim it was a partnership and never did become a corporation. This distinction is not important for the discussion here.
6. Bailey, *The Ohio Company of Virginia*, pp. 35–39. Virginia governors were often absentee, remaining in England. The lieutenant governor would stay in the province and head the government. Frequently the term governor alone was used for convenience, which will be done herein.
7. "List of Early Land Patents and Grants," *The Virginia Magazine of History and Biography*, Vol. 5, 1898, p. 241. Kiskomanett's Creek was also known as Romanettos Creek.
8. Mulkearn, Lois, compiler and editor, *George Mercer Papers: Relating to the Ohio Company of Virginia*, Pittsburgh: University of Pittsburgh Press, 1954, pp. 247–248.
9. Bailey, *The Ohio Company of Virginia*, pp. 26–31.
10. Mulkearn, p. 246.
11. Sparks, Jared, *The Writings of George Washington; Being His Correspondence, Addresses, Messages, and Other Papers, Official and Private, Selected and Published from the Original Manuscripts*, Volume II. Boston: Russell, Ordione, and Metcalf, and Milliard, Gray and Co., 1834, p. 479.
12. Mulkearn, p. 247. Spelling as in the original.
13. Mulkearn, p. 246. Spelling as in the original.
14. Bailey, *The Ohio Company of Virginia*, p. 74. Savage Mountain is west of Wills Mountain.
15. Bailey, *The Ohio Company of Virginia*, pp. 74–77.
16. Ambler, George H., *George Washington and the West*, Chapel Hill: University of North Carolina Press, 1936, p. 32; Mulkearn, *George Mercer Papers*, p. 642.
17. James, Alfred P., *The Ohio Company and Its Inner History*, New York: University of Pittsburgh Press/American Book-Stratford, 1959, p. 32. Bailey, *The Ohio Company of Virginia*, p. 70.
18. West Virginia University Extension Service, "George Washington," 2016, http://berkeley.ext.wvu.edu/r/download/224938.
19. McDonald, Forrest, *The Presidency of George Washington*, Lawrence: University Press of Kansas, 1974, p. 10.
20. Chernow, Ron, *Washington: A Life*, New York: Penguin, 2010, pp. 3–14.
21. Ferling, John E., *The First of Men: A Life of George Washington*, Knoxville: University of Tennessee Press, 1988, pp. 1–14; Chernow, pp. 18–24.
22. Ferling, pp. 15–18.
23. Bailey, Kenneth P., *Christopher Gist: Colonial Frontiersman, Explorer, and Indian Agent*, Hamden, CT: Archon, 1976, pp. 12–13.
24. Bailey, *Christopher Gist*, pp. 14–17.
25. Bailey, *Christopher Gist*, pp. 20–21.
26. Bailey, *Christopher Gist*, p. 22.
27. Bailey, *Christopher Gist*, pp. 23–24.

28. Bailey, *Christopher Gist*, pp. 23–24.
29. Bailey, *Christopher Gist*, pp. 30–32.
30. Darlington, William M., *Christopher Gist's Journals with Historical, Geographical and Ethnological Notes and Biographies of His Contemporaries*, Pittsburgh: J. R. Weldin & Co., 1893, pp. 31–32.
31. Bailey, *Christopher Gist*, p. 33.
32. Bailey, *Christopher Gist*, pp. 33–34.
33. Darlington, pp. 55–56
34. Mulkearn, Lois, ed. *George Mercer Papers Relating to the Ohio Company of Virginia.* Pittsburgh: University of Pittsburgh Press, 1954. p. 491; Galbreath, C. B., Ed. *Expedition of Celoron to the Ohio Country in 1749.* Columbus, OH: F. J. Heer, 1921, p. 50.
35. Darlington, p. 58.
36. Darlington, p. 66.
37. Mulkearn, p. 142.
38. Mulkearn, p. 143.
39. Originally all the papers seem to indicate the Logstown conference was to be in 1751. However, either because the Indians did not show up or because Gist's second journey would not be complete by then it ended up in 1752.
40. Mulkearn, p. 50.
41. Bailey, *Christopher Gist,* pp. 47–49.; Bailey, *The Ohio Company of Virginia*, pp. 97–98.
42. Darlington, p. 69.
43. Darlington, p. 69–70.
44. Darlington, pp. 70, 140.
45. Mulkearn, p. 510. Mulkearn indicates "place of crossing," but they did not cross that day.
46. Darlington, p. 141.
47. Darlington, p. 69.
48. Darlington, pp. 77–79.
49. Darlington, p. 78.
50. Darlington, pp. 77–78.
51. Darlington, p. 79.
52. Mulkearn, p. 4.
53. Bailey, Kenneth P. *The Ohio Company of Virginia*, pp. 152–153.
54. Mulkearn, p. 147. The quote does say "Forks of the Mohongaly," but this appears to be a mistake. There was never any further mention of the Forks that Gist mentioned, the confluence of the Cheat and Monongahela Rivers, after his journal entry. The company was always focused on the Monongahela and the Forks of the Ohio and never considered that route. It is most likely they were referring to the Monongahela with the eventual destination of the Forks of the Ohio. It is also possible they were referring to Turkey Foot which is also a river fork.
55. James, Alfred P., *The Ohio Company, Its Inner History*, p. 70; Bailey, *The Ohio Company of Virginia*, p. 153.
56. Mulkearn, p. 510.
57. RootsWeb, "Workman Family," 2015, http://wc.rootsweb.ancestry.com/cgi-bin/igm.cgi?op=GET&db=workman_family&id=I2245.
58. Pennsylvania Archives, Series I, p. 239.
59. Bailey, *The Ohio Company of Virginia*, p. 154.
60. Bailey, *Christopher Gist*, pp. 54, 61.
61. Wroth, Lawrence C., "The Story of Thomas Cresap, A Maryland Pioneer," *Maryland Historical Magazine* 9, no. 1 (March 1914), p. 24.
62. The Encyclopedia of New York State, "Covenant Chain," 2015, http://www.syracuseuniversitypress.syr.edu/encyclopedia/entries/convenant-chain.html.
63. "The Early Westward Movement of Virginia, 1722-1734," *The Virginia Magazine of History and Biography* 13, no. 1 (July 1905), p. 5; Early Recognized Treaties with American Indian Nations, "Ratified Treaty #1: The Great Treaty of 1722 Between the Five Nations, the Mahicans, and the Colonies of New York, Virginia, and Pennsylvania," 2016, pp. 670–675, http://treatiesportal.unl.edu/earlytreaties/treaty00001.html.
64. Early Recognized Treaties with American Indian Nations. "Ratified Treaty #3: A Treaty Held at the Town of Lancaster, By the Honourable the Lieutenant Governor of the Province, and the Honourable the Commissioners for the Province of Virginia and Maryland, with the Indians of the Six Nations in June, 1744," 2015, pp. 69–70, http://earlytreaties.unl.edu/treaty.00003.html.
65. "Treaty of Lancaster, 1722," *The Virginia Magazine of History and Biography* 13, no. 2 (October 1905), p. 142.
66. Early Recognized Treaties with American Indian Nations, "Ratified Treaty #4: Treaty of Logstown, 1752," 2015, p. 160, http://earlytreaties.unl.edu/treaty.00004.html.
67. Early Recognized Treaties with American Indian Nations, "Ratified Treaty #4: Treaty of Logstown, 1752," 2015, p. 168.
68. Galbreath, C. B., ed., *Expedition of Celoron to the Ohio Country in 1749,* Columbus, OH: F. J. Heer, 1921, pp. 5–10.
69. Galbreath, p. 16. Note: Onontio was the name used by the Indians for the Governor General of New France.
70. Galbreath, p. 17.
71. Galbreath, p. 33.
72. Galbreath pp. 34–35.
73. Galbreath, pp. 57–58.
74. Anderson, Fred, *Crucible of War: The Seven Years' War and the Fate of Empire in British North America, 1754-1766,* New York: Alfred A. Knopf, 2000, p. 25; Hurt, R. Douglas, *The Ohio Frontier: Crucible of the Old Northwest, 1720-1830,* Bloomington and Indianapolis: Indiana University Press, 1996, p. 20.
75. Anderson, pp. 25–26; Hurt, pp. 33–34.
76. Anderson, pp. 28–29; Hurt, pp. 33–34.
77. Anderson, p. 32.
78. Anderson, p. 32.
79. Yale Law School Lillian Goldman Law Library, "Avalon Project: The Second Charter of Virginia: May 23, 1609," 2015, http://avalon.law.yale.edu/17th_century/ma01.asp.
80. Yale Law School Lillian Goldman Law Library, "Avalon Project: The Charter for the Province of Pennsylvania-1681," 2015, http://avalon.law.yale.edu/17th_century/ma01.asp.
81. Craig, Neville B., *Lecture upon the Controversy between Pennsylvania and Virginia about the Boundary Line.* Pittsburgh: Printed by A. Jaynes—Franklin Head—Opposite Post Office, 1843, p. 6. Craig appar-

ently thought the fort was at the Forks when the only fort in 1752 was to be at Chartiers Creek, a few miles downstream. Also, the fort was not explicitly to repel the French, although it might have had that effect, it was to establish the Ohio Company presence in the area.

82. Volwiler Alfred T., "George Croghan and the Westward Movement, 1741–1782," *Pennsylvania Magazine of History and Biography* 46, no. 184 (October 1922), p. 277.

83. Volwiler, pp. 278–286.

84. Volwiler, pp. 287–288.

85. Darlington, pp. 34–35, 37; Volwiler, pp. 294–295, 304.

86. Lewin, Howard, "A Frontier Diplomat: Andrew Montour," *Pennsylvania History* 33, no. 2 (April 1966), pp. 153–157.

87. Lewin, pp. 163–164.

88. Mulkearn, p. 143. A pistole was a gold coin.

89. Wallace, Paul A.W., *Conrad Weiser, Friend of Colonist and Mohawk,* Philadelphia: University of Pennsylvania Press, 1945, p. 3.

90. Wallace, *Conrad Weiser,* p. 217.

91. Wallace, *Conrad Weiser,* p. 334.

Chapter Four

1. Anderson, Fred, *Crucible of War: The Seven Years' War and the Fate of Empire in British North America, 1754–1766,* New York: Alfred A. Knopf, 2000, p. 32.

2. Leyland, Herbert T. "The Ohio Company: A Colonial Corporation," *Quarterly Publication of the Historical and Philosophical Society of Ohio* 16, no. 1 (January–June, 1921), p. 9.

3. James, Alfred P., *The Ohio Company and Its Inner History,* Pittsburgh: University of Pittsburgh Press, 1959, pp. 70–71; Mulkearn, Lois, comp. and ed., *George Mercer Papers, Relating to the Ohio Company of Virginia,* Pittsburgh: University of Pittsburgh Press, 1954, pp. 271–273.

4. James, pp. 88–89; Darlington, William M., *Christopher Gist's Journals, with Historical, Geographical and Ethnological Notes and Biographies of His Contemporaries,* Pittsburgh: J. R. Weldin & Co., 1893. Reprint: Forgotten, 2012, pp. 226–231.

5. Darlington, p. 230.

6. James, p. 100.

7. Bailey, Kenneth P., *The Ohio Company of Virginia and the Westward Movement, 1748–1792: A Chapter of the Colonial Frontier,* Glendale, CA: Arthur Clarke, 1939. Republished: New Delhi: Isha, 2013, p. 202.

8. Bailey, Kenneth P., *The Ohio Company of Virginia* pp. 81, 147.

9. Chernow, Ron, *Washington, A Life,* New York: Penguin, 2010, pp. 31–32.

10. Anderson, pp. 43–44.

11. These mountains were not so named at the time.

12. Bailey, Kenneth P., *Christopher Gist: Colonial Frontiersman, Explorer, and Indian Agent,* Hamden, CT: Archon, 1976, pp. 75–76; Darlington, p. 80.

13. Anderson, pp. 18, 27–28; Hunter, William A., Dictionary of Canadian Biography, "Tanaghrisson," 2016, http://www.biographi.ca/en/bio/tanaghrisson_3E.html.

14. Chernow, p. 35.

15. Anderson, p. 44.

16. Anderson, p. 45.

17. Chernow, p. 37.

18. Bailey, *The Ohio Company of Virginia,* pp. 190–191.

19. Red Stone and Redstone Old fort are used interchangeably in the literature.

20. Bailey, *The Ohio Company of Virginia,* pp. 191–192.

21. Anderson, p. 45.

22. Chernow, p. 40.

23. Chernow, p. 40.

24. National Archives Founders Online, "Expedition to the Ohio, 1754: Narrative," 2016, http://founders.archives.gov/documents/Washington/01-01-02-0004-0002.

25. State Roads commission of Maryland, *A History of Road Building in Maryland,* 1958, p. 13.

26. Temple, Henry, "Braddock's Road," *Ohio Valley Historical Association, Proceedings of the Second Annual Meeting, Marietta, Ohio, November 28–29, 1908,* Columbus, OH: Fred J. Heer, 1909, p. 93.

27. Laurel Hill and Chestnut Ridge are sometimes confused in the literature. These are two parallel ridges, running roughly northeast to southwest, with Laurel Hill being the easterly one. However, at the southern end of Laurel Hill, at Great Meadows, Laurel Hill is very low and no longer a barrier. For this reason it is often skipped in the description of this road or sometimes mistakenly used when Chestnut Ridge is meant.

28. Anderson, pp. 51–52.

29. Anderson p. 52.

30. Anderson, Chapter 5.

31. Anderson, pp. 60–62.

32. Hunter, Dictionary of Canadian Biography, "Tanaghrisson."

33. Anderson, Chapter 5.

34. Anderson, pp. 67–68.

35. Anderson, p. 72.

36. Anderson, p. 86; Laycock, John Kennedy, "Braddock's Road," *The Pennsylvania Magazine of History and Biography* 38, (1914), pp. 3–4.

37. Hulbert, Archer Butler, *Braddock's Road and Three Relative Papers,* Historic Highways of America, Vol. 4. Cleveland: Arthur H. Clark, 1903, pp. 88–89. As Hulbert points out the words "from the French" are not in the original journal and have no meaning. Cresap owned the land so no one could recall him from it, least of all the French.

38. Laycock, p. 3.

39. Bailey, *Christopher Gist,* p. 89; Wroth, Lawrence C., "The Story of Thomas Cresap, a Maryland Pioneer," *Maryland Historical Magazine* 9, no. 1 (March 1924), p. 29; Bailey, Kenneth P., *Thomas Cresap: Maryland Frontiersman,* Boston: Christopher, 1944, p. 97.

40. Anderson, pp. 94–96.

41. Hulbert, p. 97; Laycock, p. 4.

42. State Roads Commission of Maryland, p. 15.
43. Cubbison, Douglas, *On Campaign Against Fort Duquesne: The Braddock and Forbes Expeditions, 1755–1758, Through the Experiences of Quartermaster Sir John St. Clair,* Jefferson, NC: McFarland, 2015, p. 80.
44. Cubbison, p. 80
45. Hulbert, pp. 114–115.
46. Sargent, Winthrop, *The History of an Expedition Against Fort Du Quesne in 1755,* Philadelphia: Lippincott, Grambo & Co. for the Historical Society of Pennsylvania, 1856, pp. 199–206; Baker, Norman L., *Braddock's Road: Mapping the British Expedition from Alexandria to the Monongahela,* Charleston: History, 2013, pp. 99–103.
47. Baker, p. 176.
48. Anderson, pp. 104–105.
49. McConnell, Michael N., *A Country Between: The Upper Ohio Valley and Its People, 1724–1774,* Lincoln: University of Nebraska Press, 1992, p. 122.
50. McConnell, p. 122.
51. McConnell, p. 122.
52. Lowdermilk, William Harrison, *History of Cumberland (Maryland)*, Washington, D.C.: James Anglim, 1878, p. 208.
53. Lowdermilk, p. 216.
54. Lowdermilk, pp. 227–228.
55. Lowdermilk, p. 255.
56. Anderson, pp. 233–236, 267–268.
57. Monroe County Historical Association, "Pennsylvania's Infamous 'Walking Purchase," 2016, http://www.monroehistorical.org/articles/files/070610_walkingpurchase.html.
58. Anderson, p. 78.
59. Anderson, p. 205.
60. Anderson, pp. 270–271.
61. Anderson, p. 271.
62. Anderson, pp. 274–280.
63. Anderson, pp. 274–280.
64. McGrath, Nick, George Washington's Mount Vernon: "Forbes Expedition," 2015, http://www.mountvernon.org/research-collections/digital-encyclopedia/article/forbes-expedition/.
65. Sparks, Jared, *The Writings of George Washington,* Vol. 2. Washington, George letter to Colonel Bouquet, 2 August, 1758, Boston: Russell, Odiorne, and Metcalf, and Hilliard, Gray, and Co., 1835, p. 302.
66. Sparks, p. 304.
67. Anderson, p. 272.
68. Anderson, p. 236.
69. Anderson, pp. 281–283.
70. Nixon, Lily Lee, "Colonel James Burd in the Campaign of 1759," read at a meeting of the Historical Society of Western Pennsylvania on March 26, 1936, p. 115. https://journals.psu.edu/wph/article/viewFile/1730/1578.
71. Nixon, pp. 115–116.
72. Nixon, p. 115.
73. Nixon, pp. 117–119.
74. Nixon, p. 120; Veech, James, *The Monongahela of Old: Historical Sketches of South-Western Pennsylvania to the Year 1800,* Pittsburgh: For Private Distribution Only, 1858–1892, p. 27. Veech indicates that Burd started the road at Gist's place. However, Gist's place is a few miles north of the road which everyone has going directly from Chestnut Ridge to the river. Thus it seems the road itself was not started from Gist's but probably slightly south of Gist's. It is not clear if the appellation of Dunlap's Road preceded Gist's Trace or followed it. It most likely followed it because it seems likely the name Dunlap's Creek replaced the name Nemacolin's Creek after Gist and Nemacolin had made their paths. Also, Gist is almost universally given credit for blazing the path.
75. State Roads commission of Maryland, p. 14.
76. State Roads commission of Maryland, p. 16.
77. Maryland State Archives, Proceedings and Acts of the General Assembly, 1758–1761, vol. 56, p. 105, December 15, 1758, p. 74.
78. Mulkearn, p. 395.
79. Anderson, pp. 474, 524.
80. McConnell, p. 161. A stroud is a coarse woolen cloth.
81. McConnell, p. 163.
82. McConnell, pp.167–168.
83. Anderson, p. 525.
84. Brymner, Douglas, archivist, *Report on Canadian Archives, 1889*. Ottawa Printed by Brown Chamberlain, Printer to the Queen's Most Excellent Majesty, 1890, p. 73.
85. Anderson, p. 526.
86. Mulkearn, pp. 614–615.
87. Hurt, R. Douglas, *The Ohio Frontier: Crucible of the Old Northwest, 1720–1830,* Bloomington: Indiana University Press, 1996, p. 48.
88. Anderson, pp. 536–537; McConnell, p. 220.
89. Anderson, pp. 535–546.
90. Anderson, pp. 618–619, 626.
91. Anderson, pp. 562, 574.
92. Alvord, Clarence Walworth, "The Genesis of the Proclamation of 1763," *Michigan Pioneer and Historical Society, Historical Collections, Collections and Researches,* Vol. 36, Lansing, MI: Wyncoop Hallenbeck Crawford, State Printers, 1908, p. 22.
93. Alvord, pp. 14–19.
94. Alvord, p. 26.
95. Fischer, David Hackett, *Albion's Seed: Four British Folkways in America,* New York: Oxford University Press, 1989, "Borderlands to the Backcountry," pp. 605–782; Dollarhide, William, *Map Guide to American Migration Routes, 1735–1815,* Bountiful, UT: Heritage Quest, 2000, p. 5.
96. Sparks, Jared, *The Writings of George Washington,* Vol 2. Washington, George, letter to William Crawford, September 1767. Boston: Russell, Odiorne, and Metcalf, and Hilliard, Gray, and Co., 1834, pp. 347–348.
97. Hurt, p. 55.
98. Hurt, p. 55.
99. Billington, Ray A., "The Fort Stanwix Treaty of 1768," *New York History* 25, no. 2 (April 1944), pp. 182–194.
100. Billington, pp. 182–194.
101. West Virginia Encyclopedia, "Greenbrier Company," 2016, http://www.wvencyclopedia.org/articles/2166; West Virginia Encyclopedia, "Loyal Company," 2016, http://www.wvencyclopedia.org/articles/1462; "Vandalia and the Grand Ohio Com-

pany," 2016, http://www.virginiaplaces.org/settleland/vandalia.html; West Virginia History, "Vandalia: The First West Virginia?" by James Donald Anderson, 2016, http://www.wvculture.org/history/journal_wvh/wvh40-4.html.

102. McConnell, p. 260.
103. McConnell, p. 270.
104. McConnell, p. 281.
105. Hurt, p. 57.
106. "Fort Pitt (1761–1797)," 2016, http://www.brooklineconnection.com/history/Facts/FortPitt.html; Knepper, George W., *Ohio and Its People, Bicentennial Edition*, Kent, OH: Kent State University Press, 2003, p. 33; Caley, Percy B., "Lord Dunmore and the Pennsylvania-Virginia Boundary Dispute," presented at a meeting of the Historical Society of Western Pennsylvania on April, 26, 1938, pp. 87–100, https://journals.psu.edu/wph/article/viewFile/2118/1951.
107. Hurt, pp. 59–60; Simpson-Poffenbarger, Livia Nye, *The Battle of Point Pleasant: A Battle of the Revolution, October 10, 1774,* Point Pleasant, WV: State Gazette, 1909, p. 5.

Chapter Five

1. Hurt, R. Douglas, *The Ohio Frontier: Crucible of the Old Northwest, 1720–1830,* Bloomington: Indiana University Press, 1998, pp. 76–77, 91.
2. Library of Congress, "Map of Augusta Co., Virginia, 1738–1770," https://www.loc.gov/item/99446927/.
3. McClane, Debra Alderson, *Images of America: Botetourt County,* Charlestown, SC: Arcadia, 2007, p. 9.
4. The House of Burgesses was the lower house of the Virginia General Assembly.
5. Pendleton, William C., *History of Tazewell County and Southwest Virginia, 1748–1920,* Richmond: W. C. Hill, 1920, p. 256.
6. Historical Narratives of Early Canada, "The Royal Proclamation of 1763, The Quebec Act of 1774," 2015, http://www.uppercanadahistory.ca/pp/ppa.html.
7. Library of Congress, Web Guides, Primary Documents in American History, "The Articles of Confederation," 2016, http://www.loc.gov/rr/program/bib/ourdocs/articles.html.
8. Library of Congress, *Journals of the Continental Congress, 1774–1789, Volume 9, 1777, October 3–December 31,* Washington: Government Printing Office, 1907, p. 807.
9. Giddens, Paul H., "The French and Indian War in Maryland, 1753–1756," *Maryland Historical Magazine* 30, no. 4 (December 1935), p. 287.
10. Adams, Herbert B., "Maryland's Influence in Founding a National Commonwealth, on the Accession of Public Lands by the Old Confederation," A Paper Read Before the Maryland Historical Society, April 9, 1877, Baltimore, 1877, p. 29.
11. Adams, p. 29.
12. Adams, p. 115.
13. Adams, pp. 116–117.
14. Adams, p. 31; Library of Virginia, Research Notes no. 20, The Virginia Land Office, 2017, https://www.lva.virginia.gov/public/guides/Research_Notes_20.pdf.
15. Library of Congress, *Journals of the Continental Congress, 1774–1789, Volume 17, 1780, May 8–September 6.* Washington: Government Printing Office, 1910, p. 808.
16. They learned a lesson that would apply eight years later. The Constitution required only nine states to ratify before it came into force. This was actually illegal because at the time they were still operating under the Articles, which required unanimous approval.
17. Adams, pp. 46–48.
18. Virginia's Cession of the Northwest Territory, 2016, http://www.virginiaplaces.org/boundaries/cessions.html#nine.
19. Hurt, p. 93.
20. Hurt, pp. 144–148.
21. Horsman, Reginald, "The Northwest Ordinance and the Shaping of an Expanding Republic," *The Wisconsin Magazine of History* 73, no. 1 (Autumn 1989), p. 28.
22. National Archives Founders Online, "From George Washington to James Duane, 7 September 1783," 2016, http://founders.archives.gov/documents/Washington/99-01-02-11798.
23. Historical Highlights, "The Ordinance of 1784," http://history.house.gov/Historical-Highlights/1700s/Ordinance-of-1784/.
24. Knepper, George W., *Ohio and Its People, Bicentennial Edition,* Kent, OH: Kent State University Press, 2003, p. 54.
25. Dadisman, Stanley E., "Boundaries of West Virginia," *West Virginia Review,* (October 1935), http://www.wvculture.org/history/government/wvboundaries.html.
26. Hurt, p. 148.
27. Knepper, George W., *The Official Ohio Lands Book,* Columbus: Auditor of State, 2002, pp. 7–13.
28. Knepper, *Ohio Lands Book,* pp. 7–13.
29. Knepper, *Ohio Lands Book.* p. 19. "Metes and bounds" was an old English system which depended on natural boundaries, such as rivers, and manmade markers, such as placed stones, to mark out a boundary, regular or irregular.
30. Hurt, p. 149.
31. Hurt, pp. 150–152.
32. Hurt, p. 152.
33. Hurt, p. 152.
34. Hurt, p. 155.
35. Most people were unaware of what was happening in Philadelphia as the deliberations were kept secret. Only when it was time to start the ratification process in September was the proposed constitution unveiled.
36. Horsman, p. 21.
37. Yale Law School, Avalon Project, "Northwest Ordinance; July 13, 1787."
38. "The First Federal Congress," 2016, http://www.archives.gov/exhibits/treasures_of_congress/text/page2_text.html.
39. Yale Law School, Avalon Project, "Northwest Ordinance; July 13, 1787."

40. In 1780 Virginia moved its capital from Williamsburg to Richmond.
41. Ohio History Central, "Treaty of Fort McIntosh (1785)," 2015, http://www.ohiohistorycentral.org/w/Treaty_of_Fort_McIntosh_(1785).
42. Hurt, pp. 103–104.
43. Ohio History Central, "Ohio Indian Wars," 2015, http://www.ohiohistorycentral.org/w/Ohio_Indian_Wars?rec=527.
44. Hurt, p. 121.
45. Hurt, p. 111.
46. Hurt, p. 114.
47. Hurt, p. 118.
48. Ohio History Central, "Ohio Indian Wars."
49. There are various spellings of Greenville, including Green Ville.
50. Ohio History Central, "Treaty of Greenville (1795)," 2015, http://www.ohiohistorycentral.org/w/Treaty_of_Greeneville_(1795).
51. Ohio History Central, "Treaty of Greenville (1795)," 2016; Hurt, p. 142.
52. Rice, Otis K., *West Virginia: A History*, Lexington: University Press of Kentucky, 1985, p. 19.
53. Del Papa, Eugene M., "The Royal Proclamation of 1763: Its Effect upon Virginia Land Companies," *Virginia Magazine of History and Biography* 83, no. 4 (October 1975), p. 409.
54. Neu, Irene D., "Background of the Ohio Company of Associates," retrieved from Manuscripts and Documents of the Ohio Company of Associates, http://library.marietta.edu/spc/FindingAids/Ohio_Company_of_Associates_Finding_Aid.pdf.
55. Marietta College Library, "Manuscripts and Documents of the Ohio Company of Associates," 2015, http://library.marietta.edu/spc/FindingAids/Ohio_Company_of_Associates_Finding_Aid.pdf.
56. Marietta College Library, "Manuscripts and Documents of the Ohio Company of Associates"; Knepper, *Ohio and Its People*, pp. 60–61.
57. Knepper, *Ohio and Its People*, pp. 61–62.
58. Knepper, *Ohio and Its People*, p. 62.
59. Knepper, *Ohio and Its People*, p. 62.
60. Knepper, *Ohio Lands Book*, pp. 28, 30.
61. Knepper, *Ohio Lands Book*, pp. 31–32; Knepper, *Ohio and Its People*, p. 64.
62. Ohio History Central, "Cincinnati, Ohio," 2015, http://www.ohiohistorycentral.org/w/Cincinnati,_Ohio.
63. Knepper, *Ohio Lands Book*. pp. 19–20.
64. Hurt, p. 167.
65. Knepper, *Ohio Lands Book*, p. 20.
66. Knepper, *Ohio Lands Book*, pp. 39–41.
67. Knepper, *Ohio and Its People*, pp. 48–49.
68. Encyclopedia of Cleveland History, "Cleaveland, Moses," 2015, http://ech.case.edu/cgi/article.pl?id=CM10.
69. Knepper, *OhioLands Book*, p. 43.
70. Madison was of the opposite opinion. He thought a larger republic was more sustainable (Federalist 10).
71. Knepper, *Ohio Lands Book*, p. 67.
72. Knepper, *Ohio and Its People*, p. 277.
73. Woodward, Colin, *American Nations: A History of the Eleven Regional Cultures of North America*, New York: Viking, 2011, p. 102.
74. Fischer, David Hackett, *Albion's Seed: Four British Folkways in America*, New York: Oxford University Press, 1989, p. 626. His chapter on the Borderlanders extends over pages 605–782.
75. Fischer, p. 634.
76. Woodward, pp. 174–177; Knepper, *Ohio Lands Book*, p. 24.
77. Hurt, p. 210.
78. Woodward, pp. 183–184.
79. Woodward, map on pages *x* and *xi*.

Chapter Six

1. Mulkearn, Lois, ed., *George Mercer Papers: Relating to the Ohio Company of Virginia*, Pittsburgh: University of Pittsburgh Press, 1954, p. 146.
2. Upham, Warren, "Washington's Canoe Trip Down the Potomac, Related in a Letter to Colonel Innes," *Records of the Past*, Vol. 9. Washington, D.C.: Records of the Past Exploration Society/Waverly, 1910, p. 78.
3. Smith, Claiborne T., "Innes, James," NCpedia, Dictionary of North Carolina Biography, University of North Carolina Press, 1988, http://ncpedia.org/biography/innes-james; Sparks, Jared, *The Writings of George Washington*, Vol. 1, New York: Harper & Brothers, Publishers, 1852, pp. 43, 51. Sparks claims that some artillery went by water up the Potomac to Wills Creek. This seems unlikely because up to that time there was little of no exploration of the river for transportation, and moving artillery up the river for the first time would be reckless. There are conflicting reports on who named Fort Cumberland, Colonel Innes or General Braddock.
4. Upham, p. 74.
5. Upham suggests this might have been a separate trip from the one to deliver the report to Dinwiddie. This seems unlikely considering the time periods involved.
6. Dugout Canoe, Cherokee Heritage Center, Tahlequah, OK, 2015, http://www.cherokeeheritage.org/attractions/dugout-canoe/.
7. Kapsch, Robert J., *The Potomac Canal: George Washington and the Waterway West*, Morgantown: West Virginia University Press, 2007, p. 11.
8. Upham, p. 76.
9. Upham, p. 77.
10. Upham, p. 77.
11. Kapsch, p. 14.
12. Upham, p. 77.
13. Edgar, Lady, *A Colonial Governor in Maryland: Horatio Sharpe and His Times, 1753–1773*, London: Longmans, Green, 1912, p. 1.
14. Dinwiddie to Sharpe, "Correspondence of Governor Sharpe, 1753–1757," Archives of Maryland Online, Vol. 6, p. 76.
15. Dinwiddie to Sharpe, p. 77. The letter from Sharpe to Dinwiddie does not show up in the archive of letters from Sharpe to Dinwiddie.
16. Dinwiddie to Sharpe, p. 97.
17. Gould, C. P., "Money and Transportation in

Maryland, 1720–1765," *Johns Hopkins University Studies in Historical and Political Science*, vol. 33, Baltimore: Johns Hopkins Press, 1915, p. 126; Dowden's Ordinary, http://msa.maryland.gov/megafile/msa/stagsere/se1/se5/016000/016500/016590/pdf/msa_se5_16590.pdf.

18. Hulbert, Archer Butler, *Historic Highways of America, Volume 4, Braddock's Road and Three Relative Papers*, Cleveland, Ohio: Arthur H. Clark, 1903, p. 76.

19. Edgar, pp. 23–24.

20. Cubbison, Douglas, *On Campaign Against Fort Duquesne: The Braddock and Forbes Expeditions, 1755–1758, Through the Experiences of Quartermaster Sir John St. Clair*, Jefferson, NC: McFarland, 2015, p. 5.

21. Edgar, pp. 27–28.

22. Dinwiddie to Sharpe, p. 140.

23. Sargent, Winthrop, ed., *The History of an Expedition against Fort Du Quesne in 1755, under Major-General Edward Braddock*, Philadelphia: J. B. Lippincott & Co. for the Historical Society of Pennsylvania, 1856, pp. 144–145.

24. Pargellis, Stanley, ed., *Military Affairs in North America, 1748–1765*, New York: D. Appleton-Century, 1936, pp. 62–63.

25. Sharpe to Baltimore, "Correspondence of Governor Sharpe. 1753–1757," Archives of Maryland Online, Vol. 6, p. 186. The 250 miles quoted here is in contrast to the 170 miles claimed by others. The 170 mile number is closer to being correct.

26. Pargellis, p. 61.

27. Maryland Gazette; Annapolis, MD; February 11, 1762, as cited in Kapsch, p. 302.

28. Kapsch, p. 26.

29. History World, "History of Canals," 2016, http://www.historyworld.net/wrldhis/PlainTextHistories.asp?historyid=aa19#142.

30. History World, "History of Canals."

31. Kapsch, pp. 27–29. Little Falls is downstream from Great Falls, just above Georgetown.

32. *American Heritage Dictionary of the English Language, Fifth Edition*. S.V. "sluice gates," 2016, http://www.thefreedictionary.com/sluice+gates.

33. Kapsch, pp. 32–42.

34. Hulbert, Archer Butler, *Washington and the West: Being George Washington's Diary of September, 1784*, Cleveland: Arthur H. Clark, 1911, pp. 27–29.

35. Hulbert, *Washington and the West*, pp. 27–85.

36. Hulbert, *Washington and the West*, p. 85.

37. Hulbert, *Washington and the West*, p. 86.

38. Hulbert, *Washington and the West*, p. 86.

39. Hulbert, *Washington and the West*, pp. 92–95.

40. Abbot, W. W., Twohig, Dorothy, eds., *The Papers of George Washington, Confederation Series 2*, Charlottesville: University Press of Virginia, 1992, pp. 86–99, 106–110; Abbot, W. W., "George Washington, the West, and the Union," *Indiana Magazine of History* 84, Issue 1 (March 1988).

41. He probably felt this was necessary because the Potomac lay entirely within Maryland; the Maryland boundary was on the south shore of the river.

42. Fitzpatrick, John C. ed., *The Writings of George Washington from the Original Manuscript Sources, 1745–1799*, Vol. 28, Washington: Government Printing Office, 1938, pp. 71–72.

43. Abbot, W. W., "George Washington, the West, and the Union," pp. 3–14, http://scholarworks.iu.edu/journals/index.php/imh/article/view/10855/15419.

44. Bacon-Foster, Mrs. Cora, *Early Chapters in the Development of the Patomac Route to the West*, Washington: Columbia Historical Society, 1912, pp. 51–53, 57.

45. Abbot, "George Washington, the West, and the Union."

46. Kapsch, pp. 48, 58–59.

47. Fitzpatrick, p. 184.

48. Kapsch, pp. 60–61.

49. Jackson, Donald, Twohig, Dorothy, eds. *The Diaries of George Washington*, Vol. 4, *The Papers of George Washington*. Charlottesville: University Press of Virginia, 1978, http://memory.loc.gov/cgi-bin/query/r?ammem/mgw:@field(DOCID+@lit(wd0418)).

50. Bacon-Foster, pp. 84–86.

51. Kapsch, pp. 79, 82, 85–86.

52. Kapsch, pp. 86, 90.

53. Kapsch, pp. 105–106; Bacon-Foster, p. 115.

54. Achenbach, Joel, *The Grand Idea: George Washington's Potomac and the Race to the West*, New York: Simon & Schuster, 2004, pp. 214–215.

55. Achenbach, p. 215.

56. Bacon-Foster, p. 116.

57. Bacon-Foster, p. 128.

58. Bacon-Foster, p. 139.

59. Some lists of early canals in this country don't even list this project. They start the Canal Age after 1800.

60. Inland Navigation: Connecting the New Republic, 1790–1840, "Canals," 2016, http://xroads.virginia.edu/~hyper/detoc/transport/front.html.

61. United States Resident Population by State: 1790–1990, http://lwd.dol.state.nj.us/labor/lpa/census/1990/poptrd1.htm.

62. Turner, Frederick Jackson, *The Frontier in American History*, New York: Henry Holt, 1921, p. 2.

63. Otterstrom, Samuel M., Earle, Carville, "The Settlement of the United States from 1790 to 1990: Divergent Rates of Growth and the End of the Frontier," *The Journal of Interdisciplinary History* 33, no. 1 (Summer 2002), pp. 59–85, http://www.jstor.org/stable/3656922.

64. The Erie Canal, "Clinton's Big Ditch," 2016, http://www.eriecanal.org/; Welcome to NY Canals, "Erie Canal," 2016, http://www.nycanals.com/Erie_Canal; *"The Erie Canal Story," 2017*, http://www.eriecanalcamillus.com/images/school_tours/teacher_resources/Erie_Canal_Fact_Narrative.pdf; "Canal History," 2017, http://www.canals.ny.gov/history/history.html.

65. Dungan, Nicholas, *Gallatin: America's Swiss Founding Father*, New York: New York University Press, 2010, p. 70, https://www.treasury.gov/about/history/Pages/agallatin.aspx.

66. Adams, Henry, *The Life of Albert Gallatin*, Philadelphia: J. R. Lippincott & Co., 1879, p. 350.

67. *Report of the Secretary of the Treasury, on the Subject of Public Roads and Canals; Made in Pursuance of a Resolution of Senate, of March 2, 1807,*

Washington: Printed by R. C. Weightman, 1808, pp. 5, 22.

68. *Report of the Secretary of the Treasury*, p. 22.

69. Welcome to New York Canals. Cumberland, Maryland, elevation is 627 feet.

70. Ward, George Washington, *The Early Development of the Chesapeake and Ohio Canal Project*, Baltimore: Johns Hopkins Press, September-October–November 1899, pp. 39, 40.

71. Carrying out calculations to hundredths of a foot apparently did not raise any questions. Cost estimates of millions of dollars were also carried out to the penny.

72. *Fifth Annual Report of the President and Directors of the Board of Public Works to the General Assembly of Virginia*, Richmond: Printed by Thomas Ritchie, 1820, p. 94. This report is printed verbatim in Appendix I: Guzy, Dan, *Navigation on the Upper Potomac River and Its Tributaries, Second Edition*, published online by WHILBR-Western Maryland Regional Library, http://www.whilbr.org/Potomac Navigation/index.aspx.

73. Ward, p. 46.

74. Kapsch, pp. 186–192.

75. Ward, pp. 50–51.

76. *Report of the Secretary of the Treasury*, p. 73; Sky, Theodore, *The National Road and the Difficult Path to Sustainable National Investment*, Newark: University of Delaware Press, 2013, pp. 33–34.

77. Ward, p. 71.

78. Ward, pp. 75–76, 81.

79. Ward, pp. 79–83.

80. Hahn, Thomas F., *The Chesapeake & Ohio Canal: Pathway to the Nation's Capital*, Metuchen, NJ: Scarecrow, 1984, p. 5.

81. Stover, John F., *History of the Baltimore and Ohio Railroad*, West Lafayette, IN: Purdue University Press, 1987, p. 25.

82. Ward, pp. 89–90.

83. Hahn, pp. 5–6.

84. Kytle, Elizabeth, *Home on the Canal*, Baltimore: Johns Hopkins University Press, 1983, p. 32.

85. Kytle, pp. 33–43.

86. Ward, p. 93.

87. Kytle, pp. 36–39.

88. Kytle, pp. 39–40.

89. Hahn, pp. 6–7; Kytle, p. 52.

90. Hahn, p. 7.

91. Kytle, pp. 53–56.

92. Kytle, p. 59.

93. Hahn, pp. 7–11.

Chapter Seven

1. Knepper, George W., *Ohio and Its People, Bicentennial Edition*, Kent, OH: Kent State University Press, 1989, pp. 79–81.

2. Gephart, William F., *Transportation and Industrial Development in the Middle West*, Ph.D. Dissertation, Columbia University, 1909, pp. 31–33; Knepper, George W., *The Official Ohio Lands Book*, Columbus: Auditor of State, 2002, p. 36.

3. Vance, Col. John L., "The French Settlement and Settlers of Gallipolis, an Address at the Centennial Celebration at Gallipolis," *Ohio Archaeological and Historical Publications*, Vol. 3, 1900, pp. 9–10, 45–50.

4. Doddridge, Joseph, *Notes on the Settlement and Indian Wars of the Western Parts of Virginia and Pennsylvania from 1763 to 1783*, Pittsburgh: John S. Ritenour and Wm. T. Lindsey, 1912, pp. 96, 97.

5. MacGill, Caroline E., *History of Transportation in the United States before 1860*, Washington, D. C.: Carnegie Institution of Washington, 1917, p. 118.

6. Poen was probably pone, a cornbread.

7. Veech, James, *The Monongahela of Old: Historical Sketches of South-Western Pennsylvania to the Year 1800*, Pittsburgh: For Private Distribution Only, 1858–1892, pp. 37–38.

8. Veech, p. 38. There are about 3.4 bushels per barrel.

9. Wiley, Samuel T., *History of Monongalia County, West Virginia*, Kingwood: Preston, 1883, p. 97.

10. Hulbert, Archer Butler, *The Cumberland Road: Historic Highways of America*, Vol. 10, Cleveland: Arthur H. Clark, 1904, pp. 17–18.

11. Doddridge, p. 80.

12. Doddridge, p. 81.

13. Seward, John Woodhouse, from his mother-in-law's dictation, "The Flitting of the Fenns." These family notes were provided to the author courtesy of a descendant of Seward, Dean G. Pruitt, in 2016. Fenn College in Cleveland, now Cleveland State University, derived its name from contributor Sereno Peck Fenn, who was originally from Tallmadge, Ohio.

14. Verhoeff, Mary, *The Kentucky River Navigation*, Filson Publication no. 28, Louisville, Kentucky: John P. Morton, 1917, p. 68.

15. Kentucky was formed into Kentucky County, Virginia, in 1776.

16. Verhoff, pp. 46–47, 69, 72; Kamper, Ken, Friends of Daniel Boone's Burial Site in Missouri, "Some Things in the Life of Daniel Boone," 2016, http://www.booneburialsite.org/history/dbtimeline.shtml.

17. Wills, Jack, The West Virginia Encyclopedia: "Ebenezer Zane," 2016, http://www.wvencyclopedia.org/articles/1397.

18. Kentucky was now a state, having entered the union in 1792.

19. Although the stated objective was Fort Washington, it is clear his objective was Limestone. Had it been Fort Washington he would have needed help with the ferry across the Little Miami also.

20. Hurt, R., Douglas, *The Ohio Frontier: Crucible of the Old Northwest, 1720–1830*, Bloomington: Indiana University Press, 1996, p. 255.

21. Hurt, pp. 255–256.

22. Dollarhide, William, Ancestry.com GenealogyBlog: "Getting Stumped on Zane's Trace," 2016, http://www.genealogyblog.com/?p=18354.

23. Longfellow, Rickie, U.S. Department of Transportation Highway History; Back in Time: "Zane's Trace," 2016, https://www.fhwa.dot.gov/infrastructure/back0803.cfm.

24. A Little History + Some Facts: How Cincinnati Got Its Name, 2016, http://www.cincinnativiews.net/facts.htm.
25. Gephart, William F., *Transportation and Industrial Development in the Middle West*, Columbia University Ph.D. Thesis, 1909, p. 31.
26. Knepper, *Ohio and its People*, p. 86.
27. Table 1, United States Resident Population by State: 1790–1850, http://lwd.dol.state.nj.us/labor/lpa/census/1990/poptrd1.htm.
28. Table 1, United States Resident Population by State: 1790–1850.
29. Knepper, *Ohio and Its People*, pp. 86–90; Hurt, pp. 278–283.
30. Knepper, *Ohio and Its People*, pp. 86–90; Hurt, pp. 278–283.
31. Knepper, *Ohio and Its People*, pp. 90–91.
32. Knepper, *Ohio and Its People*, pp. 91–93.
33. The Jefferson Monticello, "Louisiana Purchase," 2016, https://www.monticello.org/site/jefferson/louisiana-purchase.
34. U.S. Department of State, Office of the Historian, "Treaty of San Lorenzo/Pinckney's Treaty, 1795," https://history.state.gov/milestones/1784–1800/pickney-treaty.
35. The Jefferson Monticello, "Louisiana Purchase," 2016; Wilson, Gaye, "Jefferson's Big Deal: the Louisiana Purchase," *Monticello Newsletter* 14, no. 1 (Spring 2003), https://www.monticello.org/sites/default/files/inline-pdfs/2003spurchase.pdf.
36. Wilson, The strip of land along the Gulf of Mexico, east from the Mississippi to the Perdido River, was occupied by France as part of the original Louisiana. At the 1763 Treaty of Paris ending the Seven Years War, Great Britain received that strip from France and received Florida from Spain. Great Britain organized the Floridas into East Florida and West Florida; West Florida being the strip from the Mississippi east to the Apalachicola River. Great Britain returned the Floridas to Spain in 1783 in an agreement, separate from the 1783 Treaty of Paris, which ended the War for Independence. The United States still claimed that West Florida was part of the original Louisiana. This is probably the reason Jefferson asked Monroe to buy part of Florida from France although it apparently still belonged to Spain. Encyclopedia Britannica, "West Florida Controversy," 2016, https://www.britannica.com/event/West-Florida-Controversy; Infoplease, "West Florida Controversy," 2016, http://www.infoplease.com/encyclopedia/history/west-florida-controversy.html.
37. Wilson.
38. Abbot, W. W., Twohig, Dorothy, eds., *The Papers of George Washington, Confederation Series, 2, Washington to Harrison October 10, 1784*, Charlottesville: University Press of Virginia, 1992, pp. 92–93.
39. Abbot and Twohig, p. 93
40. Hulbert, *The Cumberland Road*, p. 17.
41. Enabling Act of 1802, http://www.ohiohistorycentral.org/w/Enabling_Act_of_1802_(Transcript).
42. Adams, Henry, ed., *The Writings of Albert Gallatin, Vol. 1, Gallatin to William B. Giles, M.C., 13 February, 1802*, Philadelphia: J. B. Lippincott, 1879, http://oll.libertyfund.org/titles/gallatin-the-writings-of-albert-gallatin-vol-1.
43. Annals of Congress, 7th Congress, 2nd Session, Appendix, p. 1589, https://memory.loc.gov/cgi-bin/ampage?collId=llac&fileName=012/llac012.db&recNum=790.
44. Annals of Congress, 9th Congress, 1st Session, Senate Proceedings, December 18, 1805, p. 24, https://memory.loc.gov/cgi-bin/ampage?collId=llac&fileName=015/llac015.db&recNum=9.
45. Annals of Congress, 9th Congress, 1st Session, Senate Proceedings, December 18, 1805, p. 24.
46. Annals of Congress, 9th Congress, 1st Session, Senate Proceedings, December 18, 1805, pp. 24–25.
47. Annals of Congress, 9th Congress, 1st Session, Senate Proceedings, December 18, 1805, p. 25.
48. Sky, Theodore, *The National Road and the Difficult Path to Sustainable National Investment*, Newark: University of Delaware Press, 2013, p. 16
49. Ninth Congress, Session 1, Ch. 17, 19 1806, Chap. XIX—*An Act to regulate the laying out and making a road from Cumberland, in the state of Maryland, to the state of Ohio*, pp. 357–359, http://legisworks.org/congress/9/session-1/chap-19.pdf.
50. Yale Law School Lillian Goldman Law Library, "Avalon Project: Thomas Jefferson: Sixth Annual Message to Congress, December 2, 1806," 2016, http://avalon.law.yale.edu/19th_century/jeffmes6.asp.
51. Yale Law School Lillian Goldman Law Library, "Avalon Project: Thomas Jefferson: Sixth Annual Message to Congress, December 2, 1806."
52. Sky, p. 18; Young, Jeremiah Simeon, *A Political and Constitutional Study of the Cumberland Road*, Ph.D. Dissertation, University of Chicago, 1902, pp. 37–41.
53. Sky, pp. 19–20.
54. Wood, Joseph S., "The Idea of a National Road," Chapter Three in *The National Road*, Edited by Karl Raitz, Baltimore: Johns Hopkins University Press, 1996, p. 109.
55. Annals of Congress, 9th Congress, 2nd Session, Miscellaneous, No. 220, January 31, 1807, p. 475, https://memory.loc.gov/cgi-bin/ampage?collId=llsp&fileName=037/llsp037.db&Page=474.
56. The choice was between Cumberland and a place called Gwinn's which was apparently on or near the Potomac about ten miles upriver. It was located on the river where the road from Winchester crossed the river. It is no longer shown on present-day maps.
57. American State Papers, 1789–1738, Miscellaneous, Volume 1, Ninth Congress, Second Session, No. 220, Cumberland Road, January 31, 1807, p. 475.
58. American State Papers, 1789–1738, Miscellaneous, Volume 1, Ninth Congress, Second Session, No. 220, Cumberland Road, January 31, 1807, p. 475.
59. American State Papers, 1789–1738, Miscellaneous, Volume 1, Ninth Congress, Second Session, No. 220, Cumberland Road, January 31, 1807, pp. 475–476.
60. Jordan, Philip D., *The National Road*, Indianapolis, New York: Bobbs-Merrill, 1948, p. 75.
61. Day, Reed B., *The Cumberland Road: A History of the National Road*, Apollo, PA: Closson, 1996, pp. 14–15.

62. American State Papers, 1789–1738, Miscellaneous, Volume 1, Ninth Congress, Second Session, No. 220, Cumberland Road, January 31, 1807, pp. 475–476.
63. American State Papers, 1789–1738, Miscellaneous, Volume 1, Ninth Congress, Second Session, No. 220, Cumberland Road, January 31, 1807, p. 476.
64. American State Papers, 1789–1738, Miscellaneous, Volume 1, Ninth Congress, Second Session, No. 220, Cumberland Road, January 31, 1807, p. 474.
65. American State Papers, 1789–1738, Miscellaneous, Volume 1, Tenth Congress, First Session, No. 243, Cumberland Road, February 19, 1808, p. 714.
66. Adams, p. 318.
67. Washington, H. A., Ed., *The Writings of Thomas Jefferson,* Volume 5, New York: Derby & Jackson, 1859, p. 272.
68. Adams, p. 424.
69. Washington, H. A., p. 333; American State Papers, 1789–1783, Miscellaneous, Volume 1,Tenth Congress, Second Session, No. 258, Cumberland Road, December 13, 1808, p. 940.
70. Sky, p. 28.
71. It never quite made it to St. Louis, stopping for lack of funds in Illinois.
72. Wood, p. 109.
73. Jordan, pp. 83–84; American State Papers, 1789–1738, Miscellaneous, Volume 2, Twelfth Congress, First Session, No. 311, Cumberland Road, February 2, 1812, p. 175.
74. American State Papers, 1789–1738, Miscellaneous, Volume 2, Twelfth Congress, First Session, No. 311, Cumberland Road, February 2, 1812, p. 176.
75. Peyton, Billy Joe, "Surveying and Building the Road," Chapter Four in *The National Road,* edited by Karl Raitz, Baltimore: Johns Hopkins University Press, 1996, pp. 139–143.
76. American State Papers, 1789–1738, Miscellaneous, Volume 2, Twelfth Congress, First Session, No. 311, Cumberland Road, February 3, 1812, p. 176.
77. Jordan, pp. 84–88; Peyton, p. 138.
78. Ierley, Merritt, *Traveling the National Road: Across the Centuries on America's First Highway,* Woodstock, NY: Overlook, 1990, p. 48.
79. American State Papers, United States Congress, Miscellaneous, Volume 2, 13th Congress, 2nd Session, No. 356, p. 226; 13th Congress, 3rd Session, No. 379, p. 262; 14th Congress, 1st Session, No.403, pp. 296–298.
80. American State Papers, United States Congress, Miscellaneous, Volume 2, 14th Congress, 1st Session, No. 406. p. 301.
81. American State Papers, United States Congress, Miscellaneous, Volume 2, 14th Congress, 1st Session, No. 406. p. 301.
82. American State Papers, United States Congress, Miscellaneous, Volume 2, 14th Congress, 1st Session, No. 406. p. 302.
83. American State Papers, United States Congress, Miscellaneous, Volume 2, 16th Congress, 1st Session, No. 486. p. 585.
84. Hulbert, *The Cumberland Road,* p. 54.
85. Searight, Thomas B., *The Old Pike: A History of the National Road,* Uniontown, PA: Published by the Author, 1894, p. 266.
86. Searight, p. 107.
87. Richardson, James D., *A Compilation of the Messages and Papers of the Presidents: 1789–1897,* Volume 2, Washington: Government Printing Office, 1896, p. 143.
88. Richardson, p. 191.
89. *A History of Road Building in Maryland,* State Roads Commission of Maryland, 1958, p. 16.
90. Ierley, p. 31.
91. Sioussat, St. George Leakin, *Highway Legislation in Maryland, and Its Influence on the Economic Development of the State, Part III of Maryland Geological Survey, Volume Three,* Baltimore: Johns Hopkins University Press, 1899. p. 162.
92. Laws of Maryland 1785–1791, Volume 204, Page 217, *Archives of Maryland Online,* 2016, http://aomol.msa.maryland.gov/000001/000204/html/am 204—217.html.
93. Laws of Maryland 1785–1791, Volume 204, pp. 217–220.
94. Sioussat, pp. 164–166.
95. Maryland Session Laws, Volume 562, November 1804, Chapter 51, p. 38, *Archives of Maryland Online,* 2016.
96. Old National Pike Milestones, United States Department of the Interior, National Registry of Historic Places Inventory-Nomination Form, 2016, https://mht.maryland.gov/secure/medusa/PDF/Baltimore%20City/B-4286.pdf.
97. *American State Papers, Documents Legislative and Executive of the Congress of the United States, Class X, Miscellaneous, No. 250, Volume I,* Washington: Published by Gales and Seaton, 1834, p. 908.
98. *A History of Road Building in Maryland,* State Roads Commission of Maryland, 1958, p. 30.
99. *A History of Road Building in Maryland,* p. 31; Archives of Maryland Legislative Records, Volume 618, November Session 1812, Chapter 79, pp. 89–92, *Archives of Maryland Online,* 2016.
100. Maryland Legislative Records, Volume 632, December Session 1813, Chapter 122, pp. 113–117, *Archives of Maryland Online,* 2016.
101. *A History of Road Building in Maryland,* p. 32.
102. Maryland Session Laws, Volume 634, January 1816, Chapter 125, p. 136, *Archives of Maryland Online, 2016.*
103. Sioussat, p. 174.
104. *A History of Road Building in Maryland,* p. 33.
105. *A History of Road Building in Maryland,* pp. 33–34.
106. Adams, pp. 84, 721.
107. Statutes at Large, 16th Congress, 1st Session, Chapter 123, pp. 604–605.
108. Statutes at Large, 18th Congress, 2nd Session, Chapter 98, p. 128.
109. Rose, Gregory S., "Extending the Road West," Chapter Five in *The National Road,* edited by Karl Raitz, Baltimore: Johns Hopkins University Press, 1996, p. 172.
110. Hulbert, Archer Butler, *The Old National*

Road: A Chapter of American Expansion, Columbus: F. J. Heer, 1901, pp. 52–53.
    111. Jordan, pp. 90–92; Searight, pp. 100–106.
    112. Searight, p. 105.
    113. Hulbert, *The Cumberland Road*, pp. 83–84.
    114. Rose, p. 173.
    115. Jordan, pp. 169–170.
    116. Searight, p. 104.
    117. Searight, p. 106.
    118. Statutes at Large, 21st Congress, 2nd Session, Chapter 63, p. 469.
    119. Table 1, United States Resident Population by State: 1790–1850.
    120. Jordan, p. 137.
    121. Zimmerman, Carrie B., "Ohio, the Gateway of the West," *Ohio Archaeological and Historical Quarterly* 40, no. 1 (January 1931), pp. 147–148. He cites Carroll Miller, *Pennsylvania Historical Magazine*, 1927, http://publications.ohiohistory.org/ohj/browse/displaypages.php?display[]=0040&display[]=137&display[]=181.
    122. Schneider, Norris F., *The National Road: Main Street of America*, Columbus: Ohio Historical Society, 1975, p. 28.
    123. Rose, pp, 170–176.
    124. Buley, R. Carlyle, *The Old Northwest: Pioneer Period, 1815–1840, Volume 1*, Indianapolis: Indiana Historical Society, 1950, p. 477.
    125. Lewman family history provided to the author by Ms. Alzada Roberts, a Lewman family descendant.
    126. "The Conestoga Wagon," *Pennsylvania Historical and Museum Commission Historic Pennsylvania Leaflet No. 15, 1997*.
    127. "The Conestoga Wagon."
    128. "The Conestoga Wagon."
    129. Searight, p. 144.
    130. Searight, p. 16.
    131. Searight, p. 109.
    132. Hulbert, *The Cumberland Road*, pp. 119–120.
    133. Hulbert, *The Cumberland Road*, p. 57.
    134. Searight, pp. 109–110.
    135. Searight, p. 112; Hulbert, *The Cumberland Road*, p. 132.
    136. Hulbert, *The Cumberland Road*, p. 132.
    137. Searight, p. 113.
    138. Hulbert, *The Cumberland Road*, pp. 126–127.
    139. Searight, pp. 147–148.
    140. Hulbert, *The Cumberland Road*, p. 144; Searight, p. 164.
    141. Searight, p. 153.
    142. Searight, p. 181.
    143. Ierley, p. 75.
    144. Ierly, p. 60.
    145. Jordan, pp. 233–251.
    146. Jordan, pp. 233–251.
    147. Dilts, James D., *The Great Road: The Building of the Baltimore & Ohio, the Nation's First Railroad, 1828–1853*, Stanford, CA: Stanford University Press, 1993, p. 283.
    148. Searight, p. 298.
    149. Hulbert, Archer Butler, *The Cumberland Road*, pp. 110–112.
    150. Colten, Craig E., "Adapting the Road to New Technology," Chapter Six in *The National Road*, edited by Karl Raitz, Baltimore: Johns Hopkins University Press, 1996, p. 197.
    151. Wood, p. 114.

Chapter Eight

    1. Railroad Museum of Pennsylvania, The Empire Builders, "Main Line of Public Works, 1834–1857," pp. 6–7, http://www.rrmuseumpa.org/education/Curriculum%20Guide%20-%20Middle%20Level.pdf.
    2. Railroad Museum of Pennsylvania, The Empire Builders, "Main Line of Public Works, 1834–1857," p. 8.
    3. Carradice, Phil, Wales History, "The Mumbles Railway," 24 March 2011, http://www.bbc.co.uk/blogs/waleshistory/2011/03/the_mumbles_railway.html.
    4. Palermo, Elizabeth, Live Science, "Who Invented the Steam Engine?" 2016, http://www.livescience.com/44186-who-invented-the-steam-engine.html; The Transcontinental Railroad, "It's All About Steam," 2016, http://railroad.lindahall.org/essays/locomotives.html.
    5. "George Stephenson," *Encyclopedia Britannica, Encyclopedia Britannica Online*, Encyclopedia Britannica, 2016, http://www.britannica.com/biography/George-Stephenson; The Transcontinental Railroad, "It's All About Steam," 2016.
    6. Dilts, James D., *The Great Road: The Building of the Baltimore & Ohio, the Nation's First Railroad, 1828–1853*, Stanford, CA: Stanford University Press, 1993, p. 26.
    7. Dilts, p. 26.
    8. Dilts, pp. 38–40.
    9. Dilts, p. 40.
    10. Dilts, p. 40.
    11. Dilts, pp. 46, 48.
    12. Dilts, p. 57.
    13. Later restrictions moved the point of intersection with the Ohio farther north, to Wheeling.
    14. Dilts, pp. 45–59, *passim*.
    15. This can be carried back further since the original railcar designers had previously designed carts, and carts go back to Roman times.
    16. Stover, John F., *History of the Baltimore and Ohio Railroad*, West Lafayette, IN: Purdue University Press, 1987, pp. 31–32.
    17. American-Rails.com, "Railroad Track, The "Highway" For Trains," 2016, http://www.american-rails.com/railroad-track.html.
    18. Stover, pp. 29–34, *passim*.
    19. Stover, pp. 37–38, *passim*.
    20. Stover, p. 39; Dilts, p. 67.
    21. Dilts, p. 150.
    22. Dilts, p. 90; Stover, pp. 31, 34–35.
    23. Dilts, pp. 90–91; Stover, pp. 35–36.
    24. Baltimore and Ohio Railroad Timeline, 2016, http://www.borail.net/Timeline.html; Stover, p. 39; Dilts, p. 187.
    25. Stover, pp. 52, 67; Dilts, pp. 242, 315.
    26. Dilts, pp. 239–240; Baltimore and Ohio Timeline.

27. Dilts, pp. 277–278.
28. Dilts, p. 291.
29. Dilts, p. 293.
30. Dilts, pp. 292–293, *passim*.
31. Dilts, p. 315, Stover, p. 66.
32. Stover, p. 68.
33. Stover, p. 67; Baltimore and Ohio Railroad Timeline.
34. Stover, pp. 69–71.
35. University of Missouri Library Systems Digital Library, John W. Barriger III, National Railroad Library, "American Railroad Journal, page 262, April 27, 1850," http://digital.library.umsystem.edu/cgi/t/text/pageviewer-idx?c=arj;cc=arj;sid=a71b2c6292e4fab157094463a5eb1401;q1=1850;rgn=date;idno=arj18500427;view=image;seq=6.
36. Stover, pp. 69–72, *passim*.
37. Dilts, pp. 387–388; Erie Railroad Company and its development, "Brief History, Timeline, Presidents, etc., of the Erie Railroad Company," 2016, http://trainmanjim.tripod.com/id13.html.
38. This was true but there was a gap at the Ohio River. The first bridges over the Ohio were started at Wheeling in 1868 and in Parkersburg in 1869 and were completed in 1871. Baltimore and Ohio Railroad timeline.
39. Baltimore & Ohio, "The Baltimore & Ohio Railroad," 2016, http://csx.history.railfan.net/history/histbo.html.
40. Dilts, p. 295.
41. United States Resident Population by State: 1790–1990, http://lwd.dol.state.nj.us/labor/lpa/census/1990/poptrd1.htm.
42. Wilhelm, Hubert G. H., and Noble, Allen G., "Ohio's Settlement Landscape," Chapter Six in Peacefull, Leonard, ed., *A Geography of Ohio*, Kent, OH: Kent State University Press, 1996, pp. 84–89. Technically the Cumberland Road went from Cumberland, Maryland, to Wheeling, Virginia. When it was extended past Wheeling it became known as the National Road. When discussing entry into Ohio on the road from the east it seems appropriate to refer to it as the original Cumberland Road.
43. Wilhelm, and Noble, pp. 83–84; Ohio Memory, "Immigration and Ethnic Heritage in Ohio to 1903," http://www.ohiohistoryhost.org/ohiomemory/wp-content/uploads/2014/12/TopicEssay_Immigration.pdf.
44. Wilhelm and Noble, p. 83; Woodard, Colin, *American Nations: A History of the Eleven Rival Regional Cultures of North America*, New York: Viking, 2011, front map; Fischer, David Hackett, and Kelly, James C., *Bound Away: Virginia and the Westward Movement*, Charlottesville: University Press of Virginia, 2000, p. 139.
45. Digital History, "The Pre-Civil War South: The South's Economy," 2016, http://www.digitalhistory.uh.edu/disp_textbook.cfm?smtID=2&psid=3558.
46. Department of Transportation, Federal Highway Administration, Highway History, "From Names to Numbers: The Origins of the U.S. Numbered Highway System," 2016, https://www.fhwa.dot.gov/infrastructure/numbers.cfm.

Bibliography

Abbot, W. W. "George Washington, the West, and the Union." *Indiana Magazine of History* 84, Issue 1, March 1988. http://scholarworks.iu.edu/journals/index.php/imh/article/view/10855/15419.

Abbot, W. W., and Dorothy Twohig, eds. *The Papers of George Washington, Confederation Series 2*. Charlottesville: University Press of Virginia, 1992.

Achenbach, Joel. *The Grand Idea: George Washington's Potomac and the Race to the West*. New York: Simon & Schuster, 2004.

Adams, Henry. *The Life of Albert Gallatin*. Philadelphia: J. R. Lippincott & Co., 1879.

Adams, Herbert B. "Maryland's Influence in Founding a National Commonwealth, on the Accession of Public Lands by the Old Confederation." A paper read before the Maryland Historical Society, April 9, 1877. Baltimore, 1877.

Alvord, Clarence W., and Lee Bidgood. *The First Explorations of the Trans-Alleghany Region by the Virginians, 1650-1674*. Cleveland: Arthur H. Clark, 1912.

_____. "The Genesis of the Proclamation of 1763." *Michigan Pioneer and Historical Society, Historical Collections, Collections and Researches*, vol. 36, Lansing: Wyncoop Hallenbeck Crawford, State Printers, 1908.

Ambler, George H. *George Washington and the West*. Chapel Hill: niversity of North Carolina Press, 1936.

American State Papers. Documents Legislative and Executive of the Congress of the United States, Class X, Miscellaneous, No. 250, Volume I, Washington: Gales and Seaton, 1834.

_____. 1789-1738, Miscellaneous, Volume 1, Ninth Congress, Second Session, No. 220, Cumberland Road, January 31, 1807.

_____. 1789-1738, Miscellaneous, Volume 1, Tenth Congress, First Session, No. 243, Cumberland Road, February 19, 1808.

_____. 1789-1738, Miscellaneous, Volume 2, Twelfth Congress, First Session, No. 311, Cumberland Road, February 2, 1812.

_____. United States Congress, Miscellaneous, Volume 2, 13th Congress, 2nd Session, No. 356.

_____. 13th Congress, 3rd Session, No. 379.

_____. 14th Congress, 1st Session, No. 403.

_____. United States Congress, Miscellaneous, Volume 2, 14th Congress, 1st Session, No. 406.

_____. United States Congress, Miscellaneous, Volume 2, 16th Congress, 1st Session, No. 486.

Anderson, Fred. *Crucible of War: The Seven Years' War and the Fate of Empire in British North America, 1754-1766*. New York: Alfred A. Knopf, 2000.

Andrews, Matthew Page. *History of Maryland: Province and State*. Hatboro, PA: Tradition, 1965.

Annals of Congress, 7th Congress, 2nd Session, Appendix, p. 1589, https://memory.loc.gov/cgi-bin/ampage?collId=llac&fileName=012/llac012.db&recNum=790.

_____. 9th Congress, 1st Session, Senate Proceedings, December 18, 1805. https://memory.loc.gov/cgi-bin/ampage?collId=llac&fileName=015/llac015.db&recNum=9.

_____. 9th Congress, 2nd Session, Miscellaneous, No. 220.January 31, 1807. https://memory.loc.gov/cgi-bin/ampage?collId=llsp&fileName=037/llsp037.db&Page=474.

Archives of Maryland Online, Dinwiddie to Sharpe. "Correspondence of Governor Sharpe, 1753-1757," Volume 6.

_____. Sharpe to Baltimore. "Correspondence of Governor Sharpe. 1753-1757," Volume 6.

_____. Laws of Maryland 1785-1791, Volume 204, 2016.

_____. Session Laws, Volume 562, November 1804, Chapter 51, 2016.

_____. Legislative Records, Volume 618, November Session 1812, Chapter 79.

_____. Legislative Records. Volume 632, December Session 1813, Chapter 122, 2016.

_____. Session Laws, Volume 634. January 1816, Chapter 125. *2016.*

Bacon-Foster, Mrs. Cora. *Early Chapters in the Development of the Potomac Route to the West*. Washington: Columbia Historical Society, 1912.
Bailey, Kenneth P. *Christopher Gist: Colonial Frontiersman, Explorer, and Indian Agent*. Hamden, CT: Archon, 1976.
_____. *The Ohio Company of Virginia and the Westward Movement, 1748-1792: A Chapter in the History of the Colonial Frontier*. Glendale, CA: Arthur H. Clark, 1939. (Reprinted in India by Isha Books, New Delhi, 2013.)
_____. *Thomas Cresap, Maryland Frontiersman*. Boston: Christopher Publishing House, 1944.
Baker, Norman L. *Braddock's Road: Mapping the British Expedition from Alexandria to the Monongahela*. Charleston: History, 2013.
Bayliff, William H. *The Maryland-Pennsylvania and the Maryland-Delaware Boundaries, Bulletin 4, Second Addition*. Annapolis: Maryland Board of Natural Resources, July 1959.
Bell, Carl D. *The Development of Western Maryland, 1715-1753*. University of Maryland Master of Arts Thesis, 1948.
Billington, Ray A. "The Fort Stanwix Treaty of 1768." *New York History* 25, no. 2 (April 1944).
Brymner, Douglas, Archivist. *Report on Canadian Archives, 1889*. Ottawa: Brown Chamberlain, Printer to the Queen's Most Excellent Majesty, 1890.
Buley, R. Carlyle. *The Old Northwest: Pioneer Period, 1815-1840, Volume 1*. Indianapolis: Indiana Historical Society, 1950.
Caley, Percy B. "Lord Dunmore and the Pennsylvania-Virginia Boundary Dispute." Presented at a meeting of the Historical Society of Western Pennsylvania on April 26, 1938. https://journals.psu.edu/wph/article/viewFile/2118/1951.
Campbell, Charles. *History of the Colony and Ancient Dominion of Virginia*. Philadelphia: J.B. Lippincott, 1860.
Chernow, Ron. *Washington: A Life*. New York: Penguin, 2010.
Clark, Jerry E. *The Shawnee*. Lexington: University Press of Kentucky, 1993.
Clark, Sandra H. B. *Birth of the Mountains: The Geologic Story of the Southern Appalachian Mountains*. U.S. Geological Survey, Department of the Interior [no date], http://www.usgs.gov.
Craig, Neville B. *Lecture upon the Controversy between Pennsylvania and Virginia about the Boundary Line*. Pittsburgh: A. Jaynes—Franklin Head—Opposite Post Office, 1843.
Cubbison, Douglas. *On Campaign Against Fort Duquesne: The Braddock and Forbes Expeditions, 1755-1758, Through the Experiences of Quartermaster Sir John St. Clair*. Jefferson, NC: McFarland, 2015.
Dadisman, Stanley E. "Boundaries of West Virginia." *The West Virginia Review*, October 1935. http://www.wvculture.org/history/government/wvboundaries.html.
Darlington, William M. *Christopher Gist's Journals with Historical, Geographical and Ethnological Notes and Biographies of His Contemporaries*. Pittsburgh: J. R. Weldin & Co., 1893.
Day, Reed B. *The Cumberland Road: A History of the National Road*. Apollo, PA: Closson, 1996.
Del Papa, Eugene M. "The Royal Proclamation of 1763: Its Effect upon Virginia Land Companies." *Virginia Magazine of History and Biography* 83, no. 4 (October 1975).
Dilts, James D. *The Great Road: The Building of the Baltimore & Ohio, the Nation's First Railroad, 1828-1853*. Stanford, CA: Stanford University Press, 1993.
Doddridge, Joseph. *Notes on the Settlement and Indian Wars of the Western Parts of Virginia and Pennsylvania from 1763 to 1783*. Pittsburgh: John S. Ritenour and Wm. T. Lindsey, 1912.
Dollarhide, William. *Map Guide to American Migration Routes, 1735-1815*. Bountiful, UT: HeritageQuest, 2000.
Donehoo, George P. "The Indians of the Past and of the Present." *Pennsylvania Magazine of History and Biography* 46, no. 3 (1922).
Dungan, Nicholas. *Gallatin: America's Swiss Founding Father*. New York: New York University Press, 2010. https://www.treasury.gov/about/history/Pages/agallatin.aspx.
Early Recognized Treaties with American Indian Nations. "Ratified Treaty #1: The Great Treaty of 1722 Between the Five Nations, the Mahicans, and the Colonies of New York, Virginia, and Pennsylvania," 2016. http://treatiesportal.unl.edu/earlytreaties/treaty.00001.html
_____. "Ratified Treaty #3: A Treaty Held at the Town of Lancaster, by the Honourable the Lieutenant Governor of the Province, and the Honourable the Commissioners for the Province of Virginia and Maryland, with the Indians of the Six Nations in June, 1744," 2015. http://earlytreaties.unl.edu/treaty.00003.html.
_____. "Ratified Treaty #4: Treaty of Logstown, 1752," 2015. http://earlytreaties.unl.edu/treaty.00004.html.
"The Early Westward Movement of Virginia, 1722-1734." *Virginia Magazine of History and Biography* 13, no. 1 (July 1905).
Edgar, Lady. *A Colonial Governor in Maryland: Horatio Sharpe and His Times, 1753-1773*. London: Longmans, Green, 1912.
Ferling, John E. *The First of Men: A Life of George Washington*. Knoxville: University of Tennessee Press, 1988.
Fischer, David Hackett. *Albion's Seed: Four British Folkways in America*. New York: Oxford University Press, 1989.

_____. *Champlain's Dream*. New York: Simon & Schuster, 2008.
_____ and James C. Kelly. *Bound Away: Virginia and the Westward Movement*. Charlottesville: University Press of Virginia, 2000.
Fitzpatrick, John C. ed. *The Writings of George Washington from the Original Manuscript Sources, 1745-1799*. Vol. 28. Washington: Government Printing Office, 1938.
Fleming, George Thornton. *History of Pittsburgh and Environs: From Prehistoric Days to the Beginning of the American Revolution, Volume One*. New York and Chicago: American Historical Society, 1922.
Galbreath, C. B., ed. *Expedition of Celoron to the Ohio Country in 1749*. Columbus, OH: F. J. Heer, 1921.
Gephart, William F. *Transportation and Industrial Development in the Middle West*. Ph.D. Dissertation, Columbia University, 1909.
Giddens, Paul H. "The French and Indian War in Maryland, 1753-1756." *Maryland Historical Magazine* 30, no. 4 (December 1935).
Gist, Christopher. *George Mercer Papers: Relating to the Ohio Company of Virginia*, compiled and edited by Lois Mulkearn. Pittsburgh: University of Pittsburgh Press, 1954.
Gould, Clarence P. *Money and Transportation in Maryland, 1720-1765*. Johns Hopkins University Studies in Historical and Political Science, Series 33, No. 1. Baltimore: Johns Hopkins Press, 1915.
Hahn, Thomas F. *The Chesapeake & Ohio Canal: Pathway to the Nation's Capital*. Metuchen, NJ: Scarecrow, 1984.
Handbook of Americans Indians. Bureau of American Ethnology, Bulletin 30, part 2.
Hanna, Charles Augustus. *The Wilderness Trail, Volume One*. New York and London: G. P. Putnam's Sons/Knickerbocker, 1911.
_____. *The Wilderness Trail or the Ventures and Adventures of the Pennsylvania Traders on the Allegheny Path, Volume Two*. New York and London: G. P. Putnam's Sons, 1911.
Hildreth, S. F. *Pioneer History: Being an Account of the First Examinations of the Ohio Valley, and the Early Settlement of the Northwest Territory*. Cincinnati: H. W. Derby & Co., Publishers, 1848.
Horsman, Reginald. "The Northwest Ordinance and the Shaping of an Expanding Republic." *Wisconsin Magazine of History* 73, no. 1 (Autumn 1989).
Hulbert, Archer Butler. *Braddock's Road and Three Relative Papers, Volume 4*. Cleveland: Arthur H. Clark, 1903.
_____. *The Cumberland Road: Historic Highways of America, Volume 10*. Cleveland: Arthur H. Clark, 1904.
_____. *The Old National Road: A Chapter of American Expansion*. Columbus: F. J. Heer, 1901.
_____. *Washington and the West: Being George Washington's Diary of September 1784*. Cleveland: Arthur H. Clark, 1911.
Hurt, Douglas R. *The Ohio Frontier: Crucible of the Old Northwest, 1720-1830*. Bloomington and Indianapolis: Indiana University Press, 1996.
Ierley, Merritt. *Traveling the National Road: Across the Centuries on America's First Highway*. Woodstock, NY: Overlook, 1990.
Iroquois Indians: A Documentary History. "July 19, 1701 Deed or Nanfan Treaty: Deed from the Five Nations to the King of Their Beaver Hunting Ground." Pp. 908-911, Reel 6, Newberry Library, Chicago. http://www.sixnations.ca/LandsResources/NanFanTreaty.pdf.
Jackson, Donald, and Dorothy Twohig, eds. *The Diaries of George Washington*. Vol. 4. *The Papers of George Washington*. Charlottesville: University Press of Virginia, 1978, http://memory.loc.gov/cgi-bin/query/r?ammem/mgw:@field(DOCID+@lit(wd0418)).
James, Alfred P. *The Ohio Company and Its Inner History*. New York: University of Pittsburgh Press/American Book-Stratford, 1959.
Jennings, Francis. *The Ambiguous Iroquois Empire*. New York: W. W. Norton, 1984.
Jordan, Philip D. *The National Road*. Indianapolis: Bobbs-Merrill, 1948.
Kapsch, Robert J. *The Potomac Canal: George Washington and the Waterway West*. Morgantown: West Virginia University Press, 2007.
Kemper, Charles E. ed. "The Early Westward Movement of Virginia, 1722-1734: As Shown by the Proceedings of the Colonial Council." *Virginia Magazine of History and Biography* 13, no. 2 (October 1905).
Knepper, George W. *The Official Ohio Lands Book*. Columbus: Auditor of State, 2002.
_____. *Ohio and Its People, Bicentennial Edition*. Kent: Kent State University Press, 2003.
Kytle, Elizabeth. *Home on the Canal*. Baltimore: Johns Hopkins University Press, 1983.
Land, Aubrey C. *Colonial Maryland: A History*. Millwood, NY: KTO, 1981.
_____. "A Land Speculator in the Opening of Western Maryland." *Maryland Historical Magazine* 48, no. 3 (September 1953).
Laycock, John Kennedy. "Braddock's Road." *Pennsylvania Magazine of History and Biography*, vol. 38 (1914).
Lewin, Howard. "A Frontier Diplomat: Andrew Montour." *Pennsylvania History* 33, no. 2 (April 1966).
Leyland, Herbert T. "The Ohio Company: A Colonial Corporation." *Quarterly Publication of the Historical and Philosophical Society of Ohio* 16, no. 1 (January-June 1921).
Library of Congress. *Journals of the Continental Congress, 1774-1789, Volume 9, 1777, October 3-December 31*. Washington: Government Printing Office, 1907.

_____. *Journals of the Continental Congress, 1774–1789, Volume 17, 1780, May 8–September 6.* Washington: Government Printing Office, 1910.

_____. "Map of Augusta Co., Virginia, 1738–1770," https://www.loc.gov/item/99446927/.

_____. Web Guides, Primary Documents in American History. "The Articles of Confederation," 2016, http://www.loc.gov/rr/program/bib/ourdocs/articles.html.

"List of Early Land Patents and Grants." *Virginia Magazine of History and Biography*, vol. 5, 1898.

Lowdermilk, William Harrison. *History of Cumberland (Maryland).* Washington, D.C.: James Anglim, 1878.

Lucas, Charles Prestwood, Sir. *A Historical Geography of the British Colonies, Vol. V, Canada-Part I (New France).* London, Edinburgh, New York, Oxford: Clarendon, 1901.

MacGill, Caroline E. *History of Transportation in the United States before 1860.* Washington, D. C.: Carnegie Institution of Washington, 1917.

Maryland Gazette. Annapolis, February 11, 1762.

Maryland State Archives, Proceedings and Acts of the General Assembly, 1758–1761, vol. 56, p. 105, December 15, 1758.

Mayre, William. "Patowmeck Above Ye Inhabitants." *Maryland Historical Magazine* 30, no. 2 (June 1935).

McClane, Debra Alderson. *Images of America: Botetourt County.* Charlestown, SC: Arcadia, 2007.

McConnell, Michael N. *A Country Between: The Upper Ohio Valley and Its People, 1724–1774.* Lincoln: University of Nebraska Press, 1992.

McDonald, Forrest. *The Presidency of George Washington.* Lawrence: University Press of Kansas, 1974.

Morse, Jedidiah. *The American Geography.* London: Printed for John Stockdale, Piccadilly, 1794.

Mulkearn, Lois, comp. and ed. *George Mercer Papers: Relating to the Ohio Company of Virginia.* Pittsburgh: University of Pittsburgh Press, 1954.

National Archives Founders Online. "Expedition to the Ohio, 1754: Narrative," 2016, http://founders.archives.gov/documents/Washington/01-01-02-0004-0002.

_____. "From George Washington to James Duane, 7 September 1783," 2016, http://founders.archives.gov/documents/Washington/99-01-02-11798.

Nead, Daniel Wunderlich, M.D. *The Pennsylvania-German in the Settlement of Maryland.* Lancaster: Pennsylvania-German Society, 1914.

Neu, Irene D. "Background of the Ohio Company of Associates." Manuscripts and Documents of the Ohio Company of Associates, http://library.marietta.edu/spc/FindingAids/Ohio_Company_of_Associates_Finding_Aid.pdf.

Ninth Congress, Session 1, Ch. 17, 19 1806, Chap. XIX—*An Act to Regulate the Laying Out and Making a Road from Cumberland, in the State of Maryland, to the State of Ohio.*

Nixon, Lily Lee. "Colonel James Burd in the Campaign of 1759." Read at a meeting of the Historical Society of Western Pennsylvania on March 26, 1936. https://journals.psu.edu/wph/article/viewFile/1730/1578.

Old National Pike Milestones, United States Department of the Interior, National Registry of Historic Places Inventory-Nomination Form, 2016. https://mht.maryland.gov/secure/medusa/PDF/Baltimore%20City/B-4286.pdf.

Otterstrom, Samuel M., and Carville Earle. "The Settlement of the United States from 1790 to 1990: Divergent Rates of Growth and the End of the Frontier." *Journal of Interdisciplinary History* 33, no. 1 (summer 2002). http://www.jstor.org/stable/3656922.

Pargellis, Stanley, ed. *Military Affairs in North America, 1748–1765.* London, New York: D. Appleton-Century, 1936.

Parkman, Francis. *La Salle and the Discovery of the Great West: France and England in North America, Part Third.* Boston: Little, Brown, 1908. http://www.gutenberg.org/files/40143/40143-h/40143-h.htm.

Peacefull, Leonard, ed. *A Geography of Ohio.* Kent, OH: Kent State University Press, 1996.

Pendleton, William C. *History of Tazewell County and Southwest Virginia, 1748–1920.* Richmond: W. C. Hill, 1920.

Pennsylvania Archives, Series I.

Porter, Frank W. III. "Expanding the Domain: William Gooch and the Northern Neck Boundary Dispute." *Maryland Historian* 5 (Spring 1974).

_____. "From Backcountry to County: The Delayed Settlement of Western Maryland." *Maryland Historical Magazine* 70, no. 4 (Winter 1975).

_____. "From Back Country to County: The Role of Economics and Politics in the Settlement of Western Maryland." University of Maryland Master of Arts Thesis, 1973.

"The Proclamation of 1763." *Michigan Pioneer and Historical Society, Historical Collections, Collections and Researches.* Vol. 36. Lansing: Wyncoop Hallenbeck Crawford, State Printers, 1908.

Raitz, Karl, ed. *The National Road.* Baltimore: Johns Hopkins University Press, 1996.

Report of the Secretary of the Treasury, on the Subject of Public Roads and Canals; Made in Pursuance of a Resolution of Senate, of March 2, 1807. Washington: R. C. Weightman, 1808.

Rice, Otis K. *West Virginia: A History.* Lexington: University Press of Kentucky, 1985.

Richardson, James D. *A Compilation of the Messages and Papers of the Presidents: 1789–1897.* Vol. 2. Washington: Government Printing Office, 1896.

Russell, William, T. *Maryland: The Land of Sanctuary; A History of Religious Toleration in Maryland from the First Settlements Until the American Revolution*. Baltimore: J. H. Furst, 1907.
Sargent, Winthrop. *The History of an Expedition Against Fort Du Quesne in 1755 Under Major-General Edward Braddock*. Philadelphia: Lippincott, Grambo & Co. for the Historical Society of Pennsylvania, 1856.
Schneider, Norris F. *The National Road: Main Street of America*. Columbus: Ohio Historical Society, 1975.
Searight, Thomas B. *The Old Pike: A History of the National Road*. Uniontown, PA: Published by the Author, 1894.
Simpson-Poffenbarger, Livia Nye. *The Battle of Point Pleasant: A Battle of the Revolution, October 10, 1774*. Point Pleasant, WV: State Gazette, 1909.
Sioussat, St. George Leakin. "Highway Legislation in Maryland and Its Influence on the Economic Development of the State." *Maryland Geological Survey*, Vol. Three. Baltimore: John Hopkins Press, 1899.
Sky, Theodore. *The National Road and the Difficult Path to Sustainable National Investment*. Newark: University of Delaware Press 2013.
Sparks, Jared. *The Writings of George Washington; Being His Correspondence, Addresses, Messages, and other Papers, Official and Private, Selected and Published from the Original Manuscripts, Volume II*. Boston: Russell, Ordione and Metcalf and Milliard, Gray and Co., 1834.
_____. *The Writings of George Washington*. Vol. 1, New York: Harper & Brothers, Publishers, 1852.
State Roads Commission of Maryland. *A History of Road Building in Maryland*. 1958.
Statutes at Large, 16th Congress, 1st Session, Chapter 123.
_____. 18th Congress, 2nd Session, Chapter 98.
_____. 21st Congress, 2nd Session, Chapter 63.
Stover, John F. *History of the Baltimore and Ohio Railroad*. West Lafayette, IN: Purdue University Press, 1987.
Temple, Henry. "Braddock's Road," *Ohio Valley Historical Association, Proceedings of the Second Annual Meeting, Marietta, Ohio, November 28–29, 1908*. Columbus, OH: Fred J. Heer, 1909.
"Treaty of Lancaster, 1722." *The Virginia Magazine of History and Biography* 13, no. 2 (October 1905).
Turner, Frederick Jackson. *The Frontier in American History*. New York: Henry Holt, 1921.
Upham, Warren. "Washington's Canoe Trip Down the Potomac, Related in a Letter to Colonel Innes." *Records of the Past*. Vol. 9. Washington, D.C.: Records of the Past Exploration Society/Waverly, 1910.
Vance, Col. John L. "The French Settlement and Settlers of Gallipolis, an Address at the Centennial Celebration at Gallipolis." *Ohio Archaeological and Historical Publications*. Vol. 3, 1900.
Veech, James. *The Monongahela of Old: Historical Sketches of South-Western Pennsylvania to the Year 1800*. Pittsburgh: For Private Distribution Only, 1858–1892.
Verhoeff, Mary. *The Kentucky River Navigation, Filson Publication no. 28*. Louisville, KY: John P. Morton, 1917.
Volwiler, A. T. "George Croghan and the Westward Movement, 1741–1782." *Pennsylvania Magazine of History and Biography* 46, no. 4 (1922).
Walden, Carl, and Molly Braun. *Atlas of the North American Indian*. New York: Facts on File, 1985.
Wallace, Anthony F. C. "Origins of Iroquois Neutrality: The Grand Settlement of 1701." *Pennsylvania History* 24, no. 3 (July 1957).
Wallace, Paul A.W. *Conrad Weiser, Friend of Colonist and Mohawk*. Philadelphia: University of Pennsylvania Press, 1945.
_____. *Indian Paths of Pennsylvania*. Harrisburg: Commonwealth of Pennsylvania, Pennsylvania Historical and Museum Commission, 1965.
Walsh, Richard, and William Lloyd Fox, eds. *Maryland: A History, 1632–1974*. Baltimore: Maryland Historical Society, 1974.
Ward, George Washington. *The Early Development of the Chesapeake and Ohio Canal Project*. Baltimore: Johns Hopkins Press, September-October-November, 1899.
Washington, H. A., ed. *The Writings of Thomas Jefferson*. Vol. 5. New York: Derby & Jackson, 1859.
Wiley, Samuel T. *History of Monongalia County, West Virginia*. Kingwood: Preston Publishing Company, 1883.
Woodward, Colin. *American Nations: A History of the Eleven Regional Cultures of North America*. New York: Viking, 2011.
Wroth, Lawrence C. "The Story of Thomas Cresap, A Maryland Pioneer." *Maryland Historical Magazine* 9, no. 1 (March 1914).
Yale Law School Lillian Goldman Law Library. "Avalon Project: Charter of Acadia Granted by Henry IV of France to Pierre du Gast, Sieur de Monts; December 18, 1603," 2014, http://avalon.law.yale.edu/17th_century/charter_001.asp.
_____. "Avalon Project: The First Charter of Virginia; April 10, 1606," 2014, http://avalon.law.yale.edu/17th_century/va01.asp.
_____. "Avalon Project: The Second Charter of Virginia; May 23, 1609," 2014, http://avalon.law.yale.edu/17th_century/va02.asp.
_____. "Avalon Project: The Charter of New England: 1620," 2014, http://avalon.law.yale.edu/17th_century/mass01.asp.

———. "Avalon Project: The Charter of Massachusetts Bay: 1629," 2014, http://avalon.law.yale.edu/17th_century/mass03.asp.
———. "Avalon Project: The Charter of Maryland: 1632," 2015, http://avalon.law.yale.edu/17th_century/ma01.asp.
———. "Avalon Project: The Charter for the Province of Pennsylvania-1681," 2015. http://avalon.law.yale.edu/17th_century/ma01.asp.
———. "Avalon Project: Northwest Ordinance; July 13, 1787," http://avalon.law.yale.edu/18th_century/nworder.asp.
———. "Avalon Project: Thomas Jefferson: Sixth Annual Message to Congress, December 2, 1806," 2016, http://avalon.law.yale.edu/19th_century/jeffmes6.asp.
Young, Jeremiah Simeon. *A Political and Constitutional Study of the Cumberland Road*. Ph.D. Dissertation, University of Chicago, 1902.
Zimmerman, Carrie B. "Ohio, the Gateway of the West." *Ohio Archaeological and Historical Quarterly* 40, no. 1 (January 1931).

Index

Numbers in **_bold italics_** indicate pages with maps.

Acadia (tribe) 28
Adams, John 125, 172, 178
Adams, John Quincy 165, 207, 215
Adena (tribe) 14
Aix-la-Chapelle Treaty 60, 84
Alabama 177, 198, 224
Albany 17, 19, 31, 106, 160, 174, 175, 211
Albany Congress 105
Alexandria 99, **_102_**, 142, 145–148, 150, 151, 153–155, 158, 171, 206
Algonkin (tribe) 16
Allegheny County 203
Allegheny Mountains (Alleghenies) 3, 5, 6, 8, 9, 11- 13, 15, 21, 23, 34, 41, 42, 44, 47, 62, 63, 73, **_74_**, 76, 78, 79, 90, 91, 95, 101, 103, 105, 106, 109, 110, 111, 114, 115, 116, **_117_**, 118, 120, 143, 145, 163, 211, 226
Allegheny Plateau 12, 13, 70, 72, 97, 101187, 200, 227n4
Allegheny Ridge and Valley 12, 13, 23, 41, 46, 72
Allegheny River 5, 21, 63- 65, 70, 80, 81, 88, 95, 96, 161
Allegheny Valley 17, 56
Alligewe (tribe) 15
Altamont 220
Anglican Church 49; Church of England 36, 37, 87, 229n7
Annapolis 46, 48, 52, 53, 58, 155, 221
Antietam 62
Antietam Creek 52, 53, 153
Antietam River 50
Antietam Valley 53
Appalachian Mountains (Appalachians) 3–5, 9, 12, 21, **_22_**, 23, 32, 44, 59, 72, 84, 87, 90, **_102_**, **_114_**, 136, 143, 177, **_190_**, 198, 211, 224, 226; Greater Appalachia 144; Plateau 227n4; Ridge and Valley 12

Appomattox River 26
Archaic Indians 14, 15
Arkansas River 32
Articles of Confederation 124, 125, 126, 127, 128, 133, 155
Atlantic 4, 5, 11, 12, 14, **_22_**, 26, 27, 34, 35, 38, 39, 40, 59, 62, 114, 160, 161, 163, 164, 182, 183, 192, 198, 199, 201, 208, 220, 221
Atlantic City 85
Avalon 35, 40
Aztec (tribe) 13

Backbone Mountain 220
Baldwin-Wallace University 142
Ballendine, John 153
Baltimore, Lord 5, 34, 35, 37, 39, 40, 42, 47, 50- 58, 68, 69, 149, 150; proclamation 54, 57
Baltimore and Ohio Railroad (B&O) 8, 165–167, 202, 209-211, 213–217, **_218_**, 219–225, 242n38
Baltimore: city and county 9, 41, 43, 46, 47, 58, 68, 69, 161–163, 165, 168, 172, 182, 183, **_190_**, 192, 194–202, 204, 206–211, 213–**_218_**, 219–221, 223, 225;
Baltimore Company 54
Baltimore Pike 8, 9, 46, 109, **_168_**, **_190_**, 197, 199, 201, **_202_**, 211, 213–216, **_218_**, 219, 225
Bank Road 196
Barcus, Daniel 206
Batts, Capt. Thomas 26, 27, 60, 65, 84
Beaver Wars 18, 19, 20, 21, 95
Bedford 203
"_la Belle Riviere_" 31, 81
Bering land bridge 13, 15
Bernard, Gov. Sir Francis 106
Big Conhaway _see_ Kanawha River
Bladen, Gov. Thomas 66

Blane, William 207
Blue Jacket 135, 136
Blue Mountain 4
Blue Ridge Mountains 5, 12, 41, 44, 49, 51, 52, 58, 103, 121
Boone, Daniel 23, 71, 175; father Squire 69
Boonesborough 175, 177, 195–197
Borderlanders 143
Boston 122, 124, 213
Boston Tea Party 119, 122
Bouquet, Col. Henry 106, 107, 108, 110, 111, 112, 113, 116
Braddock, Maj. Gen. Edward, 6, 99, 100, 105, 106, 143, 149, 150, 151, 183, 186, **_190_**, 194, 224, 236n3; expedition 58, 101, 103, 104, 109
Braddock Road 6, 101, **_102_**, 104, 106–109, 111, 118–120, 143, 154, 155, 160, 169, 170, 172–174, 183, 186, **_190_**, 194, 206, 222
Bradford, Maj. John 54
Bradford, William 18
Bradstreet, Col. John 113
Brant, Joseph 141
Brindley, James 152, 153; nephew 156
Brownsville 73, **_74_**, 108, 171, 173, 183, 184, 186–**_190_**, 192, 206, 208, 209, 225
Buffalo 19, 174, 175
Buffalo Creek 63, 70
Bunting, Redding 207
Burd, Col. James 6, **_102_**, 120, **_190_**
Burd Road 108, 109, 120, 170–174, 183, 222
Burr, Aaron 185
Butler, Richard 134

Cabot, John 38
California 204
Calvert, Cecilius (Cecil), Second Lord Baltimore 35, 37–39, 41, 42

249

Index

Calvert, Charles, Fifth Lord Baltimore 48
Calvert, George, Lord Baltimore 5, 34, 38, 40; Baron of Baltimore 35
Calvert, Leonard 37
Camden Railroad 215
Canada (Kanata) 28, 29, 32, 107, 131
Canal 48, 152, 156–*159*, 169, 181, 183, 184, 200, 214, 219, 220, 237n59; *see also* Chesapeake and Ohio Canal (C&O); Erie Canal; Potomac Canal
Cape Comfort 84
Cape Fear 84
Carleton, Gov. Guy 122
Carolinas 13, 16, 23, *45*, 47, 100, 110, 111, 113, 115, 116
Carroll, Charles 54, 165, 215
Carroll, James 165
Carter, Robert 63, 67
Cartier, Jacques 27, 32
Casselman River 72
Catawba (tribe) 4, 47, 53, 77, 89, 95
Catocin Mountain 44, 55, 58, 166, 195, 216, 217
Cayuga (tribe) 77, 95
Central Ohio Railroad 221
Chambersburg *45*
Charles I (England) 25, 35, 36, 37
Charles II (England) 38, 49, 141
Charles IV (Spain) 180
Charles County 43
Chartiers Creek 85, 93, 95, 96, 154
Cheat River 73, 154, 159, 162, 168
Checochinican 76
Cherokee (tribe) 4, 15, 110, 116, 118
Chesapeake and Ohio Canal (C&O) 2, 7, 8, 160, 162, 163–*168*, 211, 213–*218*, 225
Chesapeake Bay 5, 24, 36, 38, 39, 41, 43, 51, 99, 143, 145, 148
Chester River 41
Chestnut Ridge 72, 76, 95, 97, 101, 107, 108, 186, 189
Chicago 221, 224
Chillicothe 171, 176–179
China Sea 32
Choptank River 41
Church of England 36, 37, 87, 229n7
Cincinnati 135, 136, 140, 144, 171, 176–178, 188, 204, 207, 219, 221
Clark, George Rogers 134
Clay, Henry 187, 207, 221
Clear Spring 58
Cleaveland, Moses 141, 144

Cleveland 134, 144, 155, 174, 175
Clinton, Gov. DeWitt 88
Coastal Plain 40, 41, 43, 47
Colbert 30
Colorado 32
Columbus 13, 24, 170, 199–201, 206–208, 216, 221, 226
Company of One Hundred Associates 30
Conejohela Valley 40, 47, 52
Conestoga wagon 8, 203, 204, *205*, 208, *218*
Confederation 125, 130, 131, *132*
Confederation Congress 6, 124, 125, 126, 127, 128, 129, 131, *132*–134, 137, 138, 140–142
Congress *see* Confederation Congress; Continental Congress; United States Congress
Connecticut 7, 78, 105, 126, 128, *139*, 141, 180, 222, 223
Connecticut Land Company 141, 144
Connellsville 72, 186
Connolly, Dr. John 118, 119
Conococheague Creek 50 58, 103, 104, 145, 146, 149, 150, 196, 197
Conojocular (Conojacular) War 40, 53; *see also* Cresap's War
Conowango Creek 81
Constitution 128, 133, 141, 155, 158, 163, 164, 178–180, 182, 183–185, 193, 198, 199, 210, 235n16
Constitutional Convention 125, 131, *132*, 133, 138
Continental Congress 119, 124, 125, 141
Contrecoeur, Capt. 97
Cooper, Peter 216
Corinth 220
Cornstalk 119
Council of New England 25
Courcelle, (Governor) 31
coureurs de bois 29
Covenant Chain 78
Cresap, Daniel 63
Cresap, Thomas 16, 40, 43, 51-54, 56, 58, 62, 63, 66, 68-73, 75, 76, 79, 83, 87, 89, 92, 95, 96, 97, 99, 100, 101, 104, 112, 146, 147, 149, 152, 154, 183, *190*, 224, 226, 230n41, 233n37
Cresap, Thomas (son) 104
Cresap Road 75, 101
Cresap's War 40, 52
Cresaptown 44
Croghan, George 70, 71, 82, 83, 87–89, 96, 106, 111, 112, *117*, 118
Cromwell, Edith 68
Cruger, Lydia Boggs Shepherd (wife of Moses Shepherd) 187

Culpeper County 67
Culpepper, Lord 49, 63
Cumberland Fort 99, 100, 101, *102*, 103, 104, 106, 108, 109, 110, 119
Cumberland Gap 23, 69
Cumberland, Maryland 5, 7, 8, 46, 53, 54, 66, *74*, 145, 146, 151, 155, 158, 160, 163–168, 174
Cumberland Narrows 100, 186
Cumberland River 16, 18
Cumberland Road 7, 8, 9, 46, 71, 109, 144, 164, 169, 174, 180
Cumberland Valley 12, 41, 44, *45*, 46, 52, 58
Cutler, the Rev. Manasseh 138

Dagworthy, Capt. 104
Dans Mountain 72, 95, 101
Davis, Phineas 217
Dayton University 142
de Bienville (Blainville), Celeron 60, 80- 83, 90, 176
de Casson, Dollier 31
de Champlain, Samuel 27, 28, 29
Declaration of Independence 124, 165, 215
d'Iberville, Pierre Le Moyne 32
de Jumonville, Ens. Joseph Coulon de Villiers 97, 98, *102*
de la Galissoniere, Marquis 60, 80, 81, 83
de La Salle, Robert Cavelier 31, 32, 60, 84, 90
Delaware 126, 127, 144
Delaware Bay 35, 38, 39
Delaware River 21, 38, 39, 44, 47, 50, 85, 87, 104, 130, 142
Delaware (tribe) 3, 14–16, 21, 23, 70, 73, 75, 82, 88, 95, 100, *102*, 104, 105, 112, 113, 135
de Menneville, Ange Duquesne 83, 92, 96, 106
Demoiselle *see* Pickawillany
Denman, Matthias 140
Denny, Lt. Gov. William 106
de Saint-Lusson, Daumont 30, 32
de St. Pierre, Capt. Jacques Legardeur 96
Detroit 19, 81, 83, 88
Detroit River 15, 19, 113, 154; *see also* forts
de Vaudreuil, Gov.-Gen. Marquis 103
Dinwiddie, Gov. Robert 63, 68, 87, 89, 92, 93, 95, 96, 97, 103, 126, 146, 148, 149, 150, 236n5
Doddridge, Dr. Joseph 172, 174
Donehoo, George 15
du Gast, Pierre 28
Duke of Cumberland, William

Augustus 98, 99, 149; *see also* Cumberland
Dulany, Daniel 40, 48, 49, 53, 54, 55, 57
Dunbar, Col. 99, 101
Dunkirk 221
Dunlap's Creek 73, 76, 108
Dunmore, Gov. Lord 115, 118, 119, 174; War 119, 120, 174; fort 119
Duquesne, Marquis *see* de Menneville, Ange Duquesne
Dutch 17, 18, 29, 38, 77, 78

East Liverpool 130
Eastern Continental Divide 11, 114
Eastern Shore 36, 39, 41, 176
Easton 105, 106, 110
Easton Treaty 105, 112
Eden, Gov. Robert 58
Edict of Nantes 56
Ellicotts Mills 215
Enabling Act 178, 179, 181, 182, 185, 199
England 8, 28, 29, 34, 36–39, 42, 51, 53, 54, 56, 62, 63, 67, 80, 81, 87, 90, 95, 99, **102**, 114, 115, 142, 143, 149, 152, 153, 156, 212, 213, 215, 216, 228n46, 229n7, 231n6
Erie (tribe) 16, 18
Erie Canal 8, 155, 160–163, 165, 166, 209–213, 215, 219, 222, 257n64
Erie Railroad 221
Evitts Mountain 44

Fairfax, George 63
Fairfax, Lord Thomas 5, 49, 63, 67, 156
Fairfax Grant 49, 56
Fairfield 44
Fairmont 220, 221
Fallam, Robert 26, 27, 60, 65, 84
Fayette County 188
Filles du Roi 30
firearms 18
Five Nations 16, 18, 19, 53, 54, 77, 228n38; *see also* Indians; Six Nations
Fletcher, Gov. Benjamin 31
Florida 114, 116, 122, 180
Forbes, Brig. Gen. John 104, 106, 107, 120, 173
Forbes Road 107, 110, 113, 118, 120, 173, 174
Forks of the Ohio 6, 13, 59, 62, **64**, 66, 70, 79, 80, 82, 85, 87, 91, 93, 96, 101, 108, 109, 110, 118, 126, 146, 148–150, 154, 161, 194, 232n54; *see also* Ohio
Fort McIntosh Treaty 135, 136

Fort Stanwix Treaty 6, 115, **117**, 118, 119, 120, 121, 128, 134, 137, 173, 176
Fortieth Degree of North Latitude 28, 35, 39, 51, 52
forts **64**, 66, 83, 87, 90, 91, 96, 128; Bedford 106, 110; Le Boeuf (Waterford, Pennsylvania) 83, 95, 96, 98, 113; Detroit 112, 113, 120, 128; Dunmore 119; Duquesne (Forks of the Ohio) 83, 97, 98, 99, 101, 103, 104, 105, 107, 109; Fincastle 176; Frederick 53, 103, 107, 109, 147, 194, 217; Greenville 136; Harmer (Marietta) 135, 138; Henry 176; Jefferson 136; Ligonier 106, 110; Machault (Franklin, Pennsylvania) 83; McIntosh 134; Necessity 98, 101, 103, 105, 108, 146, 148; Niagara 110, 113; Pitt 107, 108, 109, 110, 111, 113, 120, 118, 120, 155; Presque Isle (Lake Erie) 83, 113; Recovery 136; Stanwix 116; Steuben 170; Ticonderoga 110; Tonoloway 147; Venango 113; Washington (Cincinnati) 135, 136, 176, 177, 238n19; *see also* Cumberland
Fox (tribe) 16
France 11, 17, 19, 20, 27–31, 37, 56, 60, **61**, 62, 80, 90, 99, **102**–104, 112, 113, 122, 129, 138, 160, 171, 180, 228n67, 231n93; *see also* New France
Frankfort 176
Franklin, Benjamin 56, 57, 125
Frederick 8, 44, 46, 57, 58, 99, 109, 145, 149, 151, 152, 167, 194, 195, 196, 207, 215, 216, 217; *see also* forts
French and Indian War 6, 43, 46, 47, 58, 68, 70, 88–91, 98, **102**, 108, 110, 112, 120, 121, 137, 140, 151, 168, 173, 180, **190**, 224
French Creek 95, 96
Frontenac, Count 31
Frostburg 225
Fry, Col. Joshua 79, 96, 148

Gallatin, Albert 161, 162, 163, 182, 188–**190**, 193, 195, 198
Gallipolis 144, 171
Gaspé Peninsula 27
Geographer's Line 129, 130, 131
George II (England) 99, 107
George III (England) 113, 114, 125, 149; Proclamation of 114
Georgetown 99, 109, 145, 146, 124, 149, 151, 152, 158, 163–167, 194, 214, 237n31

Georgia 16, 41, **45**, 116, 127, 142, 143
Gettysburg 44, **45**
Giles, William 182
Gist, Christopher 6, 20, 43, 66–73, 75, 76, 79, 82, 83, 85, 87–89, 92, 93, 95–98, 100, 101, 108, 143, 146, 170, 176, 183, 190, 222, 224–226, 234n74; journeys 69, 71; plantation 73, 76, 95, 97, 98, 101, 108, 186, 189, 225, 234n74
Gist, Nathaniel 68, 69
Gist, Richard 68
Gist, Thomas 68, 69
Gist's Trace 7, 9, 74, 101, 102, 107, 108; *see also* Gist, Christopher
Gooch, Lt. Gov. William 49, 50, 51, 63, **64**, 84
Gorges, Sir Fernando 25
Grafton 220, 221
Great Appalachian Valley 12, 23, 41, 44, 58; *see also* Appalachian Mountains
Great Britain 7, 27, 78, 96, 122, 125, 131, 133, 148, 152, 160, 172, 179, 180, 224, 239n36
Great Falls 146–148, 150–153, 156–159, 237n31
Great Lakes 11, 15, 16, 28, 32, 125, 131; *see also* Lake Erie; Lake Huron; Lake Michigan; Lake Ontario; Lake Superior
Great Meadows 72, 95, 97, 98, 101, 103, 154
Great Valley Road (Great Wagon Road) **45**, 46, 78, 115, 143
Great Warriors Path 23, 43
Green Briar River 93
Greenbrier Company 117, 137
Greenville Treaty 136, 141, 170
Grenada 114, 122
Guest, Christopher 68
Gulf of Mexico 13, 32, 33

Hager, Jonathon 58, 152
Hagerstown 44, **45**, 46, 53, 58, 152, 166, 194, 195, 197, 207, 217
Hagerstown Valley 12, 41, 44, 52, 58, 109
Half King *see* Tanacharison
Hamilton, Alexander 125, 161, 172, 182, 184, 185
Hamilton, Gov. James 87, 89
Hamilton County 140
Hamilton, Ohio 171; *see also* Cincinnati
Hanbury, John 63, 65, 75, 145
Hancock 109, 147, 166, 196, **218**
Hard Labor Treaty 116, 118
Harpers Ferry 44, 166, 216, 217, **218**

Harris's Ferry 88, 103
Harrisburg *see* Harris's Ferry; Paxtang
Harrison, Gov. Benjamin 155, 181
Harrison, William Henry 171, 177, 178, 207
Hayden, John 173
Henry IV (France) 27, 28
Historic Indians 14, 23
Hite, Jacob 152
Hite, Jost (Joist Hite, Joost Heyd) 50, 57
Hochelaga *see* Montreal
Hocking River 3, 13, 119, 170, 171, 176, 178
Hodenosaunee 16
Holland 50
Hopewell (tribe) 14, 15
Hudson River 8, 17, 211, 221
Hudson's Bay Company 30
Huguenots 29, 36, 56
Huron (tribe) 15, 16, 17, 18, 28
Hutchins, Thomas 130, 131

Illinois 19, 131, 177, 198, 200, 201, 202, 203, 207, 208, 210, 211, 222–224, 240*n*71
Illinois River 32, 199
immigrants 45, 50, 67, 143, 146, 171, 174, 175, 205, 223; English 122, 191; German 5, *45*, 49, 50, 55, 56, 57, 58, 63, 92, 110, 144, 145, 165, 219
Inca (tribe) 13
Indiana 19, 131, 133, 177, 178, 182, 198–201, 203, 206, 207, 210, 223, 224
Indiana Company 117
Indianapolis, Indiana 199, 201
Innes, Col. James 99, 146, 148, 149
Intolerable Acts 122
Irinakhoiw 16
Iroquois (tribe) 3, 4, 14–16, 18, 19, 47, 65, 78, 81, 84, 95, 104, 105, 106, 114, 116, 135, 224
Italy 35

Jackson, Rep. 192, 193
Jacktown 206
Jacob's Ferry 73
James, Duke of York 38, 39; *see also* James II (England)
James I (England) 4, 24, 35, 37, 38
James II (England) 39, 49
James River 26, 35, 155
Jamestown 4, 24, 34, 36, 41
Jay, John 125
Jefferson, Thomas 124, 127, 129, *132*, 157, 161, 172, 177–180, 182, 184, 186, 188–*190*, 193, 194, 197, 198

Johnson, Sir William 6, 106, 114, 116, *117*, 120
Joliet, Louis 32
Jonquiere, Gov. 88
Juniata River 70, 88

Kanawha River 26, *22*, 60, 72, 73, 81, 92, 93, 116, *117*, 119, 154, 171, 214, 217, 222
Kansas 223
Kentucky 6, 13, 23, 24, 46, 67, 69, 71, 83, 109, *117*, 118, 119, 121, 130, *132*, 134, 136, 137, 140, 142, 143, 171, 173–177, 184, 203, 204, 207, 208, 222, 223, 227*n*3
Kerr, Joseph 186
King George's War 60
Kingwood 221
Kiskiminetas Creek 63, *64*, 70, 71, 88, 92, 93
Kittanning 23, 44, 116
Knox, Henry 135

Lake Chataquin, 81
Lake Erie 8, 15, 19, 65, 81, 87, 88, 91, 96, 113, 121, 144, 160, 161, 164, 175, 179, 211, 221, 222
Lake Huron 19, 31
Lake Michigan 19, 32
Lake Ontario 161
Lake Superior 30, 31
Lancaster 44, 45, 51, 52, 78, 79, 88, 171, 176, 204
Lancaster Treaty 60, 63, 65, 72, 73
land: office 127; ordinances 6, 128, 129, 131, 132, 133, 136–138, 174; warrants 48, 53
Langlade, Charles 83, *102*
languages: Algonquian 15, 21; Iroquoian 15
Laurel Hill 97, 186, 183
Laurel Ridge 107, 174
Laurel Run 72;
Lee, Richard 63
Lee, Thomas 51, 62, 63, 66, 67, 71, 78, 79, 89, 92
Lehigh River 213
Lenni-Lenape (tribe) 76
Lewis, Andrew 119, 137
Limestone 175–177, 212, 222, 238*n*19
Lincoln Highway 225
Little Falls 148, 153, 156, 157, 159, 166, 237*n*31
Little Meadows 72
Little Turtle 136
Liverpool and Manchester Railroad 216
Lloyd, Philemon 49
Lochaber Treaty 118
Logan, Secretary 56
Logstown 70, 72, 73, 76, 79, 83, 85, 88, 89, 90, 95, 96

Logstown Treaty 66, 79, 83, 90
Lomax, Lunsford 79
London 17, 24, 56, 63, 84, 93, 96, 98, 112, 114, 115, 121, 142
Losantiville *see* Cincinnati
Louis XIII (France) 30
Louis XIV (France) 30, 32, 56
Louis XV (France) 60
Louisiana 32, 80, 81, 84, 92, 177, 179, 224
Louisiana Purchase *132*, 160, 161, 179, 180, 188, 190, 198
Louisiana Territory 172, 177, 188
Louisville 31, 69
Loyal Land Company 66, *117*, *137*
Loyalhanna Creek 70, 71
Ludlow, Israel 140, 171

Madison, James 125, 155, 164, 189
Maine 24, 28, 144, 177, 198, 224
Manitoba 32
Marietta 138, 144, 171, 177, 178, 222
Marietta College 142
Marquette, Jacques 32
Martinsburg 217
Maryland: Assembly 42, 48, 54, 59, 103, 121, 126, 196, 197; Barrens 47, 48; Charter of 37; Proprietary Province 38; 43, 46; western 34, 46- 48, 54, 57- 59, 62, 76, 103, 104, 152, 166, 167, 194, 196, 216
Maryland Monster 51, 52
Mason, George 63
Mason-Dixon Line 130, 224
Massachusetts 16, 24, 29, 34, 36, 114, 125, 137, 142, 143
Massachusetts Bay Colony 25, 29, 34, 35, 38, 78; Charter of Massachusetts Bay 25
Massie, Nathaniel 178
Maumee River 19, 83, 87
Maya (tribe) 14
Maysville *see* Limestone
McAdam, John Loudon 197
McKinley, Henry 191
Meadow Mountain 72, 95, 101
Mengwe (Minqua, Mingee) 15; *see also* Iroquois (tribe)
Mercer, George 63, 112, 152
Mercer, John 110
Mesoamerica 14
Mexico 17
Miami: Great 7, 71, 81, 179; Little 13, 20, 70
Miami Purchase 144
Miami River(s) 3, 13, 20, 71, 140, 170
Miami (tribe) 3, 14, 16, 21, 70, 71, 82, 83, 88, 134, 135

Index

Miami University 140
Michigan 19, 129, 131
Mingo (tribe) 21, 88, 98, 103, 105, 113, 118
Minnesota 131
Mississippi River and Valley 4, 11, 13, 15, 16, 20, 26, 32, 42, 62, 65, 80, 112, 122, 125, 126, 129, 131, *132*, 141, 145, 159, 173, 177, 179–181, 185, 188, 198, 199, 200, 210, 221, 224, 227n15, 239n36
Mississippian (tribe) 14
Missouri 198, 200, 201, 210, 224; River 32, 213
Mohawk (tribe) 17, 23, 70, 77, 78, 89
Mohawk River and Valley 155, 161, 175, 209, 211
Mohican (tribe) 18
Monocacy Path 43
Monocacy River 47, 54, 55, 57, 149, 152, 163
Monocacy Road *45*, 46, 53, 146, 149
Monocacy Valley 44, 54, 56, 57, 58
Monongahela River 5, 6, 13, 21, *22*, 23, 34, 54, 62, 64, 66, 72–*74*–76, 82, 90, 92, 93, 95, 101, *102*, 104, 107, 108, 109, 111, *117*, 118, 122, 138, 143, 145, 146, 148, 151, 155, 160, 161, 163, 169, 172–174, 183, 186, 187, 206, 208, 211, 220, 232n54; forks of 72, 75
Monroe, James 164, 180, 193, 194, 199, 201, 207, 239n36
Montana 32
Montauk (tribe) 16
Montgomery County 151
Montour, Andrew 70, 87, 88, 89, 106; mother 88
Montreal 27, 30, 31, 32, 80, 81, 122, 161
Moore, Thomas 186
Morgan, Gen. Daniel 174
Morgantown 225
Morris, Gov. Robert 103
Morse, Jedidiah 3
Morse, Samuel 221
Mount Vernon 67, 153, 154, 206
Murry, Zephorah 68
Muskingum River and Valley 60, 70, 81, 88, 113, 135, 138, 170

Nanfan Treaty 19
Nanticoke (tribe) 16
Nanticoke River 41
National Road 71, 72, 101, 109, 144, 169, 176, 182, 186, *190*, 197–*202*, 203–*205*, 206–211, 213–216, *218*, 219, 222, 225, 242n42

Native Americans 3, 6, 13, 17, 18, 20, 21, 23–25, 28, 41, 62, 65, 68–70, 77, 81, 84, 90, 104, 113, 134, 135, 147, 173, 224
Nebraska 223
Negro Mountain 72, 95, 101, 104
Nemacolin 73, 75, 76, 92, 95, 97, 100, 101, 108, 183, *190*, 224, 234n74
Nemacolin Creek 73
Nemacolin Path 75, 96, 97, 101, 147, 169
Nemicotton 73
Neolin 112
Neponset River 213
Neutral (tribe) 16, 18
New Brunswick 28;
New England 16, 23, 25, 28, 29, 36, 39, 137, 138, *139*, 141–144, 171, 184, 222, 223, 229n1
New France 11, 17, 20, 27, 28, 30, 31, 33, 34, 36, 60, 80, 81, 83, 84, 88, 113, 122
New Hampshire 38, 144
New Holland 30
New Jersey 12, 13, 28, 85, 106, 126, 127, 140, 144, 223
New Martinsville 220
New Mexico 32;
New Netherland 29
New Netherland Company 17
New Orleans 112, 180, 192, 193
New River 26, 27, 92
New World 5, 17, 18, 24, 34, 36, 47
New York 4, 5, 13, 20, 23, 24, 47, 56, 67, 78, 84, 85, 87, 89, 100, 105, 115, 126, 128, 133, 155, 161, 163, 208–214, 216, 219–223, 225
Newcomen, Thomas 212
Newfoundland 32, 35, 40
Niagara 81; *see also* forts
Niagara (tribe) 113
Nicholas, Miami Chief 71
North America 17, 24, 32, *61*, 62, 81, 90, 91, 104, 107, 110, 112, 143
North Branch *see* Potomac River
North Carolina 26, 69, 70, 76, 127, 136, 143, 223
Northern Ireland 115, 143
Northern Neck 49, 50, 55, 56, 62, 63, 67, 68, 84
Northwest Ordinance 3, 133, 134, 135, 178
Northwest Passage 27
Northwest Territory 3, 6, 7, 125, 131, *132*, 133, 136, 138, 142–144, 170, 171, 173, 176–179, 181, 198, 202, 209, 227n3
Nova Scotia 15, 111

Oberlin College 142
Ogle, Gov. Samuel 57
Ohio Company of Associates 137, 138, *139*, 140, 142, 144, 171
Ohio Company of Virginia 5, 6, 62, 63, 66, 69, *74*–76, 78–80, 82, 84, 85, 87–90, 92–94, 96, 97, 98, 103, 105–108, 110, 112, 115, *117*, 126, 137, 140, 145–147, 167, 170, 174, 226
Ohio Indians 14, 90, 96, 102, 105, 106, 110, 112, 113, 115, 118–120, 130, 134
Ohio: country 3–8, 11–13, 18–20, 34, 38, 42, 44, 46, 47, 54, 59, 60, 63, 66, 67, 69, 70, 71, 73, 77, 78, 82–85, 87, 88, 90, 92, 97, 101, 103, 105, 106, 107, 108, 109, 110, 112, 116, 118, 120, 122, 125–127, 130, 137, 138, 142, 150, 152, 160, 162, 167, *168*, 170, 173, 175, 179, 185, 197, 209, 221–223, 226, 227n3; "*la Belle Riviere*" 31, 81; falls of 69, 71, 175; "the great river" 3; Lake Plains 20; Oyo 81; Till Plains of 13, 70, 200; Virginia claim on 7
Ohio River 6, 8, 13, 17, 19, 21, *22*, 26, 31, 32, 60, *64*–66, 70, 71–73, 79–82, 84, 93, 94, 109, 116, 118, 120, 121, 129, 130, 135, 138, 140, 143, 151, 159, 163, 170–172, 174–177, 179, 181–183, 185–187, 189, *190*, 197–201, 203, 204, 209, 214, 215, 217, 220–222, 224, 227n3
Ohio State University 142
Ohio University 142
Ohio Valley 3, 4, 14–16, 21, 27, 31, 46, 59, 60, 62, 65, 66, 67, 76, 79, 80, 82, 83, 85, 87, 108, 110, 111, 115, 148, 173, 198, 209, 224
Ojibwa (tribe) 83, 134, 135
Old Pike 202
Oldtown (King Opessa's Town; Old Town) 16, 44, 47, 53, 56, 62, 72, 99, 104, 109, 147, 149, 158
Olmec (tribe) 14
Oneida (tribe) 77, 88, 100
Onondaga (tribe) 77, 96
Ontario 15
Opessa's Town *see* Oldtown
Oranje *see* Albany
ordinance *see* land, ordinance
Oregon 204
Orme, Capt. 100
Osage River 213
Ottawa (tribe) 16, 21, 83, 112, 134, 135
Oyo 81

Index

Paine, Thomas 124
Palatinate (Palatines) 56, 58, 89
Paleo (tribe) 14, 15
Paris Treaty 6, 112, 125, 126, 127, 128, 129, 134, 141, 168, 179, 198
Parker, Hugh 75
Parkersburg 219, 221
Parkman, Francis 31, 32
Parsons, Samuel 138
Patterson, Robert 140
Patton, James 79
Patuxent River 41
Paxtang 44
Penn, Thomas 85
Penn, William 39, 56, 85
Penns 52, 104
Pennsylvania Main Line 8, 211–214, 217, 220
Pennsylvania Railroad 212, 220, 221
Pennsylvania: border disputes 38, 39, 47, 50, 52, 53, 56, 57, 87, 118; Charter of 39, 85;
Petun (tribe) 18
Philadelphia 8, 25, 39, 40, 44, *45*, 46, 52, 58, 88, 101, 106, *132*, 138, 143, 154, 155, 161, 163, 172, 177, 182, 184, 188, 192, 203, 208–214, 220, 221, 235n35
Pickawillany 70, 71, 81, 82, 83, 88, 91, *102*; chief 83
Piedmont 12, 21, 41, 43, 47, 221
Pike boys 205
Pilgrims 25, 29, 35, 36
Piney Mountain 72, 95, 101
Piqua 71, 82
Pitt, William 104
Pittsburgh 8, 13, 59, *64*, 111, *117*, 130, 135, 164, 168, 174, 175, 188, 192, 209, 211–214, 217, 219–221, 225
Plymouth 4, 17, 18, 29, 34
Point of Rocks 166, 216, 217
Point Pleasant 214
Pontiac 109, 112, 113
Pontiac Rebellion 113, 114, 120, 121
Popham, Sir John 25
Potomac Canal 151, 153, 159, 160, 162, 210
Potomac Canal Company 162
Potomac River 5–7, 15- 17, 21, *22*, 23, 27, 34–36, 40, 41, 44, *45*, 46, 48–55, 58, 62, 65, 66, 70, 72–*74*, 85, 90, 97, 99, 103, 104, 109, 113, 145–168, 173, 176, 183, 186, 197, 209–211, 214, 216–218, 220, 222, 236n3, 237n41, 239n56; first fountain 55
Potomac River Company 155–159, 161, 162, 166, 168
Potowatomi (tribe) 83, 112, 135
Powhatan (tribe) 16

Prairie Schooner 204
Prince Georges County 149
Proclamation of 1763 121, 122
proprietors 37, 38, 40, 42, 48, 51, 59, 103; *see also* Baltimore, Lord; Calvert, George, Lord Baltimore
Puritans 25 29, 36, 14
Putnam, Rufus 137, 138

Quaker 50, 103, 143, 144, 220
Quebec 17, 28, 29, 30, 80, 114; Battle of 110
Quebec Act 122, 123, 124
Quitrents 49

railways 8, 200, 212, 215
Rappahannock River 49
Red Jacket 141
Redstone: Old Fort 76, 108, 111, 233n19
Redstone Creek 72- *74*, 76, 96–98, 108, 111, 118, 119, 173, 183, 186
Reister's-town 194
Rhode Island 127
Richelieu, Cardinal 30
Richmond 133, 182, 184, 201
Roanoke 46, 71
Roanoke River 26
Robinson, John 51
Rock Creek 99, 149, 159
Romanettos Creek 63, 93, 231n7

St. Clair, Gen. Arthur 135, 136, 138, 140, 150, 151, 177–179
St. Clair, Lt. Col. Sir John 100, 150, 151
St. Clairsville 199
St. Lawrence River 4, 11, 13, 15-17, 28, 30, 31, 33, 80, 179; Gulf of 27
St. Louis 188, *190*, 194, 197–199, 219, 221, 240n71
St. Mary's 41–43, 48
St. Mary's County 43, 48
St. Mary's River 41
San Francisco 225
San Lorenzo (Pinckney's) Treaty 180
Saskatchewan 32
Sauk (tribe) 16, 135
Sault Ste. Marie 30;
Savage Mountain 66, 72, 95, 104, 225; Big and Little 101
Savage River 164, 220
Savery, Thomas 212
Scarouady 100
Schuykill and Susquehanna Canal Company 159
Schuylkill River 39
Scioto Company 171
Scioto River 3, 13, 81, 140, 170, 171, 178

Scots-Irish *45*, 115, 143, 171, 222, 223
Searight, Thomas 202, 205, 207, 208
Semple, John 153
Seneca (tribe) 21, 70, 77, 79, 95, 98
Seneca Falls 148, 153, 156, 166
Seven Ranges 130, 131, 134, 137, 138, *139*, 140, 141
Seven Years' War *see* French and Indian War
Shannopin's Town 70
Sharpe, Gov. Horatio 99, 126, 147- 151, 194
Shawnee (tribe) 3, 14, 16–18, 21, 23, 24, 31, 47, 70, 82, 88, *102*, 105, 113, 119, 134, 135, 136, 174
Shawnee Old Town *see* Oldtown
Shenandoah River and Valley 5, 8, 12, 41, 44, *45*, 48–52, 55, 57, 63, 65, 67, 68, 78, 84, 99, 110, 147, 151–153, 156; falls 150, 156
Shepherd, Col. Moses 187
Shingas 95, 100
Shriver, David 191, 192
Six Nations 65, 66, 69, 77, 78, 89, 90, 95, 96, 104, 105, 118, 119, 232n64; *see also* Five Nations
South Branch *see* Potomac River
South Carolina 24, 84, 143, 163
South Mountain 41, 44, *45*
South Sea 26, 27, 31, 126
Spain 7, 32, 35, 36, 133, 142 179, 180, 239n36
Spendelow, Lt. Charles 100
Spotswood, Lt. Gov. Alexander 27, 49, 65, 78, 84
Springfield 200, 201
Stadacona *see* Quebec
Stagecoach 194, 204, 206, 207, 216, *218*, 219
Stamp Act 121, 122
Stanwix, Gen. John 108
Stephenson, George 212, 213, 216
Stephenson, Robert 212
Steubenville 70, 118, 170, 177, 183, 187
Stevens, Robert 215
Stuart, Col. John 116, 118
Sugar Act 114, 121
Susquehnna Canal Company 156
Susquehanna River 17, 23, 31, 41, 44, *45*, 47, 48, 50, 51, 70, 76, 87, 88, 103, 105, 116, 211
Susquehannock (tribe) 16, 18, 54
Swann, Thomas 220, 221
Symmes, Judge John Cleves 140, 142, 177

Talon, Jean 30, 32
Tanacharison 70, 79, 89, 95, 96, 98, 100; "Half-King" 70, 96
Tasker's Chance 54, 55, 57
Tea Act 119
Teays River 26
Tecumseh 136
Teedyuscung 105, 106
Tennessee 6, 12, 15, 23, 116, **117**, 118, 136, 137, 143, 223, 227n3
Tennessee River 121
Terra Maria (Maryland) 35
Texas 32, 131
Thomas, Philip E. 214
Tidewater 43, 46; Virginia 15, 25
Tobacco 5, 25, 47, 49, 57, 58; economy 5, 24, 43, 46
Tobacco (tribe) 16
Toll houses 8, 201
Tom Thumb 216
Trent, William 76, 95, 96, 97
Tresaguet, Pierre 191
Trevithick, Richard 212
Tupper, Gen. Benjamin 137
turnpike 7, 8, 194-197, 208, 219, 225
Tuscarora (tribe) 54
Twightee (tribe) 71
Twightee *see* Pickawillany

Uniontown 13, 72, 73, 76, 173, 187-189, **190**, 191-193, 207, 225
United States 3, 8, 11, 14, 29, 98, 124, 126, 127, 129, 131, 133, 136, 141, 142, 155, 157, 160, 161, 163, 171, 177, 179, 180, 184, 185, 188, 192, 193, 198, 201, **202**, 210, 211, 215 239n36
United States Congress 141, 161, 163, 176, 177, 178, 179, 180, 184, 185, 186, 188, 194, 198, 221
U.S. Route 40 (U.S. 40) 9, 72, 98, 101, 225, 226

Vandalia 190, 199, 201, 206
Vermont 41, 131, 144, 222, 223
Viele, Arnold 31, 32
Vincennes 188
Virginia: Assembly 49, 175, 220; Council 50, 51, 63, 92; Military District 130, 144, 222; Regiment 99, 104, 107; Second Charter of 24, 84
Virginia Company of London 24, 35, 37; First Colony of Virginia 24
Virginia Company of Plymouth 24, 25; Second Colony of Virginia 24

Wabash River 87
Walker, Thomas 23
Walking Purchase 104, 105
Walum Olum 15, 21
Wampanoag (tribe) 16
War for Independence 6, 7, 87, 120, 124, 135, 136, 138, 140, 141, 153, 173, 176, 198, 239n36; Ohio 130, 134, 137; Treaty of Paris 198
Warrior's Path 47, 53, 77
Washington, Augustine 51, 62, 63, 67, 68, 99
Washington, Bushrod 154
Washington, George 6, 7, 9, 66-70, 79, 89, 93, 95, 96-98, 100, 101, **102**-105, 107, 124, 125, 129, 135, 136, 137, 141, 143
Washington, Lawrence 51, 62, 63, 67, 68, 92, 95
Washington D.C. 8, 41, 148, 158, 163, 182, 183, 192-196, 206, 207, 213-215, 221, 226
Washington, Pennsylvania 188-**190**, 193, **205**, 225
Washington Road 95, 100, 101, 107, 115, 140, 146, 147, 149-151, 153-157, 159, 161, 164-**168**, 169, 172-174, 176, 179-184, 190, 209, 210, 224
Watkins Point 35, 36, 40
Watt, James 212
Wayne, Gen. Anthony 136
Weiser, Conrad 87, 89, 105, 106
West Virginia 12, 13, **22**, 73, 160
Western Reserve 141, 144, 171, 174, 222, 222
Western Reserve University 142
Western Shore 41
Wheeling, Virginia 7, 8, 9, 109, 144, **168**, 176, 181-184, 187-**190**, 192-194, 196, 197, 199-**202**, 203, 205-211, 214, 217, **218**, 219-225, 241n13, 242n38, 242n42
Wilderness Road 46
Wilkesboro 69
Williams, Eli 186
Williams Ferry 44, **45**, 58
Williamsburg 27, 68, 95, 96, 97, 99, 121, 146, 147
Williamsport 109, 146, 149, 166, 180, 183, 195, 196, 202; *see also* Williams Ferry
Wills Creek 5-7, **22**, 44, 66, 71, 72, **74**-76, 92, 93, 95, 97, 98, 99, 100, 108, 109, 145, 146, 149-151, 164, 168, 173, 183, 222, 236n3
Wills Mountain 44, 66, 72, 95, 100, 106
Wills Town 66
Winchester Virginia 16, 50, 97, 99, 103, 145, 146, 151, 171
Winding Ridge 95, 101
Wisconsin 131; glacier 14
Wood, Capt. Abraham 26
Wood, Joseph 3
Wood, Thomas 26
Woods River *see* New River
Worthington, Thomas 178, 179, 187
Wright's Ferry (Wrightsville) 44, **45**, 51, 52
Wyandot (Wendat) (tribe) 16, 21, 70, 88, 112, 134, 135
Wyoming 32
Wyoming Valley 104, 105

Xavier University 142

Yadkin River 69, 70, 71, 76
Yellow Creek **64**, 118
York 44, **45**, 51
Youghiogheny River **22**, 66, 71-73, 75, 76, 92, 93, 95, 97, 101, 138, 154, 155, 159, 161, 162, 164, 168; forks of 73, **74**

Zane, Ebenezer 171, 175, 176, 181
Zane, Jonathon 175
Zane, Silas 175
Zane's Trace 171, 175-177, 181, 184, 199, 204, 222, 223
Zanesville 199, 200, 206, 221, 225

www.ingramcontent.com/pod-product-compliance
Lightning Source LLC
Chambersburg PA
CBHW081547300426
44116CB00015B/2793